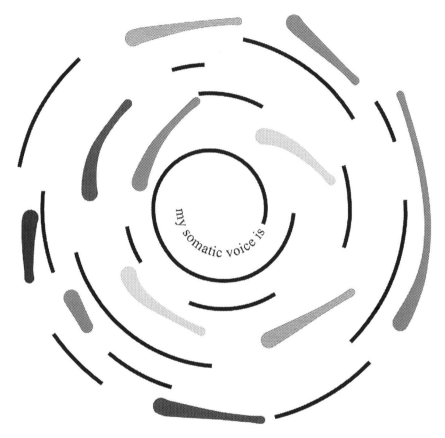

my somatic voice is. Concept by Christina Kapadocha. Co-designed with Vivianna Chiotini. © Christina Kapadocha.

Somatic Voices in Performance Research and Beyond

Somatic Voices in Performance Research and Beyond brings together a community of international practitioner-researchers who explore voice through soma or soma through voice. Somatic methodologies offer research processes within a new area of vocal, somatic and performance praxis. Voice work and theoretical ideas emerge from dance, acting and performance training while they also move beyond commonly recognized somatics and performance processes. From philosophies and pedagogies to ethnic-racial and queer studies, this collection advances embodied aspects of voices, the multidisciplinary potentialities of somatic studies, vocal diversity and inclusion, somatic modes of sounding, listening and writing voice.

Methodologies that can be found in this collection draw on:

- eastern traditions
- body psychotherapy-somatic psychology
- Alexander Technique, Feldenkrais Method
- Authentic Movement, Body-Mind Centering, Continuum Movement, Integrative Bodywork and Movement Therapy
- Fitzmaurice Voicework, Linklater Technique, Roy Hart Method
- post-Stanislavski and post-Grotowski actor-training traditions
- somaesthetics

The volume also includes contributions by the founders of:

- Shin Somatics, Body and Earth, Voice Movement Integration
- SOMart, Somatic Acting Process

This book is a polyphonic and multimodal compilation of experiential invitations to each reader's own somatic voice. It culminates with the "voices" of contributing participants to a praxical symposium at East 15 Acting School in London (July 19–20, 2019). It fills a significant gap for scholars in the fields of voice studies, theatre studies, somatic studies, artistic research and pedagogy. It is also a vital read for graduate students, doctoral and postdoctoral researchers.

Christina Kapadocha (PhD) is a Lecturer in Theatre and Movement at East 15 Acting School. She is a London-based theatre and somatic practitioner-researcher and founder of Somatic Acting Process®. Her current practice research and publications introduce new discussions on the somatic in theatre and performance studies.

Routledge Voice Studies
Series editors: Konstantinos Thomaidis and Ben Macpherson

The Routledge Voice Studies series offers a platform for rigorous discussion of voice across disciplines, practices and areas of interest. This series aims to facilitate the dissemination and cross-fertilisation of voice-related research to effectively generate new knowledge and fresh critical insights on voice, vocality, and voicing.

Composing for Voice
A Guide for Composers, Singers, and Teachers
Paul Barker and Maria Huesca

Voice Studies
Critical Approaches to Process, Performance and Experience
Konstantinos Thomaidis and Ben Macpherson

Training Actors' Voices
Towards an Intercultural/Interdisciplinary Approach
Tara McAllister-Viel

The Performative Power of Vocality
Virginie Magnat

Beethoven and the Lyric Impulse
Essays on Beethoven Song
Amanda Glauert

Somatic Voices in Performance Research and Beyond
Christina Kapadocha

https://www.routledge.com/Routledge-Voice-Studies/book-series/RVS

Somatic Voices in Performance Research and Beyond

Edited by Christina Kapadocha

LONDON AND NEW YORK

First published 2021
by Routledge
2 Park Square, Milton Park, Abingdon, Oxon OX14 4RN

and by Routledge
52 Vanderbilt Avenue, New York, NY 10017

Routledge is an imprint of the Taylor & Francis Group, an informa business

© 2021 selection and editorial matter, Christina Kapadocha; individual chapters, the contributors

The right of Christina Kapadocha to be identified as the author of the editorial material, and of the authors for their individual chapters, has been asserted in accordance with sections 77 and 78 of the Copyright, Designs and Patents Act 1988.

All rights reserved. No part of this book may be reprinted or reproduced or utilised in any form or by any electronic, mechanical, or other means, now known or hereafter invented, including photocopying and recording, or in any information storage or retrieval system, without permission in writing from the publishers.

Trademark notice: Product or corporate names may be trademarks or registered trademarks, and are used only for identification and explanation without intent to infringe.

British Library Cataloguing-in-Publication Data
A catalogue record for this book is available from the British Library

Library of Congress Cataloging-in-Publication Data
A catalog record has been requested for this book

ISBN: 978-1-138-36060-0 (hbk)
ISBN: 978-0-429-43303-0 (ebk)

Typeset in Times New Roman
by codeMantra

Visit the companion website: www.routledge.com/cw/kapadocha

Contents

List of figures   x
List of online material   xi
List of contributors   xiii
Acknowledgements   xviii
Series foreword   xix
Foreword: a phonotechnics of vocal somaticity:
   an autobiophonic note   xxi
KONSTANTINOS THOMAIDIS

Introduction: somatic voice studies   1
CHRISTINA KAPADOCHA

PART I
Vocalities in somatic studies   13

1 **Three somatic processes to voice through movement: breath, exploration, imagery**   15
BARBARA SELLERS-YOUNG

2 **Awakening grace: embodied awareness in vocal training**   28
ANDREA OLSEN

3 **Never just the body: etudes between voice and dance**   37
SONDRA FRALEIGH

4 **On Voice Movement Integration (VMI) practice by Patricia Bardi: awakening resonance in the moving body**   51
PATRICIA BARDI INTERVIEWED BY CHRISTINA KAPADOCHA

PART II
Voice work, somatics and the diverse self — 61

5 **In front of me: Fitzmaurice Voicework® as a transformative practice** — 63
ELLEN FOYN BRUUN

6 **Somatic training and resources for body-mind-voice integration: when stage fright "comes to visit"** — 76
LETICIA SANTAFÉ AND PABLO TROCCOLI

7 **Voicing with awareness: an introduction to the Feldenkrais Method** — 89
STEPHEN PAPARO

8 **My body is a map, my voice is the path: (trans)racialized somaticities and Roy Hart voice work** — 98
AMY MIHYANG GINTHER

PART III
Vocal and somatic listening in training — 113

9 **(Re)considering the role of touch in "re-educating" actors' body/voice** — 115
TARA McALLISTER-VIEL

10 **Organic voice: vocal integration through actor training** — 130
CHRISTINA GUTEKUNST

11 **Dreaming voice: a dialogue** — 140
ILONA KRAWCZYK AND BEN SPATZ

12 **Somatic logos in physiovocal actor training and beyond** — 155
CHRISTINA KAPADOCHA

PART IV
Beyond the somatic in performance research — 169

13 **Mapping the burden of vocality: french seventeenth-century vocal lamentations, Japanese meditation and somatic intra-action** — 171
ELISABETH LAASONEN BELGRANO

14 Intensive interaction: a lesson on *queered* voicing from children
with learning disAbilities 185
YVON BONENFANT

15 Vocal resonance and the politics of intercorporeality 198
ANITA CHARI

16 The somaesthetic in-between: six statements on vocality,
listening and embodiment 212
BEN MACPHERSON

PART V
Beyond this book 227

17 Beyond our somatic voices 229
CHRISTINA KAPADOCHA

Index 243

Figures

I	Mapping this book. Concept by the author. Graphic design by Vivianna Chiotini. © Christina Kapadocha	6
3.1	Shin Somatics students voicing in Snow Canyon, 2017. © Sondra Fraleigh (Photos by the author.)	44
4.1	From Patricia Bardi's workshop at East 15 Acting School, London, 17 November 2018. (Photo by Vivianna Chiotini.)	54
8.1	Moments from my improvisations during my one-on-one session with Jonathan Hart Makwaia, July 27, 2018. (Photos by Danielle Meunier.)	106
13.1	Score. Seventeenth-century manuscript Leçons de Ténèbres by Michel Lambert	173
13.2	Breathing. © Elisabeth Belgrano	176
13.3	To let. © Elisabeth Belgrano	179
13.4	Meditation. © Elisabeth Belgrano	181
17.1	my somatic voice is: the score. Concept by the author. Graphic design by Vivianna Chiotini. Following the development of the practice, the score includes the responses of: Leticia Santafé, Ellen Foyn Bruun, Jeremy Finch, Judah Attille, Jinyoung Kim, Christina Kapadocha, Fabiano Culora, Lisa Lapidge, Vicky Wright, Andrea Olsen, Anita Chari, Faye Rigopoulou, Amy Mihyang Ginther and Aphrodite Evangelatou. © Christina Kapadocha	238

Online material

Please note that the following audiovisual material that complements the reading of the suggested chapters can be found on this volume's webpage through the Routledge Voice Studies (RVS) website: www.routledgetextbooks.com/textbooks/routledgevoicestudies.

4.1   Patricia Bardi-organ work video (5:06). Documentation by Vivianna Chiotini
4.2   Patricia Bardi-Vocal Dance video (3:31). Documentation by Vivianna Chiotini
5.1   FV tremors video (1:47). Video and audio remix by Wendy Ann Mansilla
5.2   The river of blood (2:15). Media artwork by Wendy Ann Mansilla
5.3   In front of me (1:57). Media artwork by Wendy Ann Mansilla
8.1   Track _1st Improvisation_ (3:13). Voice recording by the author
8.2   Track _4th Improvisation_ (4:21). Voice recording by the author
17.1 _my somatic voice is_ (video) (7:14). Documentation by Vivianna Chiotini
17.2 _my somatic voice is_ (audio) (7:03). Extracted from the video by Vivianna Chiotini

You can also access the videos of all the activities that took place during the praxical symposium Somatic Voices in Performance Research and Beyond at East 15 Acting School in London (July 19–20, 2019) through the project's webpage on the CHASE (Consortium for the Humanities and the Arts South-East England) Training Hub: https://www.chasevle.org.uk/archive-of-training/archive-of-training-2019/somatic-voices/. Please see below a list of these twenty-one videos documented by Vivianna Chiotini:

1 Introduction by Christina Kapadocha (24:40)
2 Contribution by Andrea Olsen (30:28)
3 Contribution by Patricia Bardi (31:52)
4 Participant Response #1 by Judah Attille (09:51) (please see video no 5)
5 Participant Response #2 by Fabiano Culora (07:22) (please see video no 4)

xii *Online material*

6 Part I Reflection (48:03)
7 Contribution by Ellen Foyn Bruun (31:42)
8 Contribution by Leticia Santafé (28:33)
9 Contribution by Amy Mihyang Ginther (35:38)
10 Contribution by Stephen Paparo (34:12)
11 Participant Response #3 by Natusha Croes (17:24)
12 Participant Response #4 by Daron Oram (07:29)
13 Part II Reflection (38:14)
14 Contribution by Tara McAllister-Viel (33:34)
15 Contribution by Christina Gutekunst (31:23)
16 Contribution by Ilona Krawczyk (33:24)
17 Contribution by Christina Kapadocha (38:32)
18 Contribution by Anita Chari (36:46)
19 Participant Response #5 by Carmen Wong (13:52)
20 Participant Response #6 by Faye Rigopoulou (14:20)
21 Final Discussion (40:17)

Contributors

Patricia Bardi is the founder/director of the VMI Somatic Practice Certification Program combining Vocal Dance, Voice Movement Integration and Vital Movement Integration Bodywork centered in Amsterdam – an accredited program in somatic movement education and natural health practice. Bardi has toured extensively, teaching and performing at international festivals, universities and theatre schools throughout Europe, North America and Asia. She has received a London Arts Choreographer Award and she originated Organ Rebalancing, an accredited advanced bodywork training. She is a founding member of the School for Body-Mind Centering (US) and London's Chisenhale Dance Space and a Registered Somatic Movement Therapist (ISMETA).

Elisabeth Laasonen Belgrano is a singer and an artistic researcher with a special interest in vocal crossings between the seventeenth and twenty-first centuries. In 2011, she was awarded a PhD in Performance in Theatre and Music Drama from Faculty of Fine, Applied and Performing Arts at the University of Gothenburg. Her vocal practice and understanding of somatic vocality has developed parallel to Alexander technique studies. She is currently researching the practice of seventeenth-century vocal ornamentation as a method and a model for communicating and creating trust applicable to multiple scales and spacetimes, such as environmental, social, political and multicultural relations. She has been invited to present her work at festivals and conferences in Europe, the US and Japan.

Yvon Bonenfant makes art with non-normative voices; these days, usually, with audience's voices – where the audience members are co-artists. He applies his background and training in a variant of Gerda Boyesen's approach to body psychotherapy to thinking through acts of queered voicing. His artwork has shown in many countries and locations, and his writing has appeared in journals as varied as *Performance Research*, *Journal of Dance and Somatic Practices* and *Scan Journal*. His academic and creative work has been funded by the Wellcome Trust, Irish Research Council, Arts Council England, Youth Music and many others. He is Head of the Department of Theatre, University College Cork and Visiting Professor of Research at University of Winchester.

Ellen Foyn Bruun is an Associate Professor in Drama and Theatre Studies at the Norwegian University of Science and Technology, Trondheim. She is an Associate Teacher of Fitzmaurice Voicework® and holds an MA in Drama and Movement Therapy from the Royal Central School of Speech and Drama, University of London. As stage director, dramaturge and drama teacher, she has made theatre in a multiple of contexts over the years. In recent years, her Practice as Research has focused on integrating voice work in theatre and dramatherapy processes. Ellen has published several articles, written plays and contributed to books on drama and theatre practice.

Anita Chari is a somatic educator, political theorist and vocalist based in Portland, Oregon. She is Associate Professor of Political Science at the University of Oregon. Her work as a somatic practitioner draws from her training in Biodynamic Craniosacral Therapy, Embodiment Process work and Continuum Movement. Her scholarly writing focuses on the significance of aesthetics, artistic practices and embodiment for critical theory and practice. Her first monograph, *A Political Economy of the Senses*, was published in 2015 by Columbia University Press and her recent work appears in *Claire Fontaine: Newsfloor* (2019), *Catalyst* (2018), *The Hysterical Material* (2017) and *Social Dynamics* (in press by Routledge).

Sondra Fraleigh is a Professor Emeritus of Dance at the State University of New York (SUNY Brockport), a Fulbright Scholar and an award-winning author of nine books. Her recent editions include *Back to the Dance Itself: Phenomenologies of the Body in Performance* (forthcoming), *Moving Consciously: Somatic Transformations through Dance, Yoga, and Touch* (2015) and *Butoh: Metamorphic Dance and Global Alchemy* (2010). She also has numerous chapters in books on culture, aesthetics, ecology and cognitive psychology. Fraleigh's choreography has been seen in New York, Germany, Japan and India. She is the founding director of Eastwest Somatics Institute for the study of dance, yoga and movement.

Amy Mihyang Ginther is an Assistant Professor (University of California: Santa Cruz) and an award-winning theatre maker who has lived, taught and performed in the US, the UK, Argentina, Czech Republic, Ireland, Vietnam and South Korea. She is a *Voice and Speech Review* Associate Editor where she has published multiple articles, in addition to publishing in *Drama Therapy Review*. Amy has published in *The Toast, Transracial Eyes* and *Modern Loss: Candid Conversations about Grief* (Harper Wave 2018). She is currently working on her forthcoming edited volume on racializing and decolonizing actor training (Routledge) and a musical, *No Danger of Winning*.

Christina Gutekunst has been teaching and coaching voice for nearly twenty years in Germany and the UK. She taught voice in various drama

Contributors xv

schools and has been Head of Voice at East 15 Acting School in London (Loughton campus) since 2003. Christina has coached for both theatre and TV productions. She has worked as a voice over artist and director as well as an accent coach. She was a founder member of Beyond Words Theatre Company and Re: Actors Theatre Group. Her book *Voice into Acting: Integrating Voice and the Stanislavski Approach*, which she co-wrote with John Gillett, was published by Bloomsbury Methuen Drama. She is currently working on its second edition.

Christina Kapadocha (PhD) is a Lecturer in Theatre and Movement at East 15 Acting School and winner of the 2020 Outstanding Early Career Researcher Award in the Faculty of Humanities at the University of Essex. She is a London-based theatre and somatic practitioner-researcher, a Registered Somatic Movement Educator and founder of Somatic Acting Process®. Among others, her practice research has been published in the *Journal of Dance and Somatic Practices* and *Theatre, Dance and Performance Training* and has been presented in many national and international conferences. Christina particularly introduces new praxical discussions on the somatic in theatre-performance and voice studies. She has been working as an actress, director and movement director in Greece and the UK since 2007.

Ilona Krawczyk is a performer, singer and pedagogue. As a PhD candidate at the University of Huddersfield, she developed a process-oriented approach to vocal training and performance practice. Ilona trained with Song of the Goat Theatre and Musical Theatre School in Poland and since 2008 worked as a freelance artist for the companies in the UK, Poland, Germany, Estonia and Slovakia. She has been undertaking active roles in establishing and delivering innovative teaching programs. Notably, she is one of the Senior Artistic Instructors of Brave Kids, having developed its pedagogical model of work. For more information, please visit: www.ilonakrawczyk.com.

Ben Macpherson is a Senior Lecturer at the University of Portsmouth. He received his PhD in 2011 from the University of Winchester, in which he explored embodied reception theory and musical theatre performance. He is the founding co-editor of the *Journal of Interdisciplinary Voice Studies* (Intellect) and the Routledge Voice Studies series, and has published widely on voice, musical theatre. With Konstantinos Thomaidis, he edited the collection *Voice Studies: Critical Approaches to Process, Performance and Experience* (Routledge 2015) and his most recent monograph is *Cultural Identity in British Musical Theatre, 1890–1939: Knowing One's Place* (Palgrave 2018).

Tara McAllister-Viel is currently the Head of Voice and Speech at East 15 Acting School, University of Essex, Southend campus. Previously she was Lecturer-Voice at Royal Central School of Speech and Drama,

University of London (2005–2012) and Visiting Professor-Voice at the Korean National University of Arts [KNUA], School of Drama, Seoul, South Korea (2000–2005). The interweaving of adaptations of *p'ansori* with the Anglo-American voice practices became the foundation of her research area investigating ways of training actors' voices through an intercultural approach. She recently published the monograph *Training Actors' Voices: Towards an Intercultural/Interdisciplinary Approach*, part of the Routledge Voice Studies series.

Andrea Olsen is a Professor Emerita of Dance at Middlebury College, US, where she held the John C. Elder Professorship in Environmental Studies. Since 2016, she has also been visiting faculty at the Middlebury Institute of International Studies in Monterey, CA and at Smith College in Northampton. The author of *The Place of Dance, Body and Earth* and *Bodystories*, in collaboration with Caryn McHose, she has developed seven web-based films with Scotty Hardwig drawn from the texts (www.body-earth.org). Andrea performs and teaches internationally and offers annual Body and Earth Training Programs in the US and abroad. She is currently engaged in a two-year performance project with spoken text: *Awakening Grace: Six Somatic Tools* (https://andrea-olsen.com/).

Stephen A. Paparo is an Associate Professor of Music Education at the University of Massachusetts Amherst (US). He holds degrees from Michigan State University, Syracuse University and Ithaca College and is a Guild Certified Practitioner of the Feldenkrais Method® of somatic education. He is active as a guest conductor and regularly presents at international, national and state conferences. His research interests include the application of the Feldenkrais Method to singing instruction, non-traditional choral ensembles and LGBTQ studies in music education. He has published in *Bulletin for the Council of Research in Music Education*, *International Journal of Music Education* and *Music Education Research*, and *Musicianship: Composing in Choir* (GIA Publications).

Leticia Santafé is the director of the Postgraduate Program SOMart in Madrid. A Real Escuela Superior de Arte Dramático (RESAD) graduate, she has a Diploma in Linda Hartley's Integrative Bodywork and Movement Therapy (IBMT) and an Educator Diploma on Infant Movement Development (IDME) from the School for Body-Mind Centering®. Leticia has worked extensively in the fields of Performing Arts Research and creative expression facilitating the discovery of the Voice/Movement potentials for her students. The foundations of her work are Developmental Movement Education, Experiential Anatomy, Somatic Psychology, Linklater Voice Technique and her experience in performing arts. The discipline of Authentic Movement also supports, guides and nourishes her work.

Barbara Sellers-Young is a Senior Scholar and Professor Emerita, York University/Toronto. She is the author of two movement books for actors,

Breathing, Movement, Exploration and *Movement Onstage and Off*, which she co-authored with Robert Barton. She is also co-editor with Jade Rosina McCutcheon of *Embodied Consciousness: Technologies of Performance*. Besides teaching in Canada, she has taught movement and acting at universities in England, Australia, China and the US.

Ben Spatz (Senior Lecturer in Drama, Theatre and Performance at the University of Huddersfield) is a nonbinary researcher and theorist of embodied practice. They are the author of *What a Body Can Do* (Routledge 2015), *Blue Sky Body* (Routledge 2020) and *Making a Laboratory* (Punctum 2020). Ben is also co-convener of the IFTR Embodied Research Working Group and founding editor of the videographic *Journal of Embodied Research*. They have more than two decades of experience as a performer and director of contemporary performance, working mainly in New York City from 2001 to 2013. For more information, please visit www.urbanresearchtheater.com.

Konstantinos Thomaidis is a Senior Lecturer in Drama, Theatre and Performance at the University of Exeter. He is founding co-editor (with Ben Macpherson) of the Routledge Voice Studies series and the *Journal of Interdisciplinary Voice Studies* and founding co-convener of the Sound, Voice & Music Working Group at TaPRA. His publications include *Voice Studies* (Routledge 2015), *Theatre & Voice* (Palgrave 2017), *Time and Performer Training* (Routledge 2019) and the special issues Voicing Belonging: Traditional Singing in a Globalised World (Intellect 2017) and What Is New in Voice Training? (Routledge 2019). In 2019, he was shortlisted for the TaPRA Early Career Researcher Prize and in 2020, he won the Honorable Mention for Excellence in Editing at the ATHE Awards.

Pablo Troccoli (MA Res, RSMT) was initially educated in Fine Arts in Buenos Aires and Boston. He studied somatic disciplines applied to movement composition in Berlin and has professionally performed dance works in Germany, Belgium and France. As a somatic practitioner and researcher, Pablo holds an IBMT Diploma, the ISMETA accreditation as Somatic Movement Therapist and a Masters by Research in Art degree. He currently resides in a nature reserve in Wales, where he is simultaneously broadening the dance studio space into the landscape, affirming an embodied understanding of human existence and refining his somatic therapeutic skills immersed in a pristine natural environment.

Acknowledgements

This book is the outcome of a series of invitations and generous responses that allowed the development of research collaborations and activities. A big thank you to every single person involved in this process.

More specifically, I would like to express my gratitude to each contributor along with the contributing participants to the research activities that took place at East 15 Acting School as part of this project. A big thank you also to Vivianna Chiotini who documented and designed for this book with sensitivity and genuine enthusiasm.

The research activities that shaped the praxical and somatic identity of this volume would not have been possible without the financial support of a Pro-Vice-Chancellor (PVC)-Research and a CHASE/AHRC funds. Special thanks to Professor Tracey Loughran at the University of Essex who offered orientation and help towards these resources. In resonance, I wish to thank all the colleagues at East 15 Acting School and the Faculty of Humanities at the University of Essex who supported this project.

Many thanks to the Routledge Voice Studies series' editors Konstantinos Thomaidis and Ben Macpherson for their ongoing encouragement and advice as well as to the rest of the editing team at Routledge.

Thanks to my students with whom I learn.

Thanks to my husband with whom I grow.

Series foreword

The claim that voice is everywhere might be a truism. Voice is predominant in interpersonal and technologically mediated communications and features prominently in discussions of identity, psychological development and language acquisition. From theatrical performance to avant-garde or operatic singing, voice also offers aesthetic pleasure and, as is the case with rhetoric or journalism, it facilitates or imposes messages, arguments and beliefs. Voice is also a powerful metaphor. Feminist scholars have championed the female voice, cultural studies has lent an attentive ear to subaltern voices and the voice of the people is central to debates around politics, media, activism and religion. In the arts, voice is not merely an instrument to be perfected or enjoyed. Notions of the artist's voice or, occasionally, the author's voice permeate relevant discourses. Non-human or posthuman voices invite us to listen to animal voices, interactive voice recognition systems and vocal synthesis effected in robotics labs.

But how does one account for such plurality and multiplicity? How is voice to be discussed from a scholarly perspective? How might we move beyond bifurcated concepts of the voice in performance studies, for example?

The first, but decisive, step would be to create platforms for rigorous discussion of voice across disciplines, practices and areas of interest. The Routledge Voice Studies series offers precisely such a platform. In the past few years, attention given to voice has shifted from sporadic publications in disparate areas of inquiry to the epicenter of discourses in a variety of overlapping disciplines. This series aspires to facilitate the dissemination and cross-fertilization of voice-related research and effectively generate new knowledge and fresh critical insights on voice, vocality and voicing. To that end, we are delighted to include in the series of publications a variety of formats. We are equally interested in monographs, themed edited collections, student-focused anthologies and sourcebooks, revised and expanded editions of classic texts, and inter-medial and multimedial outputs. Our hope is that these varied structures will attract both practitioners and scholars as contributors, and find a readership among established and emergent researchers, students and artists.

We understand voice studies as a shifting landscape of questions and concerns, as a proliferative interdiscipline. Building on current initiatives, we wish to expand and capitalize on the productive debates taking place in the areas of music, theatre and performance studies, as well as cultural studies, ethnomusicology, sound studies, acoustics and acoustemology. Yet, we are equally as keen on extending an invitation to inputs from psychology, fine art, poetics and orality studies, linguistics, media and film studies, robotics and artificial intelligence, history and philosophy, translation and adaptation studies, among others. Spearheaded by the discussions across disciplines and cultures hosted in its inaugural publication, the edited collection *Voice Studies: Critical Approaches to Process, Performance and Experience*, this book series listens out for new spaces in which voice can reverberate with revitalized vigor. We hope you enjoy this fascinating journey with us.

Series editors: Dr Konstantinos Thomaidis and Dr Ben Macpherson

Foreword

A phonotechnics of vocal somaticity: an autobiophonic note

Konstantinos Thomaidis

I am in the third month of training as a physical theatre postgraduate at a UK Higher Education institution. After an intensive 7-week workshop on post-Grotowskian practices – and parallel to our ongoing classes in choreography – we are now embarking on 7 weeks of training in the Feldenkrais Method®, under the guidance of a certified Awareness Through Movement (ATM) practitioner and member of the Voice and Text Department at the Royal Shakespeare Company. At the beginning of the class, we all stand in a circle and are asked to say our names out-loud, followed by a couple of lines we have memorized. Addressing each other comes easy as we have been working as an ensemble for a while now and we all know a bit of text because we have just come out of our first practical assessment. I feel relatively relaxed in the task, since prior to the MA, I have trained for 5 years in classical acting and worked professionally for 2.

We are then instructed to lie on the floor. We are encouraged to bring our attention to specific parts of our body – the sacrum or the soles of our feet, for example – and observe how they feel, "from the inside" and "in the present," how they appear to our awareness as parts of the living whole that is our body. Our tutor's voice assumes a soothing tone, and phrasings such as "please do go gently" or "force nothing" are frequently pronounced. Between each verbal prompt, we are given plenty of time to immerse ourselves in the specificity of our affective, embodied state. I have done similar exercises in the past and, in this instance, I simply enjoy connecting to my body. One brief moment seems to thwart this flow: when asked to attend to my eye sockets, I realize I don't know what the English word means. Plus, in the Greek conservatoire setting of my previous training, I had been asked to focus on my "eyes" but never the "sockets". Momentarily, my mind wanders to familiar meanings of the word in English and for the first time I visualize my eyes as powered by electricity. But soon enough I assume it is the small cavity where the eye nests that is of interest, so I tentatively bring attention to the left, then the right one.

For the next couple of hours, our tutor will guide us through 2 ATM lessons on breath. At the beginning of each sequence, we bring awareness to our breath, primarily grounding our attention to the sternum, ribcage and lower abdomen, noticing "the function that feels natural and comfortable to us, individually". Then, each lesson builds towards an inversion of lower diaphragmatic breathing. The first invites puffing up the sternum ("reverse breathing") and the second locking the in-breath inside the torso and shifting it between the abdomen and the sternum ("see-saw breathing"). Following this, we are returned to abdominal breathing, which, by comparison, feels effortless, pleasurable even. To conclude, we stand in the circle again, repeating our names and texts. I am the last one to do so, and, upon hearing my delivery, the tutor exclaims enthusiastically: "Listen to how his voice has dropped! It is now fully in the body, isn't it?"

Encouraged by the I-voice of phenomenological description and the avowed preference of somatic disciplines for the experiential qualities of the I-body,[1] I wish to pause for a moment and listen-back to this brief episode of personal vocal history – to engage, in other words, in what I have termed as "auto-biophony" (αὐτός = self, the same + βίος = life + φωνή = sound, voice).[2] As the voicer bracketing, looping and amplifying a vocal memory from 2006, I am less concerned with presumed narrative accuracy or any opportunity to productively extrapolate first-person knowledge to other discursive domains. Rather, my attitude is *aporetic* (see Derrida, 1993): I seek to linger on the question marks raised by a somatic approach to vocality, puzzle over the simultaneous possibilities and impossibilities of yoking the somatic to the vocal or search for the conditions under which multiple physiovocal potentialities are resolved into seemingly singular answers.

Sandra Reeve identifies the conscious exploration and re-shaping of "particular movements," the provision of "a wider choice of movement possibilities" and the release of "fixed habits" (2011, 18) as the shared aims of somatic methodologies, including Body-Mind Centering, Feldenkrais or Laban/Bartenieff. Somatics help "people to be bodily aware of how they do, *as they are doing it*, rather than retrospectively, or not at all" (Reeve, 2011, 21, original emphasis). The implied temporality is that past experience has been rendered habitual bodily pattern and that tuning into the present through somatic attention opens up a future which is not a mere repetition of the habit. A similar progression was built into the structure of our ATM session: from habitual voicing, through investment in the present of breath, towards new possibilities of speaking. Meanwhile, this sequential progression was imbricated into a certain circularity. At the macrostructural level, the first ATM lesson was followed by a second which built on knowledge experientially acquired through the first; the session closed by revisiting the opening task; and six weeks of further ATM sessions, similar in structure, were to follow. Microstructurally, the "present" of guided awareness involved sustained repetition – of reversing or "see-saw"-ing the breath, for example.

Such intermingling of the linear and the cyclic is not uncustomary in performer training (see Evans et al., 2019). The inclusion of voice, however, adds further complexity. In many of the available methodologies and much writing about somaticity, the vocal ensues. The trainee undertakes body-awareness tasks and, upon cultivating an enhanced physical understanding of movement function, voicing is (expected to be) affected. This was evidently the case in the above example: we voiced at the start, moved "in the present of exploration" and concluded with spoken text. Although other strands of somatic exploration may *also* include sounding, the norm is that voice still tends to follow, even *within* the exercises offered. Anchoring the self through movement (however subtle or minimal) is the present, while voicing through the soma may be perceived as the present but is experientially a futurity. I am asked to feel my breath, "in the present," as of the body, and this new sensation is somehow transplanted to the (subsequent) moment of speaking.

And this is where aporias emerge, if we are to take somaphonics – the somatic co-constitution and inclination of the physical and the vocal towards each other – seriously: when both voices and bodies are of pedagogic interest, is the somatic, embedded in the conceptual nexus of the body-as-lived, always a way or means to vocality?[3] If somatics in physical training can fully invest in the present of movement, does the inclusion of live sonority render the voice either *a telos for* the soma (an outcome, symptom or aspiration of the bodied self) or *a measure of* the soma (a criterion retrospectively applied to check if the body operates at the level of the somatic)? How do I train as a somatic voicer if, by definition and intentionality, body somaticity exists only in the present but vocal somaticity is relegated to a future (though often discussed as pertaining to the same present)? In the moment of physiovocal presence, when is voicing experienced as somatically attuned, when as somatized and when as somatic? In other words: *when* is somaphonics and which are its implications for the trainee and their agency as vocal bodies?

If coming to voice through the soma both embraces and negates the foundational presupposition of somaticity-as-presence, how is somaphonic training achieved and who is the subject of such training? In the autobiophonic episode discussed earlier, I enter the scene as a professional, previously trained actor, I voice, I experience (new) somatic training, then voice again. I have experienced similar exercises before but not in contexts where such experiences were delineated as somatic in these terms. Even if my starting point were that of no prior training, the key tenet of somatic pedagogy would still be a methodology of de-training and re-training; I am invited to go through movement patterns that (may) feel unnatural (breathing upward in the sternum or locking the air in), and this culminates in increased functionality. The somatic at the physical level instills a move away from any blocks resulting from "kinaesthetic weakness" (Reeve, 2011, 18) or "harmful bodily manners" (Tarvainen, 2019, 8). Somatic de-patterning is intended to make the body aware of its established working modalities and, as a result, reinstate alternative neurological patterns of response that have fallen out of preference and may be more accurate, helpful and efficient. The body-future after somatic training is one of increased options through a return to the body-past prior to blocks and habits.

If trainees in somatics, as is frequently the case, are also invited to sound through humming, extra-normal vocalization or improvised text, a similar "return" to a non-prohibitive vocal state – akin perhaps to the phonic as exceeding the linguistic – can be assumed. As the autobiophonic episode indicates, however, aesthetic voicing poses a further challenge to the parallel development of somaticity and vocality. The fact that we are expected to know "some text" – against which we are to discern any improvement – is of significance: to interweave somaphonics with vocal aesthetics, a certain level of training needed to have taken place *elsewhere*. This is a recurring strategy in descriptions of somaphonic exercises: the trainee can use text or songs memorized at some point in the past or in other classes, have a print-out of a script or a score within easy reach, or learn such material prior to the somatic exploration and bookend the experience with a return to it. In some cases, the trainee already partakes in advanced, postlinguistic cultures of aesthetic vocality. When, for example, Päivi Järviö (2015) or Charulatha Mani (2019) propose ground-breaking approaches to western classical song or Karnatic singing, their turn to somaesthetics and phenomenality de-patterns abstract musicianship by foregrounding sensation and vocal materiality but can only function because a codification of the trainee's vocal embodiment has already preceded this training. Their trainees are already singers of these respective traditions – or, at least, singers-in-the-making. In my example, too, I experience these "new" lessons as somatic, because they de-stabilize aspects of my classical training, although prior knowledge of diaphragmatic breathing and (Shakespearean) text enable this very same vocal act. How can the here-and-now of the soma and that of the aesthetic vocal body coalesce if the former de-trains and the latter operates only through previous training? How is somaticity – which re-trains established movement patterns in the present – rendered aesthetic somaphonics – which presupposes a pre-existing physiovocal skillset (even if only to de-pattern it)?

Somatics, and by extension somaphonics, assume, it seems, their generative force if experienced as interruptions, subversions or ruptures – of bodily or physiovocal habituation, of canonical pedagogy, of daily or formal trainings.[4] In the domain of somatic philosophy, Richard Shusterman has argued for somaticity as the ground of all experience. His somaesthetics advocates for a move away from analyzing somatic experience, through pragmatically re-imagining new possibilities (of somatized discourse) and applying them to practice (2012). Practice, therefore, in the philosophical tradition is proposed as a rupture. By contrast, within artistic practice and inquiry, practical engagement is in place by default. Which further opportunities for subversion are, then, afforded to artist-researchers – and, more specifically, to practitioner-scholars of the somaphonic?

If, for example, the somaphonic has emerged as an interruption and critique of the abstract, reflective and logocentric and a desire for phonocentrism, can textuality be avoided altogether? Even if I were to diminish the importance of the lines our group of trainees delivered in the circle, our tutor's verbal cues acted as a constant script of the experience. To be "in the moment," to experience the lesson as a somatic one, external instruction – which could be perceived as addressing my body as an object-body or instrument – encouraged individual awareness and personalized re-training. The text of the instructions, logos-as-language, seems to operate somatically only if internally resolved: I listen to this external voice but I subsume it to my own internal voice-over; I am instructed to pay attention but, "individually," I decide to instruct my awareness accordingly, "in my own voice". Words and the way they are rendered physical sensation, matter. As a foreigner, I first become aware of the distance between the external and the internal voices when new vocabulary makes it impossible to perform the externally-instructed text as internally-motivated. To conjoin the outside voice with the felt experience of my body (and, later, with my speaking voice), a linguistic con-sensus is necessary. This linguistic gap is experienced as productive at first: I search for my eye sockets and this very searching is a process anchoring my awareness; the unknown word is a chance to attach a new visual schema to the somatic experience of my cranial structure.

I sense that my tutor finds a similar chance to acknowledge the somatic in his supportive closing statement, that my voice had dropped and was more "in the body". In this case, however, I am unmistakably reminded of the fact that words come with value judgments and encultured preferences. As a trained tenor, my vocal placement is quite high and, as a Greek, an onset with full vocal closure and less chest resonance is part of my cultural voic-escape. After two hours on the floor, I feel slightly tired and cold and I can only achieve partial glottal closure when formulating my text at the end of the session. My teacher – perhaps less keen on full-on laryngeal attack by training, culture-specific vocal habitus or class positionality? – hears a successful break into somaphonics in what I experience as a disconnection between my physicality and my voice. It is precisely such a moment, when I, as an autobiophonic voicer, live through my voice as overlappingly too close and too distanced, as expressing a singular identity but also exposing the self as an ongoing process, that provokes some further aporias: how are such discrepancies between the somaphonic as felt, as sensorially perceived and as culturally textualized be resolved in the trainee's body? How does the anti-logocentric impetus behind vocal somatics foreground the experiential, when this is always-already interwoven with a multiplicity of "scripts" – when, in other words, attending to the vocal soma through awareness and sensation is in itself a *phonotechnics*: a systematized methodology and technique of experiencing, re-organizing and perceiving vocal somaticity? More importantly, in the continuum ranging from the felt, sensual and affective aspects of vocal somaticity to its *tekhne* and texts, where can we discover possibilities, not only for new articulations of the somaphonic but also for a new politics of the vocal soma?

Notes

1 For an overview of phenomenological writing, see van Manen, 1984. For the first-person perspective pursued in somatics, key points of reference are Hanna (1973) and Eddy (2002).
2 Since 2015, I have developed a practice-research project that interrogates the ways in which a voicer understands, processes and narrates the makings of their voice. The project proposed autobiophony – roughly translating as vocal autobiography/narration of the vocal self/memoire of the self in voice – as its core methodology. This led to the creation of a performance lecture, used between 2016 and 2020 as part of my pedagogy at the University of Exeter, then more broadly circulated, for example, at the Norwegian Theatre Academy in 2018 and the University of Portsmouth in 2019 (Thomaidis, 2018, 2019, 2020). For reflexive writing on the two possible scenarios of subjectivity-making through voice, see Cockburn and Thomaidis (2017, 217–218).
3 Both somaphonics and phonotechnics are my neologisms and were developed as responses to research developed at the intersections of voicing and somatics (e.g., Boston and Cook, 2009; Tarvainen, 2019; Kapadocha, 2021).
4 It is not uncommon for the genesis of somatic methodologies to occur as such an interruption or rupture – the overcoming of his recurrent laryngeal hoarseness by Alexander or his knee injury by Feldenkrais are ubiquitous examples (see Worth, 2015, 216).

References

Boston, J. and Cook, R. (eds.) (2009) *Breath in Action: The Art of Breath in Vocal and Holistic Practice*. London: Jessica Kingsley.
Cockburn, R. and Thomaidis, K. (2017) Cross-chapter discussion: 'the subject' and voice. In: Experience Bryon (ed.) *Performing Interdisciplinarity: Working Across Disciplinary Boundaries Through an Active Aesthetic*. London: Routledge, 215–218.
Derrida, J. (1993) Aporias. Stanford, CA: Stanford University Press.
Eddy, M. (2002) Somatic practices and dance: global influences. *Dance Research Journal*, 34(20) 46–62.
Evans, M., Thomaidis, K. and Worth, L. (eds.) (2019) *Time and Performer Training*. London: Routledge.
Hanna, T. (1985) *Bodies in Revolt: A Primer in Somatic Thinking*. Novato, CA: Freeperson Press.
Järviö, P. (2015) The singularity of experience in the voice studio: a dialogue with Michel Henry. In: Konstantinos Thomaidis and Ben Macpherson (eds.) *Voice Studies: Critical Approaches to Process, Performance and Experience*. London and New York: Routledge, 25–37.

Kapadocha, C. (ed.) (2021) *Somatic Voices in Performance Research and Beyond.* London and New York: Routledge.

Mani, C. (2019) CompoSing awareness: approaching somaesthetics through voice and yoga. *The Journal of Somaesthetics*, 5(2) 67–85.

Reeve, S. (2011) *Nine Ways of Seeing a Body.* Devon: Triarchy Press.

Shusterman, R. (2012) *Thinking through the Body: Essays in Somaesthetics.* Cambridge: Cambridge University Press.

Tarvainen, A. (2019) Music, sound, and voice in somaesthetics: overview of the literature. *The Journal of Somaesthetics*, 5(2) 8–23.

Thomaidis, K. (2018) A voice is. A voice has. A voice does. *Norwegian Theatre Academy.* https://www.hiof.no/nta/english/about/news-and-events/events/tl-thomaidis.html [Accessed 27 January 2020].

——— (2019) Rethinking theatre voices. *Macmillan International Higher Education Blog.* https://www.macmillanihe.com/blog/post/theatre-voice-konstantinos-thomaidis/ [Accessed 27 January 2020].

——— (2020) Dramaturging the I-Voicer in *A Voice Is. A Voice Has. A Voice Does*: Methodologies of autobiophony. *Journal of Interdisciplinary Voice Studies*, 5(1) 81–106.

van Manen, M. (1984) Practicing phenomenological writing. *Phenomenology + Pedagogy*, 2(1) 36–69.

Worth, L. (2015) Editorial. *Theatre, Dance and Performance Training*, 6(2) 125–129.

Introduction
Somatic voice studies

Christina Kapadocha

Why somatic voice studies?

Everything started as part of my overall research. My identity is theatre and somatic practitioner-researcher. And it's very significant for me to identify myself within every activity that I'm doing because it's important to highlight that I'm not here as a voice expert, even though my first professional training in the age of fifteen was in classical singing so this is how experientially I found the first connection between my body and my voice. But this didn't become my focus […] The voice and each actor's voice is not my primary focus but I acknowledge it as an inextricable part of each actor's embodied experience. So I move and I hear, I move and I sound, I move and I speak […] In other practitioners' work voice is the starting point whereas in "our" work "we"[1] start from movement; and then movement is in holistic relation, in sequential relation with voicing.

The above draws from how I situated myself in the enactment and development of this project during the introduction of a research event at East 15 Acting School in London (May 4, 2019).[2] The reason I choose it as the opening of this book is because it helps me introduce the subject as well as the overall identity of this collection. There are two elements from this shared experience I wish to utilize in order to suggest an initial response to the subheading of this opening part "why somatic voice studies?". The first has to do with current revisions on the understanding of expertise in the sense of dominant knowledge authority in contemporary voice studies. In the recent special issue What is New in Voice Training? (2019b), Konstantinos Thomaidis introduces the need for a reconsideration of the environments that generate voice knowledge and therefore an expansion of vocal praxis[3] (2019a, 300). This is combined with the urgent necessity of acknowledging vocal polyphony, processual awareness and the significance of current transdisciplinary research and collaboration towards challenging the singular vocal expertise (Ibid., 301). The second element that adds to the previous point is that, despite the growing research interest in the embodied and experiential aspects of voice,[4] there is space for further examination of the moving-voicing-thinking potentialities through the study of diverse somatic vocalities.

This book addresses the aforementioned topics by bringing attention to the somatic field of study. Even though somatic practices have been integrating the significance of polyphonic voicing into their methodologies and could offer significant insights on the embodied understanding of voices, they have not been introduced as an area of voice research. Moreover, somatic studies have been gaining increasing popularity due to their multidisciplinary influences upon processes within and beyond artistic investigations.[5] Nevertheless, they are still broadly undocumented and therefore have not attracted enough attention regarding their impact on contemporary research. This collection fills this significant literature gap by offering a cohesive and polyphonic discussion on contemporary, emergent interactions between somatic discourses, critical voice studies and praxical methodologies. By doing so, it broadens current understandings of the somatic and the ways in which its study could advance vocal praxis. Stemming from direct dialogue with somatic lineages or various critical interrogations on vocal somaticities, this volume primarily emerges from performance contexts. At the same time, it opens up broader multidisciplinary discussions on disseminating voices, theoretical criticism and research methodologies that move beyond performance praxis. Bringing together a community of international practitioner-researchers who either find voice through somaticity[6] or somaticity through voice, it foregrounds vocal diversity and inclusion within *somatic turns*.

Somatic turns

Before moving further, I should clarify that the words *soma* and *somatic* originally derive from the Greek language with which I happen to be particularly familiar as it is my mother tongue. Soma in Greek identifies every living (at times even inanimate) body while somatic describes any process that emerges from the state of being or having a living body. Nevertheless, during the development of my research, I was re-introduced to these notions. As I began to notice that the words kept coming up in examples that spread from company names to artistic languages and broader discourses, I became interested in their relevance to multiple disciplines and essentially to advancements in the diverse use of soma/somatic in the twenty-first century. In other words, I received this shift in language, or even "trend" if you would like in some cases, as an indication that there is space for further research on what bodies could be or what embodiment may imply in the *here and now*.

I was particularly drawn to the term *somatic turn*[7] by the pragmatist philosopher Richard Shusterman (2008, 2012). According to the philosopher's idea, "the [twenty-first century] somatic turn may express the need to find and cultivate a stable point of personal reference in a rapidly changing and increasingly baffling world" (Shusterman in Loukes, 2013, 197). The interesting element to me is that Shusterman uses the term somatic in order to designate not only a physical shift in response to changes *in the world* but a general refreshed interest in what is identified as *bodymind* (see Allison, 1999). Traditionally connected to movement practices such as yoga and meditation (which unquestionably go through a current re-evaluation within a wide spectrum of contexts, from fitness to education), bodymind is used to describe the inner-outer dynamics in a potential integration between our physical and intellectual experiences.

Following further my curiosity about the current use of the term "somatic turn," it easily came to my attention that it is not confined to Shusterman's discourse. For instance, in the field of anthropology and her book *Dynamic Embodiment for Social Theory* (2012), Brenda Farnell discusses a first and a second somatic turn. The first was established in the 1970s "by the work of Michael Foucault, Pierre Bourdieu, a range of feminist theorists, and an interdisciplinary, postmodern, phenomenological valorization of the sensuous" (2012, 4). According to Farnell, "the first [somatic turn] moves us from disembodied social science to a focus 'on the body,'" while the "second somatic turn [situated in the twenty-first century] offers a theoretical enrichment of the earlier phase by re-positioning the *moving* body as central to a theoretically adequate account of embodied social action" (2012, 4, original emphasis). In contemporary archaeology, Bjørnar Olsen uses the notion of a similarly identified somatic turn in order to focus on its material potentials. Olsen adds that a crucial element is usually missing from the identification of the somatic turn "in disciplines such as philosophy, literary studies, sociology, and anthropology: the *things* that the body relates to and blends in with – in short, the material components of the world it is *being in*" (2010, 7, original emphasis).

It seems that overall "somatic turn" in the discussed discourses is used to identify various interrelations: between one's body and mind, one's bodymind and their environments, including other ever-changing moving bodies, social conditions and material objects. An inextricable part of this emerging and ongoing interrelational awareness, that brings us back to the subject of this book, is a relevant somatic turn in the contemporary study and analysis of voice. Therefore, this volume was driven by questions such as: How could somatic processes inform the understanding and communication of multiple vocal experiences and *somata*[8] in diverse contexts? How do somatic methodologies assist the development of multidisciplinary discussions, praxical research and pedagogies? How could somatic vocalities cultivate awareness of embodied identities and roles, ethical, cultural and sociopolitical implications in communication and expression? How could somatic processes offer methodological frameworks for the dissemination of vocal investigations within and beyond the field of performance studies?

Mapping somatic voices

The words *somatic* and *voice* in relation can be currently encountered in various performance-oriented projects and practices. For instance, Somatic Voicework™ founded by Jeanie LoVetri is a popular voice method.[9] During the making of this volume and while using similar vocabulary, I came across several events such as the collaborative workshop *Our Somatic Voice*[10] between the UK-based practitioners Michaela Bartovska, Zoe Katsilerou and Vicky Wright (June 17, 2018). I am also aware that the subject is present in various current praxical PhD projects, beyond the ones included here, and it keeps attracting the attention of new publications. In the existing literature, the exploration of the somatic in voice appears in edited collections on voice studies that focus on voice practices and techniques (see Boston and Cook, 2009), in volumes that introduce the contemporary field of critical and multidisciplinary voice studies (see Thomaidis and Macpherson, 2015) and in journal issues that investigate the overlaps between sound and voice studies (see Tarvainen and Järviö, 2019). This book goes further by introducing somatic voice studies as a new area of voice and somatic research and a source of theoretical advancements in the embodied perception of vocal multiplicity focusing on the significance of vocal praxis and the urgency for multidisciplinary polyphony.

Drawing from the field of contemporary voice studies, this project has been particularly inspired by the collection edited by Konstantinos Thomaidis and Ben Macpherson (2015), not only because of its critical identity but also through the editors' notion of *in-betweenness* (3–8). Whether *in-between* voice studies and other disciplines, somatics and other disciplines, theories and practices, practices and praxes, voicing and listening, voicing and writing, this volume offers numerous research methodologies for studying in-betweenness. As Thomaidis and Macpherson state: "Acknowledging the in-betweenness of voice is a provocation to methodological multiplicity" (2015, 7). The same advocation of multiplicity was prompted towards the definition of the terms *soma* and *somatic*, given that the contributors were urged from the onset of the project to offer their own perspectives on the use of the words instead of following a specific theory. Thus, while acknowledging the significant contributions of existing work within somatic studies, there was also space for further multidisciplinary possibilities and advancements. A very helpful and concise source for this overview of somatic practices, notions and ideologies during the development of this book has been the work of the academic and practitioner Martha Eddy (2009, 2016).

The first contemporary practitioner and scholar from the lineage of somatic studies who noticed interconnections between various experiential practices and worked towards creating a common space within which they could co-exist and interact was Thomas Hanna (1928–1990). Towards the end of the twentieth century, Hanna re-introduced soma in order to identify one's experienced, instead of objectified, bodymind (1970) and he used the umbrella term somatics or Somatics in order to name this new field of study (1976). Don Hanlon Johnson, who also expands upon this work through collections that allow the written dissemination of somatics (1995, 2018), notices that the added "s" to the end of the adjective somatic "created an umbrella under which many separate schools of transformational approaches to embodiment – often in conflict – could gather and deepen a collaborative work, with the kinds of dialogue that promote more grounded knowledge and better training of practitioners" (2019).[11] Especially in his recent collection *Diverse Bodies, Diverse Practices: Towards an Inclusive Somatics* (2018), Johnson argues for the significance of "difference," of more socially inclusive somatics and "a model of how voices from various places in the world and diverse bodily capacities might interact creatively with each other" (2018, 21).

In resonance with Johnson's model of inclusive somatics, this book is developed around pioneers in somatic lineages while it simultaneously creates dynamic dialogues with individuals and practices that explore vocal somaticities beyond commonly recognized somatics. This became possible only thanks to the availability and innovative contributions of the eighteen international authors, from various stages within their careers, who generously accepted my invitation to the project and shaped the first "nucleus" of this new community of work.[12] My invitation to the selected contributors was driven by the innately physiovocal, transdisciplinary and praxical identity of their work that could offer invaluable insights into this new area of practice research. At the same time, it would be process-sensitive to acknowledge that this book plants the "seed" of the emerging field of somatic voice studies which is originally identified by the work of the practitioner-researchers included here but also goes beyond this book.

Mapping this book

As part of my praxical research, I have noticed that maps could offer a smooth bridging between diverse narratives and a project's multiple components. During the practice of making and introducing this volume, which I identify as praxical, I also found myself creating a map (see Figure I). This map is developed upon *how* the book offers a new area of vocal and somatic praxis by bringing in relation somatics with other practices, practices with theoretical criticism. Ironically, it does not give geographical information on the journeys that are embedded in the project which include processes that have taken place in Amsterdam, Norway, Spain, France, Greece, Poland, Sweden, South Africa, Japan, South Korea, India, Canada, the US and the UK. The map does though offer a visualization of how this volume achieves its multidisciplinary vision of in-between potentialities.

In the middle of Figure I, you can see a rhomb with the practices that are directly connected to foundational lineages within somatics and the work

6 *Christina Kapadocha*

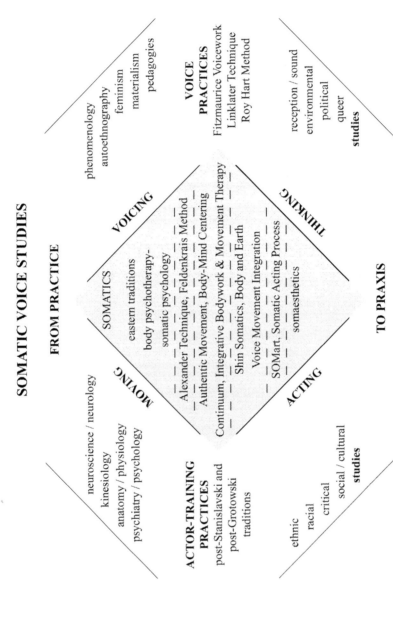

Figure 1 Mapping this book. Concept by the author. Graphic design by Vivianna Chiotini. © Christina Kapadocha.

of authors in the volume. At the top of this rhomb are eastern traditions (either ancient such as yoga or more recent like butoh) and the umbrella terms body psychotherapy-somatic psychology (see Marlock et al, 2015) that also identify contexts in which the discussed practices are employed. The ground of this somatic paradigm shift is set in the opening chapter by Barbara Sellers-Young (Chapter 1) through the shared methods of *breath, exploration* and *imagery* which underlie the whole volume. The contemporary eastern-western integration in approaches to being-moving-voicing is particularly evident in the works of Sondra Fraleigh (Chapter 3), Tara McAllister-Viel (Chapter 9) and Elisabeth Laasonen Belgrano (Chapter 13) while the way therapeutic-oriented work is applied in learning environments for special education is the source of Yvon Bonenfant's discussion (Chapter 14).

Next in this inner rhomb, you can see two practices established by the founders of contemporary somatic education F. M. Alexander (1869–1955) and Moshe Feldenkrais (1904–1984). Alexander Technique has informed Chapters 9 and 13 mentioned earlier and Feldenkrais Method towards voicing is the subject of Chapter 7 by Stephen Paparo. They are followed by practices which Eddy situates in the second and third generations of somatics: Authentic Movement by Mary Whitehouse (1910–2001), Body-Mind Centering by Bonnie Bainbridge Cohen, Continuum [Movement] by Emilie Conrad (1934–2014) and Integrative Bodywork and Movement Therapy (IBMT) by Linda Hartley.

Continuum becomes the vessel for Anita Chari's intercorporeal understanding of political resonance (Chapter 15) while the rest of the aforementioned practices appear in multiple discussions. I intentionally did not include in the above the innovative work of founders of somatic practices who contribute to this volume: Body and Earth by Andrea Olsen (Chapter 2), Shin Somatics by Sondra Fraleigh (Chapter 3) and Voice Movement Integration (VMI) by Patricia Bardi (Chapter 4). Within the same lineages, which are outlined throughout, is situated SOMart, a somatic voice and movement educational program for artists founded by Leticia Santafé (co-author of Chapter 6 with Pablo Troccoli) and my emerging practice Somatic Acting Process (Chapter 12). Finally, at the bottom of the rhomb, I add Richard Shusterman's somaesthetics as a practice within the lineage of somatics. Echoing in a way the philosophy of Chapter 1 as well as how in-betweenness exists throughout this book, Ben Macpherson in Chapter 16 maps out six statements based on the embodied thinking of the somaesthetic in-between.

Now, you may notice that none of the corners of the inner rhomb are closed and this visually suggests openness for further interrelations. The fact that somatic practices have been applied or modified as teaching and research methodologies within performance environments allowed a dynamic interaction with actor-training and voice practices, as you could see on both sides of the map. Specifically in this volume, you can find relevant discussions with post-Stanislavskian traditions in the work of Christina

Gutekunst (Chapter 10) and post-Grotowskian advancements in the work of Ilona Krawczyk and Ben Spatz (Chapter 11). The voice practices the authors employ for the investigation of vocal somaticities are Fitzmaurice Voicework (Chapter 5 by Ellen Foyn Bruun), Roy Hart Method (Chapter 8 by Amy Mihyang Ginther) and Linklater Voice Training. Due to the impact and popularity of the work of Kristin Linklater, her approach is acknowledged in various parts of this book. Nevertheless, it is specifically present in the work of Leticia Santafé and Pablo Troccoli (Chapter 6).

What I have presented up to this point are the basic somatic or somatically-inspired practices you will come across in the length of this book. Nevertheless, if you go back to the map, you will be able to notice that all the above take place within a transformative space *from practice to praxis* (or more accurately *from practices to praxes*). Therefore, at the four sides of the map, I have situated all the theoretical discussions the works within this volume either contribute to or develop further. They are positioned in groups rather than in the order they appear in the collection. These theoretical components include dialogues between somatics and medical sciences (top left), philosophical strands and pedagogies (top right), ethnic-racial and sociocultural studies (bottom left), contemporary social sciences and queer studies (bottom right). Even when chapters foreground either practical or theoretical components, the critical stance of praxis is present and is summarized in one overarching research question that navigates each of the book's four parts as follows:

- **Part I** – How does vocal urgency and awareness emerge from somatic attention to movement?
- **Part II** – How somatic processes can complement vocal training, theories and criticism?
- **Part III** – How can somatic awareness challenge unhelpful dualities and other problematics in vocal processes?
- **Part IV** – How can current somatic research in voice studies move beyond performance environments?

The aforementioned four parts and the book's developmental structure are additionally indicated through the four interrelated words at the sides of the map's inner rhomb: moving-voicing-acting-thinking. This also suggests the basic content of each part, given that the contributors of Part I come from a dance background, the contributors of Part II bring together voice work and somatics, the content of Part III unfolds within acting and performance-training environments and the works in Part IV focus on possibilities beyond performance processes. Nevertheless, moving-voicing-acting-thinking should be perceived in constant flux and in any sequence you would like to as you go through the authors' polyvocal writing. In respect to this polyphony and your diverse perceptions as readers, I choose not to include here an outline of each chapter in order to avoid any imposition of my own understanding as the editor of this collection.

Somatic voice studies 9

An inextricable part of this in-between polyphony in the context of this volume is also a multimodality in writing voices that situates this project within a lineage of current praxical investigations.[13] At this point, in-betweenness is used as a theoretical framework for the methodological multiplicity of writing that can emerge through vocal praxis. The praxical material in this book expands from layout choices (i.e. maps, boxes, indented parts) to experiential narratives (in italics or standard format, as explorations-invitations to the readers or as the main body of the text), dialogic chapters (Chapters 4, 6 and 11), images, polyphonic video and audio recordings. When it comes to the audio-visual material that complements the writing of this book, we use two ways of accessing the web spaces. The material that was specifically generated for the purposes of this project (a list of which is also included in this book's Table of Contents) is available on the volume's own webpage through the Routledge Voice Studies (RVS) website: www.routledgetextbooks.com/textbooks/routledgevoicestudies. Each file has a specific title and is included in the main body of the text of Chapters 4, 5, 8 and 17. You will also be directed to online sources authors had set up before this book's creative process through links included in the chapters' endnotes. In both cases, I would invite you to follow the suggested cross-narratives that this praxical volume, as indicated earlier, offers.

The culmination of this collection's polyvocal and intermedia identity which, among others, challenges traditional divisions between practices and theories as well as modes of disseminating practice research that tend to separate books from other media[14] is the last part (Part V) of this volume and my closing chapter (Chapter 17). The "Beyond our somatic voices" narrative is shaped *through* the integration of my writing and the "voices" of participants to a praxical two-day symposium at East 15 Acting School in London as part of this project within the conservatoire's emerging research activities (July 19–20, 2019).[15] I organized this gathering not only to bring together in one place the contributors of this book but also to open up an active participation to the *research process* of this project as a whole. In resonance with the book's overall nature, the chapter, as well as the whole collection, closes with an audio-visual documentation of the integrative practice "my somatic voice is …". In the same way, I really hope that by experiencing the invitations within this project, you would be able to explore qualities of *your own somatic voices* adding your polyphonic findings to the reflection "my somatic voice is …".

Notes

1 I use "us" and "we" in inverted commas to suggest that, at this point, I am referring to how I situate my work in relation to other somatic practices that incorporate voice as well as performance training practices that integrate physicality and voice and are identified as physiovocal or physio-vocal (see Thomaidis, 2013; Bryon, 2014). I return to how my praxis contributes to the latter in Chapter 12.

2 The specific research event was developed around a guest seminar by the founding co-editor of Routledge Voice Studies series and the Journal of Interdisciplinary Voice Studies, Ben Macpherson. The seminar entitled *Sensing, singing, streaming: six statements on somaesthetics (and a speculation about Spotify)* was inspired by Macpherson's discussion in Chapter 16.
3 Theory within or through practice (see Nelson, 2013).
4 To indicate among others the books that are included in this Routledge Voice Studies series as well as the Journal of Interdisciplinary Voice Studies founded by the same editors, Konstantinos Thomaidis and Ben Macpherson, as sources of this new knowledge.
5 A source of this growing discourse is the Journal of Dance and Somatic Practices edited by Sarah Whatley, Natalie Garrett Brown, Emma Meehan and Karen Wood.
6 Somaticity is translated as corporality, the state of being or having a body.
7 I first came across the term in Rebecca Loukes' chapter "Making Movement: The Psychophysical in 'Embodied' Practices" (2013, 194–223) as part of the volume *Acting: Psychophysical Phenomenon and Process* (Zarrilli et al, 2013).
8 Plural for soma.
9 See http://thevoiceworkshop.com/somatic-voicework/
10 See http://zoekatsilerou.com/our-somatic-voice/
11 See https://donhanlonjohnson.com/somatics/
12 Along with the additional contributions of participants to the Somatic Voices symposium (July 19–20, 2019, East 15 Acting School, London), which are acknowledged in the closing chapter (Chapter 17) of this volume, where I also revisit the notion and experience of community in this project.
13 This lineage in the field of voice studies can be identified among others in the first collection of the Routledge Voice Studies series edited by Konstantinos Thomaidis and Ben Macpherson (2015), the issues of the Journal of Interdisciplinary Voice Studies as well as the issue What is new in voice training? for the Theatre, Dance and Performance Training journal edited by Thomaidis and which is additionally complemented by a blog. In the field of somatic studies, this ongoing investigation has been present in the work of the Journal of Dance and Somatic Practices. The recent special issue Wright-ing the Somatic: Narrating the Bodily edited by Adesola Akinleye and Helen Kindred has the discussed polyphony and multimodality in the heart of its inquiry.
14 I am explicitly referring here to book publications as there are currently various online platforms (i.e. figshare for institutions), research-oriented blogs (i.e. the Theatre, Dance and Performance Training blog) and peer-reviewed journals (i.e. the Journal for Artistic Research-JAR) that allow and prompt the dynamic interrelation between various modes of disseminating practice research.
15 As also indicated in the Table of Contents, the video documentation of all the symposium activities is available through the following CHASE webpage: https://www.chasevle.org.uk/archive-of-training/archive-of-training-2019/somatic-voices/. Due to a mistake on the webpage, please note that: Response #1 by Judah Attille is video no 5 and Response #2 by Fabiano Culora is video no 4.

References

Akinleye, A. and Kindred, A. (eds.) (2019) Wright-ing the somatic: narrating the bodily. *Journal of Dance and Somatic Practices*, 1(11).
Allison, N. (ed.) (1999) *The Illustrated Encyclopedia of Body-mind Disciplines*. New York: The Rosen Publishing Group.
Boston, J. and Cook, R. (eds.) (2009) *Breath in Action: The Art of Breath in Vocal and Holistic Practice*. London: Jessica Kingsley Publishers.

Bryon, E. (2014) *Integrative Performance: Practice and Theory for the Interdisciplinary Performer.* Abingdon, Oxon: Routledge.

Eddy, M. (2009) A brief history of somatic practices and dance: historical development of the field of somatic education and its relationship to dance. *Journal of Dance and Somatic Practices*, 1(1) 5–27.

——— (2016) *Mindful Movement: The Evolution of the Somatic Arts and Conscious Action.* Wilmington, NC: Intellect.

Farnell, B. (2012) *Dynamic Embodiment for Social Theory: 'I Move Therefore I Am'.* Abingdon, Oxon: Routledge.

Hanna, T. (1970) *Bodies in Revolt: A Primer in Somatic Thinking.* New York: Holt Rinehart and Winston.

——— (1976) The Field of Somatics. *Somatics: Journal-Magazine of the Bodily Arts & Sciences*, 1(1) 30–34.

Johnson, D. H. (ed.) (1995) *Bone, Breath and Gesture: Practices of Embodiment.* Berkeley, CA: North Atlantic Books.

——— (ed.) (2018) *Diverse Bodies, Diverse Practices: Toward an Inclusive Somatics* [Play Book]. Berkeley, CA: North Atlantic Books.

——— (2019) Somatics [online]. Available from: https://donhanlonjohnson.com/somatics/ [Accessed 27 September 2019].

Loukes, R. (2013) Making movement: the psychophysical in 'embodied' practices. In: Phillip B. Zarrilli, Jerri Daboo and Loukes Rebecca (eds.) *Acting: Psychophysical Phenomenon and Process.* Basingstoke: Palgrave Macmillan, 194–223.

Marlock, G. and Weiss, H. (with Courtenay Young and Michael Soth) (eds.) *The Handbook of Body Psychotherapy and Somatic Psychology* Berkeley, CA: North Atlantic Books.

Nelson, R. (2013) *Practice as Research in the Arts: Principles, Protocols, Pedagogies, Resistances.* Hampshire: Palgrave Macmillan.

Olsen, B. (2010) *In Defense of Things: Archaeology and the Ontology of Objects.* Lanham, MD: AltaMira Press.

Shusterman, R. (2008) *Body Consciousness: A Philosophy of Mindfulness and Somaesthetics.* Cambridge: Cambridge University Press.

——— (2012) *Thinking through the Body: Essays in Somaesthetics.* Cambridge: Cambridge University Press.

Tarvainen, A. and Järviö, P. (eds.) (2019) Somaesthetics and sound. *The Journal of Somaesthetics*, 5(2).

Thomaidis, K. (2013) The vocal body. In: Sandra Reeve (ed.) *Body and Performance.* Devon: Triarchy Press.

——— (2019a) Editorial: what is new in voice training? *Theatre, Dance and Performance Training Journal*, 10(3) 295–302.

——— (ed.) (2019b) What is new in voice training? *Theatre, Dance and Performance Training Journal*, 10(3).

Thomaidis, K. and Macpherson, B. (eds.) (2015) *Voice Studies: Critical Approaches to Process, Performance and Experience.* Abingdon, Oxon: Routledge.

Zarrilli, P., Daboo, J. and Loukes, R. (2013) *Acting: Psychophysical Phenomenon and Process.* Basingstoke: Palgrave Macmillan.

Part I
Vocalities in somatic studies

1 Three somatic processes to voice through movement
Breath, exploration, imagery

Barbara Sellers-Young

I am in a dance rehearsal for the *Voices of the Disappeared* and the choreographer Gail B. hands me my script for the performance that describes a Guatemalan woman's experience of losing her eldest child.[1] The goal is to combine the words of the script with the previously choreographed gestures. I am initially confused but begin to try to integrate the choreography with my limited knowledge of breath-based vocal support and the images in the script. The final performance was only minimally successful in integrating movement and voice but it helped me to realize that in the performance style of dance theatre, the vocal life of the dancer was as significant as their movement technique.

As someone interested in pedagogical approaches to dance training, the question I asked myself was: What is the process of training that integrates sound and movement? This essay is developed theoretically and practically upon my discoveries over a thirty-year period through a review of the research on neuroscience and diverse approaches of somatic practitioners. In each area – neuroscience research and somatic practices – the historical binary of mind-body or voice-body is exchanged for a conception of the self as an integrated soma. Thus, an underlying paradigm of the essay is that movement and voice are interconnected experiences.

The suggested movement-voice interrelation is not an original concept per se and has been already present in the newly shaped field of critical voice studies.[2] Nevertheless, this essay integrates research on neuroscience with its specific reference to *embodied cognition* and an overview of somatic methods to evolve an approach to physical-vocal training based on three interactive processes – breath, exploration and imagery. The somatic basis of each process is described followed by a movement-sound exercise. This narrative provides an opportunity to separately focus on each process from both theoretical and practical perspectives. As the processes are interactive, the final exercise integrates all three.

Neuroscience and somatics: a mind-body paradigm shift

Research of neuroscientists Anthony Damasio (2000, 2005, 2010), Joseph LeDoux (2003), Shaun Gallagher (2005), Michael Gazzaniga (2008) and others has shifted Descartes' "body versus mind" paradigm with research that indicates that the development of our neural structures is the result of input from the body's sensory systems; and, in fact, that the interaction of the entire self or soma with the environment structures our neural system, a process referred to as embodied cognition. As developmental psychologist Esther Thelen phrases it:

> To say that cognition is embodied means that it arises from bodily interactions with the world. From this point of view, cognition depends on the kinds of experiences that come from having a body with particular perceptual and motor capacities that are inseparably linked and that together form the matrix within which memory, emotion, language, and all other aspects of life are meshed.
>
> (2001, xx)

Reviewing the research, Margaret Wilson (2002) concurs with Thelen and argues that cognition and its relationship to embodiment are situated in a cultural and environmental moment which is related to an individual acting in that context and that action occurs within a specific time frame. Consciousness is therefore a real-world activity that is the result of the integration of how individuals perceive the world and the actions they undertake based on that perception. In neuroscience terms, enaction is not a mind or a body in action but the totality of an integrated being as soma in responsive action.

Somatic specialists have embraced the research in neuroscience as providing evidence of the integrative states they advocate. Batson and Wilson state that "embodiment is not about the body, but rather about the generative power of movement" (2014, 75). Batson and Wilson further suggest that individuals are a sensory rich field which "[b]y sensitizing and discrimination among sensory phenomena, one learns to distinguish degrees of effort" (2014, 107). Philosopher and practitioner Shusterman states that "[t]he cultivation of skills of enhanced awareness is a central task of somaesthetics" (2012, 30). Somatic practitioners from dance and theatre – Minton and Faber (2016), Kemp (2012) and Lutterbie (2006) – agree that neuroscience's conception of embodied cognition adds to our understanding of the performer's process and the performer's enactment as an embodiment of that process.

A goal of somatic practices, including Asian physical disciplines such as Yoga and T'ai Chi, Alexander, Feldenkrais, Body-Mind Centering, Authentic Movement, Hakomi, Rolfing and Neuro-Linguistic Programming, to name a few, is that *expanded awareness* is a pathway to increased self-understanding and expressiveness.[3] Each somatic methodology has a distinct relation to the somatic experience of their founder. For example, Moshe Feldenkrais' introduction to an integrated body was Asian martial arts, more specifically jujitsu and judo. The Hakomi Method created by psychotherapist Ron Kurtz (1990) combined material derived from Taoist and

Buddhist philosophy with Bioenergetics, Feldenkrais and psychotherapy. Whether they are specifically related to dance therapy such as Authentic Movement or to body therapies that draw their conceptual framework from Asian physical disciplines, such as Feldenkrais, the theory behind each form is that attention to inner states can transform an individual's neural structures that are the result of past experience and as a consequence open an individual to new possibilities.

Although somatic approaches share some similar exercises incorporated into acting and dance classes, the goal is self-cultivation and not training in a specific aesthetic ideal such as ballet, other technical dance style and the styles of theatre from Realism to Grotowski. The underlying assumption of including somatic methods in dance and theatre courses is that enhanced awareness will increase the student's ability to engage with different styles of performance. A related goal of somatics is an integration of an experience of the sensory systems that counteracts the reliance on the visual that is common in a milieu that relies on screens, from computers to cell phones.[4] To accomplish the latter, each somatic practice involves some combination of three interactive somatic processes – breath, exploration and imagery. Integrating research in neuroscience and somatics, this essay provides theoretical and practical frameworks for these three processes.

Three somatic processes: breath, exploration, imagery

There is an interaction between two aspects of a soma – the structural self, or actual physical system, and the imaginal/social self, or the images of the world that have been stored in memory. The integration of the structural and imaginal systems through interaction with an environment creates our somatic state and related vocal life. Educational psychologist Howard Gardner (1983) suggests:

> In fact, voluntary movements require perpetual comparison of intended actions with the effects actually achieved: there is a continuous feedback of signals from the performance of movements, and this feedback is compared with the visual or linguistic image that is directing the activity. By the same token, the individual's perception of the world is itself affected by the status of his motor activities: information concerning the position and status of the body itself regulates the way in which the subsequent perception of the world takes place. In fact, in the absence of such feedback from motor activity, perception cannot develop in a normal way.
>
> (1983, 211)

By modeling the behavior of others, for example, we learn to walk, talk and practise situationally appropriate behavior. Whether individually or in a group, awareness is generally limited to the momentary joy or frustration felt at the success or failure of some social interaction. If it was successful, there is a repetition of physical and vocal gestures that brought success; if it was not successful, there is a search to discover a new vocal-physical gesture. The new vocal-gestural language creates a new self-image and related attitude. This replication of experience creates a generalized self-image that is adjusted as necessary to accommodate different social situations.

This generalized self-image is the self a performer initially animates. The goal of performance training, whether dance or acting, is twofold. The first goal is to bring self-image to a level of conscious awareness; and second, to expand awareness so that the performer can engage with a variety of voice and movement styles. Breath provides a point of concentration for expanded somatic awareness. An attitude of exploration participates in the discovery process of new modes of integrative awareness. Imagery engages the imagination to provide a depth of experience to somatic awareness that was gained through an attitude of exploration. The integration of breath, exploration and imagery evolves new neurological pathways that open the performer to new experiential conceptions of what is possible.[5]

Somatic awareness begins with breath

Breath is the basis for life and, as Kristin Linklater points out, "[b]reath is the source of your vocal sound" (2006, 43). Greeks considered the act of breathing to be connected to *psyche* and *pneuma* that suggests a combination of soul, air and spirit. Romans used *anima spiritus* to refer to breath and soul. Somatic practitioner Joseph Heller connects breath with spirit, creativity and inspiration:

> But the simple act of breathing requires no special effort, and similarly no effort is required to become connected with spirit. The body is already an inspired organism, and every moment, from your first breath to your last, is an opportunity to breathe in life's joy and fullness. Inspiration not only includes both breath and spirit, then, but is actually the meeting point at which the two merge; and the unification that takes place in you takes place automatically, unconsciously, effortlessly, and inevitably.
>
> (1986, 118)

The placement of the breath can focus and calm your mind, relax muscles, release tension and increase awareness of subtle somatic states.[6]

From the perspective of somatics, a focus on the breath and an individual's ability to attend to the somatic state of breathing is the precursor to increasing the quality of attention to other actions. The distinctiveness of a neuro-somatic method is the focus on attentive awareness. The degree and quality of attention influences the level and depth of somatic awareness or, as Linklater states, "perception must eventually be refined to extreme subtlety in order to observe the minutiae of neuromuscular behavior" (2006, 31). Breath is therefore the beginning of the majority of somatic practices towards voicing as it subtly expands kinesthetic awareness on a micro level and provides a specific point of concentration. The following exploration concentrates on the subtle sensations of the breath and the quality of attention to sensation. As with the rest of the practice that complements this chapter, it is in italics and it addresses to you, the reader, to filter through your own identity and experience.

Within the narrative of the exercise, *feel*, *fuse* and *follow* are verbs that describe the active process of integrating the breath as a point of focus, awareness and action. *Feel* is becoming aware of the kinesthetic connective state of breath. *Fuse* allows you to focus on the breath. *Follow* provides an opportunity to increase awareness of the subtle changes that take place with the exhalation of the breath. The process can be applied to developing awareness of any sensory mode or body part. This is most often accomplished in finding a connection with the subtle awareness of the breath.

Exercise 1

Feel the breath as it enters your body and note the subtle muscular changes as oxygen-laden air moves through the structures of your respiratory system via the nasal or mouth cavities, down the trachea (windpipe) to the bronchial tubes, lungs and alveoli (air sacs) housed inside the ribs. Fuse the breath with the primary muscle of respiration, the diaphragm, which lies between the bottom of your lungs and the top of your abdominal cavity. As you fuse with the breath's reach into the diaphragm, note its reaching downward towards your pelvic girdle. Also become aware of the expansiveness of the breath within the entirety of your ribcage. When you breathe out, follow the pelvis and the diaphragm as they release upward and note the release of the breath over your vocal folds and through the articulators of your lips, teeth and tongue. Repeat. With each repetition, expand your awareness to the following: the action of the diaphragm in relationship to the pelvic floor and to all sections of the ribcage, the flow of the breath over the vocal folds and through the mouth cavity. Follow the breath and expand the kinesthetic awareness of each area. For example, follow the breath's impact on the movement of each portion of your ribcage – front connected via sternum, sides and around to the back with the rib's connection to the spine; the movement of the shoulder blades. As you release the breath, follow its vibrational impact on the vocal folds. Is there a sound that flows from your vocal folds? Is there a movement of the tongue, teeth or lips that is an extension of the sound which starts in your vocal folds? With the next inhalation, repeat the process of feeling the breath move into the ribcage and fuse with the diaphragm. Engage the pelvic floor and follow the release of your breath and any sound that is the result. Allow for a

> *changing of the phrasing of the breath by slowing it down or speeding it up. Does this change the physical organization? Does it change the response of the vocal folds and the articulators of your mouth?*
>
> *Once you have established feeling, fusing and following as a process of concentration, the next stage is to extend it throughout your body. Stand in a comfortable position – head floating, spine lengthened, sternum released, tail bone dropped, hips, knees and feet aligned with each other. Breathe in becoming aware of how gravity pulls you towards the earth. Allowing the breath to match the phrasing of your exhalation, take a step forward and follow the breath as it leaves your body. Repeat several times until you have a sense of your entire being moving in phrasing with the breath. Fuse with the breath and follow it through the step of your foot. Note the subtle changes that take place from your feet up through your hips, spine, ribcage, shoulder girdle and arms, neck and head at each change of your weight from the back to your front foot. In particular, note the release in each fluid joint of the ankle, hips, along the vertebrae of the spine and with the joints of the shoulder, elbow and wrist. As you repeat, are there other physical gestures of arms, legs, head, torso that seem an extension of your breath phrasing? Are there sounds that accompany these gestures?*

Learning to attend to the breath in its act of fusing through the internal respiration process teaches "the feeling or kinesthetic state"[7] associated with reflection. As the breath is a dynamic process, the kinesthetic state of reflection is dynamic, not passive. Analogous to the movement of an idea as it penetrates and releases into the psyche, somatic reflection emerges from awareness of the movement of the breath as it penetrates and releases into the body. Breath thus becomes the method of access to increased awareness that is the beginning of an exploration. Essentially, the technique helps individuals become aware of the "background" state Damasio (2000) indicates that exists behind all actions, including thought. As such, it develops an attitude of exploration that will be taken up further in the next section.

An attitude of exploration

Anthropologist Mary Catherine Bateson (2001) points out that life is an improvisation. Each of us may attempt to plan the next moment from the previous one, but we have no certain knowledge that our perceptions and related actions will fulfill our desires. Antonio Damasio (2000) defines consciousness as an internal interplay of the soma. Describing in great detail the relationship between somatic states, reason and emotion, he provides a theoretical view point that regards people as complex organisms with interdependent systems that connect brain and body to create what he refers to as the "body-minded, brain" (2000, 223–244). As he phrases it: "The body contributes more than life support and modulatory effects to the brain. It contributes a content that is part and parcel of the workings of the normal mind" (2000, 226). Beyond well-documented laboratory tests, his conclusions are based on the realization that our neural structures are the result of thousands of years of evolution in which the primary task has been the survival of the body.

Consciousness is, according to Damasio, an extension of the body-minded brain's feedback mechanisms and is therefore related to individual's sensory and related imagistic interaction with an environment. While we, as organisms, share similar information from the environment that becomes part of these feedback loops, the manner in which we process this sensory information in highly individualized acts leads to the creation of what Damasio refers to as *somatic markers*. These markers are essentially memories evolved from interactions between individual perceptual systems and their environments. Philosopher Susan Hurley refers to the ongoing relationship between self and environment as *Consciousness in Action* (1998).

As noted by neuroscientists Thelen et al. (2001), we constantly respond to changing circumstances by creating new strategies based on new neural information that is sensorially taken in from the environment. Focusing attention on the sensory attributes of any task as an exploration immerses us in a dialogue with self and the environment. Thus, an attitude of exploration relies on the ability to take in, at any moment, new information through our sensory modalities (eyes, ears, nose, tongue and skin) and process this information simultaneously through the proprioceptor/kinesthetic devices located in the skin, muscles, joints, inner ear and along the passages of nose and throat. This combination of sense information is examined or explored by the memory in order to act.

An attitude towards exploration encourages us to examine, probe, research, analyze and study aspects of self. Exploration also helps us to stay focused on the present moment, not on what did or did not work in the previous moment or on what might work in the next. This is a somatic state, referred to in the martial arts as "open attention," in which our senses are attuned to self, other people and the environment. Attributes of exploration or open attention, identified as a "flow state" by psychologist Mihaly Csikszentmihalyi (1997), provide immediate feedback, focus or one-pointedness of mind, appropriate challenge, loss of self-consciousness and an altered sense of time. In a flow state, the exploration itself becomes "autotelic," worth doing for its own sake. Committing to the process of exploration, we dedicate ourselves to the awareness necessary for using our soma as an instrument of creation.

An attitude of exploration also enhances your ability to be simultaneously internally aware and externally focused. Acting teachers Robert Barton and Robert Benedetti call this state "relaxed readiness" (1993, 29) and "here and now" (1997, 13). Fellow acting teacher John Gronbeck-Tedesco refers to it as "getting ready to act" (1992, 1–30), a combination of security, openness and stillness. An attitude of exploration can be combined to discover the aural experience of music or the sound of your voice. Engaging the exploratory function of our imagination, any sensory system can be used to increase awareness. We can listen to our muscles and hear through our feet. We can also experience all sensory modes at the same time. Research by educational psychologist Howard Gardner (2008) suggests that each of us tends to approach the world through different organizations of our sensory systems. The following exercise is an opportunity for you to discover what vocal and physical gestures you use to explore your environment.

Exercise 2

Find a comfortable place to sit. Bring yourself to a point of focus using the breath technique of feel, fuse and follow. Allow feelings, thoughts and awareness to float freely through your experience of sitting: What sensations are you aware of? How readily do you shift your attention to something else? Try to breathe out effortlessly becoming aware of the movement of your breath. How does this change your focus? What internal muscular shifts do you note with the exhalation? Begin to focus on what you see. What sensations do you feel as you look around the space? What impact does the expanded field of attention have on your ability to focus on your breath? Add on what you hear, what you smell, the taste in your mouth, the feeling state of other parts of your body. How does each new sensory mode impact the quality of your attention in general? Do you find that you easily move from attending to the world visually to awareness of the physical space? As you change orientation between sensory systems, do you find that there is an internal desire to explore the activity with sound? Do you find that you respond via vocal gestures such as humming or singing a tune? Pick up an object and fuse your attention to that object. How do you go about exploring that object? What does the object feel like? Is there a sound that is expressive of that object? Do you find that you tend to more deeply explore it through gesture or sound or some combination of both? What happens if instead of sitting you take a walk through your home or neighborhood?

The power of imagery

Imagery is the nervous system's unifying process of our senses. As Damasio noted, information from our sensory system – eyes, ears, nose, skin, tongue and the kinesthetic/proprioceptive system – is stored in the neural structure of the brain as somatic markers. These sensory images come from a range of experiences – from family, school, church and community. They may be recalled as a sound, kinesthetic feeling, a taste, a picture, a perception on your skin or a combination of sensory-based memories. In contemporary society, among the primary distributors of images are the media – books, newspapers, magazines, television, films, radio and the Internet. In the *Evolution of*

Imagination (2017), Stephen Asma advocates that our ability to consciously engage sensory images through the imagination is the source of our evolutionary success.

Lakoff and Johnson in *Philosophy in the Flesh* (1999) argue that consciousness and the related processes of cognition are inherently embodied and that abstract concepts are expressed through imagistic metaphors which are evolved primarily unconsciously through the intersections of each soma's interaction with the environment. This discussion of cognitive embodiment is further articulated in their research which points out that much of our primary imagistic metaphoric comprehension of the world, conveyed through artistic modes of expression, is based on the goal-directed experience of a child learning to interact with the world. For instance, a child learns the concept of balance through the act of moving from crawling to walking, an experience which will ultimately be influenced by the child's interaction with parents, siblings and the texture of the walking surface as well as the organization of the space in which they learn to walk and the sounds they hear or make while learning. The child's conception of social/cultural metaphors such as "balance of forces" or "balanced justice" will be a combination of their experience of learning balance via walking and further influenced by the social/cultural environment in which they are raised. Through the integration of somatic and cultural experience, there is an unconscious response by the child to the world, as bodily-based experience of balance becomes the culturally valued conceptions such as justice or, in reference to the physical-vocal self, balance in verbal expression as a centered being.

This view of somatic development is, according to Johnson, an experience in which,

> concepts are not inner mental entities that re-present external realities [...] [but] neural activation patterns that can be 'turned on' by some actual perceptual or motoric event in our bodies, or else activated when we merely think about something, without actually [...] performing a specific action.
>
> (2007, 137)

Furthermore, Johnson cites a series of studies by Vittorio Gallese (2003, 2005) and others which indicate that our perception is multimodal as neurons fire when an individual performs a task or even contemplates its performance.

Accepting this multimodality, Lakoff and Johnson further expand on the development of movement, voice, language and metaphor. Within their theoretical framework, vocal life and language evolve in correspondence with movement. They identify a variety of image schemas that inform this process, including *container, verticality, compulsive force, source-path-goal* and *rough-smooth*. Each of these schemas could be a descriptor of an individual's vocal life. These modes of being are also the basis of language and thus ultimately of cultural formulations. For example, the simple word "in" helps us designate the difference between what is inside or not of a container, a concept a child learns early in life as they take an object and discover it can fit inside a container and often give the added gesture meaning through verbalizations. Whether walking or reaching, a child formulates an understanding between desire and accomplishment as they move from seeing to getting to voicing or verbalizing. These early contextually-specific discoveries later become the metaphoric basis of creative expression and artistic projects.

Lulu Sweigard brought the use of imagistic metaphors to dance training in a somatic approach she referred to as *ideokinesis* (2013), a combination of image and awareness. The alignment of the body evolves through a focus on imagistic metaphors that engage the related muscle groups while the body is lying completely still. Actors incorporate images in explorations to refine alignment, expand their movement vocabulary and vocal range and develop a character. Acting teacher John Lutterbie points out that the successful engagement of metaphoric images by performers is in their ability to avoid "the intrusion of discursive thought, which is seen as a negative influence that interferes with the actor's availability" (2006, 154). These discursive thoughts, as noted by Lakoff and Johnson, are the consequence of the embodiment of socially specific metaphors. The following exercise combines focus on the breath with an attitude of exploration to engage the physical and vocal possibilities of an image.

Exercise 3

Choose a metaphor from nature that is related to your personal experience – a bubbling brook, a roaring forest fire, a gentle breeze, waving grass, a frisky puppy, etc. – and you want to explore in movement and sound. Find your internal focus through feeling, fusing and following the phrasing of your breath. Become aware of the breath moving into your pelvis and extending out through the legs and soles of your feet, up through the spine, out through the arms, hands and face. Breathe in the image, fuse the image into the center of your being, your pelvis. Experience the image as attached to your pelvis. As you breathe out, follow the image adjusting your bony and muscle structures as it moves upward through spine, head and arms and downward through legs and feet. As you continue to engage with the image, follow its inclinations and allow a gesture to flow from the image. Support the gesture with a sound. Continue to explore the image discovering a set of repeatable gestures and related sounds. As you explore an image, you may find that the image changes. When it occurs, accept the change as a natural evolution of your unconscious playing with the potential of the metaphor.

The unifying power of metaphoric images can be combined with a state of exploration and an awareness of breath to create new expressive experiences.

This attention integrates with the breath and the body's systems to create new somatic states filled with energy. This energy is an invisible, silent and formless life force that combines the respiratory process with the sensorimotor and vocal systems' ability to attend to sensory images. The combination of breath, an attitude of exploration and metaphoric imagery unifies our sensory and motor systems towards vocal possibilities.

The potential of somatic knowledge

To sum up, the research of neuroscientists and the insights of somatic practitioners have created a complementary framework of a unified interactive soma that is responsive to the environment without a division of voice from movement or movement from voice. As noted throughout this essay, this paradigmatic shift is now being used by both actors and dancers to refine their craft. Influenced by the latter, modern performers participate in deeply embodied experiences that provide nuance and range to their practices but also offer frameworks of critical interrogations on related themes that could move beyond performance contexts.

The approach to experience implied by the three discussed somatic processes coincides with Shigenori Nagatomo's conception of the nature of body knowledge. His definition is not limited to mean "knowledge of the body but knowledge gained through the body" (1992, 63). Using Japanese conceptions of self, Nagatomo points out the potential of somatic knowledge to shift the "I/Other" mode that is inherent in intellectual inquiry based on limited sensory access:

> Such knowledge may be contrasted with intellectual knowledge. Intellectual knowledge is that mode of cognition which results from objectifying a given object, which propositionally takes a subject-predicate form, and which divorces the somaticity of the knower from the mind of the knower.
>
> (1992, 63)

The technique of *feel*, *fuse* and *follow*, employed within each somatic process analyzed in this chapter, aims at unifying breath, neurons, body and voice in its analytical and definitional mode.

Notes

1 The piece was part of a concert titled *Timeless Images*. It was presented at the WOW Hall in Eugene, Oregon in 1985.
2 See the works included in the Routledge Voice Studies series edited by Konstantinos Thomaidis and Ben Macpherson as well as the same editors' *Journal of Interdisciplinary Voice Studies*.
3 For more information on the history and context of Somatics as a field of work, see Eddy (2016).

4 As an example of critical interrogation on the matter in voice studies, see Macpherson (2015).
5 A text that also provides an approach that includes an in-depth discussion of this alignment in actor training and performance is Christina Gutekunst's and John Gillett's *Voice into Acting* (2014).
6 There has also been research on the relationship between breath and emotions in performance, such as Suzanna Bloch's essay on *Alba Emoting* (1993) or, in developing the phrasing of the music, the work of Víctor Manuel Rubio Carrillo (2019).
7 This phrasing, along with the feeling state reference in Exercise 2, is inspired by the teachings of the meditation and martial arts instructor James T. Kapp (1958–2006).

References

Asma, S. T. (2017) *The Evolution of the Imagination*. Chicago, IL: University of Chicago Press.
Barton, R. (1993) *Acting: Onstage and Off*. New York: Harcourt Brace Jovanovich.
Bateson, M. C. (2001) *Composing a Life*. New York: Grove Press.
Batson, G. and Wilson, M. (2014) *Body and Mind in Motion: Dance and Neuroscience in Conversation*. London: Intellect Books.
Benedetti, R. (1997) *The Actor at Work*. Boston, MA: Allyn and Bacon.
Bloch, S. (1993) Alba Emoting: a psychophysiological technique to help actors create and control real emotions. *Theatre Topics*, 3(2) 121–138.
Csikszentmihalyi, M. (1997) *Finding Flow: The Psychology of Engagement with Everyday Life*. New York: Basic Books.
Damasio, A. (2000) *The Feeling of What Happens: Body and Emotion in the Making of Consciousness*. New York: Mariner Books.
Damasio, A. (2005) *Descartes' Error: Emotion, Reason, and the Human Brain*. New York: Penguin.
Damasio, A. (2010) *Self Comes to Mind: Constructing the Conscious Brain*. New York: Pantheon.
Eddy, M. (2016) *Mindful Movement: The Evolution of the Somatic Arts and Conscious Action*. Bristol: Intellect Books.
Gallagher, S. (2005) *How the Body Shapes the Mind*. Oxford: Oxford University Press.
Gallese, V. (2003) A neuroscientific grasp of concepts: from control to representation. *Philosophical Transactions of the Royal Society of London*, 358(1435) 1231–1240.
Gallese, V. (2005) Embodied simulation: from neurons to phenomenal experience. *Phenomenology and the Cognitive Sciences*, 4(1) 23–48.
Gardner, H. (1983) *Frames of the Mind: The Theory of Multiple Intelligence*. New York: Basic Books.
_____ (2008) *Multiple Intelligences: New Horizons in Theory and Practice*. New York: Basic Books.
Gazzaniga, M. (2008) *Human: The Science Behind What Makes Us Unique*. New York: Ecco.
Gronbeck-Tedesco, J. (1992) *Acting through Exercises*. London: Mayfield.
Gutekunst, C. and Gillett, J. (2014) *Voice into Acting: Integrating Voice and the Stanislavski Approach*. London: Bloomsbury Methuen Drama.

Hurley, S. L. (1998) *Consciousness in Action.* Boston, MA: Harvard University Press.
Johnson, M. (2007) *The Meaning of the Body: Aesthetics of Human Understanding.* Chicago, IL: The University of Chicago Press.
Kemp, R. (2012) *Embodied Acting: What Neuroscience Tells Us about Performance.* London: Routledge.
Kurtz, R. (1990) *Body-centered Psychotherapy.* Mendocino, CA: Life Rhythm.
Lakoff, G. and Johnson, M. (1999) *Philosophy in the Flesh: The Embodied Mind and Its Challenge to Western Thought.* New York: Basic Books.
LeDoux, J. (2003) *Synaptic Self: How Our Brains Become Who We Are.* New York: Penguin.
Linklater, K. (2006) *Freeing the Natural Voice: Imagery and Art in the Practice of Voice and Language.* Revised Edition. New York: Dramatist Publishers.
Lutterbie, J. (2006) Neuroscience and creativity in the rehearsal process. In: Bruce McConachie and F. Elizabeth Hart (eds.) *Performance and Cognition: Theatre Studies and the Cognitive Turn.* London: Routledge, 149–166.
Macpherson, B. (2015) Body musicality: the visual, virtual and visceral voice. In: Konstantinos Thomaidis and Ben Macpherson (eds.) *Voice Studies: Critical Approaches to Process, Performance and Experience.* New York: Routledge, 149–163.
Minton, S. C. and Faber, R. (2016) *Thinking with the Dancing Brain: Embodying Neuroscience.* New York: Rowman & Littlefield.
Nagatomo, S. (1992) An eastern concept of the body: Yuasa's body mind scheme. In: Maxine Sheets-Johnstone (ed.) *Giving the Body Its Due.* New York: SUNY, 48–68.
Rubio Carrillo, V. M. (2019) *A Musical Breathing Approach with Guitar Performance.* Gainesville, FL: University of Florida.
Shusterman, R. (2012) *Thinking through the Body: Essays in Somaesthetics.* Cambridge: Cambridge University Press.
Sweigard, L. E. (2013) *Human Movement Potential: Its Ideokinetic Facilitation.* New York: Allegro Editions.
Thelen, E., Smith, L., Schoner, G. and Scheier, C. (2001) The dynamics of embodiment: a field theory of infant preservative reaching. *Behavioural and Brain Sciences,* 24(1) 1–34.
Wilson, M. (2002) Six views of embodied cognition. *Psychonomic Bulletin & Review,* 9(4) 625–636.

2 Awakening grace
Embodied awareness in vocal training

Andrea Olsen

This essay on breath and voice is framed within the performance text *Awakening Grace: Six Somatic Tools* on the same themes. The writing draws on four decades of teaching experiential anatomy, touring evening-length dance works with text internationally and creating books and films on the interconnectedness of body and earth. Breath and voice infuse all of these somatic investigations and link me directly to my creative edge as a teacher, author and performer. I write to learn and I move to know if what I am saying is true. When writing, I always make a dance. Speaking text while moving clarifies and abbreviates – words fall away. In my view, if I am not changed in the process of making something, the work is not finished. The performance text that frames this essay brought a new vocal range in its first public showing.[1] It is passed on to you – the reader and mover – to encourage fascination with the intelligence and mystery of the body as you dance your own dance with breath and sound.

Breath is exchange: you have to give something up to get something back. It is not just more, more, more. Instead, it is finding just the right amount for ease and expressivity. It is natural, like the seasons, like birth and death. And you can feel it, like the purr of a cat, humming along deep inside without your attention. Unless of course you interrupt – feel afraid.

Breath and voice begin with the body. Both are natural processes, our wild and easeful biological inheritance, if properly resourced. Body is part of Earth: our bones, breath and blood are the minerals, air and water inside us.[2] Inherent intelligence from over three billion years of evolutionary history – the origins of the first cell – is our coordinative birthright. This biological heritage is partnered with our biographical stories – our complex lived lives and cultural conditioning. Differentiating these two (biological and biographical) lineages allows us to appreciate and utilize the resources of each, sustaining easeful movement in both inherited and deeply personal breath and vocal patterns.

We share breath with others – including our plant and animal relatives. It is our first relationship with life and the last. It is part of sobbing, laughing hysterically and silence, depending on what is happening in our lives. And it is the basis of communication, both verbal and nonverbal. Breath also informs us about the quality of our environment, including air pollution, weather patterns and the impacts of people and place on our health. As a link to spiritual and mystical dimensions, it amplifies the ephemerality of life itself.

We often take breath for granted; yet, we cannot live without it. It is the source of life happening deep within us, essential for every cell and tissue. If we do not have enough breath, we cannot think effectively and we cannot speak or find our voice. Breath is a tether to awareness and consciousness (it is always happening) and our direct link to the sensations of aliveness in the body (we feel it). It occurs both consciously (we can pause) and unconsciously (without our awareness). Ultimately, breathing is beyond our control – we pass out if we do not breathe – the body takes over and breathes for us. But it can also be coached into optimal efficiency.

In communication, we can notice the primacy of breath. Our breath rhythms cue the degree of ease or discomfort we feel when interacting with others. Breathing affects stress and anxiety in our bodies through multiple neurochemical responses – if we are stressed, others notice; if they respond to stress, we become more anxious; and on it goes. Audible breath through vocalization informs others about the tone of our conversation – do you mean it or not; are you threatening or friendly? Ultimately, breath patterns communicate your degree of engagement: are you behind what you are saying and doing or conflicted? Possibly, no other aspect of embodiment can affect our physical, mental and emotional effectiveness in communication more than breath.

Memory: Maybe someone teased you as a child: funny hair, big feet or a fart. Oops! Maybe someone hit you in second grade for not paying attention – like my husband was smacked in Catholic school for daydreaming. Or someone scolded you at home, for no reason at all, except for their own pent-up voice. Or it was those fitness training techniques that made so much tension: more, more, more! Again, again, again! Faster, faster, faster! There are so many reasons to rehabilitate breathing now.

Breath patterns are established at birth and can change throughout our lives. Breathing habits might reflect the mother's breath in pregnancy, the birth process itself or later impressionable events in life that become fixed in the neural circuitry. The *breathing rhythmicity center*[3] in the brainstem (top of the spinal cord) monitors this basic pattern. Work situations and cultural norms have impact, along with our levels of comfort, need for control and opportunities for expression. This includes degrees of repression, depression and aggression in relation to context.

To change breath and vocal patterns, we begin with the ground: *grounding before sounding*. Gravity responses in the body set the *pre-movement* for breath and vocal expression – our readiness to respond. Gravity is the constant background for all movement on this planet, including the movement of breath and our ability to stand and face others. Our body has sensory receptors specifically cued for location. As we direct our attention to these foundational sensory portals in the hands, feet, head, tail and eyes that are loaded with sensory receptors (the tonic system), we receive a structural tethering for a deep full breath, the breath of location.[4] Sometimes, we need to rebuild this perception many times during the day, feeding substantial subcortical information into the system answering the question "Where am I?".

Effective voice work acknowledges the importance of pre-movement in creating the conditions for ease. Rather than tightening the body, restricting breath and increasing tension levels prior to making sound or speaking, we can stay with gravity and feel support and location, rooting our feet. Learning to release our weight into gravity, to be held and supported by the Earth, can be a stabilizing foundation. The practice is to invite ease with effective pre-movement (through imagery, language, sensation). Staying with ground and space as we meet "other" through breath and sound helps us interrupt outdated habits in the nervous system, discharging tension and rerouting pathways towards efficiency.

Inviting mind into the present moment is a perceptual act. Focusing attention on the sensations of breath leads the way to awareness. You cannot breathe yesterday.[5] Sensations link what is inside the body with the external world. Focusing on gravity-related sensations enhances our sense of body-level security and stability. Once we identify *where* we are, we can engage more complexities: *who we are, what we are doing* and *why*. In this process, we continue teasing biology from biography. Which body-level responses are pre-programmed (like a yawn) and which are unique to the moment (like tight shoulders)? All humans on the planet share ancient survival reflexes, developmental patterns and fundamental emotions that govern socialized movement, illuminating our common heritage. In vocal exchange, we can orient our awareness towards ease by remembering that we are standing, literally, on the same ground – body to body, sharing and supported by planet Earth.

"You have to go down to go up". That is my diaphragm speaking. Pinned to the inside of my ribs and tethered all the way to my tailbone, it seals up-organs from down. The heart gets a ride, the belly organs a massage. It is undulating, like a jellyfish in the ocean; there is movement involved. It is so sensual to feel yourself breathing.

Breath is our love affair with plants: we absorb the oxygen they produce on our *inbreath* and release carbon dioxide for their survival on our *outbreath*. The primary muscle to initiate breathing is the *diaphragm* with two tendinous *crus* extensions. The thoracic diaphragm creates an arched dome within the responsive ribs. In contraction (the inbreath), the muscular-tendinous diaphragm descends down towards the pelvis, tethered by the crura (plural for crus). These key extensions attach along the front of the lower spine (lumbar vertebrae) all the way to the tailbone through connective tissue. In descent, the diaphragm compresses the abdominal organs. On the release (outbreath), the diaphragm returns to its domelike shape (around nipple height in relaxation), expelling air from the lungs. Thus, the rhythmic contraction and release of the diaphragm and its attached crura massages vital organs and assists in pumping fluids throughout our structure, energizing the body.

In the breathing process, the whole spine moves, subtly responding to each breath. Any restriction in breathing, such as tight clothing, over-rigidity in the neck or abdominal muscles, or illness, interrupts efficient breath. Ultimately, every cell in the body must participate in breath: our bone cells breathe, muscle cells breathe, nerve cells breathe, exchanging nutrients and releasing waste materials in a process called *cellular respiration*. If we just bring oxygen into our lungs, we die. The muscular, spiralic heart circulates oxygenated blood to every tissue and cell, supporting fluidity, rather than rigidity, in all our movement patterns.[6]

Effective breathing in preparation for speaking and moving offers ease. Some people are "reverse breathers," lifting the shoulders up and flattening the belly to breathe in, so that the diaphragm barely moves. Some people "over-breathe," working too hard to control the process on both the inbreath and outbreath; and some of us are "shallow breathers," minimalizing movement of the ribs and organs. When we do not want to take in or be seen, we hold our breath. Although there is no "right" way to breathe in all situations, it is useful to develop an attitude of open exchange with the environments we inhabit. Tension restricts movement and masks sensation, numbing us from noticing the sensitive interplay of breath and the communicative potential of sound.

Voice is breath made audible. It is just those little vocal folds vibrating. No other tension is required. Shoulders, hips, belly, ankles, feet, your face, jaw and eyebrows can all relax! There is no muscle of exhale. And voice can be touch. We touch each other and ourselves with our sound. It is worth considering before speaking.

In sound production, the only muscles necessary beyond those of breathing are the tiny ones affecting the vocal folds. Tightening the superficial muscles of neck and shoulders, belly and back only reduces resonance and expressivity. As air moves from the lungs through the trachea (along the front of the neck), it passes through the *larynx* (at the level of the fifth cervical vertebra). This "voice box" houses the *vocal folds*, mucosa-lined ligaments, or cords, that run parallel to each other, from the front to back of the larynx, forming a horizontal vocal diaphragm in the neck. If these folds are apart and relaxed, the passageway is open and the air flows freely through from lungs to nose and mouth on the outbreath, allowing full, relaxed breathing.[7]

If, however, there is intent to make sound or speak, the folds are pulled towards each other, creating a thin space for the air to pass through, vibrating the folds. These vibrations are amplified in resonating chambers of the body, shaped by the soft tissues of pharynx and mouth and articulated by the lips, teeth and mobile tongue to produce audible sound. In speech, vowels vibrate and consonants interrupt, clip and shape the flow of the air. We map our voice from internal sensations. The way our body feels as it vibrates – resonating in relationship to particular people and places – shapes who we think we are and how we communicate with others.

Languages have different uses of vocal mechanisms for distinct sounds and flavors, reflecting the environmental sounds present in the places of origin. Feeling what we say, cycling between impression (taking in) and expression (giving out), is a fundamental rhythm and circulation in communication skills. If it is all out, you deplete your resources (there is nothing to give). If it is all in, it is hard to connect (there is no space for the other). If you merge, you lose agency (there is no differentiation). There is a contract between a speaker and a listener that involves exchange; hearing and sounding have been intricately interwoven since birth.[8]

Words can hurt. Ouch! They can also heal. When I first visited my mother in the hospital after her stroke, she looked at me directly in the eyes and said: "I just wanted you to be your own original self". Change. Thoughts twist, rearrange, reconfigure. You never know when life will change your direction. Require something new of you.

Adding the specificity of language to voice is a cortical adventure. We know so much more that we think we know. Only a small amount of what is happening around us can register at a conscious level or we would be overwhelmed at every moment. Interpretation of sound and language is personal, based on our past history. Much happens subcortically, including the deep intelligence underlying our process of meaning making and speaking. Circulating between sensation, feelings, language, judgment and conclusions creates a vocal loop. We necessarily return to sensation to be sure that our thoughts and words are grounded in actual experience, refreshing sometimes-long-held conclusions.[9] This ongoing process requires the whole self to be present, engaging embodied intelligence and possibilities for change.

Many of us identified our voice around puberty, when our bodies achieved their adult dimensions and now associate it with those particular sensations. Yet, we have changed a lot since then. Rehabilitating our relationship to voice and language is a process. Simple effective somatic skills are easy to practise but have significant impact on communication and self-identity. Do you recognize your voice at this current age? Would you like to increase resonance and adaptability? Choices around attention and tone of voice impact communication dynamics: who gets to speak and why? Recognizing the "shutdown" of voice, the hesitation, the resistance is an essential step in refreshing vocal patterns.

We can remember that people around the globe, since the origins of our species, have been killed, imprisoned or denigrated for speaking their truth. These figures are present in our myths, history books and present-day news. From Joan of Arc to Abraham Lincoln and Martin Luther King, we learned the life/death risk of big thinking and speaking. Nelson Mandela and Wangari Maathai were imprisoned for their impassioned words and daily, contemporary women in politics and young girls are denigrated – there's risk involved. When we feel the grip, the strangle, the heat rising, the tension building, the impulse to flee or to silence ourselves as we prepare to speak, it is well founded. Our bodies want to keep us alive. We likely had a good reason for the vocal restrictions made at younger ages; now there may be more resource for expression and integration.

Yet, silence is part of speech. When one's voice is not "silenced," but silent from choice, it supports the human ease of participating, creating the ground for resonant conversation. Some people need more time to formulate their feelings and thoughts into words. Feelings are slower than speech; the inner life is not tidy. For others, the quiet pause allows deeper listening, opening to unanticipated dimensions. Sometimes, silence makes space for the mystery of experience itself, larger than the words used to describe it. Pauses in speaking allow rhythm to emerge, the timing between sound and space. When we pause to feel what we say, we might just say less.

Recovering *authentic voice* involves developing a supportive, non-judgmental but discerning *inner witness*.[10] Rather than evaluating and critiquing every word you say, this witness holds a spacious view. Identifying certain qualities that you value in your inner witness can be surprising, such as humor, patience, irreverence. As we cultivate our capacity to experience ourselves with more ease, vocal range increases. Beyond our carefully constructed personality selves, the whole range of human expression is present inside each of us. Humans do not create sound; we participate in a living soundscape. Expanding our vocal range through play and exploration, we make space for spontaneous range in pitch and volume beyond construction and constriction – allowing sound to move through us and move us towards connection with others.[11]

Singing is another matter altogether. I'm not so good, wish I could...belt forth like the Swedish opera star Jenny Lind. In 1851 here in Northampton, Massachusetts, they say over 1,800 people came to hear the Swedish songbird sing. When she was just ten, a professional ballerina heard her voice and encouraged her training – knowing that you can move people through art, through voice, through believing in expressing the heart of things.

The autonomic nervous system (ANS) is considered the location for "centered" energy and authenticity. Composed of nerves and ganglia located along the front of the spine, anterior to the vertebral bodies, it governs all the vital organs and glands (affecting the heart, lungs, digestion and sexuality), and can function rapidly and continuously without conscious effort.

Learning the names of the specific parts of this system lets us recognize them as familiar – as family – inviting ease. The *sympathetic* portion of the ANS stimulates the body towards activation and engagement; the *parasympathetic* towards cycles of rest, digestion and integration. The *enteric*, the most primitive aspect, is the local nervous system of the digestive tract – the "brain in the gut". In effective functioning, the sympathetic, parasympathetic and enteric systems work together, not antagonistically, to coordinate body functioning for optimal vitality, health and coherence.

The ANS plays a central role in vocalizing, activating or inhibiting the tongue, throat, larynx and diaphragm, and connecting directly to the heart. Making friends with our ANS gives access to vocal flow with less obstruction. In this process, we understand that the nervous system exists throughout the body, a fast electro-chemical network communicating vital actions and reactions.[12] Messages go back and forth between body and brain – there is no mind/body separation. Embodied intelligence acknowledges and appreciates all aspects of the nervous system in our need for both expression and recovery. Recognizing our inherent complexity helps us to maintain a sense of curiosity about our sometimes-conflicting internal voices. With somatic awareness, we have more choices in how to inhabit the multiple voices within us.

Current discussions of the ANS focus on the *vagal nerve complex*, including the work of Dr. Stephen Porges with the *social engagement system*.[13] The social engagement system can override protective sympathetic arousal (fight/flight/freeze response) by engaging the situation or threat directly: for example, talking to the person you distrust or dislike, or speaking in public and "surviving" the process. This is called the "vagal brake". Rather than going into sympathetic (activated) defensive patterns, you can stay open to communication channels that may have shut down in a more defensive state. We can also work with a vagal tone in the parasympathetic nervous system to modulate breath and heart rate. The arts can be an avenue for balancing nervous system activity; the ventral vagus nerve involved in the social engagement system regulates activities such as singing, playing the clarinet and dancing. These practices require simultaneously regulating the breath and engaging with others – valuing both silence and sound, individuality and connection to community.

Embodiment in vocal training and singing can be seen as the encouragement to inhabit voice with authenticity. The whole intelligent body is involved in resonance and amplification in relation to the specific context of place and people, honoring past history and present experience. This includes allowing emotions, dynamic range and emphasis to inform expression for clarity and impact as appropriate and effective. Silence, breath and pauses partner speaking, not from repression but as a choice, encouraging absorption – letting you and others feel what you say. Moments of grace occur when voice emerges with no encumbrances or inhibition. Embodied vocal practices help us get conscious about voice, not self-conscious, exploring our full communicative range within the life-and-death mysteries of the human and more-than-human world.

Silence is part of sound. It's the space between sound and no sound. It's the empty circle, the dark hole of not-knowing. It's the bird singing loudly, clearly, maybe joyfully in the distant tree. It's feeling my body breathing me, speaking me and silencing me when the time is right – like now.[14]

Notes

1 This dance with text was first performed for *Historical Footnotes: Dancing through Northampton's History*, at the Arts Trust Building in Northampton, Massachusetts (September 14–15, 2018). It was also presented at the praxical symposium "Somatic Voices in Performance Research and Beyond" that took place at East 15 Acting School in London (July 19–20, 2019), as part of this book's creative process. Writings in italics throughout this essay are from the performance text.
2 See Olsen ([2002] 2019).
3 Otherwise known as respiratory rhythmicity center (see Martini, 2007, 645–646) or medullary rhythmicity center (see Patton, 2019, 845).
4 The tonic system is discussed in depth in the work of Caryn McHose and Kevin Frank (2006, 136), based on their work with Hubert Godard.
5 View *Qi Gong* videos by Lee Holden focusing on breath and sensation as avenues to present awareness: www.holdenqigong.com.
6 For Bonnie Bainbridge Cohen's views on the heart as an organ of circulation, see Olsen (2014, 225).
7 For a discussion on the descent of the larynx from C-2 to C-5 in Homo erectus and the advent of Homo vocalis, see Abitbol (2006).
8 This resonates with the understanding of *vocal in-betweenness*, as discussed by Thomaidis and Macpherson in critical voice studies (2015, 3–9).
9 See Olsen (2014, 129–131), including Samuel Bois' WIGO (What is going on?) from his book *The Art of Awareness* (1966).
10 On the notion of the *inner witness* in the practice of Authentic Movement, see Janet Adler's *A Brief Description of the Discipline of Authentic Movement* (2018) and Adler (2002, 59–82).
11 *Freeing the Natural Voice*, by voice coach Kristen Linklater, has been widely utilized in vocal training. Published in 1976 with a revised, expanded edition in 2006, it has been translated into German, Russian, Italian, Korean, Spanish and Polish. Like Mabel Todd's *The Thinking Body* ([1937] 2008), it was a foundational text in emerging somatics trainings since the early twentieth century.
12 The intertwined partner of the ANS is the endocrine system, secreting hormones into the bloodstream and orchestrating a flow or wash of longer-lasting responses.
13 See Dr. Stephen Porges' website: www.stephenporges.com.
14 For further practice, you could visit www.body-earth.org (Olsen et al, 2015) and specifically Day Three in the given process. Note that three different voices narrate the movement excursions: Alex Draper is an equity actor and teacher of voice; Mchose and Olsen are somatic practitioners and educators; together, they model differing modes of transmitting the material to the listener with voice.

References

Abitbol, J. (2006) *The Odyssey of the Voice*. San Diego, CA: Plural Publishing.

Adler, J. (2002) *Offering from the Conscious Body: The Discipline of Authentic Movement* [Play Books]. Rochester, VT: Inner Traditions.

―――― (2018) *A brief description of the discipline of authentic movement* [online]. Available from: https://disciplineofauthenticmovement.com/discipline-of-authentic-movement/a-brief-description-of-the-discipline-of-authentic-movement [Accessed 28 April 2018].

Bois, S. (1966) *The Art of Awareness*. Dubuque, IA: Wm. C. Brown.

Holden, L. (2018) *Qi Gong videos* [online]. Available from: https://www.holdenqigong.com [Accessed 28 April 2018].

Linklater, K. ([1976] 2006) *Freeing the Natural Voice: Imagery and Art in the Practice of Voice and Language*. Hollywood, CA: Drama Publishers.

Martini, F. H. (2007) *Anatomy and Physiology*. Quezon City, Philippines: Pearson Education South Asia.

McHose, C. and Frank, K. (2006) *How Life Moves: Explorations in Meaning and Body Awareness*. Berkeley, CA: North Atlantic Books.

Olsen, A. ([2002] 2019) *Body and Earth: An Experiential Guide*. Middletown, CT: Wesleyan University Press.

Olsen, A. in collaboration with McHose, C. (2014) *The Place of Dance: A Somatic Guide to Dancing and Dance Making*. Middletown, CT: Wesleyan University Press.

Olsen, A., Hardwig, S. and McHose, C. (2015) *Body and Earth: Seven web-based somatic excursions* [online]. Available from: http://body-earth.org [Accessed 20 June 2018].

Patton, K. T. (2019) *Anatomy and Physiology*. 10th edition [Google Play Book]. St. Louis, MO: Elsevier.

Porges, S. (2018) *Revolutionizing our understanding of autonomic physiology* [online]. Available from: https://www.stephenporges.com [Accessed 28 April 2018].

Thomaidis, K. and Macpherson, B. (2015) Introduction: voice(s) as a method and an in-between in *Voice Studies: Critical Approaches to Process, Performance and Experience*. Abingdon, Oxon: Routledge.

Todd, M. ([1937] 2008) *The Thinking Body*. Santa Barbara, CA: Gestalt Journal Press.

3 Never just the body
Etudes between voice and dance

Sondra Fraleigh

The body is always in the midst of acting or taking a breather, succeeding its noise and limits. The body is never just the body. And the voice is never just the voice. It is sometimes certain but often precarious. Is anybody listening? Voice is not other than body. It dances between sound and source across the same states of being and becoming the body holds. In venture, body is world, just as voice is world. And if the world is wide, it is likewise specific in cultural frames. Because of this, we find a trove of voices to believe in, or we shrink from voice and our world also shrinks.

Voice as body is unstable, risky and uncertain. To study embodiment in a somatically-close way is to hazard the "how" questions of thinking and doing: in our case, how giving attention to body as voice through a deliberate practice helps us perform better, and confidently be better. The entire range of somatic endeavor can be summarized in terms of human development and bodily knowledge. In its preoccupation with *logos* as a reason, Eurocentric philosophy has not been curious about bodily knowing or the lived materiality of voice, as philosopher Adriana Cavarero has shown (2005) and Konstantinos Thomaidis recognizes in his work on voice (2015, 10). Somatics is, among other things, about improvement of skills and performance but, more existentially, it is concerned with transformative potentials of embodied life – how we move forward with courage, emotional health and ethical awareness of our interactions – how we develop individual potentials and empathy in tandem. As a first-person relational phenomenon, somatics engages perceptual activities that encourage participants to receive and interpret sensory information as they interact with others and the environing world. Nonetheless, a phenomenologist would say that there is no such thing as self-perception in a pure sense. "Human life is we-life" in a cultural and environing world constantly in motion (Husserl, [1934] 1995, 192).

As emanating from body, voices play a role in constantly flowing matter and energy. Through voice, we flow towards otherness, especially as we are implicitly equipped to reach out. The voice develops as an extension of the personal body and its already assimilated world. My world expands in voicings – joy and sadness sound aloud as I teach, write, dance, heal and sing. Singing is in fact a large metaphor for the way I dance and write: if it doesn't "sing," I don't want it on the stage or the page.

In this essay

This essay is a phenomenology of voice – or study of experience – in two etudes. Each etude studies a different aspect of somatic methods relative to voice and includes somatic practices for the reader to do or consider. Practices are indented and set apart in the text. In all parts, I ask myself what my background as a dancer, yogini, Feldenkrais teacher and founder of Shin Somatics methods might add to the aims of this volume. *Shin* means oneness in Japanese, which links cross-culturally to non-dualism in phenomenology. As an author in the fields of phenomenology and somatics, I have wondered how the experiential standpoints of these two discrete endeavors might be applied in practice, and whether somatics might be interpreted as phenomenology in action. Here, phenomenology provides theoretical/descriptive scaffolding for the sensory/reflective core of somatic experience. From the field of critical voice studies, as introduced by Konstantinos Thomaidis and Ben Macpherson (2015), the essay is also motivated by Thomaidis' critical question: "[...] how do we think and do voice [...]?" (10).

Voice is most common and taken for granted, yet ever special when we bring it to conscious attention. Performing consciously in theatre arts and vocal practices affords somatic first-person attention to affective powers of voice. It also concerns how otherness is embodied and engaged, whether playfully or agonistically. This text expands somatic intentionality from self towards others and the environmental world. Relative to this, it develops two corresponding concepts in phenomenology: *enworlding*, engaging in the world or "living the world," as Edmund Husserl put this ([1932] 1995, 167), and *worlding*, an active term and mythic image advanced by Husserl's student, Martin Heidegger. Worlding is "a gathering dance" of the near and far, of earth and heaven. The worlding dance gathers in to move out and fold back again: "The world presences by worlding" (Heidegger, 1971, 77). In every detail, the world shows itself in everything, in dance and song, in meadows and deserts, chairs, brooms and jugs.

Enworlding and worlding imply subtle differences and overlapping meanings. The prefix "en" moves towards "in" – "within" and "in having" – while worlding is wide and moving. The very thought of *world* might draw an inward or outward accent in perception. We are not passive recipients of an already constituted world, which does not mean that the world is not already constituted and in process. Husserl writes that human subjectivity is active. We *experience* and come to *know* the world "in fashioning a world through activity," thereby constituting and possessing a consciousness of the world, whether through the strife of politics or the soil of nature and history. Human subjects bear every sense of what is meant by *world*; the world of nature itself is alive and has ontological being (Husserl, [1932] 1995, 167–189).

In the etudes

Worlding, Etude I, explores convergence of voice with body and world through two somatic practices. The first practice, *worlding voice* and *truth telling*, concerns emergence of personal truth through psychosomatic aspects of voice and imagistic yoga. It derives from a short section of *Land to Water Yoga* (2006), my synthesis of yoga sources with somatic processes and visualizations, from walking on land to floating in water and rising in air.

In a turn of emphasis, the second practice explains a dialogic process of voicing with partners and in group work. This practice, *worlding voice through dialogics*, describes *Contact Unwinding*, a polyphonic dialogical process in my teaching of movement with voice. Key somatic pedagogical principles enter in through Mikhail M. Bakhtin's dialogical phenomenology, particularly his identification of "extralinguistic utterance" and silence (1986, 108–109). Contact Unwinding is, as implied, an uncoiling of body and voice, whether calm or agitated, and ready for surprise.

Sounding, Etude II, shifts cultural emphasis to Japan, introducing *butoh* in a metamorphic somatic practice of *becoming other*. Butoh is a form of dance and theatre arising in the ashes of Japan after World War II. Eschewing power in the wake of America's postwar occupation of Japan, butoh dancers identify with weakness and death, decay and regeneration, performing the body as evolutionary and somatically relative (Fraleigh, 2010, 63–78). Butoh processes are metamorphic and increasingly global in participation. One of the founders and beloved grandfather of butoh, Ohno Kazuo (1906–2010)-sensei, said in our workshops that "butoh doesn't belong to culture; it is the dance of everyday life" (1986).

Etude I: worlding

Worlding dives beneath performative attributes of voice, reaching back conceptually to the lifeworld (*lebenswelt*) philosophy of Edmund Husserl who produced the root text of phenomenology (*Logical Investigations*, [1900] 1970). It would be a mistake to dismiss Husserl as an essentialist. Rather, he brings precariousness to light through his unfolding of several lifeworld horizons, all somatically based in changing constitutions of the body. He proposed somatology as a body-based study, particularly pertinent to various approaches to soma/somaticities in this volume and somatics as a field of study. Husserl described "the environing world" through various interrelated horizons or ways of knowing, ecological, social and cultural (Husserl and Fink, [1932] 1995, 154–165). He called these horizons "lifeworlds" in their relationship to the somatic life of the body, which he also named "the lived body" ([1952] 1989).

Martin Heidegger (1971) popularized "worlding" as a floating signifier for the "uncovering" and "becoming" of phenomena, as we come to know the familiar and imagined things of our ever-changing yet still present world. His major work, *Being and Time* (1927), heightens significance of present time consciousness, since our "being in the world" holds uncommon potential, as past and future coalesce in "the ecstasy" of the present ([1927] 1962, 401–403). From Heidegger's phenomenology in *Being and Time* to Tim

Ingold's anthropology of *Being Alive* (2011), semantics of worlding crosses from philosophy into the arts, bridging to literary criticism, cultural studies and anthropology.

Enworlding (*verweltlichung*) is Husserl's concept for the ongoing incompletion of the world in its convergence with the lived body ([1932] 1995, li). The "voice" of his original phenomenology had a time-conscious meditative ring in such phrases as "the flowing live present" (Ibid., xiv). Husserl writes copiously of enworlding in one of his last works, the *Sixth Cartesian Meditation* ([1932] 1995, 188–192). He broaches a transcendental idea with this, not pointing to otherworldliness, but to how deeply we might penetrate and appreciate the world we live. He sought to open eyes and hearts to what is apparent, but easily passed over in what he called the taken-for-granted "natural attitude". Our body of perception and action is ever incomplete, never just body, but in pause and suspension of belief (in bracketing the natural attitude), *as body*, it can soundlessly reveal our fragile, precious life.

Voicing body and world

Voice, as body, converges with the world, suggesting somatic states of attunement through movement and affective registers. Voices world in action, in vibration, speech, song and story – no less through commitment and opinion. The voice is a natural power and also a cultivated one. Certain voices thrill us; others might sound sweet, gruff or perhaps tired. Through deliberate practice, voice can signal expertise. Voice, like dance, is not just any kind of movement. The conscious use of voice makes every breath count, every movement, every sound and word (Fraleigh, 2015, 10–14).

The voice presences by sounding. Whether in stammers or flows, the voice plumbs possible worlds of otherness and interchange. The physical body cannot pass through walls but the voice can. Its sound penetrates objects and soaks surroundings. Vibrational movements of voice are multidirectional, physical and at the same time psychosomatic. Voice is never just of the physical body, particularly in non-dual phenomenology. As thought poured through sound, the voice circulates and encompasses mind. In speech and song, voice reflects rough percussive hues and signals historic melodies in cultures around the world. The spoken voice might harass but, like a mother's cooing, it also caresses and soothes and thus is tactile-kinesthetic. Through sensing the voice and understanding the contextual physicality of sound, we might realize the effects for good or ill we have on others when we use our voice in effects that redound. The voice is alive with intention and orientation, even in a mumble. The tone of voice can heal or hurt: can clear mental and physical expression, develop the imagination and bring consciousness to both wild playfulness and meditative mantra. These are a few ways to describe the vast phenomena of voice *via* body and world.

The voice worlds in time and is never just the voice. It evolves, and we are responsible for how we develop its wide array. Use of voice is a practice, just as life is a practice. We perform voice: willing it, if you will, while hopefully not being willful. Husserl speaks to nuances of will: "Willing as willing something in the world, weighing in the world worldly possibilities – as personal capabilities, assessing them, making up one's mind, actualizing them in action" ([1932] 1995, 187).

Land to water yoga

Accordingly, in my cross-cultural searches for ease of will in performance, I created a somatic form of yoga that mostly anyone can do, called *Land to Water Yoga.* Infused with nature and animal imagery, the somatic practices of this yoga can be done anywhere but are best performed outdoors in nature. Through my Eastwest Somatics Institute, I continue to develop this dancelike and highly adaptive yoga method. I began to teach yoga creatively in community and not as virtuoso achievement through my experiences with Sri Aurobindo's Integral Yoga at his first ashram in Baroda, India. This personal transition marked my travels and lectures in India during the year 2000 in the new millennium. In its variety, yoga has become mercurial for me, never just of the body, and like dance and voice, not one thing but many. Yoga's ancient Indian sources evolved diversely through a confluence of languages, teachers and customs but its core meaning of *yoke and unification* still crosses all forms.

In *Land to Water Yoga,* I teach the following practice as a visualization of voice through chakra five, or the throat chakra in physical yoga. Chakra is a Sanskrit term identifying seven primary energy centers of the body with metaphorical and psychological significance. The throat chakra relates to the thyroid (butterfly) gland, the voice box, the tongue and jaw, and is associated symbolically with living and voicing one's truth. The short practice I develop here also includes Craniosacral Therapy, hands-on restorative techniques of the head, neck and spine that I learned in certifying as a craniosacral therapist. The practice below references the significance of the throat chakra and is described further through "Chakra Unwinding" in *Land to Water Yoga* (2006, 91–106).

Undertake the following exploration through contemplation of sound and source, as Paul Barker has written about the importance of the *sound of the voice* "as a harbinger of meaning, before and beyond the word itself" (Barker, 2015, xxi). This is a craniosacral somatic process for freeing and vitalizing the throat chakra through attention to the jaw, which is part of the throat chakra. It is also quite literally a remedy for jaw tension and TMJ (temporomandibular joint) discomfort, sometimes called "lock jaw".

Worlding voice and truth telling

The throat chakra symbolizes truth telling. Through this chakra, one says: *"I speak my truth,"* at the same time, recognizing that truth arrives on the heels of responsibility. In teaching, I share my truth with students through dance, word and music, and this requires that I listen to their truths. In telling my truth, I am mindful that *what* I say is not the only thing that matters; *how* I say it is important. The words I choose are conveyed qualitatively through body language and somatic tone of voice. I realize that truth is not unidirectional but arises contextually and dialogically between people.

First move your hands up to gently cradle the sides of your face. Place the tip of your long fingers in front of the top of the ears. Rest the other fingers where they fall naturally on your face. Let your hands find an easy fit. Then feel the pads of your thumbs under the jaw line. Notice the comfort of holding your own face with care. When you are ready, take a deep, down-through-your-body easy breath. Then exhale completely. Inhale again with more awareness and glide the flesh of your face up towards the fingers as you inhale. Maintain a steady contact and do not slide the hands along the face. Rather, move your hands, cheeks and jaw with lightness and awareness. You will be closing the jaw slightly, as you move the hands gently upward. On the outbreath, descend your hands, barely moving the jaw with the flesh of your face. Keep moving the hands down until they leave the face and trace easily down the throat. You will be left with a relaxed open jaw and a slightly stupid look, as your face and mouth sag and give up. Let your eyes relax, your ears tingle and enjoy looking silly.

When you finish the process above, or if you facilitate this very easy exploration in a class, take time after finishing to sit quietly. Breathe softly. Close your eyes and attend to sounds in the silence, to any vague impressions, pre-voices or well-formed voices that arrive in your body consciousness. Imagistic prevalence comes to people in individual ways. Let any realizations develop in your perceptual awareness without judgment or allow a meditative silence. When you are ready and out loud, experience the fullness of saying to yourself: "I speak my truth. I have a voice".

Worlding voice through dialogics

Voice is intrinsically before language and characterized by changes inseparable from expressions, emotions and beliefs. Such affective extralinguistic elements contribute to unique genres of somatic communication. Somatic practices are particularly rich in extralinguistic, aesthetic and kinesthetic aspects of utterance; the sphere that falls between linguistic and purely semantic analyses that Mikhail Bakhtin sees has entirely disappeared for science. "The utterance as a whole," he says "is shaped as such by extralinguistic (dialogic) aspects. These extralinguistic dialogic aspects pervade the utterance from within" (1986, 108–109). In Bakhtin's phenomenology, "intelligible sound (a word) – and the pause constitute a special logosphere, a unified and continuous structure, an open (unfinalized) totality" (1986, 134).

To link such extralinguistic utterances – movements and sounds – I teach a somatic partnering process that I identify as *Responsive Voice*. Bakhtin's work on utterance and expression respects linguistic context and a wide spectrum of possible genres of communication. As he puts it, "we speak in diverse genres without suspecting they exist" (1986, 78, 98). The somatic genre I describe here has several layers of utterance all imbued with aesthetic/affective imprints and mindful of ethical distance between participants in somatic settings where body contact is involved. Emotional distance (the space between) can be an objective part of care and curiosity in teaching and learning through contact and touch. My question is ever how to create connections that are responsive, playfully alive and respectful.

Responsive Voice relates to Contact Unwinding in Shin Somatics, a unique development of interactive contact and movement with partners and in groups. Responsive Voice adds voice to the process and is structured in three simple phases: (a) voicing through sound and movement, (b) voicing back and (c) summary. Partners designate *guides* and *primary movers*. The *mover* initiates the movement and vocal expression (a) and the *guide* moves alongside, voicing back (b), responding as a witness and encouraging – listening, moving and sounding, matching in supportive contact (assisting an arm to reach further or take a new direction, for instance, or perhaps aiding stability with a hand on the back). As part of contact, the guide might match or contrast the voicings of her partner or wait in silence at will. The summary phase (c) is a short reflection or verbal dialogue between the partners. Partners are authors in reflections of insight and change during this summary. The whole of the dialogic process waits upon the unknown, as partners find words for responsive transfers of movement, melodies, drones and muttering.

Everyone understands that contact is a choice, and we also explore moving and sounding at a distance, remembering to change partners a few times. I sometimes participate, but alternate this with observation, also giving reminders about the process. Our improvisations use *call* and *response* in a polyphonic way; the *mover* letting sound and movement be whatever it wants to be in the moment, the *guide* listening and voicing back in supportive and tactile dialogues that often overlap. The process might be soft and indistinct or robust and roiling. If the class is large, pairs take turns, and those on the outside circle become witnesses to the whole, with one or more pairs on the inside. Of course, people often feel vulnerable and we recognize this as an aspect of performance. This is why we call it "a practice" instead of a finished performance. We agree to make our work space a safe place psychologically and we laugh a lot.

Moving, listening and sounding in dialogue with others, I feel like a vine, interconnecting, holding, falling, fading and stretching wide. Our movement-sound improvisations might be performed in the studio or in evocative surroundings outdoors. I take students to Snow Canyon near my home in Southwest Utah (Figure 3.1), where we improvise in whorled red

44 Sondra Fraleigh

Figure 3.1 Shin Somatics students voicing in Snow Canyon, 2017. © Sondra Fraleigh (Photos by the author.)

sandstone, feeling our way softly barefoot amid occasional songs of birds. We also visit abandoned construction sites, barking like tin and wailing softly in the lonely atmospheres of rusty pipes. Waiting, holding our arms close to our bodies, we consciously pause the in-breath. Letting the arms go, we relax and hum through the out-breath.

For me, the teaching process is like a dance, and voicing is like dancing with rich choreographic challenges and improvisatory elements. In teaching, I match in my body the movement images and sounds that arise in others but with aesthetic distance. When the process comes to conclusion, I sometimes structure a class summary by asking students to share some aspect of their experience in small groups. This way, everyone gets to speak and to listen and I am not the one to say what insights have arrived. Somatic learning supports polyphony as it varies among individuals who bring with them different experiences and expectations. Being a practitioner-phenomenologist, I stay ready for surprise.

Etude II: sounding

A voice is never just a voice. It is always being oriented through intention: sounded, spoken, sung, discovered and understood in a particular circumstance. Piersandra Di Matteo (2015) writes of sound and discovery through "the capture of speech," noticing how voice is situated between the body and language at the level of "utterance" (90). This is "the voice understood not as a signifying power but as sound" (Ibid., 91). Like Bakhtin, Di Matteo sees how encoding such corporeality "traces words back to physical events which give them life" (Ibid.). The insights of these authors resonate with my own experience, as I trace back to somatic matters of voice.

In the small town where I grew up, my father was the wedding and funeral singer and an actor in awful Gay Nineties melodramas. Needless to say, he took pride in his voice, even as his main occupation was that of raising cattle on our ranch. As for me, he liked to say: "Sondra can do anything except sing". Well it has all come true. I can do anything except sing. When I try, my body tenses and suddenly I cannot hear a thing. Is anybody listening? Sometimes, I get lucky and remember to relax, use my breath consciously, listen and imagine. I listen for the sound I want to make and imagine it becoming real. More than anything, I have wanted to be able to sing well. But as fate or circumstances would have it, I have become good at dancing. It was always easy for me, and so much fun, even in its awesome challenges. Gradually, as I grew older, dancing became my way of singing. I could sense my father's mellow rose and golden voice come to life in my movement, and eventually hear him in my teaching voice. I can connect to people with my voice when I teach and tell stories, and I am convinced that voice is both given and earned. It is something to be developed – as signaling immediately the tone of personality: unprepossessing, persuasive, whining, pleasant, shy or bold, bullying (unfortunately) and so much more.

On butoh

Di Matteo's idea of *tracing sound back* to the physicality of utterance also draws me towards butoh as a metamorphic form of dance and theatre.

The butoh body does not idealize the body, as in classical ballet, nor is it overtly expressive as is the early modern dance. Butoh is an original Japanese postmodern development and not pedestrian in the sense of European and American postmodern dance. It brings imagistic metamorphosis and the body of crisis to theatre and therapy. Butoh encourages performances of becoming other, including other than human. Applications of butoh can facilitate the voice *becoming other*, not just the voice we expect, as we explore in the final section, *sounding other*.

Butoh is adventurous in its metamorphic core. At the moment, it occurs to me that I would like to become an amoeba or a potato, anything to escape my habitual self. What a relief! Through its transformational ethos of becoming other, butoh offers an antidote to the West's focus on the personal self. The self that appears in butoh is basic. One grapples with rudimentary movement most people can do: slow bent-knee-glide-walking, squatting, leaning-off-center, falling-way-off-center, turning, twisting, shaking, grimacing, bobbling, disappearing and much more (Fraleigh and Nakamura, 2006, 101–143). Such root creativity has allowed butoh an international participation and eclectic development (Fraleigh, 2010, 16–34).

Butoh means "dance step," and is also called "ancient dance," as the dance already and always worlding inside and around us. In holding the stories of our ancestors, our butoh bodies hold everything. They attest that our human nature is not above environmental nature, that human natures and voices world along with the ecology of the planet. My butoh body dances in the shadow of nuclear crises in Japan and in protest of nuclear testing wherever it takes place. In the 1950s into the 1960s, the United States government tested nuclear weapons in a crucible close to me at Frenchman's Flat in Nevada, dousing the majestic red cliffs, verdant valleys and ranches of my home in Southwest Utah. I give voice and dance to this story, to witness and to warn (Fraleigh, 2004, 170–173).

Transforming

Here, I shift from the voice of the educator/philosopher (in the first etude) to the phenomenological voice of the dancer and vocal improviser, expanding the *metamorphic intentions* and creative values that sustain butoh. The value of directing vocal intention towards otherness, to become other (the sound of a brook or growl of an imagined monster) whether morphing in butoh or acting in theatre, derives from practice of intention but not intention simply as such. Metamorphic intention involves something more dialectic and tremulous. In morphing (transforming) through sound, I tune to unseen yet present vibrations, and let my body/voice take any shape in the moment. I am sometimes surprised and often incredulous as movement and voice coalesce in simultaneity with my intentions. In butoh, as in other expressionist improvisations, I often court grotesque transmogrification, but I do not insist on particular outcomes. To morph in transformation from a place of abject weakness in butoh is to exercise great power – as in a flash, empathy strengthens belief towards otherness, whether other people or races, or the sound of water embodied in flesh. Flesh is never just flesh and I am never just my body, my self.

Early in this section, I said I would like to become a potato (maybe) or an amoeba. When I image this, suddenly I laugh a little and relax. I could even become a potato-amoeba. I do not actually become anything other than myself, but I can practise changing my ordinary sway of mind as I direct my intentions creatively and, with kinesthetic empathy, get down on the floor and morph into one smiling cell. I might even wield my breath towards the benefits of potassium in the squeeze of every heartbeat or feel blobby and gooey to disappear my organs and edges. When I get up, I can test how I feel in the new one-cell me. In becoming a potato-amoeba, I move my intentional capacities to original ground, disrupting my habitual sense of a normal self. In retrospect, I might wonder how this one cell sounds and try voicing it. Ouch! In this absurd example, I encounter *values of morphic intentionality* in extending imagination, experiencing embodied change and empathy, outwitting habit, extending choice and inviting surprise and belief in body and world. To this, we could add the importance of practising the creative freedoms, constraints and choices of any intentional performance.

Husserl studied intentionality as the main theme of phenomenology and the fundamental property of consciousness (McIntyre and Smith, 1989). Intentionality refers to how acts, including voiced actions, are oriented, not simply where the sounds go but also the fullness of attention and affectivity that informs them. The body is already and always materially relational, as I write about with others in delineating several phenomenologies of performance in a recent work (Fraleigh, 2018). Nature is not taken for granted in phenomenology neither is it a fixed concept (Husserl and Fink, [1932] 1995, 189). Nature as embodied in complexity and change is never just nature. Our body has a history relative to the environing world and material nature and (I add) so have the morphing contours and expressions of any voice.

Paul Ricoeur carries bodily-lived relativity still further. During his imprisonment by the Nazi occupation of France, he translated much of Husserl's phenomenology. Later, Ricoeur's own work, *Freedom and Nature: The Voluntary and the Involuntary* ([1966] 2007), drew phenomenology towards physiology. This work is concerned with how sensorimotor habits inform individual habitus. It studies how habit and skill interact as individuals bring what seems natural to attention and consciously improve on it or else join the obscure involuntary habitus. In either case, *we become what we do.* I walk every day, for instance, and pay attention as I go. More to the point of intentionality, I often stop along the way to find the horizon with my eyes or roll my feet from heel to toe in order to sensitize my connection to the ground. The times I fine-tune my walking, dance and voice, remind me of my freedom.

Ricoeur shows how movement and knowledge are bound together in voluntary effort, as the mental and physical bring about "an undecipherable unity, beyond effort" ([1966] 2007, 249). The voice sounds right and true; we can speak and sing as we intend. The writing flows. In Ricoeur's phenomenology, the voluntary dimensions of human existence – willing, acting, intending and orienting – are systemically interactive with the involuntary body at an organic level. This realization is fundamental to transformative potentials of somatic practice. Somatic transformation is lived as an effective embodied change, not an ideal. Freedom is lived as "situated" (Fraleigh, 2004, 214–216). Choices are embodied organically through repetition – and in consent or refusal, Ricoeur states in a full section titled Motives and Values on the Organic Level (1966, 104–122). In tracing back to intention, I can practise my freedom to change. Future time is already stirring in what I do now. My invisible future voice is constantly unfolding.

Enworlding sound itself

Finding voice is a discovery that continues over a lifetime, from the time of infancy when we learn how to make sounds and finally to talk and sing, to old age when we often have difficulty articulating words and meanings, as we might like. Finding voice is at root a search for sound, and this is the sound that is ours, a sound that identifies our uniqueness while engaging us with others and the world. Voice is connective, dialogic and enworlding.

My butoh-inflected processes of *tracing sound back* often evolve in nature as part of the more than human world, voicing "the more" through "becoming other". Butoh can be highly theatrical but it also attunes to nature, even as it moves beyond nature/culture dichotomies in exploring liminal states and morphic intentionality. In convergence with the ongoing world, my butoh body is unfinished, never just my body, my voice. My voice, sometimes enraptured, awkward, ever present and vanishing, thuds and waits, its *butoh-fu* (poetic marks) trembling.

Butoh is not about acting a part or mirroring or imitation. The butoh way of becoming other is about disappearing any sense of solidity and entering into other objects and happenings while intentionally exploring all that is not neatly, habitually human. To this end, butoh dancers often powder their faces with white rice powder. Butoh is indeed a study in depersonalization, directing intentionality below surface appearances. My butoh mentor, Ohno Kazuo-sensei, teaches a metamorphic process that he calls "Be a Stone". "Be a Stone" is the single instruction for his dance of becoming other. As a Japanese veteran of World War II, he tried to dance for healing at the Auschwitz concentration camp in Poland. He could not express anything, he sometimes said in workshops, until he sensed the suffering in the stones.

Sounding other

Go to a place away from city life, outside, near the sea, on a mountain, in a forest or in the desert. Lie down, sit or stand, but be ready to change positions as you wish, or move minimally and with attention to dissolving your body. Butoh is generally slow but it can spark speed. Listen to whatever sounds are present in the environment. Just let them be. Absorb the sounds. Ask yourself how you feel in this absorption. The sounds will morph and move, as they do in open environments. Dancers will be tempted to move a lot. Might I ask you to do less? This exploration is about sound primarily and moving minimally.

Notice how your body wants to move as it disappears into the external and internal sounds, or maybe you want to be still. Be carried by the sounds you hear. Move a little towards them if you wish or move away. Can you split the difference between conscious action and dream? If you fall asleep, that's OK. You will wake up and find where you are, what you remember and what is sounding through you. Hum softly to yourself if you want to. Feel the vibrations of your voice enveloped in sound surroundings.

Like my mentor, Ohno Kazuo-sensei, I am often drawn to stones and find voice through them. Some stones sound mineral metallic, others ring hollow or echo with space and history. I relax to become the soundings and colors of stone. Stone is never just stone.

As a somatic practice, let your voice embody something other; however, this comes to you. Be in your sounding body for a while. Return rested and resilient. You can do this exploration alone, of course, but might want to experience it with others. If you do, at the end of your sounding event, sound together in community. Finally, check in with the group to share your impressions.

References

Barker, P. (2015) Foreword (With one voice: disambiguating sung and spoken voices through a composer's experience) in *Voice Studies: Critical Approaches to Process, Performance and Experience*. Abington, Oxon: Routledge.

Cavarero, A. (2005) *For More than One Voice: Toward a Philosophy of Vocal Expression*. Translated by P.A. Kottman. Stanford, CA: Stanford University Press.

Di Matteo, P. (2015) Performing the *entre-deux:* the capture of speech in (dis) embodied voices. In: Konstantinos Thomaidis and Ben Macpherson (eds.) *Voice Studies: Critical Approaches to Process, Performance and Experience*. London: Routledge, 90–103.

Fraleigh, S. (2004) *Dancing Identity: Metaphysics in Motion*. Pittsburgh: University of Pittsburgh Press.

——— (2006) *Land to Water Yoga*. New York: iUniverse Press.

——— (2010) *BUTOH: Metamorphic Dance and Global Alchemy*. Urbana: University of Illinois Press.

——— (2015) *Moving Consciously: Somatic Transformations through Dance, Yoga, and Touch*. Urbana: University of Illinois Press.

——— (2018) *Back to the Dance Itself: Phenomenologies of the Body in Performance*. Edited with essays by Sondra Fraleigh. Urbana: University of Illinois Press.

Fraleigh, S. and Nakamura, T. (2006) *Hijikata Tatsumi and Ohno Kazuo*. London: Routledge.

Heidegger, M. ([1927] 1962) *Being and Time*. Translated from German by John Macquarrie and Edward Robinson. New York: Harper & Row.
—— (1971) The thing. In: Martin Heidegger (eds.) *Poetry, Language, Thought*. Translated from German by Albert Hofstadter. New York: Harper and Row, 163–180.
Husserl, E. ([1900] 1970) *Logical Investigations*. Translated from German by J. N. Findlay. London: Routledge & Kegan Paul.
—— ([1952] 1989) *Ideas Pertaining to a Pure Phenomenology and to a Phenomenological Philosophy,* Book 2 (Ideas II). Translated from German by R. Rojcewicz and A. Schuwer. Boston, MA: Kluwer Academic Publishers.
Husserl, E. and Fink, E. ([1932] 1995) *Sixth Cartesian Meditation: The Idea of a Transcendental Theory of Method*. Textual notations and appendix by Edmund Husserl. Translated from German with introduction by Ronald Bruzina. Bloomington: Indiana University Press.
Ingold, T. (2011) *Being Alive: Essays on Movement, Knowledge and Description*. Abington, Oxon: Routledge.
McIntyre, R. and Smith, D. W. (1989) Theory of intentionality. In: Jitendranath N. Mohanty and William R. McKenna (eds.) *Husserl's Phenomenology: A Textbook*. Washington, DC: Center for Advanced Research in Phenomenology and University Press of America, 147–179.
Ohno, K. (1986) *Butoh Workshop* [workshop]. Yokohama, Japan.
Ricoeur, P. ([1966] 2007) *Freedom and Nature: The Voluntary and the Involuntary*. Translated from French by Erazim V. Kohak, foreword by Don Ihde. Chicago, IL: Northwestern University Press.
Thomaidis, K. (2015) The Re-vocalization of logos? Thinking, doing and disseminating voice. In: Konstantinos Thomaidis and Ben Macpherson (eds.) *Voice Studies: Critical Approaches to Process, Performance and Experience*. London: Routledge, 9–21.

4 On Voice Movement Integration (VMI) practice by Patricia Bardi
Awakening resonance in the moving body

Patricia Bardi interviewed by Christina Kapadocha

Patricia Bardi has occupied a significant position in the development of somatic movement and voice integration. One of the earliest protagonists in the field, she has been developing and honing her understanding and practice for over forty years. Originally a dancer, in her explorations she has combined scientific information with rigorous somatic understanding and creative dance artistry. The fruits of her discoveries are her accredited educational program, VMI – Voice Movement Integration,[1] and her unique, improvisatory performance approach entitled "Vocal Dance," which is both a training method and her own performance practice.

A note to the reader (Christina Kapadocha)

While witnessing a workshop held by Bardi at East 15 Acting School in London (November 17, 2018) as part of this book project, I am drawn to the practitioner's rhythmical and rhyming words: "Let the sound and the action have some interaction" (Bardi, 2018). This diverse interaction is at the heart of the following material which is developed upon Bardi's written responses to my questions combined with video documentation and transcribed thoughts after the workshop. In resonance with the overall identity of the volume, my intentions as witness of our interactive process were not only to bring forth the originality and innovative contributions of Bardi's practice but also how it can interact with and inform theoretical perspectives on voice and somaticity. For the facilitation of your navigation throughout this cross-narrative, I integrate some notes to the reader in the main body of the text.

The background of a dance-voice artist

Christina Kapadocha (CK): Could we start by you briefly telling us about your background? I am interested in your connection to dance and in how voice emerged in your practice.

Patricia Bardi (PB): In 1972, upon completing my university study in psychology in New York, I started to pursue my lifelong dream of learning to dance. From the start I was drawn to experimental, improvisatory performance and wanted to absorb as many diverse influences as I could. So, over five years I participated in a wide spectrum of dance classes including: modern dance technique with Nancy Meehan, a soloist with Erick Hawkins; ballet with Colette Barry and Susan Klein; improvisation and dance making with Trisha Brown; and composition with Daniel Nagrin. Also having direct interaction with early seminal practitioners of Contact Improvisation such as Lisa Nelson and Steve Paxton had a profound influence on my development.

In 1974, while I was studying dance with Nancy Meehan, I was introduced to Bonnie Bainbridge Cohen and her work at the time on body alignment. I was intrigued by the description of her approach and subsequently joined her first Body-Mind Centering® (BMC®) teacher training group in New York. This led in 1977 to my working one-on-one with Bonnie to prepare the courses I was teaching in her first BMC® certification program in Northampton, Massachusetts. This wonderful opportunity gave me a first-hand, invaluable experience of what it means to research into body presence and its relationship to somatic movement integration. Also, upon moving to London, I began my long association with the exceptional osteopath and educator Ernest Keeling who has been a seminal influence in my understanding of the significance of touch and physical integration in my somatic practice.

The initial somatic work on Cohen's experiential anatomy included working with the organs. This had a significant effect on my movement integration and influenced my approach to dance. I experienced how important it was to include a deep understanding of internal body awareness in my dancing. The internal world of the body was opening up for me, leading me through a growing awareness of breath, breath support and vocal anatomy to the start of my creative adventure with voice.

In my earliest experiences of voice, I can clearly remember the moment, in my dance training in New York with choreographer Miki Goodman, when I realized that sound for me was a physical instrument. My aim at the time was to bring a totality of body awareness into my dancing. The questions arising were "why am I leaving out the capacity of my breath and sound? Why am I silent?" This new insight opened up my explorations. Bringing voice into my dancing both astonished and invigorated me. I was no longer a silent dancer and began developing into a *dance-voice artist*.

My early dance practice with voice was intuitive and solo-based. I was interested in making my own dances and started exploring the organs' potential for influencing my movement language. By including sound in this exploration I experienced a new level of sensory perception, vitality and direction. These explorations became my first *Vocal Dances*. At that point voice became a key element in my somatic movement practice – opening a new path to my creativity and self-development.

The exploration of organs as source of dance-vocal interaction

CK: You mentioned that when you started making your own Vocal Dances you began exploring the organs' potential. Could you explain what you mean by that? Why specifically organs and how is this possible in practice?

PB: Originally my research into the presence of the organs included the voice as a means for encouraging more attuned responses. I was a conventional dancer and using my voice was not included in my dance training at all. Initially my aim was to integrate sound to stimulate organ presence in my movement experience. This created a different sensory experience within my physicality which significantly influenced my movement vocabulary. Through this early research, I could sense how voice had the capacity to integrate my attention and intention far more deeply and richly than working solely with movement. Bringing the awareness of the organs by including the vibrational impact of sound transformed my movement experience. Through this exploration, I discovered the organs are a three-dimensional inner volume filling the space of our torso, a rhythmical, moving and pulsating inner presence. As a mover-dancer I was perceiving how the inner, fluid weight of the organs participated in my movement and vocal expression; and I realized that this sensory awareness was a bridge for subcortical autonomic functions and able therefore to influence my musculoskeletal, conscious abilities.

This interactive exploration featured strongly in my solo dance performance. Through the awareness of my organs, I was able to connect with the inner dialogue of my thoughts and feelings. What arrived was the potential to bring my voice into my capacity to interact and express more directly with musicians or play with a character. It fostered my ability to articulate my point of view through sound and language, which transformed the abstraction of dance with another layer of meaning and expression. The boundaries between theatre, dance and music were dissolving and a clearer, more fully-realized interdisciplinary approach came into being.

At this point I conducted an in-depth inquiry into the anatomical and physiological science of the body and from this knowledge base investigated my own body systems through movement and sound. From these personal discoveries I developed the methods and practice for my Voice Movement Integration program. Working with students, including performing artists, movement educators and therapists, I have found that it is essential to offer and to guide them through a series of well-defined somatic movement and voice practices in order to develop this interdisciplinary awareness and conscious alertness. It is important to guide this vocal-physical practice to awaken their sense of a resonant body moving actively in space. My somatic educational program therefore provides the student with a rigorous understanding of anatomy, physiology, human motor development and perception to build a foundation for actively integrating movement with voice into a whole-body experience (Figure 4.1).

Figure 4.1 From Patricia Bardi's workshop at East 15 Acting School, London, November 17, 2018. (Photo by Vivianna Chiotini.)

To the reader: For further insights on the practice, see Patricia Bardi-organ work video (5:06). Accessible through the Routledge Voice Studies (RVS) website. Documentation by Vivianna Chiotini.

From a performance to a teaching practice

CK: So, how was your Vocal Dance further developed from a performance practice to a training process?

PB: As students started becoming more interested in experiencing and learning how to combine voice and movement, I developed the tools for communicating my practice. I was touring throughout Europe teaching somatic movement to dancers as well as performing my Vocal Dances. I became increasingly aware of how essential the interconnections were between these practices for myself and the dancers I was teaching. I was inspired to design an educational training program that would systematically and rigorously teach performers and aspiring practitioners how to develop their body, voice and movement through somatic practice. It developed into a four-year course in which graduates become qualified somatic movement educators-therapists and bodyworkers.

My solo Vocal Dance performance practice was the source for developing the Vocal Dance ensemble practice which is a key component in the program. It is a creative practice that aims at freeing one's voice to be fully alive and reflected in one's expressive vitality and active movement. Bringing breath and voice into the experience of moving integrates a new level of sensory attention and influences the students' motor intention. They discover breath and voice aligned with movement is a profound unifier of internal awareness and active expression. It is an integration of dance, voice and language, while combining compositional elements with the immediacy of improvisation.

Within the frame of a live interactive performance, this combination opens the potential for further discovery and innovation of the material to emerge and deepen. By engaging with this somatic process and responding to qualities and variations of flow, rhythm and texture streaming through the body, vocal presence arrives from a heightened physical state of awareness and inspires a resonance of feeling, thought and action in the performer.

To the reader: By returning to the volume's webpage, you could watch a video on how the practitioner included the specific practice in her workshop. See Patricia Bardi-Vocal Dance video (3:31). Documentation by Vivianna Chiotini. The editing of the video follows the development of the practice from group to partner work and then back to group.

CK: How would you describe the integration of sound, movement and language in your teaching?

PB: In my understanding of it, the very nature of sound while moving in an acoustical space is gravity-free. The resonance of the sound is felt in the body as a vibrational fluidity moving equally and fully in all dimensions. Whereas the body's movement has to engage with gravity, the sound is a living force that animates the cellular presence (full and effortless attention) and this sense of fluidity is potentially received through the entire body. The vibration of sound can move more freely with less tension and effort within the body and influences our sensory attention.

Functionally the neural circuits of the eyes, vestibular system and proprioception sense receptors connect directly to the cerebellum, modulating our movement effort and coordination. I look to bring the internal awareness of the movement flow stimulated by sound to inform and guide the movement through the body. Within this interactive and active listening process, the performer becomes more aware of how their entire body – hands, eyes, ears, spine, ribcage, pelvis and feet – is receiving and animating. Thus, the sound they generate influences their movement presence and also the reverse, enabling the quality of sensation in the movement to influence the interactive vocals.

Within the vocal-physical interaction of Vocal Dance, written and spoken language becomes a potent element. The interaction of language with movement profoundly impacts the sensory information the body is experiencing. This is due to the many levels of brain activity being awakened in the process – conscious, cortical, imaginative, subconscious associative, deep memory and poetic filters. These awakened areas activate a symbolic world incorporating memory and sensation as a source and pool of images, reflecting personal history and felt experience. This is information the cortical mind does not readily retain yet actively receives from the associative power of images, memory and vocal-physical presence. This fosters a wellspring of new sources of creativity and unleashes new patterns of vocal-physical response.

Outlining Voice Movement Integration as somatic training

CK: You have already spoken about Vocal Dance as an important part of your somatic training program. Could you also outline how you further support one's vocal-physical responses within the additional strands of your VMI training?

PB: Within the ongoing development of my research-led practice, in 1993 I founded the VMI Somatic Practice Certification Program centered in Amsterdam. The program attracts a diverse group of students from different backgrounds and ages including performing artists – dancers, actors and singers – movement educators and therapists, speech and physical therapists, holistic health practitioners, body psychotherapists, Pilates and yoga teachers. The training combines Vocal Dance with VMI and Vital Movement Integration Bodywork (VMIB). These three strands are interrelated yet distinct in the way they approach vocal-physical presence.

Vocal Dance is a creative expressive approach, while VMI aims at vocal-physical self-awareness and integration. It supports the development of perceptual, observational and expressive skills from an internal presence informing our self-knowledge. This encounter with the self emerges from well-defined, accumulative and progressive somatic practices integrating holistic understanding of each of the body systems. The VMI practice incorporates *Active Breath*, a key aspect of the work integrating guided movement sequences, whole-body breathing, physical rhythms and voice.

The third strand, VMIB, is a bodywork technique and therapeutic process the students develop for applying in their professional practice. It focuses on specific protocols for each body system incorporating hands-on touch and physical repatterning skills for working directly with another person's embodied experience. In receiving this level of sensitive touch, along with guided movement sequencing, the practitioner guides a person to open their perceptual filters to new arenas of sensory perception through the entire body. The interconnecting core of all three strands is how we live and perceive through our vocal-physical presence and how this enhances our core sense of self.

CK: It seems to me that the word somatic in your practice suggests a combination of lineages and processes with notions of perception, expression and self-awareness. You have been using the term in order to describe your work while being a contemporary somatic practitioner who primarily focuses on vocal-physical interaction. How would you identify the notion of somatic in your work?

PB: As a frame of reference, the word somatic did not emerge in the vernacular of common understanding and as a specialized field until the 80s and 90s. People would ask what somatic means and if I mentioned the word "psychosomatic" the gap in the understanding was bridged. Before somatics as a field was specifically-identified, dance-movement practitioners, including myself, saw the exploration of internal processes as a potent resource: to guide our sense of embodiment; as a welcome tool for developing our creative skills with more clarity; and a source of insight into our capacity for movement and expression. In working with my students integrating voice with movement through guided somatic practices, I started shaping my insight about how different cultural traditions have evolved their rhythms and expression through the body.

CK: So, if I understand correctly, the somatic in your practice includes, among others, the awareness of diverse cultural expressions? Have you focused at all on this culture-related insight in your work?

PB: Early in my development I often visited the Jacques Marchais Museum of Tibetan Art located in Staten Island, New York. I was enthralled looking at the Tibetan sculptures' multifaceted expressions. While living in Massachusetts I attended a concert by the extraordinary South Indian singer Subbalakshmi. This was my first encounter with Indian vocal music and it profoundly moved and inspired me. Upon moving to London, the spectrum of Indian music and dance being offered exponentially broadened by curiosity and interest.

In the early 80s I received an Arts Council England grant and conducted a research project on North Indian vocal music. It was an invaluable and priceless experience studying voice and observing the Indian music culture. The outcomes were a performance that took place in Pune and Delhi and a film about my research for which I collaborated with young Indian filmmakers. Being exposed to a non-Western form of music and dance opened up a whole new perspective for me about expression and presence. Indian dance originated in temple dancing and has a direct relationship with music and the gesturing language of *mudras*. One of the most important influences was to see how the voice and the movement approached space. There was a far more articulated response to how each sound and movement related to the use of space. I personally had never experienced this specificity in the Western cultural style of expansiveness, of filling the available space, initiating outward without the sense of return. This experience has had a lasting effect on my vocal-physical approach without trying to imitate or consciously include elements of Indian culture.

CK: I hear it clearly in the way you have developed your language around the interrelation between voice and space. This also brings to mind the "inner space" of one's vocal-physical presence and of the body systems you mentioned before.

PB: The key here is to look at how somatic movement enhances the capacity of the voice beyond vocal production into a more realized felt experience that has the power to inform and develop one's sense of self more profoundly. A somatic approach that includes the organs and nervous system's subconscious processes informs the functional anatomy of the voice and also enhances our vocal resonance and power to express more directly. The process informs our sense of self and aligns our movement awareness more precisely. Anatomically speaking, we know that the brain is connected to the organs through the autonomic nervous system (ANS) sustaining our homeostatic balance via the vagus nerve. Structurally, the organs' inner volume and three dimensionality occupies the inner space of the torso surrounded by the core muscles.

By somatically connecting to this internal interaction, we can follow more fully the physical and emotive possibilities of our voices. This potentiality, in my perspective, opens a dimension of emotional content that is felt directly and without interpretation. As the artistic voice is conventionally conveyed through song or text, it already carries some kind of interpretation. When we are more aligned with the richness of a fuller physical presence in our voices, beyond functional anatomy, we can work more directly with our inner resources, finding our own original physical voice.

CK: I understand what you mean by one's own original physical voice while witnessing your practice. I am also curious about the choices of the sounds in your Vocal Dances as they bring up for me once more cultural or intercultural qualities.[2]

PB: Again, it's not about trying to imitate world music but to my observation world music has a visceral source because it emerges from the experience in the body. Music and vocalization developed through dance and movement. So, in working with different rhythms and qualities in sound and movement, you arrive at some recognizable world-music traditions without copying them. This is a very different orientation as the quality of the voice and the quality of the rhythm are interacting with body presence. It is not prescribed in the sense of "what do I select?". It is essentially about the felt experience – what is engaging the presence, what rhythm, what quality of sounds are getting stimulated and sustained.

I incorporate animated polyrhythms as a springboard and initial frame for people to have a chance to both develop their vocal skills and integrate their vocal-movement skills. As the students become more familiar with bringing their voice actively into space, they can open up the experience through improvising in the ensemble interaction and discover a far bigger spectrum of how they can relate to sound, rhythm, syntax, even textures of sound. The initial vocal frame could potentially be a limitation but as the interactive experience unfolds, I can guide them to extend their range and experiment more freely in their expression. In an experienced ensemble that is working compositionally with improvisation, the roles of mover and sound maker are constantly intermingling and the audience may not distinguish between who is moving and who is vocalizing. It is an animated whole experience. The soundscape that comes out of this impetus from the body through movement is also a response to qualities of vocal phrasing. It can be a very dynamic and exciting interaction. It is a hybrid form that gives it its quality and its genre.

More possibilities for *sound-action interaction*

CK: I guess in the support of this dynamic quality also reside the multidisciplinary potentialities of your work. You mentioned that the artistic voice is conventionally conveyed through song or text. What about other artists, such as dancers, for whom voicing is not traditionally integrated in their training and expression?

PB: I see the activity of the breath and voice as a genuine unifier of attention and intention for all creative artists who use their bodies as an instrument of expression. But of all worlds of artistic expression the dancer is indeed the most "silent". Why shouldn't dancers be given more experience of their breath and voice in their training; why be left out of the voice's vital link in their awareness and expression? To me, "having a voice" is a metaphor for communicating who we are and what we know with clarity and authenticity. Voice is our signature in sound and our vehicle for how we bring forth our ideas, and how we share our understanding with the world. In working with embodied breath as the silent source of the sound, the relationship between breath awareness and vocal presence engages in a continuum; it guides and informs our capacity to express ourselves.

The option for dancers using voice in performance is secondary to the core impact of the physical-vocal integrative work of the dancer – freeing the breath, building breath support and accessing the power of the voice in defining and refining their physical presence. Approaching and identifying voice as a physical experience activated through body presence helps to dissolve the dancer's fears of using the voice. The feedback a somatic voice can give is not muted and inhibited. Instead, it offers the possibilities of a more vivid physical presence which heightens awareness of creative self-empowerment. Having a relationship to their voice gives the dancer a clearer capacity and further access to knowing, expressing and articulating their thoughts and feelings.

CK: Focusing on self-empowerment and given that you identify yourself as a female dance-voice artist, I am also thinking about how your practice could interact with the writings of feminist philosophers such as Julia Kristeva (1984) and Hélène Cixous (1986). How do you see your work contributing to modern discussions on inclusion of the female vocal soma?

PB: A central theme throughout my artistic work has been questioning and opening the boundaries of the traditional role assigned to the female archetype. Initially having the courage to pursue dancing came directly from participating in a consciousness-raising women's group we called the

"Self-Development Group" in New York. My work with voice in dance started from an innocent place and has evolved over the years into a defined somatic approach integrating voice with movement that opens new sources of awareness and self-knowledge for both women and men. These are tools of empowerment for everyone.

For women being fully embodied in their voice and physical presence is fundamentally important in fully achieving equality and freedom of expression in the world. She feels her power: has confidence and the ability to express who she is; knows what she observes and understands with more articulated skills. She has the courage to be heard as well as seen and knows herself more fully. She can acknowledge and be conscious of the woman she is, inside the presence of her vocal-physical body.[3] I see my work as part of an exciting wave of transformational thinking and practice involving the body which gives women new tools for knowing and living their strength.

Notes

1. See http://patriciabardi.com/.
2. You may wish to return to the video on the practitioner's Vocal Dance group practice in relation to this question.
3. This does not aim to confine womanhood within its universal biology but acknowledges the intricate politics of fourth-wave feminism. See, among others, Phipps, 2014; Threadcraft, 2016; Hussein, 2018.

References

Bardi, P. (2018) *Workshop on Voice Movement Integration (VMI)* [workshop]. East 15 Acting School-London, November 17.

Cixous, H. and Clément, C. (1986) *The Newly Born Woman*. Translated from French by Betsy Wing. Mineapolis: University of Minnesota Press.

Hussein, N. (ed.) (2018) *Rethinking New Womanhood: Practices of Gender, Class, Culture and Religion in South Asia*. Cham, Switzerland: Palgrave Macmillan.

Kristeva, J. (1984) *Revolution in Poetic Language*. Translated from French by Margaret Waller. New York: Columbia University Press.

Phipps, A. (2014) *The Politics of the Body: Gender in a Neoliberal and Neoconservative Age*. Cambridge: Polity Press.

Threadcraft, S. (2016) *Intimate Justice: The Black Female Body and the Body Politic*. New York: Oxford University Press.

Part II
Voice work, somatics and the diverse self

5 In front of me
Fitzmaurice Voicework® as a transformative practice

Ellen Foyn Bruun

In the vocal "forest of Arden"

In an interview from 2004, the founder of Fitzmaurice Voicework® (FV), Catherine Fitzmaurice, says that her work allows "anything to happen. Anything that wants to happen. It's creating chaos. It's throwing people into the forest of Arden" (2004, 4). The "forest of Arden," an imaginary place known from William Shakespeare's *As You Like It* (1603 [1963]), becomes in Fitzmaurice's words a metaphor of vocal instability, blurred realities and messy interactions – a deconstruction of the orderly reality to create new possibilities of vocal transformation. During a five-day workshop in London taught by Fitzmaurice in 2007, I went through a profound emotional and physical experience that in the end left me craving for more. I was literally thrown into the "forest of Arden" – a place of bewilderment, turmoil and new orientation in terms of my relationship to my voice and its physicality. As a certified FV teacher myself, now based in Scandinavia, I still find the work puzzling due to its ongoing transformative potential regarding vocal presence through somatic awareness. Hence, the FV practice has become for me an embodied and vocal anchor in my professional life as a drama and theatre practitioner-researcher and scholar. This means that I have been engaging in an open-ended identity process of curiosity and new discoveries while deepening my own embodied and vocal presence.

FV is a comprehensive approach to voice with equal emphasis on vocal *freedom* and *focus of expression* which transgresses performance on stage and in daily life. It was originally developed for actor training and is at present used in various fields, including supporting people with a wide range of vocal needs. There are over 300 certified FV teachers working internationally (The Fitzmaurice Institute, 2018). FV aims for inner somatic listening as well as for communication on stage and in life. The approach is not exclusive; it can contribute to contemporary voice studies as a method of its own and as a vehicle in combination with other approaches. In this chapter, I do not intend to outline all the elements of FV (for this, see, among others, Morgan, 2012; Watson and Sadhana, 2014; Holmes, 2016; Morrison et al, 2017). My present discussion draws from a study conducted in 2018 in the context of the arts and technology strategy at my university in Trondheim, Norway (*NTNU ARTEC*, 2019). The study addressed my personal transformative experience in the encounter with FV and how my relationship to my voice developed and asserted itself consequently. I wanted to use my vocal and embodied presence as an autonomous transformative phenomenon towards broader awareness of the reality of voice.

Within the same project, I also wished to explore multimodal ways of disseminating the research process and its transformative potentialities based on how the FV practice integrates the physical, emotional, intellectual and vocal body. To do this, Performance as Research (PAR) seemed the most appropriate methodology as it combines theory, interdisciplinarity and transdisciplinarity with "its embodied, affective, and interactive nature" (Barton, 2018, 11). As part of this interactive nature, I invited a collaboration with the digital media artist Wendy Ann Mansilla. Her role was to witness my investigations and translate (or transform) my research practice into digital narrative segments. These segments became part of the devising material for the PAR In front of me (Bruun, 2018) and they reappear in this reflexive narrative on the project.

This chapter is developed around the overall research question: how can intuitive performance practice contribute to the emergence and dissemination of new knowledge on the transformative potentialities of FV? I structure my writing by outlining the theoretical ground and the process towards the performance, then I reflect on the performance itself and lastly, I filter my own reflections through audience feedback to achieve an informed understanding of the reception of the study. I conclude by returning to *how* my PAR study provided an opportunity to make my intuitive learning process explicit heightening awareness and deepening understanding of vocal presence as an innate part of human identity. With this chapter, I wish to propose this kind of intuitive performance practice as a useful research method for the field of critical voice studies.

Theorizing an intuitive inquiry

My PAR methodology combines theoretical ideas that underlie FV with research methods employed in the social sciences: autoethnography (Jones et al, 2013), intuitive inquiry (Anderson, 2000) and Jungian-inspired phenomenology (Romanyshyn, 2010). Autoethnography is in line with qualitative research methodology that emphasizes the subjective, socially-constructed narrative as poly-vocal and reflexive (Gergen and Gergen, 2000, 1037). It requires that "we interrogate what we think and believe, and challenge our own assumptions, asking over and over if we have penetrated as many layers of our own defenses, fears, and insecurities as our project requires" (Holmes, 2016, 191). I take this further by adding the possibilities intuitive inquiry could offer to the study of transformative experience (Anderson and Braud, 1998). The proposed strategies invite any kind of intuitive responses to the studied phenomenon: rational and non-rational, dream images, visions, kinesthetic impressions, felt proprioceptive responses and inner contemplation (Anderson, 2000, 2). All these are elements already present in my FV practice.

Another approach that acknowledges unconscious dynamics in the research process is proposed by Jungian psychologist Robert Romanyshyn (2010). For my study, Romanyshyn's integration of embodied phenomenology with Jung's notion of active imagination addresses the researcher's unconscious process and supports research informed by dreams, symptoms, synchronicities, "the functions of intuition and feeling, alongside the functions of thinking and sensation" (Romanyshyn, 2010, 275). Romanyshyn suggests the intentional use of the *transference field* in the research process, a field mediated by unconscious images, fantasies, complexes and archetypal material. This mediation was vital for my PAR as during the devising process, I focused on exploring FV as a creative and reflexive motor based on the imagery surfacing from my embodied vocal explorations. The performative outcome was eventually shaped upon nine image-based units: (1) Breathing Body, (2) Floating Windows, (3) Perceptions, (4) Fragments, (5) Frozen, (6) Snow, (7) River of Blood, (8) Cracked Glass and (9) River of Life. The interaction of my live performance with the digital narratives, inspired by the emergent imagery in my research process, formed a dream-like whole that underpinned the significance of the conscious-unconscious interconnections towards the understanding of the complexity of vocal phenomena.

Both Anderson and Romanyshyn recommend a layered, cyclic process that systematically encircles the studied phenomenon with open-minded self-reflexivity that can render learning and eventually transformation (Anderson, 2000, 5; Romanyshyn, 2010, 283). In my view, this kind of reflexive research practice represents a bridge between the artistic process of devising and performing with the performative research paradigm (Barton, 2018, 14). With reference to the FV allegiance to teach what is *in front of you* in the sense of being somatically present and able to act appropriately in each present moment, my study committed to somatically deal with what was *in front of me*. The aim was to devise a performance that would interweave practice, personal narrative, reflections and theoretical framing in a multimodal format to advance the understanding of the contribution of FV to one's voice-based transformative journey, and subsequently the inclusion of unconscious experiences in the critical analysis of voice.

Destructuring-restructuring: the blood poem

For the practical ground of my praxical investigation, I employed the two basic features of FV, *destructuring* and *restructuring*, systematically and in dialogue (Morrison et al., 2017). The alternation between destructuring and restructuring is essential in this practice. While destructuring seeks to develop freedom in the voice and a sense of letting go of unhealthy and unhelpful habits, usually connected to previous learning processes, restructuring aims for focus and clarity of thought and emotion in verbal communication (Watson and Sadhana, 2014, 149). This is achieved by containing the energy released in the destructuring phase that is often experienced as chaotic, unpredictable and without specific direction. The intention of the restructuring is to focus this energy by centering it and giving it direction via the central nervous system to the rest of one's embodied and vocal expression. Here, the legacy of traditional European breathing techniques, such as *bel canto* and rib reserve, plays an important role (Fitzmaurice, 2015, 67).

Due to the intuitive nature of my research that aims at including unconscious input into vocal transformation, I began the process foregrounding the destructuring work, also commonly known as the FV tremorwork®. Destructuring became particularly significant for my project because of its potential to integrate chaos with flow serving as a "butterfly effect," disturbing the mundane, armored persona by throwing it into a fragmented world of rough edges where mind and body move towards union (Morgan, 2012, 142). The FV tremors are intentional and can be stopped at any point by the person tremoring. They are induced by physical postures inspired by yoga with the explicit purpose of releasing the breathing reflex and sensitizing somatic awareness of vocal sounding (Fitzmaurice, 2015, 64). By watching the FV tremors video (1:47) on the volume's webpage through the RVS website, you could get an idea of how this work may look and sound like through my own experience. The specific visual and vocal extract (as a video and an audio recording interweave) is from the project's creative process. You see me lying on top of the words of the poem which I discuss as part of my destructuring-restructuring work below.

When I first experienced this kind of generated tremors in the 2007 workshop, I noticed a lot of unfamiliar activity inside my body, like waves of movement leading to intensified sensations and feelings from the intuitive responses of my autonomous nervous system. The building up of my experience seemed to resonate with the step-by-step research process proposed by Romanyshyn, during the first phase of which the focus is on the bridge between the researcher's conscious and unconscious or, in Jungian terminology, the researcher's *active imagination* (Romanyshyn, 2010, 292). In this state, the researcher allows daydreaming and reverie to come to the foreground by spurring free association and imagination, being sensitive to the inner imagery and emotional responses. In my current work, I wanted to investigate tremorwork and its input on my active imagination while learning to use it intentionally and somatically releasing unhelpful tension held in my body.

Within the first stages of my destructuring work, I observed that images and metaphors which were familiar from my past practice surfaced. Hence, in a sort of a modified restructuring step, I decided to vocally and physically explore these images through the structure of a poem I wrote during the 2007 workshop. This step seemed like an appropriate bridging between my unconscious and conscious processes that Romanyshyn suggests, triggered by my intuitive present response to tremorwork. The following poetic reflection is not meant to offer a logical and comprehensive structure. Instead, it is embedded here to suggest how the specific voice work can trigger an openness to the unconscious that, when restructured, could enable a deeper understanding of one's embodied identity and process.

> *Living on air*
> *Where there is only air*
> *How can you make life where there is only illusion*
> *Bursting the myth of my family*
> *Frozen grief*
> *Frozen water*
> *The green spiral thing penetrates*
> *The red drop porous ball*
> *Skin fragile skin*
> *The green knife cuts through*
> *Ball bursts and becomes the river of blood*
> *Amalgamates with other blood drops*
> *Flows into the open landscape*
> *Ocean*
> *Black earth*
> *The river of blood*
> *Finds its way into the dark earth*
> *Creates dark traces dries up disappears*
> *Into the soil for insects to feed themselves from*
> *The red river*
> *Nourishment for the invisible creatures*

I called it The blood poem because of the physical and vocal shifts I experienced with the image of blood as life-giving and life-threatening source; it reminded me of Jung's archetype of rebirth (Jung, 2014). When I first wrote The blood poem in 2007, it was automatic and associative writing with no conscious reflective intention. Still, it came up as an aesthetic-poetic response to my first encounter with the Fitzmaurice tremorwork. Even though its revision in my 2018 process could be described as logic or cognitive, it was guided by intuitive intention and embodied necessity. As a result, it helped me towards my practical objectives. The feeling of entering a warm and embracing landscape through the image of the *red river of blood* enabled me to immerse myself consciously with enhanced somatic awareness in the process of softening muscular rigidity. I then explored the poem vocally while switching from destructuring/tremorwork to its counterpart restructuring. While destructuring, I spontaneously improvised with the sounds trying to overlook the semantic meaning of the words and put focus directly on the somatic experience of breathing, sounding and voicing from within my body. The restructuring part of my explorations emphasized intentional breathing paying attention to the personal meaning of the metaphors and their associations.

My main surprise while exploring The blood poem was that it felt as if I had just written it, or even that I re-wrote it again and again while destructuring and restructuring. How could this re-writing interact with and inform my perception of FV as a transformative practice? It seemed to me that the intuitive and confusing premonition underlying the 2007 practice had found its own direction and purpose that I was now ready to fully understand. Through the video The river of blood (2:15), you could have a visual and audio experience of the poem. The visual background is how Mansilla digitally transformed my imagery while simultaneously embedding extracts of my practice. By following the cursor, you could also observe how she enabled me to interact with the digital interface during the performance (I will return to this later in this chapter). On the right of the screen, there is a bit of the poem, partially restructured. Water sounds and a melodic dream-like music mingle with my recorded voice. Inspired by the emerged associations, my voice is heard in the background singing Narrow daylight (2004) by Elvis Costello and Diana Krall. At the same time, you could hear and see the lines of the poem in red letters at the bottom of the screen. My voice does not have one sole quality; it explores the words, it repeats, it overlaps with my singing and interacts with the digital interface. Many things are happening simultaneously in a chaotic yet connected structure that intends to disseminate the transformative and intuitive nature of the research project.

The significance of the digital narrative

It was interesting for me to notice that, during the creative research process, Mansilla's work became something beyond a digital translation of my imagery, supporting the emergence of new findings. Focusing on such transformative potentialities, I made three main observations: that change comes from a non-linear process, that transformation requires self-exposure and that self-exposure eventually brings a sense of ongoing vocal homecoming.

Through the devising process and the study of the emergent metaphors while developing the digital narrative, my understanding of the transformative potentiality of FV shifted from a linear process in a chronological order (from 2007 to 2018), to a more dynamic, circular and organic phenomenon. When exploring the tension between two main metaphors, the red fluid blood and blue frozen water, based on the dialogue between the embodied FV practice and the digital translations or transformations of the metaphors into audio-visual material, I found that the offered access to my imagination enabled me to connect to my somatic and vocal transformation in a new way. This new way of connecting somatically to my voice seemed to be independent of linear time encouraging a state of timeless-ness and intuitive freedom of expression from within. I became aware of the intuitive intention of my body to reorganize itself topographically, recognizing its capability to do so through an experiential state of time *as* space.

The second theme that came up was my willing for self-exposure. I wanted to convey my FV-induced transformative process of daring to be exposed, unpacking the fragmented and disjointed process of delving into chaos, and to explore the emerging metaphors through body, voice and visualization (in both the present experience and the digital format). As the theme of exposure came up in the creative process, I recalled another pivotal moment in my vocal learning, namely working with the song It's good to see you (2002) by Allan Taylor during the FV Teacher Certification Program in 2014.

When I sang the song to my co-students, I felt overwhelmed by a vivid connection to the image of a "constant thread that's never broken". I revisited the song within this PAR project through the destructuring and restructuring process, responding to the intuitive emergence of the memory from my training. My focus was an experiment with the relation between the *you* and the *I* in the song, of the singer imagining that I was both the *I* and the *you*, subject-object in one. I suddenly understood an aspect of the aim to dissolve binaries in artistic research as proposed by Robin Nelson (2013, 21). I also got a new experiential understanding of the somatic aspect of FV in terms of overcoming the body-mind binary (Fitzmaurice, 2015, 68) in line with Thomas Hanna's notion of soma as a self-regulating *and* self-sensing unity (1988, 32).

The creative process brought up a deep sense of vocal homecoming, not only in relation to my past experiences but also in a spiritual way that transgressed my phenomenological body. I realized that for me the transformative impact of FV had overcome the binaries of being *at home* and *away* in a very concrete way. From the first encounter with FV in 2007, I had felt at home with the practice although my body obviously resisted to "let go" of learned, unhelpful habits of "holding back". In this sense, FV had represented something very strange and unfamiliar, yet at the same time a welcoming place of comfort, curiosity and pleasure. Throughout the devising process of my performance research, it became clear to me how my intuitive knowing had guided me into trusting myself in terms of *leaning into the unknown* and giving up previous habits little by little. One could say that I had immersed myself somatically and vocally in the *creative chaos of the forest of Arden* and by this I discovered new layers of experiential realities within. As a result, I understood that *coming home to one's vocal and embodied self* is not an end result but rather *a continuous state of being and becoming*. Therefore, for the performance, my intention became to convey this layered, non-hierarchical experience of chaos and order, mess and structure, unconscious and conscious, integrating the digital elements of metaphorical narratives with my embodied vocal expression.

The digital narrative in the performance happened through my interaction with a screen and was based on Mansilla's perceptions of my praxical explorations, including a choice of collected images, diaries and writings of different kinds. The digital aspect of the performance had a proactive function in terms of rendering the actual visualization of my intuitive imagery and transformative process into visual material for the audience. As intended, the digital narrative became an important anchor for me while performing, along with the prepared script of spoken text, movement and singing. In the following section, I outline the performance with a focus on the interrelation between my presence and the digital narrative. In order to get a sense of this simultaneous interaction in the performance, you could watch the video In front of me (1:57) before moving on to the narrative in italics below.

In front of me: the performance

My breathing body is shown on a big screen facing a set of window frames. The recorded sound of my breathing body is mixed with the sound of my present breathing, facing myself on the screen with my back turned to the audience. I turn around and narrate a dream from one of my diaries. It is about a girl in the streets at night. She discovers that her body is made of rubber, like a doll. The dream ends when the girl is threatened by a group of violent men. After that, my body appears on the screen tremoring with unstructured and breathy sounds, multiplying itself and sounding together with itself into a crescendo, before disappearing. I also watch this rather surreal sequence as a witness with the audience, before I turn to them to share a poem by Tami Spry (2011, 15–16) on autoethnography:

> *Autoethnography is body and verse.*
> *It is self and other and one and many.*
> *It is ensemble, acapella, and accompaniment.*
> *Autoethnography is place and space, and time.*
> *It is personal, political, and palpable.*
>
> *It is art and craft. It is jazz and blues.*
> *It is messy, bloody, and unruly.*
> *It is agency, rendition, and dialogue.*
> *It is danger, trouble, and pain.*
>
> *It is critical, reflexive, performative, and often forgiving.*
> *It is the string theories of pain and privilege*
> *   Forever woven into fabrics of power/lessness.*
>
> *It is skin/flints of melanin and bodies*
> *   in gendered hues of sanctuary and violence.*
> *It is a subaltern narrative revealing the understory of*
> *   hegemonic systems*
> *It is sceptical and restorative.*

It is an interpreted body of evidence.
It is personally accountable.

It is wholly none of these, but fragments of each.
It is a performance of possibilities.

Spry's poetic-theoretical text is intended to give the audience a suggestive way of locating the performance in the performative research paradigm. Then a collage of personal photos, postcards, writings and notes appears on the screen. The collage is randomly put together and appears in different combinations. The window frames reappear with a big hand reaching out towards them while snow is falling. After this, only white snow is falling lightly on the screen. I interrupt this poetic atmosphere with a short presentation of the creative process of the PAR project to convey the step-by-step research to the audience (similarly to what I do in this chapter). While I am doing this, a part of myself regrets the choice as it feels like I need to legitimize the artistic research with theoretical conceptualization. On the other hand, I feel that the audience listens and seems interested in the research narrative too. Then I return to the poetic mode and choose deliberately to intensify my emotional presence as performer. I quote lines from The blood poem while some of these also come up on the screen in writing:

Thoughts in images
River of blood
                        Frozen grief
                                    Frozen water
Skin fragile skin
The green knife cuts
                          Ball bursts and becomes the river of blood
    Flows into the open landscape

The words are shown on a black frame with moving red drops (similar to those in the River of blood video). *Mansilla's interface technique gives me the possibility to change the image in real time when I move the cursor on the screen. The red drops transform into flowing red rivers as if the drops burst open and emerging red rivers meander on to the black frame. Then the frame changes and now the imagery of glass and frozen water appears with sounds like cracking or thawing. In the background, my recorded voice is singing Narrow daylight. The frozen water is now melting and flows with a dripping sound like melting icicles. My voice in this sequence alters between Jacques' monologue "all the world's a stage" from As You Like It (Act II, Scene VII) and a dialogue between Catherine Fitzmaurice, other FV teachers and myself, composed from my diaries. I reflect upon my frustration, resistance and difficulties in letting go of learned, unhelpful habits for free vocal expression and breathing. While doing this sequence I notice a shift in my own presence through the presence of the audience, including Catherine Fitzmaurice herself among them. The sequence ends in a climax with me shouting at myself in frustration for holding on to rigid patterns and chronic tension.*

Then, I release to free breathing. With that the somatic response of letting go comes up and I can finally surrender to the transformative experience of embodied vocal freedom without resistance. In the final black frame, the red drops are transformed into blue drops visible in and around the window frames. I can interact with the interface as I did before. After the intensity of the previous frame, I move the cursor over the blue drops and the fluid image of rivers is now filling the screen. I look straight at the audience. I aim at taking them into my experience and in a calm voice I say: In front of me – now – are you. I sing It's good to see you. By the second verse: "when a man is down, he stands alone," my voice cracks and I am in tears. Ironic, I'm thinking. The suggested resolution in the prepared digital narrative and the wobbly reality of the moment. Restructuring, I invite the audience to join me in the last chorus.

In front of me: reflections

By the end of the performance, I felt that I had been able to communicate the multilayered complexity of my FV-induced transformative process of *coming home* and *being at home* with my own vocal presence. The performance itself also had a transformative impact on me. The theme of daring exposure that emerged during the devising process was present as well throughout the performance and became even more prominent during its final part. I exposed myself in a way I had not planned and allowed an integration of all the phases and findings in the research process. It was as if I found a way to embody the tension of my transformative journey with FV from opacity (red thick blood) to transparency (blue clear water).

I performed In front of me for around sixty people at *The Fifth International Freedom and Focus Fitzmaurice Voicework Conference – Listening Beyond Borders* at the Rose Bruford College in London (July 23, 2018). The performance marked a significant step in the research process because it tested the effective communication of my transformative learning with FV – with its struggles, resistances, emotional triggers and vulnerabilities – towards broader understandings on vocal transformation. In line with PAR and "its embodied, affective, and interactive nature," as argued by Barrett and Bolt (in Barton, 2018, 11), the knowledge production between the mediated me, my presence and the audience was available only in the moment of performance. The example of my voice cracking in the end reveals how this kind of situated knowledge resides "always in the making, focusing on the process but situated wherever it engages an audience" (Hunter in Barton, 2018, 12). This kind of moments cannot be planned but happen intuitively. In that "chaotic" moment, I *knew* I was *at home* – totally present to my embodied vocal self and the audience.

Concentrating on the audience, the dynamic dialogue between my transformative journey and the digital material in the performance was meant to generate for them a multilayered and multimodal experience. From the feedback I collected, it appeared that the layering of presences during the performance came across and stayed with the audience afterward. It was significant for me that they all acknowledged that my PAR gave them insights not only on my own transformative experience and the impact upon my vocal individuation, but also on their own understanding through affect and somatic resonance during the performance. Some pointed out how the digital material supported the personal narrative by making the invisible visible. There were also references to the creation of productive and wider aesthetic associations with the use of archetypal imagery and metaphors. It became clear to me that the strength of this kind of combined narrative within PAR can create an aesthetic outcome that enables not only the researcher (me) but also the audience to connect to a shared transformative experience through their own subjective associations. One audience member wrote,

> [t]his piece was deeply vulnerable and surrealistic in its presentation. Conventional assumptions of how technology is experienced kind of "went out the window".
> I felt connected in a human way [...] which I was surprised by.
> [...] When the invitation to sing came, it felt natural – as in a dream – and fluid, like the liquid of the blood and the water from the river.
> (Audience Member A, email, July 28, 2018)

This quote, in my understanding, highlights the relational capacity of PAR to reinvent social relations and dismantle disciplinary distinctions that create conditions for the emergence of new analogies, metaphors and models for understanding objects of inquiry (Barton, 2018, 11). It takes me back to my research question and my wish to investigate my intuitive and somatic drive for transformation and vocal individuation spurred by my initial FV experience "of being thrown into the forest of Arden" (Fitzmaurice, 2004, 4). Vocal individuation is therefore discussed here according to the Jungian understanding of an intuitive, self-regulatory and embodied transformative practice (Jung, 1969, 173–184). Based on my praxical investigations, it also becomes apparent that vocal individuation is not an isolated or static process but rather a dynamic state of being and becoming.

My PAR ends up emphasizing the significance of each individual voice, as argued by Catherine Fitzmaurice, through the "desire for community and communication. To voice is personal. It is both physical and intellectual. It is social" (Fitzmaurice, 2015, 68). In earlier writings, I have discussed the connection between FV and the emphasis on the individual voice as analyzed in the ideas of the feminist philosopher Adriana Cavarero (Bruun, 2015). In voice studies, Konstantinos Thomaidis has been working on what he calls the "Cavarerian project" with emphasis on the re-imagination of voice praxis in research and higher education (2015, 10–11). So, in comparison to earlier stages of my research on vocal individuation, this PAR project gave me an opportunity to examine the experiential transformative process from a first-person and relational perspective. As a result, it contributed to my increased somatic capacity and at the same time to a deeper understanding of vocal presence as an innate part of human identity.

The process and reflexive analysis of In front of me has also allowed me to locate my project and findings within a broader theoretical and practical framework of somatically-oriented voice studies. Somatic thus, in my understanding, suggests the integration of body, mind, psyche and vocal individuation. This is significant because, in combination with the performance-research practice discussed here, it offers an appropriate methodological framework for the study of voice-induced transformative processes. *Vocal homecoming* is ultimately the objective and there is always more space for *arriving*. This PAR project and the opportunity to share it in detail through this chapter has been a rewarding journey for me as a scholar and practitioner-researcher. I am left with compelling trust in the impact of this kind of artistic research that bridges disciplines and modalities – trust and somatic awareness stemming from the initial choice of listening to my body and its somatic, intuitive intentions towards vocal individuation. This last audience input indicates the further aspiration of my research:

> I reflect on your piece and I think: Yes, do it again and again and mix and match with the academic side, that is really exciting. To mix it up. To dare to mix it up. To inspire the academic heady world to open up and communicate more with the whole body.
> (Audience Member B, email, July 31, 2018)

References

Anderson, R. (2000) Intuitive inquiry: interpreting objective and subjective data. *ReVision*, 22(4) 31–40. Available from: http://search.ebscohost.com/login.aspx?-direct=true&db=a9h&AN=3182992&site=ehost-live [Accessed 27 August 2019].

Anderson, R. and Braud, W. (1998) *Transpersonal Research Methods for the Social Sciences: Honoring Human Experience*. Thousand Oaks, CA: Sage Publications.

Barton, B. (2018) Introduction I. Wherefore PaR? Discussions on "a line of flight". In: Annette Arlander, Bruce Barton, Melanie Dreyer-Lude and Ben Spatz (eds.) *Performance as Research*. London: Routledge, 1–19.

Bruun, E. F. (2015) Listen carefully. *Dramatherapy*, 37(1) 3–14.

——— (2018) In front of me. In: *The Fifth International Freedom & Focus Fitzmaurice Voicework Conference – Listening beyond Borders*, July 20–24, London: Rose Bruford College for Theatre and Performance.

Costello, E. and Krall, D. (2004) Narrow daylight. *The Girl in the Other Room*. The Verve Music Group, a Division of UMG Recordings, Inc.

Fitzmaurice, C. (2004) *The actor's voice* [interview]. www.actingnow.com. Interviewed by Eugene Douglas. Available from: https://static1.squarespace.com/static/5569e19fe4b02fd687f77b0f/t/5a754963085229a6161ecdb6/1517636311816/Douglas-Fitzmaurice+ActingNow+Interview+2018.pdf [Accessed 3 July 2018].

——— (2015) Breathing matters. *Voice and Speech Review*, 9(1) 61–70.

Gergen, M. M. and Gergen, K. J. (2000) Qualitative inquiry: tensions and transformations. In: Norman K. Denzin and Yvonna S. Lincoln (eds.) *Handbook of Qualitative Research*. London: Sage, 1025–1046.

Hanna, T. (1988) What is somatics? *Journal of Optometry*, 2(2) 31–35.

Holmes, S. (2016) Autoethnography and voicework. *Voice and Speech Review*, 10(2–3) 190–202.

Jones, S. H., Adams, T. E. and Ellis, C. (eds.) (2013) *Handbook of Autoethnography*. Walnut Creek, CA: Left Coast Press Inc.

Jung, C. G. (1969) *The Structure and Dynamics of the Psyche*. Volume 8, 2nd edition. Translated from German by R. F. C. Hull. Edited by Herbert Read, Michael Fordham and Gerhard Adler. London: Routledge and Kegan Paul.

Jung, C. G. (2014) *Four Archetypes*. Oxon: Routledge Classics.

Morgan, M. K. (2012) *Constructing the Holistic Actor: Fitzmaurice Voicework: Actor Voice Training*. Scotts Valley, CA: CreateSpace Independent Publishing Platform.

Morrison, J., Kotzubei, S. and Seiple, T. (2017) Vocal traditions: Fitzmaurice Voicework. *Voice and Speech Review*, 11(3) 339–347.

Nelson, R. (2013) *Practice as Research in the Arts: Principles, Protocols, Pedagogies, Resistances*. Basingstoke: Palgrave Macmillan.

NTNU ARTEC (2019). Available from: https://www.ntnu.edu/artec [Accessed 11 June 2019].

Romanyshyn, R. D. (2010) The wounded researcher: making a place for unconscious dynamics in the research process. *The Humanistic Psychologist*, 38(4) 275–304.

Shakespeare, W. and Furness, H. H. (1603 [1963]) *As You Like It*. New York: Dover Publications.

Spry, T. (2011) *Body, Paper, Stage: Writing and Performing Autoethnography*. London: Routledge.

Taylor, A. (2002) It's good to see you. *Out of Time*. Pudsey, West Yorkshire: T.Records.

The Fitzmaurice Institute. (2018) Available from: https://www.fitzmauriceinstitute.org/ [Accessed 3 July 2018].

Thomaidis, K. (2015) The Re-vocalization of logos? Thinking, doing and disseminating voice. In: Konstantinos Thomaidis and Ben Macpherson (eds.) *Voice Studies: Critical Approaches to Process, Performance and Experience*. London: Routledge, 10–21.

Watson, L. and Sadhana, N. (2014) Fitzmaurice voicework: theory, practice, and related research. *Voice and Speech Review*, 8(2) 149–156.

6 Somatic training and resources for body-mind-voice integration
When stage fright "comes to visit"

Leticia Santafé and Pablo Troccoli

Introduction

Performing for an audience is a much-desired experience that requires thorough preparation. Being in the spotlight, however, can cause distress, discomfort and can severely disrupt artistic potential and limit careers (Studer et al, 2011). This paradox has to be addressed and negotiated as a form of anxiety inherent to public performance. How is it possible for the professional to fully communicate challenging material on stage in front of an audience while feeling safe enough to remain available, playful and savoring a sense of personal satisfaction? And how can one draw on one's inner resources in order to regulate such challenging situations? Focusing particularly on voice performance, this chapter proposes that a stage performer can playfully "survive" moments of performance-induced anxiety by practising somatic awareness. This study is a practice-led research on body-mind-voice integration epistemologically contextualized within the field of somatic practice, where embodied first-person experience is the principal source for knowledge formation (Fernandes, 2015; Parviainen and Aromaa, 2015).

As a starting point, we wish to acknowledge that the stressful effects of public performance elicit complex physiological and cognitive responses in individuals, which manifest in different ways and degrees of severity (Steptoe et al, 1995; Goodman and Kaufman, 2014). Furthermore, the modality of this stress response varies across different stage-related professions, cross-cultural differences and performance contexts (Seo et al, 2016). Due to these complexities, the specialized literature tends not to use the term "stage fright" uniformly and connects it with a variety of anxiety manifestations (McNeil, 2010). Across this chapter, we will use the terms performance anxiety and stage fright to refer to different phases of the stress response in individuals. Performance anxiety will apply to the study of pre- and post-performance stress responses and stage fright to the actual performance experience.

Our observations are shaped by a series of workshops we have set up as a laboratory on somatic co-regulation of performance anxiety and stage-fright manifestations.[1] At this stage of research, the evidence we have gathered suggests that performance anxiety and crucially the stage-fright experience imply a temporary loss of body-mind-voice integration, which is directly connected to self-regulation of the autonomic nervous system (ANS).

In this brief chapter, we will outline just two elements from the wider somatic methodology we apply to address stage-fright disintegration during our workshops. The first element refers to body-mind-voice development, which is studied in movement through the sequence of Basic Neurocellular Patterns (BNP) proposed by Bonnie Bainbridge Cohen (2018). The second element draws on psycho-physical exercises of the Linklater methodology (2006), from which we focus on the use of imagery, the sense of vibrational touch and the support that bodily fluids provide to vocal expression. These materials are grounded and further developed by our experience in stage performance and work as somatic practitioners, which has given us an embodied understanding of the impact that performance anxiety and stage fright can have on the performer.

The set of movement explorations we briefly introduce here aims to recognize the physiological, cognitive and emotional complexities of our responses to performance-related anxiety. The practice progresses towards facilitating a first-person experience of body-mind-voice integration during performance. Modern findings in neurophysiology (Porges, 2017; Porges and Dana, 2018) provide theoretical support to our discussion regarding the ontogenetic relevance of the ANS to our first perceptions of security and fear and our mature responses to stress (Caldwell, 2014).

From performance anxiety and stage fright to co-regulating body-mind-voice integration

A study on the impact of stage fright among student actors (Steptoe et al, 1995) has found that manifestations of pre-performance anxiety can induce different coping strategies. The desired state of calmness backstage is sought through various means such as meditative practices, breathing exercises, drinking alcohol or the use of sedatives. On the other extreme of this coping spectrum, as another study suggests (Studer et al, 2011), some performers feel the need to match the challenge of being on stage by seeking to elevate their physiological tone through engagement in strong physical activity. The same study draws attention to an increase in substance-based coping strategies among young artists in the beginning of their careers, involving the use of illicit drugs and medication.

Sociologist Susie Scott, working with a small yet heterogeneous and multicultural group of performing artists, suggests that the stage-fright experience "involves a sense of vulnerability to exposure" (2017, 722). She analyzes stage fright before performance, during performance and after performance. Expanding upon Scott's research, we wish to propose that performance anxiety operates within each individual as an undercurrent of adaptive responses to stress that are already sensed and experienced during rehearsals. We suggest that this underlying state reaches its expected peak on stage, especially during a premiere, and then transitions and continues to transform backstage after the public performance. Eventually in some cases, the severity of stage fright is linked to anxiety attacks that "freeze" the performer and even lead to show cancellations (Hines, 2018).

As the demands and complexity of public performance continue to evolve through time, it seems that whatever the circumstances involved in triggering a performer's physiological response to stress, this response is dominated by inner anxiety and fear. It also appears that even the most rigorous training methods and the strategies learned across life-long performing careers might not offer an antidote to it (Goodman and Kaufman, 2014). An alternative perspective on regulating stage-induced stress is suggested by the Alexander Technique® (AT) practitioners Michael Frederick and Elaine Williams (2017). Their application of AT principles to stage-fright regulation emphasizes the importance of creating a space for self-reflection and slowing down that enables the performer to witness the body-mind-voice build-up of a stage-fright response. Voice teacher Michael McCallion has described the physiological response to stage fright as "a phenomenon produced by a *disturbance* of our use" (1998, 33, added emphasis). Considering the above along with the spectrum of the phenomenon (Steptoe et al, 1995; Studer et al, 2011; Goodman and Kaufman, 2014), we argue that this *disturbance* can be identified as body-mind-voice disintegration.

We propose that performance anxiety and stage fright emanate from a healthy physiological response to stress and have to be accepted as factors at play in one's integrated body-mind-voice creative experience in front of an audience. The proposed methodology and practice do not intend to make performance anxiety or stage fright disappear nor are they aimed at redressing anxiety-related symptoms. Instead, practising somatic awareness will modulate our physiological response when public performance-related anxiety comes to "visit" us. An actual experience of co-regulation in training can set new templates for our stress responses and offer us the potential for playfulness, relationship and integrated vocal expression during stage performance. We start by outlining theory that informs our body-mind-voice integration training for drama students, while the chosen elements of our discourse are necessarily adapted to the brevity of this chapter.

A brief anatomy of the stage-fright experience: the ontological roots of our responses to fear

Vibration: the birth of voice

Somatic experiential research developed by the founder of Body-Mind Centering® (BMC), Bonnie Bainbridge Cohen, proposes that the BNP that underlies the entire human developmental sequence is *vibration* (2012, 5).

Cohen suggests that the presence of vibration can be sensed by inward attention as a subtle movement beneath stillness or as a sound that underlies all visceral and cardio-circulatory murmurs. The vibrational pattern can often be experienced as a non-verbal poly-sensory blend of information which involves imagery. According to BMC, at every stage of human development, vibration ebbs and flows through every tissue, organ and function of the living body (Bainbridge Cohen, 2018, 7). Therefore, the vocal expression of every individual carries imbedded in it the signature of its underlying vibrational support.

Our voice methodology proposes an encounter in the present with the vibrational ground of our vocal expression through somatic awareness and practice. This learning journey will lead us to become acquainted with "the source of our voice in earth" (Santafé, 2014) to develop trust and inner security.

Fluids: the ground substance of communication

In the womb, the amniotic fluid acts as the first and principal medium of communication between the organisms of mother and child. Our first experiences of fear and bonding take place in utero where the fetus is *in-formed* by being bathed in movement, touch, vibration and emotional information (Grof and Bennett, 1992). This fluid-neural communion is mirrored in the central nervous system (CNS) with its own specialized fluid medium, the cerebrospinal fluid (Martini et al, 2018, 481–483). A keystone in the progression of exercises proposed by Linklater's methodology and included in our somatic approach is called "the touch of sound" (Linklater, 2006, 29–84). Linklater offers step-by-step guidance to link psycho-physical imagery with the feeling of an organic impulse towards vocal communication. The practice asks the student to direct attention to the feeling of vibrations in the body, an approach that we use in our methodology to support the awareness of body fluids as ground substance and medium of vocal and emotional communication.

Emotion: fluid flesh in movement

Performance anxiety and stage fright, at any degrees, are complex emotional events. They begin within us as chemical information transported by fluids and thus are brought to the attention of the CNS (Fredrikson and Gunnarsson, 1992). An instant later, emotion manifests as a way of knowing coupled with a specific physical sensation, sometimes located in a certain area of the body (Nummenmaa et al, 2013). Human viscera, bodily fluids and tissues, underpinned by vibration, are the locus and "theatre" of human emotional life and communication. This is the "inner playground" of the stage performer, from which vocal communication and embodied emotion emerge (Bainbridge Cohen, 2012, 38). Often, the performer on stage can find difficulty in keeping in touch with her emotional life and remaining available for vocal communication. Linklater offers guidance on this integration saying that "the performer has to be the captain of her emotional ship, so she can feel that her vulnerability is her strength" (2019).

Performance anxiety and stage fright: primitive reflexes in action

Five weeks after conception, primitive reflexes begin to activate in utero, allowing a limited set of movement patterns the fetus can use to defend against a perceived threat or to bond for safety and comfort (Santafé, 2014). In parallel to the activity of these motor responses in utero, heart-rate variations of the fetus have been recorded (Kisilevsky et al, 2003). Echoing the research of the American psychiatrist Bruce Perry (2004), we believe that the circumstances through which this defense/relationship reflexive polarity reaches maturity are patterned in the lived experience of the infant and become the experiential foundation for further neurophysiological development which will be expressed as behavior thereafter.

In adult life, mature primitive reflexes mediate our responses to stress and their corresponding motor responses (Porges, 1995). The experiential evidence we are collecting in our workshops confirms that variations in the heart rate are often involved in performance anxiety and stage-fright events. In line with our observations, if stage fright takes for the performer the dimension of an existential threat, an autonomic reflexive response is enacted which is rooted in personal life circumstances (Perry, 2004).

Surviving stage fright in comfort: the gut feelings on stage and the wandering (Vagus) nerves

The ANS with its three distinctive neural networks – the enteric, sympathetic and parasympathetic – leads early neural development in utero and foregrounds the survival of the organism at every developmental stage (Damasio, 2012, 307–314). The Vagus nerves, part of the ANS, are of relevance to the anatomy of performance anxiety and stage fright. Porges describes them as "a family of neural pathways" (1995, 8). Vagal enervations reach to all the anatomical structures involved in phonation, cardiopulmonary regulation, liver, kidneys and the gastrointestinal duct (Martini et al, 2018, 764). All of these organs and functions are commonly involved in experiential testimonies of stage fright (Fredrikson and Gunnarsson, 1992; Steptoe et al, 1995), including the observations of the participants in the workshops presented below. When stage fright overwhelms a stage performer, to ensure survival, the ANS rapidly changes the physiological tone by removing vagal control to the heart rate; metaphorically speaking, the vagal brake is switched off (Porges, 2017, 127–168). Then, as cardiopulmonary function intensifies, vocal communication is shut down or compromised and fight or flight becomes the only available behavioral options. In extreme cases, the performer is engulfed by an "autonomic storm" (Caldwell, 2014, 141) when the body-mind-voice, involuntarily and in self-defense, engages in a freeze response and the performer can even faint.

Our somatic methodology sets the experiential basis for surviving stage fright by keeping the vagal brake on, which translates in leaving behind defensive behavior and achieving self-regulation on stage through relationship, eye contact and vocal communication.

The inherent plasticity of physiological tone

Medical terminology defines physiological tone as a precise level of activity that underpins and precedes any movement or organic function (Martini, 2006, 305–306). In our somatic approach to performance-related anxiety, we make use of the inherent plasticity of physiological tone to attain self-regulation through modulation of autonomic responses to stress. During the practice, students are led to observe their internal experiences and to identify the tonal quality which can support the perception of a challenging performative environment as "safe enough". The objective is for them to remain playful, efficient and open to vocal and emotional expressions.

Practising body-mind-voice integration on performance anxiety and stage fright

> [...] we experience our world as it is and ourselves as we are. It is not practical but it has a different virtue: it is true.
>
> (Hanna, 1970, 203)

Our somatic methodology intends to support two aspects of perception: what an experience means for a single individual, identified as subjective experience and how the other perceives that person's experience, identified as intersubjective experience. Both perspectives are indispensable in the research process of somatic body-mind-voice integration, something that tends to become evident to the participants when the training requires them to work in dyads. The following examples of exercises are taken from a series of workshops that involved independent drama students in research on somatic awareness and performance anxiety. Every participant was required to prepare in advance a short monologue, something we used for the opening of our workshops as discussed below. In the studio, a keyboard was used as didactical aid.

Day 1: an exercise on observation

Participants were told that after an individual warm-up, they had to perform their monologues one by one to the rest of the group as an audience.

In resonance with Scott's study discussed earlier in this chapter, attendants were given the task to observe themselves on body-mind-voice and emotion while transitioning through their pre-performance, performance and post-performance moments. The exercise was designed to cultivate in the trainees conscious awareness of autonomic behavior. Each participant was encouraged to unravel the "anatomy" of their individual "survival" strategies and was each invited to feel how their jaws, tongues, dried lips, sweaty hands, posture and cardio-respiratory pattern became involved in the composition of their autonomic responses to stress (Linklater, 2006).

After the monologues, the trainees were invited to notice whether they had experienced any form of pre-performance anxiety and to describe in detail their body-mind condition during the event. All participants noticed some form of anxiety and below are some of the descriptions of the sympathetic arousal experienced by individuals before performing their monologues:

> As my turn to perform approaches, my heart is racing, my hands and feet get very sweaty.
> I lose confidence about remembering the text, starting to say it to myself to remember it.
> If I breathe I calm down. My heart goes much faster than in normal life.
> I start laughing hysterically and try to calm down.
> I am scared about forgetting my text, my stomach, chest and throat are very tense.
> I feel a sudden burst of energy in my body, tension in my eyes and jaw.
> My heart pumps so hard that I feel it in my head, my mouth is dry.

With all this accumulated pre-performance energy, one might expect a vivid outcome, full of textures and colors. Instead, when the trainees in the audience were asked what they witnessed, they made the following overall observations: *quiet and monotonous sound, rigid and disengaged voices, physical tension, impairment of the voice*. When participants were asked what was impeding them from thriving on stage, they often used the word *fear*. One participant described her experience as something that took her away from what she wanted to do. When questioned as to how they managed their individual responses to anxiety in order to perform their texts, participants said they tried to calm down by either trying to ignore or push through the fear. Others expressed that they felt the urge to constantly anchor their attention to the text, fearing that they were going to forget it on stage.

This observation exercise seemed to suggest that none of the coping strategies the participants came up with were an effective solution to their performance anxieties. They showed difficulties in sustaining body-mind-voice integration and some of them "survived" their performance while immersed in a state of heightened mental activity. The exercise allowed us to propose to the attendants that an accepting and witnessing attitude towards our stress responses before and during a stage performance and acknowledgment of their impact on our body-mind-voice integration is necessary for the development of somatic awareness and self-regulation of our performance-related anxiety.

Day 4: a practice on the Vagus nerves in vocal performance

To offer you an orientation towards this practice, in this part we shift the narrative to invite you, the reader, to explore an exercise the workshop participants went through on the fourth day of the process. It is a partner exercise in two parts, developed upon supportive, nonjudgmental witnessing. The written description of the practice is adapted to the brevity of this chapter.

Part 1: Co-regulation, an organic home for my voice

1   Lie on the floor, take your time to shift your present attention to your physical sensations, emotions and mental processes. Enjoy transitioning towards lying on the surface of the earth and invite the judge or critic within you to step aside for a moment, to just witness the ongoing process.
2   Curl yourself on one side, into a semi-fetal position, take care that cervical vertebrae rest in a relaxed curvature towards the sternum. Move your attention to your relationship with gravity. Yield to the support the earth provides you through the floor, maintain an active interaction with it and allow yourself to be nurtured. Notice how this unconditional support allows your breath to perfectly respond to your physiological needs, without you *having to do* anything with it. Consider your breath as your *voice in silence.*
3   Your partner sits down next to you while you are in this position. She uses one hand to make contact with the front part of your body. The intention is to support the movement of your attention towards the softness of the organic content. It is very important for you both to negotiate between you the quality of this contact in order to offer support in the way it is needed.
4   Take your time to direct your awareness into the soft, fluid content of the front part of the body. Notice how sensation is followed by feeling and how the breathing pattern changes. Allow the possibility of expressing what you feel with the sound of your voice in a very basic non-articulated way. Yawn and sigh with relief as you please, feeling the way in which the expressive nature of your organic content(s) finds an unobstructed fluid connection with your voice.
5   Pause for a moment to share with your partner. Make eye contact and describe what you have noticed in the front part of your body. Let your experience shape your verbal description, allow yourself to be the witness of your subjective experience without analyzing or judging it.
6   Go back to the same semi-fetal position and start exploring with the thumb and index finger the inside and outside of the mouth at the same time. Travel with your sense of touch in your fingers through the landscape of the mouth, feeling and seeing the proprioceptive scene of the

mouth. Take pauses and notice the feelings and sensations arising from the tactile exploration. Express (to motor out) with your voice whatever is there, in a non-articulating manner. Be aware of the mouth first, then of the whole face and the rest of the digestive tract (organ content) all the way to the anus.

7   Move if you need to with the front soft part of your body and allow the vocal expression that emerges to be part of your research. Remember that breathing what you are sensing and feeling gives you the possibility to express it through your voice. Allow yourself to notice that the sounds and feelings arising through your voice come from the soft fluid organ content of your body. Consider the possibility that the community of organs inside of you that helps you stay alive have space and time to sound their stories. Let those sounds/stories travel through the fluids of your body and to color your vocal expression.

8   Pause and take a moment to taste in fine detail the type of organic tone you are experiencing. Decide if you want to increase or lower this tone and tell your partner your preference. Sound, guiding your voice towards yourself, into the soft, fluid tissue inside your body, as if you were bathing your organs. Give them what they need right now, while the supporting partner invites you to open the range of your voice using a keyboard, playing different semitones around the sound quality you are exploring. Pause and sense the underlying vibrational quality within you, right now. Witness your vibrational being. Be nurtured by it.

9   Align your organic (visceral) desire for vocal communication with any loose fragment, passage or word of the text (for the workshop participants, this was an invitation to revisit the monologue they performed on Day 1). Do not analyze or compose the outcome, let your body-mind motor out your voice.

After this practice, the workshop participants were asked to share something about their experiences. Reflections included the following:

> The emotions have a flow in my body; I feel my voice is mine and real.
> I enjoy being at home with my body and voice; I feel pleasure,
>   playfulness and connection.
> Vibration is present in me.
> It took me to a place of really wanting to communicate with my voice.
> I am honestly feeling and expressing what I own.
> I can feel my words having weight and time to be spoken.

Part 2: Playing between physiological flexion and extension, sharing my voice

1   Start in the same semi-fetal position. Your partner makes contact with your feet and actively massages them. Imagine or feel a connection between your feet and the mouth and let the sucking reflex be activated.

2   Using your partner's hands for resistance, start pushing through your feet to uncurl yourself to reach full extension. Stay on the same side and try not to arch backward. During this unfolding journey, imagine/follow your voice traveling in a fluid way from the ventral part to the dorsal side of your body. Allow the "sounding food" that you have cooked beforehand in the semi-fetal position to unfold and travel through the dorsal part of the body outward, into space.
3   Remain on that side in full extension and open the senses to the space around you. Pause, sense your breath. For a moment, be curious about your relationship and connection with your partner through space.
4   Research through flexion and extension the journey of your voice from the inside-emotional content to the outside-communicative space. Start slowly and play with different paces. Let your partner support you once again using a keyboard. She could suggest semitones and you could develop a dialogue with them as you move. Turn to the other side and follow the progression described in Parts 1 and 2. Notice your body's asymmetrical distribution of organic volumes and weights. Sense and experience what might be different on this side.

Once we switched roles and the practice was complete during the workshop, we gave time to the participants to integrate their experience through a verbal reflection with their partners. A gradual transition to standing up followed, orienting and opening the senses into the entire working space. Then, the participants were asked to re-perform their Day 1 monologues. Once again, the trainees performed one by one, while the rest of the group was their audience. We were curious to witness the impact the practice may have had on their body-mind-voice integration. After their performances, the participants were asked to report their experiences. Individual accounts included:

> When I stand up and move, I feel completely different. I feel soft, free, full of sensation in my body.
> Playing with the text I am very present with the different emotions traveling through it. I have a strong sense of direction, depth and truth.
> I am very imaginative and emotions came to the text with great ease; lots of satisfaction.
> When I stand up in front of the audience I feel ready to speak the words.
> My voice sounds organic, easy and feels honest, it gives truth to my words and I can feel it; my desire of exploring and playing with the spoken text is there with me.
> When I approach the text I feel freedom of voice and imagination circulating my body.

Ending the workshop, we asked the trainees to reflect upon their body-mind-voice experience during the last monologue performance. Accounts of individual experiences included:

> I notice I feel freedom to follow my impulse.
> I sense pleasure in my body while speaking.
> I now feel secure to speak out.

Closing thoughts

This ongoing body-mind-voice integration research is rooted in our own experience of performance anxiety-related contexts and its unpredictable triggers. We designed this workshop series as laboratories for somatic research to investigate if a somatic methodology could facilitate self-regulation of stress responses during performance. The workshops have focused on experiential study and practice in dyads tending towards self-regulation of the ANS and body-mind-voice integration. What has become evident is that somatic awareness requires a gradual familiarity with the individual modalities of physical, emotional and cognitive performance-related anxiety responses. Furthermore, it seems that this familiarity can strengthen our capacity for self-regulation of our stress responses.

On the path to experience self-regulation, our research suggests that encountering our unique vibrational quality provides a foundation to experience and relates to our "earth voice". This recognition, rooted in the unconditional support we receive from the earth, brings along the freedom that our breath possesses. By exploring the raw contents of our organic voice and by engaging in physiological flexion and extension, we have observed that the voice moves through a fluid medium of emotion towards a space of shared communication. Our workshop series has *provided* the trainees the opportunity to become familiar with a "safe enough" co-regulated physiological tone. This awareness can become an essential embodied quality for the contemporary performer in order to "survive" body-mind-voice challenges within a sense of playful security.

Dedication

In memory of Kristin Linklater (1936–2020).

Note

1 "The unpredictable life of words on stage" workshops first took place in Madrid in 2018 (September 17–21) and the research was revisited in 2019 (September 16–19). This chapter draws from both of these contexts.

References

Bainbridge Cohen, B. (2012) *Sensing, Feeling and Action: The Experiential Anatomy of Body-Mind Centering.* 3rd edition. Northampton: Contact Editions.

——— (2018) *Basic Neurocellular Patterns: Exploring Developmental Movement.* Torrance, CA: Burchfield Rose Publishers.

Caldwell, P. (2014) *The Anger Box: Sensory Turmoil and Pain in Autism.* Shoreham-by-Sea: Pavilion Publishing and Media.

Damasio, A. (2012) *Self Comes to Mind: Constructing the Conscious Brain.* London: Vintage Books.

Fernandes, C. (2015) When Whole(ness) is more than the Sum of the Parts: somatics as contemporary epistemological field. *Brazilian Journal on Presence Studies,* 5 9–38.

Frederick, M. and Williams, E. (2017) Alexander Technique interventions for stage fright. In: Kathy Madden and Kathleen Juhl (eds.) *Galvanizing Performance. The Alexander Technique as a Catalyst for Excellence.* London: Kingsley Publishers, 179–201.

Fredrikson, M. and Gunnarsson, R. (1992) Psychobiology of stage fright: the effect of public performance on neuroendocrine, cardiovascular and subjective reactions. *Biological Psychology,* 33(1) 51–61.

Goodman, G. and Kaufman, J. C. (2014) Gremlins in my head: predicting stage fright in elite actors. *Empirical Studies of the Arts,* 32, 133–48.

Grof, S. and Bennett, H. Z. (1992) *The Holotropic Mind: The Three Levels of Human Consciousness and How They Shape Our Lives.* San Francisco, CA: Harper Collins.

Hanna, T. (1970) *Bodies in Revolt: A Primer in Somatic Thinking.* San Francisco, CA: Holt, Reinhart and Winston.

Hines, R. (2018) *Frozen actress cancels Broadway performance due to massive anxiety attack.* Available from: https://www.today.com/health/frozen-actress-cancels-broadway-performance-due-massive-anxiety-attack-t127339 [Accessed 26 March 2018].

Kisilevsky, B. S., Hains, S. M. J., Lee, K., Xie, X., Huang. H., Ye, H. H., Zhang, K. and Wang, Z. (2003) Effects of experience on fetal voice recognition. *Psychological Science,* 14(3) 220–224.

Linklater, K. (2006) *Freeing the Natural Voice: Imagery and Art in the Practice of Voice and Language.* London: Nick Hern Books.

——— (2019) Private conversation with Leticia Santafé, Valladolid, September 29.

Martini, F. H. (2006) *Fundamentals of Anatomy and Physiology.* 7th edition. San Francisco, CA: Benjamin Cummings.

Martini, F. H., Nath, J. L. and Bartholomew, E. F. (2018) *Fundamentals of Anatomy and Physiology, Global Edition.* 11th edition. London: Pearson.

McCallion, M. (1998) *The Voice Book: For Everyone Who Wants to Make the Most of Their Voice.* Revised edition. New York: Routledge.

McNeil, D. W. (2010) Evolution of terminology and constructs in social anxiety and its disorders. In Stefan G. Hofmann and Patricia Marten DiBartolo (eds.) *Social Anxiety: Clinical, Developmental and Social Perspectives.* San Diego, CA: Elsevier Academic Press, 3–21.

Nummenmaa, L., Glerean, E., Hari, R. and Hietanen, J. (2013) Bodily maps of emotion. *Proceedings of the National Academy of Sciences of the United States of America (PNAS)*, 11(2) 646–651.

Parviainen, J. and Aromaa, J. (2015) Bodily knowledge beyond motor skills and physical fitness: a phenomenological description of knowledge formation in physical training. *Sport, Education and Society*. Available from: http://dx.doi.org/10.10 80/13573322.2015.1054273 [Accessed 26 March 2018].

Perry, B. D. (2004) Violence in childhood. In: *Understanding Traumatized and Maltreated Children: The Core Concepts* [DVD]. Houston, TX: The Child Trauma Academy.

Porges, S. W. (1995) Orienting in a defensive world: mammalian modifications of our evolutionary heritage. A Polyvagal Theory. *Psychophysiology*, 32(4) 301–318.

―――― (2017) *The Pocket Guide to the Polyvagal Theory: The Transformative Power of Feeling Safe*. New York: W. W. Norton and Company.

Porges, S. W. and Dana, D. A. (2018) *Clinical Applications of the Polyvagal Theory: The Emergence of Polyvagal-Informed Therapies*. New York: W. W. Norton and Company.

Santafé, L. (2014) *Infant Development Movement Training (IDME): Ontogenetic Development Module* [class notes]. Tuscany, Italy: School of Body Mind Centering®.

Seo, M., Young-Hoon, K. and Kim-Pong, T. (2016) I am dumber when I look dumb in front of many (vs. few) others: a cross-cultural difference in how audience size affects perceived social reputation and self-judgements. *Journal of Cross-Cultural Psychology*, 47(8) 1019–1032.

Scott, S. (2017) Transitions and transcendence of the self: stage fright and the paradox of shy performativity. *Sociology*, 51(4) 715–731.

Steptoe, A., Malik, F., Pay, C., Pearson, P., Price, C. and Win, Z. (1995) The impact of stage fright on student actors. *British Journal of Psychology*, 86(1) 27–39.

Studer, R., Gomez, P., Hildebrandt, H., Arial, M. and Danuser, B. (2011) Stage fright: its experience as a problem and coping with it. *The International Archives of Occupational and Environmental Health*, 84(7) 761–771.

7 Voicing with awareness
An introduction to the Feldenkrais Method

Stephen Paparo

> Improvement of talented people comes through their awareness of themselves in action. Their talent arises from their freedom to choose their modes of action. New modes of action are available to those who have discovered themselves, or who have had the good luck to meet a teacher who helped them to learn to learn.
>
> (Feldenkrais, 1981, 96)

This chapter posits how the Feldenkrais Method® (FM) can develop technical and expressive skills that result in greater possibilities for self-expression in speaking and singing. It does so by acknowledging Moshe Feldenkrais (1904–1984) as both a practitioner and a theorist. In brief, the FM is a learning process through which participants develop awareness of themselves by observing how they move as they explore various movement sequences. In keeping with the experiential nature of this approach, the chapter offers a self-directed movement and voice exploration developed by the author. Its purpose is to provide an experience of the somatic voice – that is, how the voice emerges as a result of thoughts, feelings, sensations and movements that are embodied physically – and to demonstrate how awareness of oneself is the foundation to learning how to learn. Firsthand experience of the FM will give context to the subsequent discussion of its key principles and strategies in relation to the exploration. The chapter then concludes with suggestions for exploring an embodied approach to singing through practice and research.

The Feldenkrais Method

Dr. Moshe Feldenkrais (1904–1984) developed his method over several decades beginning in the 1930s in an effort to regain his mobility after a knee injury left him unable to walk. He theorized that the introduction of new sensorimotor experiences would lead to greater functional awareness of how he moved. Drawing on his expertise as a physicist, mechanical engineer and judo expert, he experimented with his own movement patterns and eventually taught himself how to walk again. He first published his experiential theories about the relationship between human movement and the nervous system in *Body and Mature Behavior* (1949). In *Awareness Through Movement* (1972), Feldenkrais posited that humans act according to their self-image, which he defined as an integration of thinking, sensing, feeling and moving present in every action. He believed that the mind and body are inseparable and constitute the embodied self. Through his own self-exploration and subsequent work with others, he realized that the use of movement and guided attention were means to clarify habits and learn alternatives that are more efficient. He understood the brain's innate capacity for lifelong development and anticipated what is now known in neuroscience as brain plasticity or neuroplasticity (Doidge, 2015).

Feldenkrais created two practical applications called Awareness Through Movement® (ATM) and Functional Integration® (FI) (Lynn, 2017). Both ATM and FI lessons are designed to explore a specific function, ranging from early developmental movements (such as crawling, rolling and turning) to highly complex and sophisticated skills (such as standing on one's head, and rolling while balancing a book on each hand and foot). In ATM lessons, the Feldenkrais practitioner (or teacher) verbally guides students through a sequence of movements and directs their attention to the sensations while moving. These lessons may be taught individually or in a group setting. When working one-on-one with a student, the practitioner uses gentle touch and tailors the lesson to the individual's needs. Feldenkrais ATM and FI lessons generally are done lying in various positions (on the back, side or front), but also can be done sitting or standing. They are exploratory, are non-competitive and allow students to progress at their own pace. Outcomes following a lesson or series of lessons vary from student to student and may include decreased tension and chronic pain, improved posture, better motor coordination, increased range of motion and an overall positive sense of well-being. Over time, these improvements contribute to an expanded and new repertoire of movements, sensations, feelings and thoughts.

Clarifying the "ah"

This self-directed ATM lesson designed specifically for this chapter based on Feldenkrais principles explores the relationship of the jaw, head and spine while singing. In order to increase your sensitivity while doing the lesson, do the movements slowly with minimal effort and observe the quality of your movement and sound of your voice. Rest briefly as indicated so that your attention is fresh at the start of each new movement sequence. As a result of doing the lesson, you may notice changes that include more erect alignment and skeletal support, fuller and more efficient use of the breath, ease of phonation and distinctions singing with different attitudes. Your observations provide valuable information about your unique self. Ultimately, the goals of this lesson are to convey how somatic focus can create a more resonant

Voicing with awareness 91

and embodied sound and to demonstrate how the FM can be incorporated as a part of practice sessions, voice lessons and choral rehearsals.

1 Sit comfortably towards the front of your chair with both feet on the floor and hands resting in your lap. Notice the contact of your pelvis and buttocks with the chair. Sense the curves of your spine in your lower back, upper back and neck. To begin, recite a short text or sing a simple song using a moderately loud voice. Listen to the sound and feel the vibration of your voice as you speak or sing. Remember what this feels like so you can compare that with the feeling at the end of the lesson.
2 Beginning with your lips together, sustain a hum on a comfortable low pitch for the length of your exhalation and then inhale. Repeat this a few times and notice the movement in your chest, ribs and abdomen as you exhale and inhale. Next, begin to hum and slowly open to create an "ah" sound. Feel how your jaw opens as your lips part. Repeat this a few times, making as little effort as possible to create the "ah". Stop and rest for a moment.
3 Slowly nod your head forward and down towards the floor as if you were nodding "yes" and then return to the starting position. Continue this movement and each time allow more of your spine to round. Tilt your pelvis backward and round your back. Feel how your ribcage widens in the back and gathers in the front. Stop and rest for a moment.
4 Continue the same rounding movement and add the humming as you move. Sustain a comfortable low pitch with your lips together as you round yourself and return to the starting position. Hum for the length of your exhalation and then inhale. Repeat this a few times and notice how it is possible to round yourself as you hum. Then stop and rest.
5 Slowly nod your head back and look up towards the ceiling and then return to the starting position. Continue this movement and each time allow more of your spine to arch. Tilt your pelvis forward and arch your back. Feel how your ribcage widens in the front and gathers in the back. Stop and rest for a moment.
6 Continue the same arching movement and add the "ah" sound as you move. Sustain a comfortable low pitch on an "ah" as you arch yourself and return to the starting position. Feel how your jaw opens as you arch. Sustain for the length of your exhalation and then inhale. Repeat this a few times and notice how it is possible to arch yourself as you sing. Then stop and rest.
7 Combine the rounding and arching movements. Begin rounding your spine and continue through the starting position and then arch your spine. Stay within a comfortable range of movement and feel each part of yourself as you move (e.g. head, ribs, back, pelvis). Then add the humming as you round and open to the "ah" as you arch. Observe the timing of opening and closing of the lips and jaw. As you arch, allow the jaw to open and the "ah" to emerge without any effort. Then as you

round, allow the jaw to close and the hum to emerge. After a few repetitions, stop and rest.

8 Now reverse the coordination. Create the "ah" as you round and hum as you arch. Feel how you must actively open and close your lips and jaw relative to the rounding and arch of the rest of your body. Repeat this a few times and then stop and rest.

9 Return to the original coordination so that you hum as you round and open to the "ah" as you arch. Notice if there are any changes in the quality of your movement or in the sound of your voice. Repeat this a few times and then stop and rest.

10 Explore saying "ah" with different attitudes. Try a *satisfied* "ah" and an *angry* "ah". How does a *curious* "ah" sound and feel different than a *surprised* "ah"? Try some on your own. Notice how you organize yourself to express each attitude that you want to communicate. What differences do you feel from one attitude to another? How does the *satisfied* "ah" feel different than the *angry* "ah," for example?

11 Once again, recite the text or sing the song that you did at the beginning of the lesson. Listen to the sound and feel the vibration of your voice as you speak or sing. How does this compare to the beginning of the lesson? Are you able to express the meaning in a more nuanced way? Notice any difference in the contact of your pelvis and buttocks with the chair. Sense the curves of your spine in your lower back, upper back and neck. How have they changed? Do you have a more detailed awareness of yourself? Does your voice feel more integrated as a part of yourself? What other differences are you aware of as a result of this lesson?

Core Feldenkrais principles

The FM is a means to "learn to learn" because it posits both theoretical principles and practical applications for human improvement. It is grounded in the fact that humans have the capacity for growth, change and improvement throughout our lives because of the plasticity or malleability of our brains based on our experiences. Feldenkrais explained:

> My way of looking at the mind and body involves a subtle method of 'rewiring' the structure of the entire human being to be functionally well integrated, which means being able to do what the individual wants.
> (Feldenkrais, 1981, 26)

The knowledge that it is possible to "rewire" ourselves to improve our ability to do what we want and to function with greater skill and ease can be liberating and inspiring. When applied to singing, the FM provides greater insight into the process of learning how to sing and eradicates the belief that a person is either "born with a voice" or not. This section discusses several pedagogical principles and strategies of the FM in relation to the self-directed ATM lesson and offers suggestions for how these can complement vocal training.

One principle, as stated in the quote at the beginning of the chapter, is that *awareness of oneself in action is key to learning and improving.* Put another way, it is not possible to change our action without conscious knowledge or awareness of what it is that we are doing. The ATM lesson provides numerous opportunities to observe oneself in action. Observing the sensations and feeling in the body as well as listening to the sound and quality of the voice primes one's attention for what to notice to during the lesson and provides points of comparison between the beginning and end of the lesson. Directives, such as "notice the movement in your chest, ribs, and abdomen as you exhale and inhale," help to focus one's attention on specific sensations, feelings and movements. By exploring different thoughts and emotions, it is also possible to observe the automatic, physical response that manifests in the tone of one's voice. When expressing the angry "ah," for example, you may have noticed a general tightening and contracting in the abdomen and chest in order to expel the air with greater force. You may also have felt a forceful downward movement of the jaw and a scrunching of your brow, eyes and nose. These actions contributed to the loudness and sharpness of the sound. When expressing the satisfied "ah," in contrast, you may have felt a general sense of release in the abdomen and chest and a softening of the muscles in your face. These actions likely produced a softer and more soothing sound. Noticing the sound of our voices is another way we can observe our state of being and gain awareness about ourselves.

Another principle is that *freedom of expression comes from the ability to choose from a variety of options.* Though it may seem obvious, the more options one has, the greater one's ability to select the best or most appropriate option in any given situation. In the ATM lesson, you explored different ways to create the "ah". In addition to exploring different emotions, the lesson employed two specific movement-based strategies – the exploration of seemingly random movements and differentiation – in order to elicit more coordinated and efficient action and to expand your repertoire of possibilities. Though the rounding and arching movement may seem extraneous to creating the "ah," the movement is important because it involves the entire spine in supporting the head by balancing the flexors and extensor muscles. It also helps clarify the relationship of the head and the jaw, which is unconsciously held closed by muscles that work against gravity. Creating the "ah" while rounding and humming while arching changes the overall organization of the action and differentiates the jaw from the movement of the head and spine. When the head is less supported by the spine, the muscles of the jaw have to work harder. Conversely, when the head is more supported, the jaw can open and close with less effort. Learning how these parts can move both in tandem and in opposition builds brain maps, creates a variety of options and results in more efficient coordination when speaking and singing.

Yet, another principle is that *new options are possible through self-discovery.* The FM provides a framework for exploring rather than suggesting what learning should take place. Though the lesson in this chapter has possible outcomes, those who do the lesson will have different experiences because each is a unique individual. What is central to the experience is the process that creates conditions for learning. The more adept at the process one is, the more interesting and fruitful their learning can become. To that end, it is important to be curious and embrace mistakes in order to more fully understand what helps or hinders an intended action. Ithaca College Professor of Voice and Feldenkrais Practitioner Carol McAmis uses the phrases "make friends with the mistake" and "do the mistake on purpose" to help reframe the importance of errors and to remove self-judgment, to invite more willingness and openness to learn.[1] In the lesson, the discovery that the spine supports the head in order to release the jaw easily results from expanded awareness of how the spine moves in tandem with the jaw and by intentionally doing the opposite (i.e. doing the mistake). After experiencing the support of the spine and the independence of the jaw, for example, it is then possible to consciously weed out unnecessary effort that inhibits the jaw from opening and closing with ease. A new, more preferable option results from this intentional self-exploration.

These key principles and strategies are the foundation of the FM and support learning that results in the overall improved human function. They differ from physical exercise and rote movement training that emphasize strength, speed and agility. They also differ from traditional voice training that tends to focus on outcomes rather than the learning process. When put into practice in the context of singing study, the FM offers singers the opportunity to improve by gaining awareness of how they sing and to develop their own personalized vocal technique regardless of experience level or musical genre. The FM offers teachers of voice (in choral or studio settings) a vast set of tools with which to empower students to engage in their own learning process and to make discoveries on their own.

Further explorations

Though the research on the uses of the FM is limited, recent studies suggest positive outcomes for singers and teachers (Worth, 2015; Paparo, 2016; 2020; Mingle, 2018). In continuing to expand this line of research, I offer the following suggestions for future exploration. The examination of the implementation of FM in a variety of settings such as voice studios and choral rehearsals would widen our understanding of possible applications and benefits. This could help to determine some universal pedagogical strategies among singers across various contexts. Though the experiential nature of this somatic practice lends itself well to qualitative research paradigms, future research could develop pre- and post-test measures of certain dimensions of singing, such as posture, breathing and range, which might provide useful data to evaluate changes in performance and substantiate self-reported descriptions of singing. Additionally, with its potential to enhance well-being, foster healthy vocal function and develop metacognitive skills, as Grant (2014) suggests, research examining each of these aspects through quantitative and qualitative designs would be warranted. In continuing my own research agenda, I am currently working with a professional learning community of choral music educators to develop pedagogical structures for implementing the FM in choral settings. I also plan to conduct a qualitative investigation among voice teachers who are certified in the FM in hopes of developing a comprehensive model for implementation in voice training.

In closing, the incorporation of the FM as a part of voice training has been an established practice among teachers and students (Darnley, 2015; Neely, 2016). It is becoming more widely recognized and valued in the voice community as evidenced in part by the listing of Feldenkrais experience in voice teachers' biographies in professional organizations, such as the National Association of Teachers of Singing and Voice and Speech Trainers Association. As I have hopefully demonstrated in this chapter, the FM can provide individuals with a theoretical foundation and practical means for developing their potential as singers. It can give voice teachers and choral conductors additional tools to work with students with a variety of needs and to help them to engage in their own learning process. It can also help singers to personalize their learning process to build a vocal technique and become more expressive performers.

For those interested in further exploring the FM, I offer a few possibilities and provide a list of resources at the end of the chapter. To learn more about the FM, I suggest reading books written by Dr. Feldenkrais and secondary interpretations by Feldenkrais practitioners, partaking in ATM lessons via audio and video recordings or online sessions, and finding a practitioner for in-person ATM or FI lessons. For those interested in applications of the FM to voice training specifically, I suggest reading the handful of articles, chapters and books about the potential of the FM as a complementary approach to develop self-awareness and vocal efficiency (Linklater, 1972; Vittucci, 2002; Grant, 2014; LeBorgne and Rosenberg, 2014; Neely, 2016). In addition, the vocal pedagogy literature posits rationales as well as numerous practical strategies for incorporating Feldenkrais in voice training to complement traditional teaching and learning (Gilman, 2014; Grant, 2014; Nelson and Blades, 2018). A final possibility would be to seek out a voice teacher who incorporates FM into their teaching.

Note

1 Carol McAmis, a former teacher and mentor, has extensive experience incorporating the FM in her teaching of singers at all levels. These phrases are part of *The Singer's PlayBox^{tm}* practice cards, an original invention designed to help singers be more productive in the practice room.

References

Darnley, L. (2015) What is voice studies? In: Konstantinos Thomaidis and Ben Macpherson (eds.) *Voice Studies: Critical Approaches to Process, Performance and Experience.* New York: Routledge, 208–210.

Doidge, N. (2015). *The Brain's Way of Healing: Remarkable Discoveries from the Frontiers of Neuroplasticity.* New York: Penguin Books.

Feldenkrais, M. (1949). *Body and Mature Behavior.* New York: International Universities Press, Inc.

——— (1972). *Awareness Through Movement.* San Francisco, CA: Harper San Francisco.

——— (1981). *The Elusive Obvious: Or, Basic Feldenkrais.* Cupertino, CA: Meta Publications.

Gilman, M. (2014). *Body and Voice: Somatic Re-education.* San Diego, CA: Plural Publishing, Inc.

Grant, S. J. (2014). Vocal pedagogy and the Feldenkrais method. In: Scott D. Harrison and Jessica O'Bryan (eds.) *Teaching Singing in the 21st Century.* Dordrecht, The Netherlands: Springer, 175–185.

LeBorgne, W. D. and Rosenberg, M. (2014) *The Vocal Athlete.* San Diego, CA: Plural Publishing, Inc.

Linklater, K. (1972) The body training of Moshe Feldenkrais. *The Drama Review: TDR*, 16(1) 23–27.

Lynn, G. (2017) *Awakening Somatic Intelligence: Understanding, Learning and Practicing the Alexander Technique, Feldenkrais Method® and Hatha Yoga.* London: Singing Dragon.

Mingle, A. J. (2018) *Applications of Somatic Education Principles to Voice Pedagogy.* PhD. Rutgers University.

Neely, D. W. (2016) Body consciousness and singers: do voice teachers use mind-body methods with students and in their own practice? *Journal of Singing*, 73(2) 137–147.

Nelson, S. H. and Blades, E. L. (2018) *Singing with your Whole Self: A Singer's Guide to Feldenkrais Awareness Through Movement.* Lanham, MD: Rowman & Littlefield.

Paparo, S. A. (2016) Embodying singing in the choral classroom: a somatic approach to teaching and learning. *International Journal of Music Education*, 34(4) 488–498. doi:10.1177/0255761415569366.

Paparo, S. A. (2020) *Singing with Awareness: A Phenomenological Examination of Singers' Experience with the Feldenkrais Method.* Submitted for publication.

Vittucci, S. (2002) Accessing the organic logic of the vocal mechanism: the teaching of Cornelius Reid from the perspective of a Feldenkrais practitioner. In: Ariel Bybee and James E. Ford (eds.) *The Modern Singing Master.* Lanham, MD: The Scarecrow Press, Inc, 260–288.

Worth, L. (2015) Moshe Feldenkrais. *Theatre, Dance and Performance Training Journal*, 6(2).

Suggested Feldenkrais method resources

Corbeil, R. (2007) *Vocal Integration with the Feldenkrais Method* [CD]. Seattle, WA: Richard Corbeil.

Feldenkrais, M. (1972) *Awareness Through Movement.* San Francisco, CA: Harper San Francisco.
Nelson, S. H. and Blades, E. L. (2018). *Singing with your Whole Self: A Singer's Guide to Feldenkrais Awareness Through Movement.* Lanham, MD: Rowman & Littlefield.
Reese, M. (1987) *Moving out of Pain* [CD]. Berkley, CA: Feldenkrais Resources.
Wildman, F. (2000) *The Busy Person's Guide to Easier Movement.* Berkley, CA: The Intelligent Body Press.
Zemach-Bersin, D., Zemach-Bersin, K. and Reese, M. (1990) *Relaxercise: The Easy New Way to Health and Fitness.* New York: HarperCollins.

Additional online resources

Feldenkrais Resources (www.feldenkraisresources.com)
Feldenkrais Guild of North America (www.feldenkrais.com)
International Feldenkrais Federation (www.feldenkrais-method.org)

8 My body is a map, my voice is the path

(trans)racialized somaticities and Roy Hart voice work

Amy Mihyang Ginther

> Courage in the not knowing is
> a type of emancipatory pedagogy.
> It feeds permission. It encourages
> play. It dances in what we are
> present to in this very moment, not
> where we hope to arrive.
>
> When we are not afraid, our curiosity
> can flourish. It can be the fertile soil for
> discovery, transformation, for creation.
>
> My question, my wish for this week, was to see:
> Where do the voice, body, self meet?

This is an excerpt from my reflexive writing during a week-long workshop I took with Jonathan Hart Makwaia (JHM) at Centre Artistique International Roy Hart (Malérargues, France, July 24–29, 2018). It encapsulates my inquiry into my voice practice and subsequent pedagogy with regard to how my transracial adoptee identity intersects with my soma, my living body. I use my participation in this workshop as the practical component of a Practice-as-Research (PaR) project which informs the content of this chapter.

It is challenging to succinctly describe Roy Hart voice work because it is often improvisational in nature and many teachers who worked with Roy Hart and his contemporaries teach variations of the practice.[1] In this chapter, I will focus on a few key points of the workshop, which illustrate a pattern to JHM's interpretation to the guiding principles of Roy Hart, which I summarize as playful improvisation, fully-embodied expressivity and increased range that accesses sounding beyond something aesthetically pleasing that is often deeply personal (Pikes, 1999). The intention is to deepen my own voice practice as a person who has a number of intersectional, historically-marginalized identities and to further develop my pedagogy for my students. I endeavor to see how the guiding principles of Roy Hart and JHM's teaching can create space for me and my students to explore and express an increased spectrum of who they are in relation to their bodies and their voices in performance.

My body is a map, my voice is the path 99

Scholars from postcolonial, critical race and adoption studies have theorized around the body as a site of racialization, colonization and globalization as it relates to power (Ahmed, 2002; Fanon, 1986; Kim, 2010). PaR methodology (Nelson, 2013) illuminates how these ideas are embodied through, in this case, voice as it relates to transracial identity, which offers potentially-reimagined ways of framing voice and acting pedagogy.

In addition to being a queer woman of color, I am a transracial Korean American adoptee.[2] *Transracial* in this context means that I was adopted into a family whose racialized identity was different than my own, often being white where the adoptee is of color. I was adopted at three months old and was raised in a predominantly white town in Upstate New York. I identify as *transnational* (South Korea to the US) and *translingual* (Korean language to English). During my training as an actor, I was given little opportunity to explore my racialized identity or the potential somatic trauma related to my adoption. I did not feel like I had the words (or even sounds) to express the entirety of my identity using the English-dominant, postcolonial[3] training modalities I assimilated into to be a "successful" student.

I currently teach voice, speech and acting at the University of California: Santa Cruz, with an undergraduate population that identifies as 66 percent non-white. Like me, my students seek voice and acting methodologies that engage with the entirety of who they are in relation to their race and other sociopolitical identity locations. And yet, postcolonial actor and voice-training practices often continue to perpetuate the sociopolitical environments that ironically silence these students. In this chapter, I will theoretically racialize the soma and deepen this investigation through my PaR project in Malérargues. My current observations, reflections and contextualizations from this workshop expand discourse around pedagogical practice for acting and voice students with racialized somaticities, with the intention to create space for them to be more fully expressive and powerful in their training and subsequently their performance work.

Locating current voice and engaged pedagogies

Currently, mainstream voice practice in postcolonial actor-training spaces is founded in the belief that the vocal soma is intrinsically linked to individual identity that is influenced by enculturation. The main goal is to free or release the voice from habitual tension caused by socio-cultural factors. This efficacy varies outside these modes of somatic thinking/feeling (McAllister-Viel, 2009) and falls short for two major reasons in postcolonial spaces: the changing student population and the continued institutional power of what Pierre Bourdieu calls *nomos*: "Middle Class Normativity; Heteronormativity; White Privilege; Racism; Classism; Sexism; Patriarchy; Neoliberalism; Ableism; Normative Bodies; Colonialism; Xenophobia; English Hegemony; Globalizations; Ageism" (in Jones and Woglom, 2017, 49). Acting students from diasporic and/or multilingual backgrounds are applying and attending drama programs at increasing rates; they are also more aware of and forthcoming in expressing these identities along with gender, disability and sexuality. They continue to express dissatisfaction with current actor-training practices (Ginther, 2015; Adamucci, 2017; Levingston, 2018; Masso, 2018) and advocate for equitable training that addresses and honors all of these identity locations so they may reach their full potential as theatre artists.

In response to the aforementioned problematics, *engaged pedagogy* potentially offers more emancipatory teaching philosophies that center students, their experiences and their complex identities. Drawing from critical and feminist pedagogical theory (Friere, 1995; Giroux, 2005), bell hooks writes that engaged pedagogy stresses the importance of both teacher and student well-being (1994, 15) and "highlights the importance of independent thinking and each student finding his or her unique voice" (2010, 21). This is particularly resonant for postcolonial voice practitioners as the theorized, political voice (as a means of liberation) is often collapsed with the somatic voice. She believes that erasure and neutralization of the living body perpetuate hegemonic biases:

> We must return ourselves to a state of embodiment in order to deconstruct the way power has been traditional orchestrated in the classroom, denying subjectivity to some groups and according it to others. By recognizing subjectivity and the limits of identity, we disrupt that objectification that is so necessary in a culture of domination.
>
> (1994, 139)

In centering the soma in this pedagogical conversation as a means of going beyond theory and into reflective practice, hooks emphasizes the import of the living body (which I argue is inclusive of voice). In my voice training as a transracial adoptee of color, I aim to engage with my own practice of Roy Hart work with the intention for this to impact and nurture my pedagogy for my current voice students. This seeks to fully acknowledge and center the racialized living body as a way to de-center *nomos* within learning spaces.

Mapping the (trans)racialized soma

For the purposes of this chapter, I use Martha Eddy's definition of the soma: a living body that "can remember experiences as well as respond with awareness to life events" (2016, 7). Eddy goes on to argue that within somatic educational spaces, practitioners utilize "somatic tools of touch, movement (including the movement of the breath), vocalization and language to further awareness" (Ibid., 15). In including breath and vocalization as part of somatic practice, Eddy views the voice as part of the living body. Theorist and dramaturge Piersandra Di Matteo argues for this association between voice and soma:

> The voice [...] is enriched by the respiratory and bodily sources active in the language, and by encoding specific dimensions of corporeality, it

traces words back to the physical events which give them life. The voice is thus always written by the body. Closely bound up with the place of utterance, the voice is the art of guiding the body.

(2015, 91)

In framing the voice as both a result of the living body and its mechanisms and a somatic event itself, Di Matteo creates space for further investigation with regard to how these connections may relate to somaticities as they engage with identity, characterizing the voice as "the gesture which exhibits the relational uniqueness of being" (Ibid., 92). Communications studies scholar B. Hannah Rockwell additionally connects voice and soma, arguing that human voices are "the preeminent site where a dynamic relationship between mind and body are most notably exposed" (2011, 5). So not only is the voice sprung from the corporality of the living body, it acts as a bridge between the soma to the outer world; it is an expression of the living, conscious body and its unique history and identity locations. Rockwell goes as far to say that, "definitions of self, ideological orientations, social identities, speech and social action are nonexistent without a human body to speak up, take shape" (Ibid., 14). Without a soma that exists and interacts with a larger world, our "relational uniqueness of being" would not exist. Theatre scholar-practitioner Awam Amkpa approaches this concept from the opposite direction, writing, "this body belongs to a place, but places are socially constructed, so by that token the body is socially constructed" (Alker et al, 2010, 85). In the same essay, Gwendolyn Alker argues, "the body is messy, boundaried and porous, historicized, contextualized, simultaneously individual and culturally embedded" (Ibid., 76). If the living body interacts with, exists through and is defined by its engagement with sociopolitical and historical contexts, how do acting students' somaticities become racialized as a result of social and institutional power? How does this affect their ability to train their voices and bodies to fully express limitless stories and characters?

According to Sara Ahmed, whose research lies within feminist, queer and critical race studies, "racialization involves the production of 'the racial body' through knowledge, as well as the constitution of both social and bodily space in everyday encounters we have with others" (2002, 47). Racialization is therefore a social construction created through sociopolitical hegemonic power, not through genetic or physical features; it is how others *read* a soma within specific contexts and how that soma responds. Many theorists see European colonialism and its ongoing impact as a root cause for how bodies are racialized (Ahmed, 2002; Fanon, 1986; Hook, 2008; Lugones, 2010). In her article "Towards a Decolonial Feminism," Lugones writes: "the colonial 'civilizing mission' was the euphemistic mask of brutal access to people's bodies through unimaginable exploitation, violent sexual violation, control of reproduction, and systematic terror" (2010, 744). Derek Hook adds that colonial embodiment occurs when "the balance of the body's relation to the world, to other bodies, to its own positive identity, to an array of cultural and historical values, is almost completely obliterated" (2008, 148). Both Lugones and Hook here emphasize the profound negative impact colonialism has on the racialization of bodies.

In his book *Black Skin, White Masks*, Frantz Fanon deepens this theory, situating this racialized power dynamic in his own body through his description of his experiences living in France as a Black man, writing:

> In the white world the man of color encounters difficulties in the development of his bodily schema. Consciousness of the body is solely a negating activity. It is a third-person consciousness. The body is surrounded by an atmosphere of certain uncertainty.
>
> (1986, 83)

What is striking here is how Fanon calls his racialized awareness a third-person consciousness or what Du Bois calls "double consciousness" (2015, 9). So if, according to Eddy, we define the soma through its consciousness, racialized soma has additional consciousness because it is constantly being defined through a white, colonial gaze as *other*. This additional consciousness can manifest in a number of disconcerting ways: in the form of "anxiety, anger, rage, depression, shame, or guilt" (Carter and Forsyth, 2009, 36) "that may rise to the level of trauma" (Ibid., 38).[4] It is crucial to note how a living body may be impacted through racialization with regard to training an actor's voice where the aim may be to release habitual blocks from physical and mental tension as a result of enculturation, a common goal in postcolonial voice work in places like the US and the UK. Ahmed writes that the process of being racially othered "is to feel pressure upon your bodily surface; your body feels the pressure point, as a restriction in what it can do" (2007, 161). Hook views the "body as a surface of experience that undergoes anxieties, visceral responses, symptomatic episodes" (2008, 149) and that the "lived experience of racism […] is not easily contained, or assimilated into the symbolic domain of speech, language, signification" (Ibid.). If this is true, that racialized somaticity complicates vocal and linguistic expression through (often both) resistance or assimilation, this may pose significant pedagogical challenges within voice and speech classes in postcolonial contexts. Before discussing that further, I will illuminate ways that transracial adoptee identity further complicates how somaticities become racialized.

Sociologist Eleana J. Kim has theoretically characterized the transracial Korean adoptee body as a complex one, writing, "adoptees embody and expose the contradictions of the global" (2010, 8) and that "for many of them, their origins are constructed out of socially grounded notions of kinship, citizenship, and histories of connection and disconnection" (Ibid., 6). This is unsurprising when one reflects on how racialization manifests not only within a larger, sociopolitical setting, but also within a transracial adoptee's nuclear family and immediate community, which are often predominantly

My body is a map, my voice is the path 103

white. I felt this deeply in my body when I first returned to Korea to meet my biological family, starkly feeling aspects of my US assimilation internally while reading as racially Korean.

Growing up in my family and hometown, my body read as *other* and in Korea, my voice and ways of thinking/doing read as *other*. Kim notes:

> [F]or many of these adoptees the project of creating a coherent self in an 'as-if' family as an 'as-if' white person was undermined by their own material embodiment. The Asian or Korean body of the adoptee itself destabilizes the coherence of self-identity.
>
> (Ibid., 92)

As a result of this, Kim argues that "essentializations of Korean-ness are [...] never acquired but presumed to be deeply embodied and rendered inaccessible to the adoptee" (Ibid.) and that this creates a block, for example, in learning or reclaiming Korean language.[5] Thus, the soma of the transracial/transnational/translingual adoptee further complicates somatic consciousness referenced by Eddy and racialized consciousness by Fanon and Du Bois. If our students enter an actor and voice-training space with this level of somatic complexity, what types of voice practices can address these complexities in a comprehensive, emancipatory manner? How can praxis within PaR generate more embodied understanding of these critical theories in dialogue?

Navigating with PaR as a compass

It is not enough to theorize about racialized somaticities and resulting implications in actor-training spaces without actual engagement with embodied voice practice because "theory is not inherently healing, liberatory, or revolutionary. It fulfills this function only when we ask that it do so and direct our theorizing towards this end" (hooks, 1994, 61). Conversely, voice practice without theory is not sufficient when we aim to look at larger sociopolitical structures that impact racialized somaticities in actor-training spaces because "the language of working practitioners [...] with its tendency towards the technical, has appeared shallow" (Boston, 1997, 248). Praxis[6] invites me to triangulate and contextualize my experience in the workshop with theoretical assertions about the body, voice, transracialized identity and engaged pedagogy from earlier sections, in order to argue for voice methods and teaching language that create space and permission for participants to explore aspects of their identity such as race and language. I engage in a type of reflexivity called *standpoint epistemologies*, which is what PaR expert Robin Nelson believes "leads researchers to reflect upon their own ideology and values [...] in relation to the cultural practices of the object of study" (2013, 53) that emphasizes "awareness of an inevitable interrelatedness between subject and object" (Ibid.). This lens creates space for my multiple identities of performer-participant-pedagogue-theorist-woman of color-transracial adoptee to live within and among the embodied experience of the workshop with the intention to generate more engaged vocal pedagogy for my students in relation to their racialized somaticities.

Returning to my written reflections that opened this chapter inquiry, I will focus on JHM's specific pedagogical interpretation of Roy Hart voice work during this particular workshop in Malérargues.[7] JHM has been a Roy Hart Voice Teacher since 1978, studying directly with Roy Hart, his step-father, and was a member of the Roy Hart Theatre. I intentionally wanted to study with him because he is one of the few master teachers of this work who is a person of color with such a complex cultural and national background. JHM has lived in Tanzania, the country of his biological father, the US and the UK; his own artistic vocal creations are an embodiment of these aspects of his identity (Kozinn, 1993). During the six-day workshop with him, I documented my experience through daily reflexive writing and post-workshop writing. Additionally, I recorded audio of my one-on-one session with him and evidence this in support of my reflexive writing and recollection of my workshop participation. I combine these methods with the theoretical ideas analyzed here and additional contextual information on Roy Hart-inspired pedagogies as praxis.

Reimagining terrain through vocal discovery

Every day followed roughly the same progression: individual voice and body warm-up, partnered warm-up, group improvisations and hour-long one-on-one sessions with JHM in front of the rest of the group (every participant would have one of these individual sessions at some point during the week). The one-on-one sessions would always begin with JHM asking the participant to physically place themselves, him and the group in any area of the room they felt was best. He would generally check in with the participant, asking them to locate themselves in the work physically, vocally and emotionally and would ask what their wish was for that session. Being invited to set up the space and intention engendered a sense of agency within me. During my one-on-one session, JHM asked:

> How are you feeling now? [...] What's feeling most relevant to you, in this moment? [...] Do you have any specific wishes? [...] Are you fluent in Korean? [...] Are you comfortable [inaudible], even if you're not fluent, are you comfortable speaking with — speaking Korean? [...] I feel like it would be great in some way to include Korean in this now — but I'm not sure yet, the best way — [...] So let's begin by the moment, just following your intuition, your wish. You don't need to know why. When it feels like a good moment to pause, you can pause. We'll just listen.[8]

Throughout the week and particularly during my one-on-one session, JHM built on this Roy Hart convention with his choice of language which evoked

My body is a map, my voice is the path 105

a gentle presence in the space. This presence created a space of pedagogical permission for me, which encouraged my authority over my own readiness to explore and engage with aspects of my transracialized somaticity. This sense of permission additionally encouraged moving and sounding that evoked personal images to emerge organically, flowing in a cyclical way, feeding into each other, resulting in (and an increased awareness of) a fuller, more released and embodied voice. Often in postcolonial voice work, images come from the instructor and/or methodology, often relating to metaphorical depictions of anatomy. I argue that the space JHM created allowed images to emerge from my own somaticity, which engendered the kind of deeply personal engagement that is characteristic of Roy Hart voice work. One of these images emerged during my first improvisation and was in relationship with audible changes in vocal pitch and timbre. I invite you to bear this in mind as you listen to my first vocal improvisation [Track _1st Improvisation_ (3:13), RVS website] while reading my written reflection about my 엄마 (Korean mother) and my adoptive mother:

> I saw my 엄마's face and went back to the memory of my reunion with her. The time was already non-linear because I saw her face as I heard her running down the hall crying in anticipation of meeting me. Then my mom was there too. She also reunited with 엄마, beyond her lifetime, beyond her death. My voice brought them together.

I reunited with my 엄마 in 2004 and my US mother died in 2008 without being able to meet her. In this first improvisation, my voice evoked my memory of my reunion with my 엄마 and as my voice and original images created a dialogue with each other, a "new" memory emerged that connected my two mothers. Much like my transracialized identity feels unreconcilable and contradictory, my embodied voice acted here as a way to transcend both space and time to connect these two mothers, who embody the polarities of these racial/national/linguistic identities. This bridge between these aspects of my identities is arguably heard through my voice. In the early stages of the improvisation on the same track, I begin in quite high pitches (00:18), finding some time to venture into my break for brief moments (00:55; 1:11). Towards the end (2:15), I hover more on the break of my voice to see what lies in that space, gradually intensifying this exploration (2:50). This part of my practice was consistent with Di Matteo's argument that "the voice is thus always written by the body. Closely bound up with the place of utterance, the voice is the art of guiding the body" (2015, 91). Personal images (deeply related to my transracialized identity) emerged from my sounds and movement which altered this memory which, in turn, impacted my voice (Figure 8.1).

During my first one-on-one improvisation, I only engaged with sound and image, even though JHM invited me to play with Korean language.[9]

106 *Amy Mihyang Ginther*

Figure 8.1 Moments from my improvisations during my one-on-one session with Jonathan Hart Makwaia, July 27, 2018. (Photos by Danielle Meunier.)

I did not do so until the fourth improvisation where he gently suggested it again, asking: "Do you feel like sounding in Korean at the moment?" (note how this is a question I can say "no" to as opposed to a direct request). As someone who has only taken Korean language classes as an adult, improvising in Korean can be challenging and disembodied for me. This emerges out of a complex transnational, transracial, translingual space where I am expected to speak fluent Korean in both Korea and the US because of my racialized somaticity, and I have internalized my inability to satisfy these expectations as a stress-inducing sense of inferiority.[10] This is supported by Alfred Wolfsohn's belief that Western culture limited an adult's vocal expressivity, arguing that "one's rebirth comes about through conscious vocal expression" (in Pikes, 1999, 39). He clarifies, "when I speak of singing I do not see it as an artistic exercise […] but as a possibility and a means of recognizing oneself and of transforming this recognition into conscious life" (Ibid., 34). This argument frames this voice work as a way of unearthing aspects of self that were effaced through enculturation and in the case of (trans)racialized somaticities, white, colonial spaces. Because of this, it is rare for me to feel safe to engage with Korean language, particularly through improvisation and in front of a group of co-participants. By the time I started my fourth vocal improvisation during my one-on-one session (which took place on the fourth day of the workshop), I felt emboldened by JHM's consistent pedagogical space, internalizing the permission I could give myself to speak as much or as little Korean as I wanted, and that it did not need to be understood as a speech act, which is rare in my daily lived experience of my multiple consciousnesses characterized by Fanon, Du Bois and Kim. As you listen to the following [Track _4th Improvisation_ (4:21)], I have provided these translations as reference.

Hangul	Romanization	Translation
엄마	Omma	Mother
어떻게	Ohtohkae	Why
나는 난다	Nanun nanda	I am who I am
마음에집	[Maom] eh jip	My [mind, heart, feeling, emotion] as home
다리있어요	Tari issaeyo	You are/It is a bridge.
안녕	Anyeong	Hi
괜찮아	Guenchana	It's okay
열심히	Yeolshimhee	With difficulty

You will notice in this fourth improvisation, JHM vocally engaged with me more actively, moving from verbal/nonverbal encouragement (00:58, 1:05) to sounding in response (1:31), matching my sound (3:08) and bringing in piano accompaniment (3:20 to end); at some points, the sounding was almost a dialogue between us. In reflecting upon this after the session, I interpret this vocal dialogue as a thoughtful engaged pedagogy that supported my own vocal journey; it was an embodiment of JHM's validation and encouragement of the way I was sounding with Korean. It also provided me with external impulses to respond to. Post-workshop, I wrote:

> My body is a map
> My voice is the path
> The moments I had freedom
> To move
> and to sound
> Reminded me of how rare they are
> [...]
> I cannot believe the depths of discovery
> Still within myself
> My voice touched places I could
> not venture before

Charting future courses through new territories

Through a praxical analysis of my reflections and experiences of this workshop, I demonstrate that JHM used Roy Hart voice work in a way that created an emancipatory space for me to explore aspects of my (trans)racialized somaticity. This six-day workshop in Malérargues was consistent with other experiences I have had with Roy Hart voice work, in that they all emphasized improvisation, fully-embodied sound and increased range; this transcended my experience of my voice and self far beyond my formal training as an actor in my undergraduate and graduate institutions. I felt like I had permission to make sounds and express emotionality around my identity that were perhaps not acceptable for someone with the identity locations I embody in white, postcolonial spaces. My voice not only felt fully integrated with my personal images and body, but it became a vehicle to transcend aspects of my embodied transracialized identity that are difficult to reconcile. Notably, I observed a physical openness and release in sounding, a major tenet of contemporary, postcolonial voice work, indicating a usefulness of this work with regard to training actors with racialized somaticities as I engaged with aspects of my identity. Roy Hart believed that actors and singers must vocally explore these aspects of themselves to be more authentic in their performance work: "I know that my role is to teach people to be aware of the political explosives within themselves before they can be of any use to the cause of human progress" (in Pikes, 1999, 101).[11] If the goal for actors is to have a fully expressive soma with a vocal apparatus free of excess tension, and racialized somas may have such tension due to oppressive structures in a hegemonic culture, I posit that an engaged voice pedagogy will have some way of addressing this beyond a level of physical engagement.

Lastly, I argue that JHM's complex identity and transnational-translingual-transcultural embodied experience enrich his pedagogical interpretation of this type of voice work and create a unique space of permission for me to explore new depth and place with my voice in relation to my transracialized somaticity. There is no way I can claim this with certainty – that JHM's own identity further impacted his embodied way of dialoguing with my voice with his own voice and with the piano – but from my positionality, my awareness of his identities impacted how openly I related to this vocal and instrumental dialogue between us. I do not believe it is necessary for a voice practitioner to have such complex and racialized somatic experiences as JHM and I have had to create the kind of pedagogical space he created during my workshop in France. I will continue to argue, however, for sweeping measures to recruit, mentor and retain voice teachers of color as their experiences and resulting pedagogy are vital for current and more inclusive actor-training practices. I simultaneously advocate for a deeper examination of current practitioners of how their embodied self, impacted by racialization (which includes whiteness and colonialism), manifests in their ways of doing, being, knowing and speaking in their teaching/learning spaces. As we continue to explore how somaticities relate to rapid technological advancements and increasingly fraught sociopolitical climates, more nuanced research on identity and vocal somaticities urgently demand our attention and resources. After decades of theorizing the soma, we are only beginning to tap into the lived, breathing, voicing body as a cite of complex identity, power, trauma, memory in relation to all that it is capable of: collectively, creatively, politically.

Acknowledgments

I am in deep gratitude for Jonathan Hart Makwaia and my participatory cohort during my time at Centre Artistique International Roy Hart, for bearing witness and offering love and generous guidance. Thank you from the bottom of my heart to Morné Steyn: without his wisdom, provocations and inspiration, this chapter would not have been possible.

Notes

1 Alfred Wolfsohn, Roy Hart's predecessor, created this voice work as an embodied way of processing his trauma as a veteran of World War I. After Wolfsohn's death in 1962, Roy Hart carried his work forward, ultimately establishing a community who practised this type of voice work, teaching it and using it as a basis to devise new performance work in Europe, until his death in 1975. I want to acknowledge the questionable methods Wolfsohn and Hart allegedly engaged in with their students and their controversial beliefs they held with regard to sexuality, for example, and separate these concerns with their guiding principles taught by their successors. For more on this, see Pikes, 1999; Kalo et al, 2000.
2 I am one of over 161,000 Korean adoptees who have dispersed across the world. This phenomenon began in the 1950s during and post-Korean War, and is a result of colonial, economic and gendered forces. For a comprehensive history of this, please see Kim, 2010.
3 Categorizing this type of voice work as Euro-American, Western, US/UK, mainstream are all imperfect as they do not fully encapsulate what I am referring to here. When I use postcolonial, know that I nod towards these terms, while intentionally stressing the remnants of European colonialism in how we create and internalize hierarchies in our ways of doing and knowing.
4 For a more comprehensive overview of this, particularly with regard to voice work, see Ginther (2015).
5 Neurolinguistics have recently provided scientific findings that support that lost language for translingual adoptees remains in their somas (Pierce et al, 2014; Choi et al, 2017). Something particularly striking from the aforementioned 2017 study: "Early development of abstract language knowledge: evidence from perception-production transfer of birth-language memory" was that there was no difference in language retention between those adopted in pre-verbal phases and those who had begun to speak Korean, which intimates an impact of the language from an earlier, even fetal developmental stage. For more about this in depth, see Kim and Ginther (2019).
6 Robin Nelson defines praxis as "theory imbricated within practice" (2013, 5).
7 Before working with Hart Makwaia in Malérargues, I took workshops with Margaret Pikes, who was a founding member of Roy Hart Theatre, Phil Timberlake (Roy Hart Voice Teacher since 2013) and Marya Lowry (Roy Hart Voice Teacher since 2010). I also took numerous workshops with Ros Steen, a master teacher of Nadine George Technique (George is a founding member of Roy Hart Theatre).
8 In this quote, […] generally denote my responses, which have been deleted for brevity and to focus on JHM's prompts. I have omitted nonverbal thinking words that I do not believe interfere with content and intention.
9 The fact that I did not accept JHM's invitation to use Korean is a testament to the idea that I felt empowered enough to do what I wanted when I was ready.
10 Please see Endnote 5, Kim and Ginther (2019), Ginther (in press) for more on Korean language in relation to my adoptee monolingual identity.
11 This quote also connotes the therapeutic benefits of Roy Hart voice work (Newham, 1994; Bruun, 2015), all of the Roy Hart teachers I have worked with primarily trained actors, which is consistent with its pre-existing pedagogical theory (Lewis, 2013; Holmes, 2016).

References

Adamucci, S. (2017) Theater students face racial microaggressions in department [online]. *The Ithacan*. Available from: https://theithacan.org/news/theater-students-face-racial-microaggressions-in-department/ [Accessed 1 June 2017].

Ahmed, S. (2002) Racialized bodies. In: Mary Evans (ed.) *Real Bodies*. London: Palgrave, 46–63.

——— (2007) A phenomenology of whiteness. *Feminist Theory*, 8(2) 149–168.

Alker, G., Martin, R., Browning B. and Amkpa, A. (2010) Dialogues: the state of the body. *Dance Research Journal*, 42(1) 75–88.

Boston, J. (1997) Voice: the practitioners, their practices and their critics. *New Theatre Quarterly*, 13(51) 248–254.

Bruun, E. F. (2015) Listen carefully. *Dramatherapy*, 37(1) 3–14.

Carter, R. T. and Forsyth, J. M. (2009) A guide to the forensic assessment of race-based traumatic stress reactions. *The Journal of the American Academy of Psychiatry and the Law*, 37(1) 28–40.

Choi, J., Cutler, A. and Broersma, M. (2017) Early development of abstract language knowledge: evidence from perception-production transfer of birth-language memory. *Royal Society Open Science*, 4(1) 1–14.

Di Matteo, P. (2015) Performing the entre-deux: the capture of speech in (dis)embodied voices. In: Konstantinos Thomaidis and Ben Macpherson (eds.) *Voice Studies: Critical Approaches to Process, Performance and Experience*. London: Routledge, 90–103.

Du Bois, W. E. B. and Marable, M. (2015) *Souls of Black Folk*. London: Routledge.

Eddy, M. (2016) *Mindful Movement: The Evolution of the Somatic Arts and Conscious Action*. Bristol: Intellect.

Fanon, F. (1986) *Black Skin, White Masks*. Translated from French by Charles Lam Markmann. London: Pluto Press.

Freire, P. (1995) *Pedagogy of the Oppressed, New Revised 20th-Anniversary Edition*. Translated from Portuguese by Myra Bergman Ramos. New York: Continuum.

Ginther, A. M. (2015) Dysconscious racism in mainstream British voice pedagogy and its potential effects on students from pluralistic backgrounds in UK Drama Conservatoires. *Voice and Speech Review*, 9(1) 41–60.

——— (in press) A pedagogy of trans-orality: reflections on the development of embodied EFL pronunciation possibilities from a Korean adoptee perspective. In: Curt Porter and Rachel Griffo (eds.) *The Matter of Practice: New Materialisms and New Literacies in Linguistically Diverse Classrooms*. Charlotte: Information Age Press.

Giroux, H. A. (2005) *Border Crossings: Cultural Workers and the Politics of Education*. 2nd edition. New York: Routledge.

Holmes, S. (2016) Autoethnography and voicework: autobiographical narrative and self-reflection as a means towards free vocal expression. *Voice and Speech Review*, 10(2–3) 190–202.

Hook, D. (2008) The 'real' of racializing embodiment. *Journal of Community and Applied Social Psychology*, 18(2) 140–152.

hooks, b. (1994) *Teaching to Transgress: Education as the Practice of Freedom*. New York: Routledge.

——— (2010) *Teaching Critical Thinking: Practical Wisdom*. New York: Routledge.

Jones, S. and Woglom. J. F. (2017) *On Mutant Pedagogies: Seeking Justice and Drawing Change in Teacher Education*. New York: Springer.

Kalo, L. C., Whiteside, G. and Midderigh, I. (1997) The Roy Hart Theatre: teaching the totality of self. In: Marion Hampton and Barbara Acker (eds). *The Vocal Vision: Views on Voice.* New York: Applause Books, 185–199.

Kim, E. J. (2010) *Adopted Territory: Transnational Korean Adoptees and the Politics of Belonging.* Durham: Duke University Press.

Kim, O. M. and Ginther, A. M. (2019) I am who I am - 나는 나다': archetypal drama therapy workshops for Asian American adoptees. *Drama Therapy Review*, 5(2) 251–266.

Kozinn, A. (1993) Review/music; Tanzanian folk songs meet American jazz [online]. *The New York Times.* Available from: https://www.nytimes.com/1993/03/06/arts/review-music-tanzanian-folk-songs-meet-american-jazz.html [Accessed 20 August 2019].

Levingston, M. (2018) Tisch students encounter racial insensitivity in drama program [online]. *Washington Square News.* Available from: https://nyunews.com/2018/04/08/04-09-news-tisch/ [Accessed 1 June 2018].

Lewis, R. (2013) Dark voices in revolt. *Theatre, Dance and Performance Training*, 4(3) 368–380.

Lugones, M. (2010) Toward a decolonial feminism. *Hypatia*, 25(4) 742–759.

Masso, G. (2018) Central principal Gavin Henderson faces calls to resign over diversity quotas remarks [online]. *The Stage.* Available from: https://www.thestage.co.uk/news/2018/royal-central-principal-gavin-henderson-faces-calls-resign-diversity-quotas-remarks/ [Accessed 6 June 2018].

McAllister-Viel, T. (2009) Voicing culture: training Korean actors' voices through the Namdaemun market projects. *Modern Drama*, 52(4) 426–448.

Nelson, R. (2013) *Practice as Research in the Arts: Principles, Protocols, Pedagogies, Resistances.* New York: Springer.

Newham, P. (1994) Voice Movement Therapy: towards an arts therapy for voice. *Dramatherapy*, 16(2–3) 28–33.

Pierce, L. J., Klein, D., Chen J., Delcenserie, A. and Genesee, F. (2014) Mapping the unconscious maintenance of a lost first language. *Proceedings of the National Academy of Sciences*, 111(48) 17314–17319.

Pikes, N. (1999) *Dark Voices: The Genesis of Roy Hart Theatre.* New Orleans: Spring Journal Books.

Rockwell, B. H. (2011) *The Life of Voices: Bodies, Subjects and Dialogue.* London: Routledge.

Part III
Vocal and somatic listening in training

9 (Re)considering the role of touch in "re-educating" actors' body/voice

Tara McAllister-Viel

The use of touch to train actors' voices in popular voice pedagogy is an accepted pedagogical tool within the US and the UK acting conservatoires. Influential master voice trainers, Cicely Berry, Kristin Linklater, Michael McCallion and Patsy Rodenburg, all use touch in their practices (Berry, 1973, 63–64, 79–80; McCallion, 1988; Rodenburg, 1994; Linklater, 2003). The use of touch increases a student's awareness of excessive muscular contraction, or "tension," which inhibits the process of vocalization, by directing her awareness to a certain part of her body/voice and keenly observing the student's behavior (McAllister-Viel, 2019, 1, 43–46). This fundamental observation becomes the foundation for the next step: learning how to release this "tension" and "re-educate" the body/voice by substituting inefficient or "habitual" muscular usage with more efficient usage. This learning process is also the necessary preparatory work for further learning. Linklater wrote:

> How do you *teach* relaxation? By touching the pupil's body and feeling whether the muscles are responding to the messages being sent to them. How do you induce a new use of the voice? By taking hold of the body and moving it in new directions which break conditioned, habitual movements.
>
> (1976, 4; 2006, 10–11, added emphasis)

The use of touch to heighten a student's awareness of her "conditioned, habitual movements" has a variety of influences but one influence I would like to examine for the purposes of this chapter is the adaptation of FM Alexander's approach, the Alexander Technique, into popular contemporary voice training. Linklater wrote: "His [Alexander] influence is clear in much of the voice work that has developed since then" (1976, 2). Alongside my actor training, which included the practices of Berry, Linklater, McCallion and Rodenburg, I had the privilege of three years private Alexander training. From my experiences, I have adapted my understanding of Alexander's "hands-on" approach in my teaching practice, as well as adapted my understanding of touch in training actors' voices from the approaches of master voice trainers.

Simultaneously, I trained in a variety of Asian modes of practice at the Asian/Experimental Theatre program, University of Wisconsin-Madison, which included understandings of the use of ki [energy] as awareness within Hatha yoga (Wu style), *taiqiquan, kalarippayattu* (a traditional Indian martial art), and later in my career Korean *p'ansori* (a traditional Korean vocal art form), and Zen meditation at Hwa Gye Sa [temple], both in Seoul, South Korea. Over the course of my career, I have looked for ways of interweaving Anglo-American voice training with my understandings of the Asian modes of training in both my acting technique in performance and my teaching practice (McAllister-Viel, 2019).

I teach in a variety of different multicultural and multilingual contexts in which I sometimes struggle to find word choices and/or translations during my instruction to articulate *the experience of experiencing* an exercise. Alexander had identified the issue of language in his practice. Edward Maisel, editor of Alexander's collected writings, suggested that the practitioner introduced his method of touch as "directing awareness," because verbal instruction when teaching the experience of experiencing was inadequate. Maisel wrote:

> Initially, Alexander had attempted – in words, futile words – to teach the new feeling by *telling* his pupil how to attain it [...] But instead of relying upon words in situations whereof one cannot speak, might there not be some other form of communication? Might it not be possible to impart one's message in some other way? In meeting and solving this problem, Alexander developed a means for conveying kinesthetic experience – which is perhaps the most valuable part of this work.
> (1969 [1974], xxix, original emphasis)

I sometimes do away with language instruction during an exercise or support my verbal instruction with role modeling of behavior and touch to bring focused attention to a student's conscious awareness of her vocal function. Another reason I use touch in my classrooms is because the ephemeral voice can be realized in concrete ways through touch and this can help students who might find voice difficult to pin down. Students can locate "voice" by mapping, through touch, the vibrations over the hard surfaces of their bodies (e.g. secondary resonance or "bone conduction"). Voice can be realized through touch as vibration. Touch grounds voice in body and this helps realize a major principle in contemporary, popular voice training, often characterized as "embodied" voice.

"Re-educating" body/voice

I have struggled with using touch in tandem with Alexander's concept of "re-education" ([1910] 1918, 107) of the body/voice, a major principle underpinning his use of touch and a concept also adapted by many contemporary voice trainers. The student begins training by examining "conditioned, habitual movements" (Linklater, 1976, 4; 2006, 10–11). McCallion warned that in the beginning of training, "the first problem is that because what we do is habitual, it feels right, and so is difficult to detect as a wrong" (1988, 8–9). The student brings into the voice studio habits that feel "right" but are "wrong," setting up a way to understand muscular usage within a right/wrong or good/bad binary, which I find problematic. The student learns that she must initially distrust what feels "right," or distrust her embodied feeling. She cannot "trust [her] judgement" but instead she must rely on "some external and trustworthy guide" (Linklater 1976, 4–5). In my experience, this adaptation of "re-educating" the body/voice undermines student agency, her responsibility for her own learning and her confidence in coming to know her body/voice.

Recently, voice trainers have been (re)considering the use of touch in training actors' voices. Master voice trainers, David Carey and Rebecca Clark Carey, discuss problems with the use of touch in their voice training texts, *Vocal Arts Workbook and DVD* (2008) and *The Verbal Arts Workbook* (2010). In their 2008 publication, they wrote:

> Until recently, this training culture assumed that it was acceptable, for example, to require students to wear specific types of clothing, to work in bare feet, to touch each other […]. However, in our contemporary context of multiculturalism and diversity, many of these practices are rightly being questioned.
>
> (Carey and Clark Carey, 2008, xvi)

In dealing with this issue in class, Carey and Clark Carey suggest: "If it is inappropriate to ask students to touch each other, feel free to be creative with those exercises which require it – or simply don't do them" (2008, xvi). Not using touch in teaching is always an option, but what are tutors missing if they ban touch from their classrooms as a means of avoiding the complex issues that touch brings into their classrooms? If tutors find value in teaching through touch, how might they "be creative" adapting touch in the voice studio?

Master voice trainers Micha Espinosa and Antonio Ocampo-Guzman point out in their writing the "complex relationship most Latinos have to the physical body" that they argue is not being addressed in most popular US actor-training programs (2010, 151). In an interview, Espinosa discussed some of the questions that guide her use of touch in studio:

> I am aware and structure my courses or classes with an understanding of my situated perspective and the cultural context […]. Even if there is a culture of touch [in the classroom] there is a tremendous amount to learn. What do I represent? What are the power structures at play?
>
> (2019)

For voice trainer Electa Behrens, who teaches in English within multilingual classrooms at the Norwegian Theater Academy/Akademi for Scenekunst, the question that guides her use of touch in studio becomes,

> how do we make space for and respect cultural difference and at the same time invite sensual strategies? [...] Not just say 'no touch,' but rather ask; who touches? How? When? And celebrating the diversity of response touch offers the voice.
>
> (Behrens, 2019)

One aim of this chapter is to examine the concerns I have surrounding the use of touch in my teaching, particularly focusing on the multicultural and diverse training environments in which I work. In the first half of this chapter, I investigate the ways touch is used in popular, contemporary voice practice, as a departure point for how I have, in the past, adapted practices to my multicultural/multilingual classrooms. I begin with those aspects of prominent approaches that I have struggled with, prompting me to look for additional ways to address the use of touch and feeling in my teaching. Specifically, I examine the following:

- the student can touch the surface of the skin, and may feel activity underneath the skin, for instance, the way the muscles contract and release, but many other functions integral to voicing happen within the depths of her body where touch cannot reach and where feeling is elusive. How might "touch" and the "awareness" brought about by touch and feeling be understood more broadly than simply skin-to-skin contact through a corrective method?[1]
- Part of the training of contemporary practices asks the student to observe her body as an object (e.g. object-body) through a Western biomedical model. But within my multicultural/multilingual classrooms, not all students understand their body only through this model; they bring in other mappings of the body through diverse world views. How might this popular approach interact with other understandings of body/voice to include various body knowledges?
- The messages that touch sends to the learner are delivered through "feeling," which some master trainers rightly find problematic, in part because the feeling of touch is subjective and culturally influenced. However, relying on anatomy and physiology to carry the messages of touch invests in the body as a stable site for learning. How might multiple interpretations of the experience of experiencing touch offer greater agency to the multicultural/multilingual student in her learning journey?

The second half of this chapter attempts to articulate my ongoing explorations interweaving well-known, contemporary Anglo-American voice training with certain Asian modes of training, specifically in regard to the role of touch in learning. The focus here is to propose alternative ways of addressing bodies/voices and touch. I propose that cultivating focused awareness through breath/ki and applying it to touch can help the learner understand "outside" and "inside" (e.g. "object-body" and "subject-body") in a more joined-up way. By applying meditative breathing methods to touch, the student magnifies her awareness of her musculature in the beginning of the training. However, through long-term practice, she can shift from muscular awareness to a cultivation of ki as awareness.

One benefit of adding meditative practices to current, popular voice practice is to reach more diverse student populations that many voice trainers feel are not being satisfactorily addressed (Burke, 1997, 58, 61–62; Brown, 2000; 2001, 124–128; Espinosa and Ocampo-Guzman, 2010, 150; Ginther, 2015, 41–60; Klemp et al, 2015, 82–90). Another benefit is that the conceptual model for what touch and feeling can do and how it can do "it" is augmented. Touch and feeling are no longer located in individual investigations of physiological function but open up to include ways of "forming one body" with others, leading to more connected communication and empathetic listening. Ultimately, this chapter hopes to add to ongoing discussions within popular contemporary voice training about the role of touch as a pedagogical tool within the UK and the US acting conservatoires.

Touch as "universal" human experience

Within many popular voice-training exercises, anatomy and physiology is the foundation for shared phenomenological experience (McAllister-Viel, 2019, 21). Rodenburg wrote: "The biology, mechanics and hydraulics of the human voice are the same everywhere" (1992, 107). The body becomes the site for the voice, the producing mechanism for sounding and voicing and the kinesthetic awareness of physical acts which influence the training of voice. In short, body mediates the experience of experiencing voice. Berry wrote: "That is why I said that our common ground was the experience of the voice through the movement of muscles" (1973, 14). Exercises can transfer between bodies during training because it is assumed that the bodies involved have the same materiality which makes transmission of skills possible. Touch, as a pedagogical tool within this conceptual model, helps work towards a necessary reduction of experience between bodies and acts as a founding principle for transferring technique from one body to another. The transmission of skills is successful when learning outcomes can be seen, heard or felt.

This is also one of the ways in which voice is understood as "embodied". For Linklater, "[t]he voice is forged in the body" (Linklater, 2016: 59). The voice is "embodied," literally "in" and "of" the body. When this singularly body is understood through anatomy and physiology, conceptualized through a Western, biomedical model, it can be hard to integrate other world views of body/voice. Phillip Zarrilli noted:

> We organize 'the world' we encounter into significant gestalts, but 'the body' I call mine is not a body, or the body, but rather a process of embodying the several bodies one encounters in everyday experience as well as highly specialized modes of non-everyday, or 'extra-daily' bodies of practices such as acting or training in psycho-physical disciplines to act.
> (2004, 655)

If a student has "several bodies" she encounters through an ever-becoming process of her "everyday experience" as well as during training, "extra-daily bodies of practices," then, relying on anatomy and physiology as *the* singular body of reference during training is inadequate. Additionally, the information gathered from touch is not necessarily understood in the same way between all those who are touching the same thing. How a student organizes "the world" through her body affects how she experiences that "world" through her senses and how she understands or "reads" the "sensing/experience". Zarrilli wrote:

> The Latin sentire means "to feel." To be sentient is to be open to "feeling," that is, to "sensing" and thereby experiencing "a world." But precisely how many senses there are, how they are understood, and how a "world" of sensing/experience is defined varies widely across cultures, histories and religious-philosophical perspectives.
> (2016, 121)

When body/voice is universalized and trained through object-body exercises, the experience of experiencing body/voice is problematically universalized.

Inside/outside

According to Linklater, in the late 1930s, Iris Warren, her former voice tutor at LAMDA (London Academy of Music and Dramatic Art), added a psychological understanding to physiologically-based voice exercises. She wrote:

> [T]he voice exercises remained, but were gradually altered by the shift from external, physical control to internal, psychological ones. The criterion for assessing progress lay in the answer to the question 'how does it feel?' rather than 'how does it sound?'
> (Linklater, 1976, 2–3)

By the 1970s, acting training had been characterized in popular voice texts as processes that were either outside/inside or inside/outside (Linklater, 1976, 3; 2006, 1–2; Berry, 1992, 288; Rodenburg, 1992, 113; McAllister-Viel, 2019,

8–9, 68–71). This referred to the differences between the technically-proficient British actor (outside-in approach to acting) who trained to embody muscular skill in contrast to the psychologically-motivated, emotionally-driven American actor within American Method approaches (inside-out approach to acting). This characterization set up a way to think about voice training as a divide between the technique of the body/voice and its outward appearance and the expressive body/voice driven through internal psychological and emotional motivation, "the need to communicate" (Linklater, 1976, 12) or the "need for words" (Rodenburg, 1993).

As an actor trained in both the US and the UK, I have some understanding of this inside/outside binary. This way of thinking about embodied skill was challenged when studying Zen meditation in Seoul. I began attending Zen meditation classes for foreigners soon after I arrived in Seoul in 2000, while teaching voice training for actors at The Korean National University of Arts (KNUA), School of Drama (2000–2005). Part way through the meditation class, the class would break and take tea in an adjoining room where we could put questions to the monks in English, Danish and French about our experiences, an extension of the Dharma talk.[2] When we drank tea from our small cups, we were asked to be attentive to the journey of the tea as we drank it, to focus on the experience of drinking tea and not drink the tea thoughtlessly.

In my "beginner's mind," this meant increased sense of awareness of how I drank tea, the temperature of the tea, the flavor, the texture of the cup at my lip, the action of my tongue and throat as I swallowed, and the warm feeling as it traveled down inside my body to places I could not touch with my hands but could feel inside. At that time, I focused on how the tea journeyed from outside of me to inside of me. Zen Master Seung Sahn in dialogue with his students (recorded and compiled by Stephen Mitchell) instructed: "Where is inside? Where is outside?" The student answered: "Inside is in here; outside is out there". Seung Sahn replied: "How can you separate? Where is the boundary line?" The student answered: "I'm inside my skin, and the world is outside it". Then Seung Sahn said: "This is your body's skin. Where is your mind's skin? [...] Don't make inside or outside" (1976, 19–20).

I took this lesson from my meditation practice and brought it into my voice classrooms at KNUA. How might I help my students understand a spectrum of ways of perceiving touch beyond the binaries of inside/outside, good/bad, right/wrong that I found so problematic? The use of touch as "directing awareness" satisfies the need to find technique in the body, how to direct one's awareness to the muscles so that their behavior can be observed, felt and changed, if necessary. This kind of "awareness" of how the muscles work anatomically and physiologically is different from how I have experienced ki as awareness in Asian modes of training. Integrating adaptations of Alexander's "directing awareness" from voice training with my own training in meditation practices made it possible to knit together ways of shifting awareness through the use of ki cultivation. Understanding ki as awareness opened up possibilities of the use of touch as well.

Breathing and being breathed

I started by adapting a traditional exercise from Cicely Berry's practice my students already knew – the first exercise from her first book (1973, 23). Berry instructed:

> Lie on the floor on your back with your buttocks flat. Feel the back as spread as possible. Crook your knees up a little apart, aware of them pointing to the ceiling. This should help to get your back flat. Do not push it down by tensing, however, just get it as flat as you can. Try to be aware of your back spreading over the floor, and not sinking down into it. Let it spread. Let the shoulders spread, try to feel the shoulder joints easing out, and not cramped in. It helps if you allow the elbows to fall away from the body, with the wrists inwards […]. Now think of your back lengthening along the floor---become aware of your spine and try to feel each vertebra slightly easing away from the other. Feel this right to the base of the spine--- to the tail in fact. Allow the head to lengthen out of the back.
> (1973, 23)

The teaching language in Berry's exercise is similar to Alexander's "orders," asking the student to feel the back spread, the spine lengthen, etc. Also notice her use of the teaching word "aware". She asks the student to "feel" and become "aware" of certain sensations. Here, touch, such as how the back touches the floor and/or the feeling of the back spreading along the floor, is used in order to increase the student's kinesthetic awareness of the experience of her body's function, in this instance spinal alignment. Touch, and the awareness it brings, is an external, outward experience brought into the internal reasoning "self" of the student.

In order to move the students' awareness from their observing mind on an object-body to sensing ki within the body, I ask the student to become attentive to her back. First, I ask her to focus on her experience of her back as it rests on the floor. She may notice the messages that touch delivers from her back touching the floor. She might notice the temperature or the hardness of the floor against her back. She might feel uncomfortable and need to shift to make herself comfortable. Next, I ask her to become aware of her back by "breathing into her back". She may notice the back of her ribs spread along the floor as she breathes. So far, her observing mind has reflected on the anatomy and physiology of her body as an object. Next, I ask the student to continue to breathe, increasing her awareness of *how* she is breathing. This exercise takes a long time. The more she breathes, the more she is likely to notice her breath. At some point during the length of this process, she may get bored and her mind may start to wander or she may "zone out". But I keep asking her to stay aware of the breath.

Actor/trainer Jeungsook Yoo, who integrates her meditative practice with her acting practice, points out that the request to focus on the action helps to give the mind something to do and keep it from wandering. In her case, when asked by a director or trainer to put her awareness "in the soles of your feet" or in "the center of your palms," she directed her awareness to that part of the body and observed it. She wrote: "In both cases, these instructions provided a specific aim for concentration so that the practitioner's mind does not need to wander. It knows where to go. Therefore, the awareness functions as a magnifier to gather the concentrated mind" (2018, 71). By instructing my student to stay aware of her breath or her back on the floor, her observing mind has something to do. But the student must stay with this task. She must (re)commit to this action each time it happens – to commit to being attentive and not allowing the mind to wander.

This description of attentive awareness could also apply to a characterization of Alexander's "orders" – how a student learns to become consciously aware of parts of her body by being attentive to its movement. In Alexander's training model, the observing mind consciously controls the physical matter of the body. So too, for Yoo: "I directed my awareness to the part of my body and observed it [...] awareness was perceived as a mental activity" (2018, 71). At this point, interweaving meditative practice and "directing awareness" is possible because they seem to share a similar beginning. Also, through repetition over a period of time, the student is giving her body the opportunity to teach itself how to breathe in this position – how to breathe "efficiently" under these conditions. Efficient muscular use is a value shared by Alexander practice, its adaptation into Anglo-American voice training and my experience with meditation: breathing should not be effortful.

At this point, there is a "temporal gap" (Yoo, 2018, 71) between the observing mind and the act of cultivating ki as awareness while becoming immersed in the act of breathing. This is where the different practices begin to diverge. Yoo wrote:

> As I repeated the exercise, the gap disappeared. Once I put my awareness on the centre of my palms, it senses that the awareness is touching it as a form of ki, and I sense the ki of the centre of my palms. The awareness as a magnifier itself is experienced as a ki. As a result, awareness comes to have a double meaning: both a 'mental' function and ki. This magnifier can be located depending on our intention, and therefore we can send ki to a specific place.
>
> (2018, 71)

For Yoo, this discovery in her training led her to conclude:

> It shows how awareness, more than other states of mind, can be shaped. We can modulate its direction, location, size and it is immediately accompanied by ki, which contain information about other states of mind. In this way, awareness is an initial method to build the route in space for moving ki.
>
> (2018, 71)

In Alexander's training model, the observing mind consciously controls the physical matter of the body. Although Alexander characterized his training as "psycho-physical" and insisted on a non-separation of "'mental' and 'physical' operations (manifestations) [...] of the functioning of the human organism" (1924, 29–30), this is not the same as a symbiotic relationship between mind and body. The premise of "re-education" belies the assumption that mind and body are ontologically separate and points to the way in which mind and body have been traditionally understood in the West as dualistic.

Within Yoo's conceptual model of training "mind" through body, she develops ki so that wherever mind goes, ki follows. This understanding of "mind" is different from Alexander's conscious-controlled behavior (McAllister-Viel, 2007, 105). Conscious bodily movement is a key difference between Eastern and Western practices (Yuasa, 1993, 28). In Western practice, like Alexander's process of "re-education," the "mind that is subject dominates and moves the body that is object," but in Eastern "body-mind oneness" there is no longer a felt distinction between "the mind qua subject and the body qua object" (Ibid.). A level of body/mind integration is assumed at the beginning of training. The function of training then is not to create a body/mind relationship, but instead to train towards further levels of integration (Kasulis and Dissanayake, 1993, 303; Sellers-Young, 1998, 177).

While the student continues to breathe, I ask her to imagine that the floor is an extension of her ribcage; the floor is not "outside". She is breathing the room. As Yoo points out, there may be a temporal gap between the observing mind and the act of cultivating ki as awareness while becoming immersed in the act of breathing. Through attentive repetition, the student can slowly release her observing mind and, in the act of breathing, release the feeling of the floor beneath her, the weight of her body, noticing how the ribcage rises and falls. She can begin to soften her focus. She is working towards a feeling of *being breathed*. She is working towards the deeper levels of bodymind integration and ki cultivation. Sometimes a student reports after the exercise feeling very warm on a floor that was previously cold against her back, or feeling like she is light and floating when previously she noticed the heaviness of the weight of her body on the floor. Her experience of touch and feeling is changing, not through touching her muscles and observing their behavior but through bodymind immersion of a task.

Forming "one" body

The benefit of thinking about touch departing from the binary of outside/inside is that the student moves from objectifying her body and its experience. Her "self" is not a psychological, internalized place in binary opposition to her outside material body. This act of attentiveness is a kind of "extra-daily" training. The daily acts of drinking tea or laying on her back breathing extend beyond the daily experience of those acts when the student is trained to focus her attention on the immediacy of the experience, the moment-by-moment ever-becoming action. The student is asked to remain present in the *here and now* of the experience. It is difficult for the learner to remain in the moment because there are distractions, mind wanders or the student "zones out" and becomes inattentive. She must work towards softening the hard line between perceiving her "self" apart from her environment (inside/outside) and instead expand her awareness. As Yoo noted, "the concept of awareness [is] enlarged" (2018, 71).

Students can then work towards "forming one body" (Leder, 1990, 156). Effortful action gives way to an overall feeling of effortlessness – being breathed as much as she is breathing. Leder characterized the process in this way:

> Physiologically, respiration stands at the very threshold of the ecstatic and visceral, the voluntary and involuntary. While we can modulate our breathing at will, it is primarily an automatic function […]. Watching breath come in and go out for minutes or hours, one is saturated by the presence of a natural power that outruns the "I". Breathing simply happens and happens and happens. There is no need for willful management; all is accomplished without effort on one's part.
>
> (1990, 171)

The doer of the action and the action merge into one. Leder wrote, using his understanding of Wang Yang-ming:

> We form one body with all things not simply because we share the same ch'i [ki]; we also do so by way of an expansive awareness through which we incorporate the surrounding world […]. As subject, I do not inhabit a private theatre of consciousness but am ecstatically intertwined, one body with the world [….] interconnectedness is innate.
>
> (1990, 158–159)

Forming one body emerges from an already present sense of oneness with the world, and is "evidenced by the human propensity for compassionate identification […]. Our consanguineous relation with all things finds expression in intuitive empathy" (Leder, 1990, 159). This kind of empathy and the way in which to deepen connection is different from McCallion's understanding of empathy as an "inside" versus "outside" training (e.g. mimicry). McCallion wrote:

> The interesting thing about the process of empathy, as distinct from mimicry, is that although you are working initially from your perception of externals, of how the body moves, how the voice sounds and so on, the straight imitation of these externals is only a means to achieving some interior knowledge of who the subject is; you have to feel at

the end of the process that you know how to behave as the subject in all circumstances. This may not *be* so; but the character must *feel* that complete to you.

(1988, 188, original emphasis)

Mimicry is discouraged and is characterized as an external action, an outward appearance. Empathy is characterized as an internalized understanding, or psychological motivation, that triggers emotional response. But how does the student bridge the distance between "working initially from your perception of externals" to "*feel* at the end of the process that you know how to behave as the subject?" "Forming one body," as I have experienced it, can help students build that bridge in part because it moves the student away from "inside" and "outside" to become "ecstatically intertwined" with the world.

Placing Anglo-American prominent contemporary voice training on a continuum of training with meditative practices is one way in which different trainings from different world views might interact in the voice studio. Touch and feeling move from observing the body as object towards blurring the distinction between "outside" and "inside". The feeling of "myself" breathing gives way to "being breathed" – outrunning the "I" of ego-identification. The feeling of empathy with others "forms one body," leading to a feeling of connectedness in studio training that can become a template for "connectedness" with an audience during performance. "Awareness" magnifies the experience of experiencing and "is the initial method to build the route in space for moving ki" (Yoo, 2018, 71) not only within the student-actor but between the actors and the audience during performance. Ki is a tactile, felt experience between actor and audience, and at the highest level forms one body between performer and spectator.

(Re)visiting touch

When training actors' voices through adaptations of Alexander's "re-education," the body of the student is understood through a Western biomedical model and is touched on the outside in order to feel how the muscles contract and release. This physiology is understood as the same or similar to all learners because the material of the body is understood as the same or similar in all learners. The student learns to release muscular contraction through the information touch brings. The muscle is taught the feeling of "release" through the observing mind.

The use of touch in "re-education" is a corrective model of experience. The student is asked to notice an "incorrect" or inefficient muscular use, or "habit," and replace that behavior with more efficient muscular use or better "habit". Because the student is advised not to trust themselves to decide if muscular contraction is "natural" or "habitual," or in short, good or bad muscular usage, the power to interpret experience lays with the teacher as a guide. This power dynamic can curtail a student's agency and undermine her confidence.

The advantages of touch in this approach are many, not the least of which is Maisel's observation that verbal instruction is like sending a kiss by messenger,

> [t]he experience he [Alexander] sought to impart was one which by its very nature eludes utterance [...]. How do you convey a new feeling, a new pattern of physical sensation, to a man [sic] who has never known it?
> (1969, xxvii)

For Alexander, touch was a technique that helped him solve this problem and for some of my students in studio the method of laying hands on their own body, or having others lay hands on them in this way is unproblematic. But for those students and teachers who want to use touch "in a generative exercise which explores how the performer with agency can employ touch to release their own, very unique creativity, association and voice" (Behrens, 2019), adapting traditional methods embedded within popular voice training is necessary. What is offered here is a small contribution to an ever-growing body of work by voice trainers seeking to address diverse populations in their classrooms.

Notes

1 Maisel insists that "[t]he Alexandrians reject all forms of physical manipulation [...] likewise reject corrective exercise as a path to good use of the self" (1969, xxvi).
2 The "dharma talk" at Hwa Gye Sa sits within the tradition of Korean Seon (zen) which is an interpretation of Buddhism distinct from the meditation traditions of Japanese Zen or Chinese Ch'an. Part of a beginner's meditation practice includes instruction through a question/answer format. For the beginner, this is intended to strengthen her "sensation of doubt" which "is the indispensable core of hua-t'ou meditation through hearing an exposition of the enlightened man's understanding" (Ku San, 1978, 3). Ku San wrote that if the dharma talk is not understood with this purpose in mind, "it will be easy to dismiss these discourses as paradoxical or incoherent nonsense, rather than seeing them for what they are in reality – advanced meditation directions" (Ibid.).

References

Alexander, F. M. ([1910] 1918) *Man's Supreme Inheritance*. London: Chaterson.
—— (1924) *Constructive Conscious Control of the Individual*. London: Methuen & Co, LTD.
—— ([1969] 1974) *The Alexander Technique: The essential Writings of F. Matthias Alexander*. Edited by Edward Maisel. London: Thames and Hudson.
Behrens, E. (2019) *Use of Touch* [email]. Sent to Tara McAllister-Viel, February 14.
Berry, C. (1973) *Voice and the Actor*. New York: Collier Books.
—— (1992) *The Actor and the Text*. New York: Applause Books.

Brown, S. (2000) The cultural voice. *The Voice and Speech Review: Standard Speech*, 1 17–18.

——— (2001) The cultural voice: an interview with Danny Hoch. *The Voice and Speech Review: The Voice in Violence*, 2 124–128.

Burke, K. (1997) On training and pluralism. In: Marion Hampton and Barbara Acker (eds.) *The Vocal Vision: Views on Voice*. New York: Applause Books, 57–62.

Carey, D. and Clark Carey, R. (2008) *Vocal Arts Workbook and DVD*. London: Methuen.

——— (2010) *The Verbal Arts Workbook*. London: Methuen.

Espinosa, M. (2019) *Use of Touch* [email]. Sent to Tara McAllister-Viel, February 26.

Espinosa, M. and Ocampo-Guzman, A. (2010) Identity politics and the training of Latino actors. In: Ellen Margolis and Lisa Tyler Renaud (eds.) *The Politics of American Actor Training*. New York and London: Routledge, 150–161.

Ginther, A. (2015) Dysconscious racism in mainstream British voice pedagogy and its potential effects on students from pluralistic backgrounds in UK Drama Conservatories. *Voice and Speech Review*, 9(1) 41–60.

Kasulis, T., Ames, R. and Dissanayake, W. (eds.) (1993) *Self as Body in Asian Theory and Practice*. Albany: SUNY Press.

Klemp, S., Ginther, A., Battles, J. and Shane, L. (2015) We've only just begun: reflections and insights 'Giving Voice to International Students' roundtable from the 2013 VASTA conference in Minneapolis. *Voice and Speech Review*, 9(1) 82–90.

Ku San. (1978) *Nine Mountains: Dharma-lectures of the Korean Meditation Master Ku San. Song Swang Sa Monastery*. Chogye Chonglim (Republic of Korea): International meditation Center.

Leder, D. (1990) *The Absent Body*. Chicago, IL and London: The University of Chicago Press.

Linklater, K. (1976) *Freeing the Natural Voice*. New York: Drama Book Publishers.

——— (2003) *Teaching Voice* [video]. Devon: Arts Archives.

——— (2006) *Freeing the Natural Voice: Imagery and Art in the Practice of Voice and Language*. London: Nick Hern.

——— (2016) The art and craft of voice (and speech) training. *Journal of Interdisciplinary Voice Studies*, 1(1) 57–70.

Maisel, E. (ed.) (1969) *The Alexander Technique: The Essential Writings of F. Matthias Alexander*. London: Thames and Hudson.

McAllister-Viel, T. (2007) Casting perceptions: the performance of the gendered voice as career strategy. *Voice and Speech Review*, 5(1) 216–223.

——— (2019) *Training Actors' Voices: Towards an Intercultural/Interdisciplinary Approach*. London: Routledge.

McCallion, M. (1988) *The Voice Book*. London: Faber and Faber.

Rodenburg, P. (1992) *The Right to Speak*. New York: Routledge.

——— (1993) *The Need for Words*. London: Methuen.

——— (1994) *A Voice of Your Own* [video]. New York: Applause Books.

Sahn, S. (1976) *Dropping Ashes on the Buddha*. Compiled and edited by Stephen Mitchell. Cumberland: The Providence Zen Center, Inc.

Sellers-Young, B. (1998) Somatic processes: convergence of theory and practice. *Theatre Topics*, 9(2) 183–187.

Yoo, J. (2018) *A Korean Approach to Actor Training*. London: Routledge.

Yuasa, Y. (1993) *The Body, Self-Cultivation and Ki-Energy*. Translated by Shigenori Nagatomo and Monte S. Hull. Albany: SUNY Press.

Zarrilli, P. (2004) Towards a phenomenological model of the actor's embodied modes of experience. *Theatre Journal*, 56(4) 653–666.

—— (2016) "Inner movement" between practices of meditation, martial arts, and acting: a focused examination of affect, feeling, sensing, and sensory attunement. In: Michael Bull and Jon P. Mitchell (eds.) *Ritual, Performance and the Senses*. London: Bloomsbury Academics, 121–136.

10 Organic voice

Vocal integration through actor training

Christina Gutekunst

Psycho-physical techniques like deep breathing, relaxation and body work are widely employed by vocal coaches when teaching how to train and improve vocal ability. The so-called somatic practices like the Alexander Technique (AT), Yoga and T'ai Chi are also employed in actor training with the aim of engaging an actor's physical, mental or emotional expression and freeing body and breath through various points of attention. For instance, AT primarily aims at improving alignment and vocal habits by altering the reaction of the individual to the stimuli of the environment, while Yoga and T'ai Chi focus on the energy and flow of the breath. Somatic and psycho-physical techniques can stimulate imagination and are working with impulse to support emotional responses through breath and voice. They have influenced the work of pioneers in voice training such as Kristin Linklater (2006) and Cicely Berry (1997).

In my experience as a voice and voice-into acting trainer at East 15 Acting School in London, where I am the Head of Voice (Loughton campus), a problem of integration arises when these techniques – however beneficial in themselves – are employed in isolation from the actual acting process. As a result, students can find it difficult to apply these practices in rehearsal or performance. This is significant not only for acting but for *how* one needs to study voice as a diverse and broader field of work. Whether when acting or looking at a wider spectrum (e.g. doing presentations, giving a speech or even learning a new language), responding *organically* out of the experience of the present moment's stimuli *specific to each context* is the key for complete vocal integration.

When it comes to acting, vocal integration arises for each actor when they manage to challenge any possible problematic gap between their experience and the play text or script. The challenge is that the words are not *our own*. This chapter is a small sample of how a *vocal organic response* – my contemporary modification of traditional Stanislavskian techniques for voice – can bridge *the gap* between the actor and the text. To this end, I do not look particularly at how I apply specific somatic practices in my voice work but on how breath (the basis of both psycho-physical and somatic approaches) can become the crucial link to the *imaginary, sensory* and *spatial experience* of any specific context, while offering the energy for the vocal communication of the actor's impulses and psycho-physical actions.[1]

Drawing from the fundamental theoretical and practical components of my work, I argue that we need to allow our voice to be more than a *mere technical tool* that runs in *parallel* to the acting performance or the delivery of a speech and to tap into its full communicating potential instead. To do so, I propose that we would need to *skillfully* respond to each context rather than objectifying and distancing ourselves from what is said. Subsequently, my perspective suggests that drama schools could encourage further interaction between skill classes and the acting process instead of keeping them as separate units.

The actor's *intellectual* and *creative* mind: theoretical inspirations for vocal integration

I perceive the gap between the actor and the text as a conflict between the individual's *intellectual* and *creative* mind when processing an author's written language. For this understanding, I have been inspired by the ideas of the psychiatrist and scholar Iain McGilchrist in his book *The Master and his Emissary – The Divided Brain and the Making of the Modern World* (2010). McGilchrist explains how the two hemispheres of the brain may look symmetrical but are different. He refers to an actual physical barrier, the corpus callosum, which simultaneously keeps the two hemispheres independent but also, paradoxically, acts as a bridge between them so that information can be transferred from the one to the other (McGilchrist, 2010, 210–213). Therefore, it is crucial to understand that the left and right brain hemispheres do distinctive but complementary tasks; *what language says* is processed in the left hemisphere and *how language is said* involves the right hemisphere. In order to allow *integrated vocal response*, we would need as well an integration of this brain activity.

For the theoretical understanding of vocal integration, I have been additionally inspired by the popular perspectives of the neurologist Antonio Damasio (2000). Damasio's ideas help me support that an actor's mind and body are placed firmly within oneself as a unified whole, affecting each other in a constantly changing way as they interact with the world. He asserts that

> a mind, that defines a person requires a body, and that body [...] naturally generates one mind. A mind is so closely shaped by the body and destined to serve it that only one mind could possibly arise in it. No body, never mind.
>
> (Damasio, 2000, 143)

Moreover, complementing McGilchrist's take on the brain function, Damasio notes that consciousness and self are not an "all-knowing little person" sitting in the brain (2000, 190). In other words, one's brain is not the locus of the individual's mind (in the broader sense of the word) while both are not dualistically separated by each body. Thus, vocal integration additionally requires the significant awareness of one's individuality. It is crucial for voice tutors to understand that each actor's self and identity lead to unique responses to the given text and circumstances – no actor's response to the same circumstances will be alike.

The *organic* versus the *representational* vocal response in actor training

Based on the above, the main question that arises in actor-training pedagogies is "How can we support actors find their uniquely creative responses?" To this end, we would first need to answer the question "What is the voice responding to?"; an intellectual mode that *represents* a premeditated vocal pattern; or a creative mode – a rich, sensory, present and inspired vocal response – that arises out of direct experience with the context? I identify the latter, a state that allows actors not to intellectualize *how* words are said while performing, an *organic* vocal response.

An organic approach to voice work in acting has its roots in the actor-training process first established by the Russian theatre practitioner Konstantin Stanislavski (1863–1938) and further developed by his student Michael Chekhov (1891–1955).[2] Stanislavski understood the reasonable gap that occurs between the actor and the text resulting into an intellectual response, as a phenomenon that comes up because of the fact that the author's words are, at least in the first place, something separate from us. He says:

> [O]ur own words are the direct expression of our feelings, whereas the words of another are alien until we have made them our own, are nothing more than signs of future emotions which have not yet come to life inside us.
> (Stanislavski, 2013, 84)

The integrated activity outlined in the previous part enables the actor to respond through the words as if they are an organic and inevitable outcome of their own experience of the given circumstances.

If we decide predominantly intellectually how a script should be delivered, the intellectual brain describes the world of the script sealing language as a self-sufficient entity. In this case, the representation of the form becomes the prime focus: the voice externally describes and represents structure, rhythm, sounds, figures of speech, images and literal meaning. According to Stanislavski's criticism, "[t]he [representational] actor does not live, he plays. He remains cold toward the object of his acting" (2008, 26). In this representational experience, the vocal response is expressed through technical and intellectually-controlled tools such as appropriate articulation, phrasing, intonation, accentuation and pitch range. This technical focus can often result in early speech patterns, vocal mannerisms and "faked" emotions – prompting the vocal response into a *representational* result rather than a spontaneous and *organic* response to psycho-physical acting impulses.

The organic as opposed to the representational vocal response, along with the rest of the theoretical ideas discussed in this first part of the chapter, will now be seen directly through the actor-training practice and, more specifically, four Stanislavskian acting elements: the elements will be approached through somatic and psycho-physical principles in the organic voice approach, followed by exercises for the reader to explore how to work towards vocal integration.[3] I see the dynamic interaction between somatic and psycho-physical principles in the acting process in the same way I theoretically perceive the actor's vocal integration. The somatic to me represents the physical (the body) while the psycho-physical brings forth all the connections between mind (psyche), body (soma), voice and acting impulses. Try to keep this interaction in mind while exploring your organic voice in the following sections.

Ease and focus: somatic and psycho-physical principles in the organic voice approach

> There can be no question of true subtle feeling or of the normal psychological life of a role while tension is present.
> (Stanislavski, 2008, 121)

The state of released muscular activity enables not only sustained focus but also psycho-physical responsiveness to vocal and acting impulses. The ground for this responsiveness is a deep somatic breath which carries the voice and the words while informing the action that is communicated. In doing so, creative impulses can be connected to our deepest experiences, heighten our senses and lead to the most present vocal expression. What is important here is that the mind-body-breath interaction is in a *receiving-creative* mode rather than in a *disconnected-intellectual* mode that focuses on expected results.

The principles:

Balanced alignment: The somatic principle of aligning all the components of the bone and muscular structure to achieve balance, stability and ease in the most efficient way creates the basis for the psycho-physical principles of our work. Optimum alignment uses a minimum of muscular activity to sustain itself. The somatic work on alignment enables creative communication between the mind and the body because the muscles are free to respond to creative impulses.

Rooted breath support: It is the somatic work on strengthening the core muscles of the pelvic floor, spine and abdominal muscles to create the optimum breath support. Rooted breath support offers the physical basis for the psychological impulse to find a direct connection to the muscular and vocal responses. This support should not become *mechanical* skill but the *root* for a voice that *reacts* to acting impulses with ease.

Centered onset of sound: This sound is initiated by somatic breath flowing with ease up to the closed vocal folds, creating air pressure and making them vibrate. It has to be voiced (not breathy), free of constrictions and unwanted noises. The psycho-physical principle is that the *centered sound* can support the expression of the speaker's identity as themselves or the character. It is the *me* of the vocal identity of the actor and asserts unique reactions to the circumstances.

How to explore ease and focus:

Stand with your feet parallel, hip width apart and check that your knees are unlocked. Try to release your tailbone downward and gently lift your spine by imagining a golden string pulling you up from the crown of your head towards the sky. This is how you can quickly find your balanced alignment adopting what can be described as a supported, neutral stance.

Now you can find your rooted breath support. To do so, you can imagine a balloon filling out your pelvis, your lower back and belly; allow your breath to drop into your pelvic floor, into your back and all around this middle area of your body. The breath balloon is an image that can help you locate where the breath should go and find a sensation for what it feels like when you use your full-breath capacity. Follow your natural impulse to breathe.

In order to start finding the connection with the centered onset of your sound and open your vocal channel, lift your soft palate through a yawn and place a smile in the back of your throat. Shape a silent "aw" sound and try to breathe through this into your deep core breath balloon.

Say "this is me" to further connect with your centered onset of sound. The centered onset of sound needs to have sharp precision.

The magic *if*: somatic and psycho-physical principles in the organic voice approach

> Real acting begins [...] when there is no character as yet, but an "I" in the hypothetical circumstances. If that is not the case, you lose contact with yourself, you see the role from the outside, you copy it.
>
> (Toporkov, 2001, 110)

Organic voice 135

The significance of imagery and the engagement of an actor's imagination towards organic vocal expression became already present in the previous part with the use of the image of the breath balloon. Moreover, when it comes to character work, one of Stanislavski's quintessential components is that the actor is asked to place themselves into the imaginary circumstances *as if* they were real. You can ask yourself: "What would I do if I were in theses circumstance?" He called this process the *magic if*, because of its far-reaching creative effect on the actor's inner-outer life connection through imagination and expressed actions. If actors do not use such a connection relating to their own human experience, observation and imagination, they will be "locked" into a purely intellectual processing of the circumstances which leads into representational vocal responses.

The principles:

The creative connector: The somatically-rooted breath outlined earlier becomes the psycho-physical *creative connector* between an actor's imagination and their organic vocal expression.

The sensory experience: Highlighting the psycho-physical interconnection between breath-images-voice-words moment by moment, the actor can "plant" in the space imaginary focus points. In response to these focus points, the actor creates sensory experience.

How to explore the magic if:

Taken from a more classical context, imagine your text would be: "There is a storm brewing". Try to respond to these circumstances as if they were real through your immediate experience. Ask yourself: "If I am in this situation what am I seeing, experiencing, doing – how do I respond?"

What can give rise to these words organically for you? How can you find them out of your experience as if they were real? I suggest you try and create images such as the dark foreboding night sky, the flashes of lightning, the claps of thunder, the wind bending the trees and the arrival of torrential rain. Place the images into the space around you so that they create different focus points.

Receive and breathe in the images. Notice the sensory experiences that come up for you and can give rise to the words. Speak the words from your deep breath balloon and centered onset of sound out of the specific sensations in response.

The important element here is that you should not imagine the circumstances inside your head but surround yourself with them as if you were encountering the world of the storm. This way you can breathe in spatially and sensually what the circumstances are as well as support your vocal ability to fill the space.

Be careful not to premeditate the response but to find the immediate response out of your present-moment experience. The voice needs to respond with skill rather than demonstrate skill. The desired outcome will be responding to impulses with detail, color and variation, while vibrating the experience.

Communication: somatic and psycho-physical principles in the organic voice approach

> Acting is action. The basis of theatre is doing, dynamism.
> (Stanislavski, 2008, 40)

Once placed in the circumstances, we need to *interact* with other people, creating a dynamic and spontaneous responsiveness to achieve real communication in performance. The opposite would be to have worked out how to say the lines in a particular way without really listening or reacting to others. Out of this dynamic interaction comes what the character wants to achieve in the situation, the narrative and the actor's vocal response.

The principles:

Breathing in the other person: This somatic and psycho-physical principle sets the tone for a dynamic interaction not only with the other person's presence but also with the experienced circumstances or problem the other person presents.

Breathing in the impulse: Adding to the above, the actor should be open to breathe in and speak on the impulse that arises from an immediate rather than a premeditated response.

In both cases, communication is achieved while the inbreath receives and the outbreath transmits.

How to explore communication:

With all the somatic and psycho-physical principles explained up to now in place, explore the following vocal responses with a partner. In the beginning, you can be A and your partner could be B. Then feel free to switch.

With your attention focused on your partner, use your breath in order to create a bridge between you and the other person on a both sensual and spatial level. Try to take in your partner through your present experience and the response of your senses. At the same time, attune to your spatial awareness through your breath by sensing the distance between you and the other person. When ready, use your breath to aim and connect your vocal response to your partner. Seek attention from each other through the following text:

A: You!
B: Me?

A: Yes, you!
B: Me!

Make sure that you find your own vocal action and reaction through the words. Now you can try to experience and breathe in together the circumstances of the brewing storm, given in the exercise of the previous part. You can heighten the stakes by adding that one of you has a lover riding in the forest who might be in danger. Connect again with your voice by breathing in the other person and the circumstances. Find the organic experience of the words while interacting and responding to each other. Explore the following text:

A: A storm is brewing!
B: Is Sebastian still out there?
A: Yes! We need to search for him!

The objective: integrating the principles in the organic voice approach

> […] the nature of theatre […] is entirely based on the relationships among the characters and of individuals with themselves.
> (Stanislavski, 2008, 232)

Out of the circumstances arises a *problem* for the character. A whole chain of objectives – wants, aims, needs, intentions or tasks – drive us through the imaginary life of the play. The objectives are pursued through *actions* – psychological, physical and verbal or silent. Nonetheless, the choice of actions and how the problem will appear to be solved would depend on each actor's individuality. Understanding that diverse individuals respond differently to given circumstances would also further encourage organic vocal response.

The principle:

Breathing in the individual: Summarizing as well as integrating all the previous somatic and psycho-physical principles towards organic voice, breath becomes the *specific* energy that combines all the elements of the individual actor and communicates *active* words through the ability of their voice.

How to explore the actor's objective:

Taking the previous exploration further, we now play with psychological actions within the imaginary objective of "I want to help my friend".

Working again with a partner, decide who is A and B. Both partners would need to breathe in the problem and breathe out the psychological action in their lines. As a reminder, the suggested text is:

A: A storm is brewing!
B: Is Sebastian still out there?
A: Yes! We need to search for him!

Breathing in your individualities and present communication, try to find five different actions to respond and interact with each other. For instance, for the line "Yes! We need to search for him!" the psychological actions could be "I instruct you," "I warn you," "I implore you," "I rush you," "I affirm and galvanize you".

Keep your rooted breath support and centered onset of sound under every syllable. Focus on affecting and changing the other person by using your breath and making the words active. Having a varied range of actions at your disposal as you are driven by an objective, can help you create an integrative and organic vocal response rather than intellectually over-controlling the expression of the words.

Returning to the question "what is the voice responding to?"

Let's conclude this brief organic voice practice by imagining sunshine and sense it as if it was real.

Breathe in the sensation of warmth, light, pleasure and relaxation into your deep breath and let it fill your whole body. Sound out a voiced sigh in response. Find the vocal response and reaction to the sensation by saying the word "sunshine". Let the vowels express the experience that comes directly out of your senses and through the word.

Now find the centered onset of your sound in your pelvic floor and spine. Say "sunshine," finding and asserting your unique response.

Respond only through the vowels of the word. Do this several times. Then say the word again and let yourself respond through different pitches. Make sure that this is not an external decision but comes spontaneously out of your experience.

Try to allow yourself to discover the word out of the generated sensation. The general cycle is:

- *the word "sunshine" offers you an impulse*
- *breathe in the word through its sensation*
- *allow "sunshine" to become an active word through your rooted breath support*

Returning now to the question "What is the voice responding to?" it may be evident that in this organic approach, we encourage voice to respond to multiple and simultaneous impulses: thoughts, senses, feelings, imagination, will. It is an ongoing investigation which remains the key towards *vocal organic response* that can bridge *the gap* between the actor and the text within training as well as during the performance process. Such an approach to voice that supports the expression of language in both form and content while communicating circumstances of human experience can help the actor and, furthermore, the speaker to express themselves through active words. Therefore, it may be practised here in relation to the acting experience, but it can also be easily seen in relation to the needs of each speaker's creative expression.

Notes

1. For a detailed step-by-step guide to how every element of voice can be integrated with the organic acting approach, see Gutekunst and Gillett (2014).
2. For a detailed analysis of how I make Stanislavski's practice the foundation of my work with voice, along with the influence of Michael Chekhov's technique and of other practitioners related to the field of somatics such as Rudolf Steiner (1861–1925) and Rudolf Laban (1879–1958), please refer to Part Three of my book (Gutekunst and Gillett, 2014, 169–291).
3. Please note that a detailed description of the practice goes beyond the scope of this chapter and the objective is a brief practical exploration of the ideas outlined in the first part of this discussion.

References

Berry, C. (1997) That secret voice. In: Marion Hampton and Barbara Acker (eds.) *The Vocal Vision: Views on Voice*. London: Applause, 25–36.

Chekhov, M. (1953) *To the Actor: On the Technique of Acting*. New York: Harper and Row.

Damasio, A. (2000) *The Feeing of what Happens: Body, Emotion and the Making of Consciousness*. London: Vintage Books.

Gutekunst, C. and Gillett, J. (2014) *Voice into Acting: Integrating Voice and the Stanislavski Approach*. London: Bloomsbury.

Linklater, K. (2006) *Freeing the Natural Voice: Imagery and Art in the Practice of Voice and Language*. London: Nick Hern Books.

McGilchrist, I. (2010) *The Master and his Emissary: The Divided Brain and the Making of the Modern World*. New Haven and London: Yale University Press.

Stanislavski, C. (2013) *Creating a Role*. Translated by Elizabeth Reynolds Hapgood. London: Bloomsbury.

Stanislavski, K. (2008) *An Actor's Work*. Translated by Jean Benedetti. Oxon: Routledge.

Toporkov, V. (2001) *Stanislavski in Rehearsal*. Translated by Jean Benedetti. London: Bloomsbury.

11 Dreaming voice
A dialogue

Ilona Krawczyk and Ben Spatz

The context for this co-authored chapter includes the authors' distinct but related experiences with post-Grotowskian theatre companies in Poland, our current relationship as PhD researcher (Ilona Krawczyk) and supervisor (Ben Spatz) and our mutual interest in voice and movement as practitioner-researchers. To accommodate this diversity of perspectives, the essay is structured as a dialogue, allowing us each to draw out what matters to us individually. The first and third sections are written by Ilona Krawczyk, introducing Arnold Mindell's processwork and the notions of *dreambody* and *dreamvoice*, and tracing them through a series of case studies from her Practice as Research (PaR). The second and fourth sections are written by Ben Spatz, reflecting on the place of somatics in the post-Grotowskian traditions and exploring the inextricability of technique and identity in even the smallest kernels of voice.

Dreambody, dreamvoice (Ilona Kraczyk)

A heightened state of sensory attention is one of the key aims of training and performance practice within post-Grotowskian theatre companies, which attempt to achieve what Grotowski called "freedom from the time-lapse between inner impulse and outer reaction in such a way that the impulse is already an outer reaction" (Grotowski, 1982, 16).[1] Taking as an example the Coordination Technique (CT) developed and taught by the Song of the Goat Theatre, the intention of such training is to release a performer from self-censorship and inner resistance, allowing them to focus on picking up incoming sensory impulses and "establishing relationships with oneself and others, by staying in the present, tuning-in, listening and reacting within exercises, improvisations and text" (Dowling, 2011, 245). "Tuning in" to the details of moment-to-moment experience is in this context most often achieved through physically demanding improvisational work, which later extends to include text and singing. Nevertheless, in the moment of expressing voice, whether through text or song, some resistance often appears, creating a "time-lapse" between impulse and expression. This disruption of "flow" (Csikszentmihalyi, 2002) in the moment when the voice is introduced has two distinct causes or aspects. One is related to the difference between movement and voicework in post-Grotowskian processes of creative devising. The other lies in the way performers in general perceive their own vocal expressivity. In the following paragraphs, I elaborate on these two aspects, drawing on my experience as a performer working with post-Grotowskian companies.

From 2011 to 2012, I trained with the Song of the Goat Theatre (Teatr Pieśń Kozła) as part of a Master's degree program at Manchester Metropolitan University.[2] In the process of generating material for performance, our work with movement began from traditional folk dances and other choreographies proposed by the directors, but the actual process of building up scenes was predominantly based on improvisation. The emphasis on improvised movement was aimed at developing intimate human connection within the ensemble and allowing spontaneity to emerge in moment-to-moment encounters, exposing the "inner life"[3] of the performers. The same human connection was sought in voicework, which emphasized listening and attuning to each other's intentions and reactions. Within training, this was often done through spontaneous group explorations of vibration, resonance, breath, range and harmony. However, when it came to devising material for performance, these spontaneous vocal expressions most often gave way to existing material constituted by the structure of texts and songs composed for the performed piece and/or borrowed from folk music. The performance was developed by finding the "line of life" within this pre-composed musical material and integrating it with movement material developed through improvisation. Thus, in this process, the main difference between movement and voicework manifested in the fact that, while physical and vocal training both made use of improvisation, the improvisation of movement continued into the generation of performance material, whereas the voice was first subjected to a musical or textual structure and only then to a search for the "line of life" in performance.[4]

The second aspect mentioned earlier – the performer's moment-to-moment perception of their own expression – relates to a more general difference in the way in which sensory feedback is received during physical and vocal practices. An exceptional feature of vocal expression is the immediate feedback received by the vocalizing person through the auditory system as well as that of felt vibration in the body. When voicing, auditory perception takes place simultaneously with expression. This process of sending and receiving circulates continuously, as long as sound is being made, creating a loop of mutual interdependence, which I call the *perception-expression loop* of voice. This concept is inspired by Jean Piaget's idea of reflexive action, defined as "a dynamic concept of circularity that brings together perception and action in a continuous process of sense-making and interaction with the environment" (Lesaffre et al, 2017, 63). The phenomenon of circularity has gained recognition in recent studies of music interaction and cognition (Leman, 2016; Lesaffre et al, 2017) as well as in the emerging area of interdisciplinary voice studies (Thomaidis and Macpherson, 2015). For example, Piersandra Di Matteo refers to the "unsettling experience of *listening to oneself*, recalling the perceptive chiasmus that places the voice at the same time inside and outside the subject" (2015, 92, original emphasis). My own conception of the loop of vocal perception-expression refers not only to the sensory interaction of a practitioner with the environment or world outside their body, but also to the loop of interaction with their own internal world – that is, moment-to-moment psychophysical processes, manifesting through what we call in this chapter *dreamvoice*.

The dreamvoice is an idea inspired by Arnold Mindell's notion of *dreambody* (1992). It refers to an empirical phenomenon that appears through unintentional expressions, such as an unexpected crack in the voice during spoken or sung performance. The dreamvoice may reveal a performer's perception of their own voice's quality and capabilities, arising out of their personal life experience and also linked to their cultural background. In my PaR training and performance practice on embodied voice, I have found that the integration of inner impulse and outer performance happens within and between what one intends to express and what one expresses unintentionally. Keeping in mind that this process is not static or singular but continuous and recurrent throughout a given session of training or performance, the perception of each sound necessarily influences those that follow through adjustments made by the performer – whether consciously or not – and through psychophysical reactions appearing in this process. These adjustments and reactions may create a time-lapse between impulse and expression, especially when a performer attempts to get rid of unintended sounds. In a process-oriented approach to voicework, unintentional expressions are not necessarily to be avoided. Instead of fighting them, a performer may choose to follow them, amplify them and transform them.

Process work (or "processwork") is another term for process-oriented psychology, which expands the Jungian concept of the unconscious and the methods of Gestalt psychology. Additionally, building upon Jungian dream analysis (see Mindell and Mindell, 1992, 1), picking up sensory signals and feedback from the outside world and from the body is an essential element of processwork. As Mindell states, "our job [as human beings] is to become aware of how we and others perceive things" (Ibid., 25). Bodily phenomena such as illness and pain, as well as unconscious movements and gestures, are understood to reveal the same kinds of messages from unconscious processes that are manifested in dreams. In other words, waking bodily "symptoms" are understood by Mindell as manifestations of the same process as that of dreaming while asleep. Within processwork, this is called the dreambody. "The dreambody is first a sensation and, then, finally, a message which appears in your body, in your dreams and in many other channels too" (1992, 29). The "channels" to which Mindell refers are different kinds of awareness: *proprioception, visualization, hearing, seeing, movement, relationships* and *world phenomena*.[5] Distinguishing these allows the practitioner to observe where their attention is directed. For example, when attention is turned to the action of singing or speaking, the hearing channel is "occupied". But if, while using their voice, a person makes a gesture or movement without being aware of it, this means that the movement channel is "unoccupied" in that moment. According to Mindell, an unoccupied channel is one that can reveal a *dreambody message*.

An important aspect of processwork is the transformation of *ego* into a *fair observer*. Ego is that which can observe what Mindell calls "primary" and "secondary" processes: that is, both I, me, doing what I want to do or was planning to do (primary processes) and distractions, internal and/or external events that arise and get in the way of what I want to do (secondary processes). When ego becomes a fair observer, there is no conflict between these two processes (Mindell, 1990, 19–21). In reference to the performer, this is the state of flow, or "no time-lapse" in moment-to-moment action. Returning to the example used before: in the moment when a performer breaks the flow of action while introducing voice to physical action, a change of channel from movement to hearing has occurred. In processwork, changing channels is conceptualized as an *edge*, with attention shifting between different modes of perception. The edge is a state, moment or place in which unconscious messages from the dreambody can break through into consciousness (Mindell and Mindell, 1992, 43–63). In improvisation or physically demanding training, moments of *I cannot do this anymore* or *I am bored* can then become opportunities to "change channels" or to "amplify the symptom," bringing to consciousness what the dreambody wants to communicate.

Although the aim of processwork is to improve a person's overall wellbeing, this is achieved by understanding the causes of existing tensions, resistances and symptoms rather than by trying to release or eradicate them, as the latter approach is understood to invite the recurrence of that same symptom in the future. Amy Mindell writes:

> Process work is based on the idea that processes contain their own inherent wisdom. Even the most intractable relationship problems or body experiences contain a great deal of meaning and wisdom, hidden within what otherwise might seem like intolerable events. In order to unfold the details of any particular experience, it is important to notice our everyday approach to experiences as well as the *dreamlike or unknown background* aspects of those events of which we are not quite aware. Only when all aspects of an experience are unfolded with awareness does the wisdom embedded in the experience reveal itself most fully.
> (2008, 214, original emphasis)

The "unknown background aspects" of events, manifesting through dreamvoice, are a central focus in the process-oriented approach to voicework developed within my research. Following processwork theory, it is not enough to train how not to do things, or how to do them in a "right" way. Indeed, I begin from the premise that there is no right or wrong expression. Every expression exposes the practitioner's moment-to-moment process through the dreamvoice. Until one understands the hidden causes behind an unintended expression, it may come back again and again, particularly in stressful moments. According to Mindell, focusing on disruptions, receiving them as expressions and even amplifying them can help to change our perception of the so-called "mistakes" and integrate their function into our identity. This involves letting unintentional sounds be understood and transformed in creative ways, changing one's approach from *it sounds right* or *it sounds wrong* to *what does it mean?* In the context of theatre, I propose that this shift of attention has potentially significant implications for training as well as for the dramaturgy of performance, when unintentional sounds can become the intentional focus of a compositional process.

Dreaming in post-Grotowskian practice (Ben Spatz)

I am interested in the progression Ilona traces, in the Song of the Goat's Coordination Technique and devising process, from dynamic improvised physical interaction to more structured work on text and song. What is it that makes this particular juxtaposition so compelling for me and for others working "after" Polish visionary director and master teacher Jerzy Grotowski? Years ago, I wrote that song, in diverse post-Grotowskian practices, functions as a kind of "vessel": an "essential type of structure through which alertness and receptivity are expressed, spontaneity becomes perceptible, and an extended encounter can unfold" (Spatz, 2008, 217). The idea that *receptivity is expressed* suggests one way of making concrete and practical what Ilona calls the perception-expression loop of voice. In terms of Mindell's channels, we might characterize this as a juxtaposition of improvisation and play in one channel with precisely repeatable structure in another. Not only in the Song of the Goat work but in many other post-Grotowskian practices, the expressiveness of receptivity is trained and developed through a combination of improvised physical interaction and precisely repeatable song. In this sense, terms as different as *coordination* (as in CT), *mutuality* (Staniewski and Hodge, 2004, 75–77), *encounter* (Salata, 2012) and *tandem* (Richards, 2008, 93–94) could be said to share as a principle or threshold technique the *expression of receptivity* through a particular synthesis of improvised and scored interaction.[6] Grotowski referred to the quality of expressive receptivity as the joining of

> two aspects: movement and repose.[7] When we are moving, and when we are able to break through the techniques of the body of everyday life, then our movement becomes a movement of perception. One can say that our movement is seeing, hearing, sensing, our movement is perception.
>
> (Grotowski, 1997, 263)

This *movement as/of perception* is a particular approach to what Ilona calls the perception-expression loop. Perception here is understood as one aspect or pole of action, always in tension with the opposite pole of dynamic action. While in everyday life we might find ourselves either in repose, perceptive but not expressive, or in movement, active but not perceptive, the specific quality of the heightened state to which many performers aspire is one in which perception and expression are bound tightly together. And the particular strategy through which this is attained, in many post-Grotowskian practices, is the combination of improvised, open, playful or relaxed movement with complex, musically-orchestrated, multivocal or polyphonic singing.

Song "plays a singular role" in what theatre scholar Tadeusz Kornaś calls the "Grotowski and Gardzienice Strand" of Polish alternative theatre, including the Gardzienice Centre for Theatre Practices, Studio Theatre, Song of the Goat Theatre, Chorea Theatre Association, Węgajty Theatre, Music of the Borderlands Foundation, The Grotowski Institute and its resident company Theatre ZAR (Kornaś, 2007, 44), as well as the Workcenter of Jerzy Grotowski and Thomas Richards in Italy (Richards, 2008; Spatz, 2015, 136–147). Even Grotowski's early theatrical works, which did not involve composed songs, were experienced by their performers as "one long song": not simply a dramatic text but "a sort of music" in which "the words are very precise and very important at the same time" (Campo and Molik, 2010, 17). This was certainly my experience of the creative process in Gardzienice, where I lived from 2003 to 2004, working on the performances *Metamorfozy* and *Elektra*. Włodzimierz Staniewski, director of the Gardzienice Theatre, writes:

> Song is a being; it is not just a composition or melody which must simply be sung. Nor is it a pretext for an actor to express his or her ability as an actor. Song is not illustration: it is not only words and melody. [...] When I speak about the "line of life of a song", I am referring to its inner contents, which we have to discover. Song is a hidden territory itself, it is inhabited by a lot of lives.
>
> (Staniewski and Hodge, 2004, 67)

Song is more structured than text, but in either case the voice functions as a vessel for a "line of life" that flows through it. This life may appear as a quality of physical movement or dynamic action that is simultaneously perceptive, open and relaxed: a movement that is a repose. Through movement – and through fluctuations of the voice within the song – what Mindell calls the dreambody (perhaps "associations" is the Grotowskian equivalent) appears. In the context of the present volume, it seems pertinent to ask whether it would be right to call this process somatic.

In post-Grotowskian practices, we find ideas of receptivity in references to the "inner sounding" of the song and the "vibrating energy and magnetic power" of "mutuality" between performers (Staniewski and Hodge, 2004, 71, 74); to the integration of the voice "with the body, through song, song and text, use of breath, resonance, range and harmony and establishing relationships with oneself and others, by staying in the present, tuning-in, listening and reacting" (Dowling, 2011, 245); to a work in which songs themselves can "appear in this moment like two persons made of flesh," with a "tangible presence, beyond the reach of words, beyond images, beyond meanings" (Kosiński, 2008, 68); to a kind of human connection, grounded in song, in which one can experience "a feeling of freedom," like "stepping out of all the chains," an approach to singing that is "based in part on resonance and on the way the song's resonance develops as the song is repeated" (Richards, 2008, 132, 139). Yet rarely do we encounter any explicit mention of somatics. Everywhere in such practices, we encounter the body, embodiment, physicality (as in physical action), corporeality and even the "carnal" (Richards and Grotowski, 1995, 15, 123) – but not the *soma* as it is used in fields of somatics, to name "the body as perceived from within by first-person perception" (Hanna in Johnson, 1995, 341). Why this absence? What is it that seems to separate post-Grotowskian practices from the world of somatics?

In many forms of movement-based embodied practice, such as dance and martial arts, a distinction can be drawn between pre-choreographed forms and responsive, partner-based interactions.[8] The latter (as in aikido, capoeira and contact improvisation) both influenced and were influenced by post-Grotowskian practices during the late twentieth century.[9] But the improvisational or relational dynamic is less evident in theatrical songwork.[10] There are fewer approaches to partner-based vocal improvisation that would correspond to the modes of partner and ensemble physical training for which many of the ensembles mentioned earlier are known. The tendency in post-Grotowskian practice is to follow an order according to which physical training precedes, prepares for, leads into and underpins songwork. Accordingly, the development of perceptive, receptive and sensitive qualities is undertaken first and more broadly through a range of movement techniques and then bridged or carried into the act of singing. As Ilona suggests earlier, this is likely due both to the specific historical and aesthetic development of these practices and to the material characteristics of movement and vocality. In any case, this ordering of work assumes and/or produces the reification of songs as complex wholes. While movement and physical action can be broken down into the tiniest fragments (as can sound and vocal action), song is more like dance when it comes to fragmentation: when a dance or song is dissected into small pieces, at a certain point, it loses its coherency and one is no longer working with *that* song or *that* dance but with pure sound or movement.

All of this points to a certain lacuna in post-Grotowskian practices, a gap that marks a limit or boundary of a particular territory of technique: insofar as these practices are structured by song, the somatic dimension of the voice – as the recessive pole of a sought-after *expression of receptivity* or *movement of perception* – is always, perhaps intentionally, hidden or unacknowledged. Moment-to-moment channels of receptivity, perceptivity and sensitivity are crucial to these practices and are arguably what distinguishes post-Grotowskian songwork from other forms of song-based theatre, such as musicals and opera. Yet, a somatic or receptive voice is rarely cultivated on its own in these contexts. Instead, receptivity is carried into songwork from elsewhere. Considering that, what would it mean to develop the somatics of voice in a post-Grotowskian vein? How might receptivity and sensation be brought to the foreground in a practice that is organized by singing as distinct from a more general sounding or voicing? This is what I understand Ilona to be exploring in her doctoral research at the edge of song and in her extension of *dreambody* to *dreamvoice*. She uses Mindell's processwork to pry open the voice, revealing points at which both dramaturgical and musical structures break down and from which both may then be reconstructed. This approach has implications not only for the development of post-Grotowskian pedagogies and aesthetics but also for how we understand the cultural and political dimensions of somatics. I will return to this point in the fourth part of this chapter.

Case studies (Ilona Krawczyk)

The following case studies are examples of how a process-oriented approach to voicework can be applied in the context of voice pedagogy. The first comes from a private, individual training session in Poland, part of a series that I led as a voice tutor in March and April 2018. The student presented a high level of analytical understanding of his own vocal patterns. In attending our sessions, he stated a desire to work on relaxation and on the capacity to deliver vibrant, open sound, resonating in the so-called "mask" (from the nasal cavity to the top of the head). I recall:

> During this session, the student's attention gradually focused more and more on the channels of visualization and proprioception, acknowledging his posture and position in the space. He said that he realized that not only the voice but also his whole physical body was shifted backwards. This manifested in his standing with his weight transferred onto his heels and his head leaning slightly backwards. His chest balanced against this posture by protruding forwards. Standing for a long time in this position, the student encountered pain and reported that he felt as if he had a metal stick in his spine. He was extremely precise in defining where the stick began (the occiput, or back of the head) and where it ended (the thoracic spine, between the shoulder blades). The student mentioned a felt need to "connect the upper and lower parts" of his body. I proposed some exercises aimed at supporting such integration, focusing on grounding the body to the floor and developing the student's awareness of his pelvic area muscles. We began an exercise

> that involved leaning and pushing towards each other with the hands, accompanied by the student vocalizing single notes. Gradually, the top of his head began to lean on my shoulder, pushing against me instead of his hands. At that point I observed a change in the student's vocal expression. His voice became loud and vibrant. I asked him to start singing the song he had brought to work on. Whenever he returned to his previous form of vocal expression, I asked him again to vocalize only single notes. We carried on with this process, the student pushing with more strength and excitement, until I lost my strength and could not hold my position anymore.
>
> Afterwards, the student reported an association that had arisen during the exercise: "keeping the border." He stated that he felt confused and could not analyse what happened, but that he could not feel the metal stick anymore.

According to Mindell's processwork, confusion often comes in the moment of encountering an "edge," when the dreambody reveals a message from unconscious processes. As the dreambody and, respectively, the dreamvoice most often manifest in symbols, I suggest that the message was revealed in this case by tension and pain in the body, with attention shifting to the channel of visualization when the image of a stick and "keeping the border" came to consciousness. In terms of vocal pedagogy, this session of individual vocal training suggests how the implementation of a process-oriented approach – with attention to the role of the practitioner's own perception-expression loop – can empower students in the self-exploration of their voices.

The next example suggests how working with the awareness of the fair observer and process-oriented approach to vocal training can also be applied in a group session. This case study is from a training session I led with a group of undergraduate Drama students in early Spring 2018 at the University of Huddersfield in England.

> During one of the exercises I asked everyone to sit in a circle and pass along a vocalized note in such a way that, at least for a moment, each giver and receiver would vocalize together, searching for one voice in terms of pitch and timbre. This is a vocal exercise commonly used by post-Grotowskian practitioners, including the Song of the Goat Theatre. In the first round, some students changed the given pitch. At some point, one student trained in music commented on her partner's difficulty in reproducing the note, trying to explain how far she had strayed from the original. I responded by inviting everyone to observe, listen and focus on searching for a relationship with their partner: to acknowledge how close or distant their voices might be without commenting on it. Following the premise that there are no right or wrong sounds, I proposed that students should listen to how their voices meet and blend together even if they are not making the same note. I added that I also

would not make any comments on their expression. The only source of assessment would be their process towards their vocal relationship and they would have to rely on their own perception in executing the task. In this way, as the facilitator of the process, I invited the group to work on their voiced *relationships* channel, instead of focusing on the indicated "distance." When we started again, after the third round, all the students managed to match the transmitted pitch.

In terms of processwork, this example shows how shifting attention to a different sensory channel, from hearing to relationship, can influence and transform vocal expressions. This transformation can also lead to reflection on another aspect of interdependence between perception and expression, namely how external assessments of quality influence a person's beliefs and perceptions regarding their own and others' capabilities. Throughout my years of pedagogical work, I have encountered many examples of how someone's critique – expressed through words like *you are out of tune, you cannot sing, your voice sounds horrible* and the like – would stop a person from singing or would have a tremendous influence on the way they express vocally. This example demonstrates how the application of a fair observer and process-oriented approach in a group session enabled the participants to fulfill the task once the external assessment of vocal quality was removed.

The two aforementioned examples present applications of a process-oriented approach to voicework in pedagogical situations (individual and group). The outcomes of these sessions suggest how the implementation of a fair observer can develop self-awareness in embodying voice, reveal hidden causes of unintentional expressions and integrate them in the performance. A significant aspect of this work is the shifting dynamics in the teacher-student relation. By taking the role of a facilitator, I followed the student-practitioners' processes. Instead of assessing what is right or wrong, I created a space for non-judgmental discovery, in which the students could engage attentively with their perception-expression loop and trust their dreamvoice. This eventually led to released and attuned vocal expressions. A similar shift in dynamics can also inform the dramaturgy and composition of performance, as explored in other areas of my PaR not addressed here.[11]

Kernels of the voice (Ben Spatz)

In the aforementioned examples, Ilona offers a way to conceptualize what might be the core of a process-oriented voicework practice: the way in which the *sensation* of the self always goes beyond mere haptic and interoceptive stimuli to include what our bodies and actions *mean to ourselves*. As Ilona suggests, Mindell's work invites us to recognize the inextricability of sensation and meaning, perception and imagination, body and "psyche," within the somatic field. This territory of indifferentiation, which Mindell calls the dreambody, is at once the source and the first target or impact point of the sounds we emit, whether in performance or in daily life. Any account of vocal somatics must therefore grapple not only with the feedback loop that ceaselessly operates between perception and expression, but also with the unknowability of the layers of embodiment that are woven into and through this loop. Even when vocalizing the simplest of sounds, the relationship between perception and expression is not static but continually changing, as the tiniest waver in sound, or the smallest distraction, may provoke a cascade of associations which, in turn, influence the next moment of sounding. The elements or "kernels" of voicework practice are therefore not separable into perceptive and expressive units. Rather, perception and expression are already indistinguishable in such micro elements. Like the act of standing, even the simplest vocalization – such as humming a single pitch – is the result of a complex and iterative process. One cannot begin to hum without immediately both hearing and feeling the sound, and these feelings and sensations cannot help but inform whether and how the sound continues.

One clear benefit of this analysis is that the dreamvoice can be enlisted to improve performance skills and to expand the range of what counts as performance. In the aforementioned examples, Ilona shows how apparently simple exercises that link the act of vocalization to intentionality, encounter and association can unlock hidden meanings of the difficulties that performers sometimes experience during vocal performance. She also demonstrates the permeability of the border around "song," which as I previously noted has been one of the defining features and structuring principles of post-Grotowskian practices in Poland, Italy and elsewhere. The idea of the "fair observer" and the premise that "there are no right or wrong sounds" seem to be in productive tension with the very idea of song. If we take this assertion seriously, then a given song can no longer be approached as a form to be mastered, or an act to be achieved, but rather as something like a reference point, a tool or a measuring stick in relation to which the meaning and function of any performance can only be *interpreted* and not assessed. Notes that were "out of tune," intervals that were "disharmonic," sounds that were "unmusical" then become meaning-laden differences worthy of substantive consideration. In Staniewski's words: "Everything which sounds beyond the 'edges' of the codified system is musicality" (Staniewski and Hodge, 2004, 64). But the perception-expression loop goes both ways. We would be remiss if we considered only what a greater focus on perception can bring to expression and did not also ask how expression shapes perception at the deepest levels of embodiment. I am thinking here of how cultural and artistic meanings shape the somatic kernels of the voice.

A common trope of vocal pedagogy, whether post-Grotowskian or not, is that of "freeing the natural voice" (Linklater, 2006). This image emphasizes one half of the perception-expression loop: that in which a better perception or understanding of the voice leads to its stronger, richer or more organic expression. The assumption underpinning this trope is that an artificial voice, which has been trained or imposed by less perceptive means, must be dissolved in order for a more natural or authentic voice to be freed and expressed. But the image of the "loop" contradicts the trope of vocal freedom by asserting that the path of meaningfulness runs in both directions. As a continuous feedback loop, the act of voicing or singing can never be simply the expression of a somatic kernel, because that kernel is continually formed and shaped by what is heard and perceived. Given the iterative, processual and *dreamlike* way in which the perception-expression loop gives rise to associative and representational (or hermeneutic) meaning, any quest for a natural voice that fails to recognize the meaningfulness and diversity of vocalities is privileging expression over perception to the detriment of understanding. The claim that "there are no right or wrong sounds" requires a very different approach to vocal practice and pedagogy: one in which the immediate task is not to help the student express in a certain way – not even their own individual way – but rather to help them *perceive and recognize what is already being expressed.* Although Ilona emphasizes the value of this in a rehearsal or training process that moves ultimately towards performance, I am equally interested in pursuing a radical reversal of the ontology and teleology of voicework/songwork, according to which expression serves perception and the cultivation of diverse vocalities remains open to interpretation rather than being channeled into any sort of musical or theatrical composition.[12]

During a studio session led by Ilona in early 2017, in which she was leading our shared practice, she invited me to begin singing a song silently, in my mind, while moving through space. Her next suggestion was to let the song begin to resonate quietly, mumbling the words and vocally "touching" the melody without letting either fully develop. I found this experience to be remarkable and noted that, in all my experiences with post-Grotowskian and more mainstream approaches to singing, I had never been asked to sing a song *subvocally* or *submusically* in this way. I had broken down songs into rhythms and fragments, made them faster or slower and louder or quieter, synchronized songs to movements and vice versa, sung "as if" to a certain person or with a certain intention and used songs as meeting grounds for encounters – but I had never been invited to mumble, murmur or half-sing a song. Something even struck me as blasphemous in this request, because of the way it violated the integrity of the song. The song was unmistakably present to me, since I was singing it, but it was not allowed to appear in an audible way. It was, in other words, *perceived without being expressed* – or expressed in a way that was only perceptible to me. This exercise, which I have since taught under the rubric of "subvocality," changed my understanding of what it means to work with a song. I wrote earlier that, when a song is broken into small pieces, at a certain point it loses its coherency and becomes pure sound. The most interesting point however comes just before that, when a kernel or fragment of vocality balances at the edge of meaning: between lexical and nonlexical, between sound and song. At this point, we cannot deny that the meaning of what is happening is an indeterminacy of perception and expression.

The perception-expression loop destabilizes the division between somatic and semiotic and the assumption that an organic or natural bodyvoice can be secondarily or incidentally channeled into culturally-specific forms. Of course, the somatic is a field of emergence that continually bubbles up into the semiotic forms of culture, but equally, the performance or expression of cultural forms continually sediments into the somatic, forming vocal kernels – nuggets and layers of dreamvoice – that are in no way universal, neutral or simply individual. These kernels, in which perception and expression are indistinguishable, are at once somatic and cultural. They are not only psychophysical phenomena that can be cultivated into performances, but also fragments of culture that become embodied through experience and perception. Thinking ecologically, this means that our bodies not only draw from our environments to generate performances – in a sense transmuting earth, water and air into songs and dances – but also convert received cultural practices into our very material being. The body and its techniques compose and contest identity, but, on a larger scale, identities are also the roots and sources of our bodies, their "*from*-ness" (Erçin, 2018). In a time of material ecological crisis, perhaps this suggests that our collective need to renew embodied arts is in no way "merely cultural" (cf. Butler, 1998). And perhaps, through a reframing along these lines, that which we call "the body" – not a physical object, but the dreambody/dreamvoice in all its terrible meaningfulness – could be foregrounded in a post-Grotowskian practice that would approach song from both directions, no longer hiding the somatic as the secret resource of an expressive power but revealing it as an indispensable pole of action: individual, cultural, ecological.

Notes

1 Following Ben's usage, we mean "post-Grotowskian" in the sense that Hans-Thies Lehmann defines the post-Brechtian: "not a theatre that has nothing to do with [Grotowski] but a theatre which knows that it is affected by the demands and questions for theatre that are sedimented in [Grotowski]'s work but can no longer accept [Grotowski]'s answers" (Lehmann, 2006, 27).
2 In addition to this program, my discussion of Coordination Technique and of post-Grotowskian practice draws on practical experiences working with the Song of the Goat Theatre and the Brave Kids project, as well as with Anna Zubrzycki Studio, Chorea Theatre Association and individual practitioners associated with either the Gardzienice Centre for Theatre Practices or the Workcenter of Jerzy Grotowski and Thomas Richards (e.g. Agnieszka Mendel, Pawel Passini, Ela Rojek, Jacek Timingeriu and Przemek Wasilkowski).
3 The notion of "inner life" in the Song of the Goat Theatre practice reflects on the connection between performers through "a highly tuned-in, constant state of openness" (Dowling, 2011, 247). My application of this term emphasizes the inner psychophysical process of a performer.
4 The phrase "line of life" also appears in a quote from Włodzimierz Staniewski, cited in Spatz's section below.
5 This is the order in which the channels are listed in Mindell (1990, 17). In practice, all the channels are of equal importance.

6 The Workcenter's practice is complex in this regard, as in my experience physical training in no sense precedes their singing. Nevertheless, the centrality of song in their practice sustains a two-level synthesis in which song (rather than voice or sound) is combined with action (rather than movement or dance).
7 The phrase "movement and repose" comes from the apocryphal Gospel of Thomas, a key text for Grotowski.
8 For more on this distinction, see Mroz (2011).
9 One expert on late twentieth-century performance art in the US told me half-jokingly that contact improvisation was "America's response to the *plastiques*" – a set of exercises developed and taught by Rena Mirecka, Ryszard Cieslak and other core actors in Grotowski's Theatre Laboratory.
10 I borrow the term "songwork" from Garry Tomlinson (2007), as described in Spatz (2019). Like voicework, it is intended to suggest the wide range of potential explorations and practices that can be developed outward from voice/song as a starting point, as distinct from a narrower focus on voice/song as sound alone.
11 My application of a process-oriented approach to voicework in performance devising was most fully developed through the *Dreamvoice* performance/sound installation, presented at the University of Huddersfield in 2019 as a final part of my Practice-as-Research PhD. For reasons of space, that project is not discussed here.
12 I note that Ilona's sections have focused more on voicework and mine more on songwork. This surely reflects our different positionings and research projects and highlights the dialogic approach of this essay as a whole – especially given that the border between song and voice is precisely one of those "edges" at which signals from the dreambody are likely to manifest.

References

Butler, J. (1998) Merely cultural. *New Left Review*, 227(1) 33–44.

Campo, G. and Molik, Z. (2010) *Zygmunt Molik's Voice and Body Work: The Legacy of Jerzy Grotowski*. London: Routledge.

Csikszentmihalyi, M. (2002) *Flow: The Classic Work on How to Achieve Happiness*. London: Rider.

Di Matteo, P. (2015) Performing the *entre-deux*: the capture of speech in (dis)embodied voices. In: Konstantinos Thomaidis and Ben Macpherson (eds.) *Voice Studies: Critical Approaches to Process, Performance and Experience*. New York: Routledge, 90–103.

Dowling, N. (2011) Teatr Piesn Kozla and its integration into Western European theatre training. *Theatre, Dance and Performance Training*, 2(2) 243–259.

Erçin, N. E. (2018) From-ness: the identity of the practitioner in the laboratory. *Journal of Interdisciplinary Voice Studies*, 3(2) 195–202.

Grotowski, J. (1982) *Towards a poor theatre*. Reprinted edition. London: Methuen.

––––––– (1997) Theatre of sources. In: Richard Schechner and Lisa Wolford (eds.) *The Grotowski Sourcebook*. London: Routledge, 252–270.

Johnson, D. H. (ed.) (1995) *Bone, Breath and Gesture: Practices of Embodiment*. Berkeley, CA: North Atlantic Books.

Kornaś, T. (2007) *Between Anthropology and Politics: Two Strands of Polish Alternative Theatre*. English edition. Warsaw, Poland: Zbigniew Raszewski Theatre Institute in cooperation with Ministry of Foreign Affairs.

Kosiński, D. (2008) Song from beyond the dark. *Performance Research*, 13(2) 60–75.

Lehmann, H. T. (2006) *Postdramatic Theatre*. Translated from German by Karen Jürs-Munby. Oxon: Routledge.

Leman, M. (2016) *The Expressive Moment: How Interaction (with Music) Shapes Human Empowerment*. Cambridge: MIT Press.

Lesaffre, M., Maes, P. J. and Leman, M. (eds.) (2017) *The Routledge Companion to Embodied Music Interaction*. New York: Routledge.

Linklater, K. (2006) *Freeing the Natural Voice*. London: Nick Hern Books.

Mindell, A. (1990) *Working on Yourself Alone*. London: Penguin Arkana.

—— (2008) Bringing deep democracy to life: an awareness paradigm for deepening political dialogue, personal relationships, and community interactions. *Psychotherapy and Politics International*, 6(3) 212–225.

Mindell, A. and Mindell, A. (1992) *Riding the Horse Backwards: Process Work in Theory and Practice*. London: Arkana.

Mroz, D. (2011) *The Dancing Word: An Embodied Approach to the Preparation of Performers and the Composition of Performances*. Amsterdam: Rodopi.

Richards, T. (2008) *Heart of Practice: Within the Workcenter of Jerzy Grotowski and Thomas Richards*. London: Routledge.

Richards, T. and Grotowski, J. (1995) *At Work with Grotowski on Physical Actions*. London: Routledge.

Salata, K. (2012) *The Unwritten Grotowski: Theory and Practice of the Encounter*. New York: Routledge.

Spatz, B. (2008) To open a person: song and encounter at Gardzienice and the Workcenter. *Theatre Topics*, 18(2) 205–222.

—— (2015) *What a Body Can Do: Technique as Knowledge, Practice as Research*. London: Routledge.

—— (2019) Molecular identity: digital archives and decolonial Judaism in a laboratory of song. *Performance Research*, 24(1) 66–79.

Staniewski, W. and Hodge, A. (2004) *Hidden Territories: The Theatre of Gardzienice*. London: Routledge.

Thomaidis, K. and Macpherson, B. (eds.) (2015) *Voice Studies: Critical Approaches to Process, Performance and Experience*. Abingdon, Oxon: Routledge.

Tomlinson, G. (2007) *The Singing of the New World: Indigenous Voice in the Era of European Contact*. Cambridge: Cambridge University Press.

12 Somatic logos in physiovocal actor training and beyond

Christina Kapadocha

Initiating logos from somatic attention

If you are with someone you feel comfortable with, invite them to the following relational exploration that is intended to help and, more precisely, complement your current reading experience. Start by identifying your roles in the process as if you are about to begin a physiovocal improvisation or a scene exploration. As the reader of this chapter, you could initiate the somatic attention by taking the role of the actor-mover and giving your partner the role of the actor-witness. What this means in simple terms is that even though the suggested process, at least in the beginning, is meant to evolve around the actor-mover's investigation and expression, the actor-witness should not lose connection to their own somatic experience. This could be achieved by simply letting the actor-witness know that they do not have to direct all their attention to you but as much as it is easy for them. They could navigate this attention by focusing on their tactile experience in relation to the actor-mover and the space, observing how this ongoing communication shifts. As you go along with the practice, you may want to move through the subtle shift of somatic attention and intention in both roles, allowing yourselves to simultaneously become movers-witnesses of self and other.

For now, go back to the role of the actor-mover and try to choose a comfortable starting position in the space, maybe sitting or standing. The actor-witness comes close to you in a negotiated distance. You can both take a moment to check where your weight is in relation to the support of the space and very softly notice the movement of your breath. Try to stay in the simplicity of the rising and falling, opening and closing movement of your lungs in a rhythm that feels comfortable for each of you. Take the next moment to notice very gently the volume and the size of your lungs shifting your attention to the roundness of your ribcage, from the front to the back, from the one to the other side of your torso. Observe how this subtle focus may affect your presence in the space and in relation to your partner.

The actor-witness starts observing your presence and very gently positions their whole palm on your hand, arm or back. For the beginning, I suggest these common points of contact as part of our relational daily lives. The tactile intention is to simply be with the actor-mover without applying pressure or pushing towards change. Can you both slowly direct you full attention to the first point of contact? In order to do so, you may want to visualize the contacted surfaces of your skins as being composed by tiny breathing cells that constantly move and change shape. Ground yourselves in this shared moving image for a moment. Now, as a receiver of this contact, you may want to start moving slowly from this point, gradually releasing your present senses, thoughts, feelings and imagination. After a while, you can start voicing from this same point as if your contacted cells can actually sound. Try not to have expectations from this sound and allow it to just be. Ask your partner to stay present as much as they can to this one point of contact. As you develop the exploration, they could move to another point of cellular contact, attuning to your unfolding communication. If you feel like closing your eyes, try to move in-between your outer and inner vision. Do you start sensing your sound? If so, allow yourself to play with its qualities trying not to judge.

For the next step, the invitation is a gentle transition from sound to words and eventually the communication of a piece of text, whatever may be available to you at this moment. So, if it comes up or when it comes up, allow your sounding-through-contact to become a syllable, a word, a phrase, a lyric, a song, a poem, something that is present for you, something you would like to share with yourself and your partner. If you are an actor, you may want to go for a monologue that you wish to explore. If you are a singer, you may choose a song. Allow the development of voicing-through-contact improvisation. If you have enough space where you are, dance through the contact and the vocal experience of the words. As your physicality might now become more active, the actor-witness should respond to that but without getting stressed about having to keep contact throughout. Enjoy the flexibility of possibly losing each other for a moment and then find contact again. At some point, the actor-witness should give you space to continue the exploration without their direct contact, keeping though the memory of it. When the active physicality passes, allow yourselves to transition to rest. Without external movement, simply voice the words, keeping the experience of words as inner movement. You may want to find eye contact with your partner or only sense their presence in the room. Can you hear yourself differently? Can you sense the actor-witness listening to you? The conclusion of the exploration will emerge at its own time. Would you like to reflect? Try to ground your words into your experiences using first person and present tense. Do you speak differently? Do you feel more present to yourself and your partner?

If so, I would suggest that you have just experienced qualities of your somatic logos.

This opening invitation emerges from the *cellular text* exploration in my current teaching through which I support the grounding integration between each individual actor's movement, sounding and embodiment of play text. It opens this chapter in order to offer an indication of how, as an educator-researcher,

Somatic logos 157

I aim at encouraging actors' awareness as diverse, moving, voicing and acting selves. For the identification of actors' experiential and expressive multivocality, I introduce the plural word *somata*. *Soma*, the Greek word for body, was first re-conceived by the philosopher and Feldenkrais practitioner Thomas Hanna who used the term in order to distinguish between experienced "bodily being" from objectified perceptions of *the body* (1970, 35). In my present praxis, I further refine actors' somaticities by highlighting not only experiential and holistic aspects but also their interrelationally emerging polyphony. I develop my practice by modifying somatic processes of *witnessing in acting* based upon Body-Mind Centering® (BMC®) and Authentic Movement principles. I formally started practising these somatic methodologies through Linda Hartley's Integrative Bodywork and Movement Therapy (IBMT) training (2012–2016). I combined the training with a parallel Practice-as-Research (PaR) doctoral project on my process of becoming a *trainer-witness* through an actress's awareness (Kapadocha, 2016). As a result, I found myself interrogating the shaping of a somatic actor-training approach introduced as Somatic Acting Process®.

Inspired by recent academic discourses on *in-between-ness* within the burgeoning field of voice studies (Thomaidis and Macpherson, 2015a), in this chapter I suggest that BMC-informed somatic contact could provide a *listening* methodology for the awareness of a voicer-listener dynamic of interrelation and the perception of vocal logos as a somatic process. By using the word *listening*, I refer to an integrative, interrelational presence and understanding that could benefit not only actors but also actor-trainers' contribution to each actor's physiovocal learning. Additionally, drawing on Merleau-Ponty's phenomenological approach to logos, I discuss how we can theoretically and practically (or praxically) shift our attention from the single and hierarchical logos to qualities that advocate *embodied* and subsequently *somatic logos*. This experiential perception of logos in the context of this chapter aims at broadly revisiting the dynamics between learners and educators within and potentially beyond actor-training environments.

From *the one* logos to *somatic logos*

The problematic distancing between voicer and listener that is still present in our culture and daily understanding has been established by the classical perception of logos or Logos (in Christian theology). Rooted in the Greek classical thinking of Plato and Aristotle, traditional perceptions of logos advocate an objectified *phone* (voice) or *homilia* (speech) that carries universal characteristics and "truths" that should reside in an intellectual rationale. In twentieth-century philosophical and scientific thought, logocentrism has been mainly associated with the thinking of Jacques Derrida who defines this tradition as "the exigent, powerful, systematic, and irrepressible desire" for a transcendental signified ([1967] 1997, 49). His deconstruction argued against the *one* universal thought, which transcends all external signs, as a paradox inherent in language that overlooks plurality, diversity and the aforementioned in-between-ness. Derrida's ideas have been complemented by other modern philosophers such as Adriana Cavarero's criticism on the *devocalization of logos* (2005, 33–41) in her discussion on a vocal ontology of uniqueness. This criticism, when examined in relation to actors' multiple somaticities and voices, reveals that contemporary actor-training discourses could afford further advancements.

One prominent logocentric example, when it comes to voice in actor training, is the established use of the term *apparatus* for the description of the actors' vocal, breathing, speech, articulatory and sound processes. Apparatus, "[t]he technical equipment or machinery needed for a particular activity or purpose,"[1] was a term broadly used by Konstantin Stanislavski (1863–1938) within the shaping of the first systematic actor-training discourse in the twentieth-century Europe. Stanislavski's influential heritage for contemporary theatre and acting education was unavoidably infused with the scientific ideas of his time, combined with his stated intention to establish acting as a "formally" acknowledged *episteme*.[2] Thus, when it comes to the section on voice and speech in the recent edition of Stanislavski's *An Actor's Work* (2010), the reader can come across various expressions of the actor's *vocal* and *physical apparatus* (382, 394–395). By no means do I argue that Stanislavski's current impact upon actors' embodied training and the development of somatic theories in acting is not enormously helpful (see, among others, Sellers-Young, 2010; Gutekunst and Gillett, 2014). The problematic element that I find in the use of scientifically-informed vocabulary, such as apparatus or instrument, in the twenty-first-century actor training is that it perpetuates the identification of actors' multiple experiences as *singular, unified* and *objectified*. This objectification and unification does not only affect each actor's own expression but also their in-between communication as well as the actor-educator dynamics. Therefore, from an educator's perspective, I propose that it would be helpful for actors' awareness if more attention was directed to additional critical elements such as each actor's uniqueness, ethical aspects of diversity and the significance of interaction as dynamic and multisensory process.

The analysis of *logos* in the last work of phenomenologist Maurice Merleau-Ponty, *The Visible and the Invisible* (1968), helped me contextualize the embodied dynamics of the term in actors' learning processes in my doctoral thesis. According to Merleau-Ponty, logos could be re-examined through his notion of *flesh* (1968, 126–127), which represents "an 'element' of Being," an *exemplar sensible* that is simultaneously sensible and sensate and exists even before the formation of language (1968, 135, 139, 147). His *logos as flesh*[3] suggests an integration between embodied and intellectual aspects of perception through which we develop a sequential sense of self in relation to the world and the others. Merleau-Ponty's intercorporeal understanding of logos gave me the ability to start exploring responses to the logocentric problematics of mind and body, inner and outer, self and other dualism in actor training. Nevertheless, within this intercorporeality, the philosopher did not take into account elements of diversity and uniqueness regarding the problematics of *the one-universal body*. In order to fill this gap and highlight characteristics of individuality and uniqueness in each actor's experience and expression, I added to Merleau-Ponty's discussion by introducing the term *embodied logos*.

In this chapter, I should like to go even further and indicate more diverse *in-between* potentials of logos through the interrelational experience and perception of *somatic logos*. My aim is to propose how contact-based somatic witnessing, like in the opening invitation, can facilitate more complex phenomenological awareness and generate a fuller *listening* to the unique physiovocal idiosyncrasy of each self and other. Talking through my ongoing personal development as a trainer-witness in group actor-training environments, I propose that this complementary somatic perspective can be very helpful for both actors' learning processes and educators' pedagogies.[4] I have witnessed that it benefits not only actors' intellectual-embodied integration but also a fuller understanding of acting as a dynamic of receiving-responding between every individual involved in training and creative processes. This in-between somatic awareness ultimately results to each actor's softening of self-consciousness while boosting self-awareness and confidence. Revisiting Merleau-Ponty's thinking for the purposes of this discussion, I identify the ground for the suggested somatic in-betweenness in the philosopher's flesh-based experiential reversibility:

> I experience – and as often as I wish – the transition and the metamorphosis of the one experience into the other, and it is only as though the hinge between them, solid, unshakeable, remained irremediably hidden from me. But this hiatus between my right hand touched and my right hand touching, between my voice heard and my voice uttered, between one moment of my tactile life and the following one, is not an ontological void, a non-being: it is spanned by the total being of my body, and by that of the world; it is the zero of pressure between two solids that makes them adhere to one another.
>
> (1968, 148)

Somatic logos in physiovocal actor training

Echoing Merleau-Ponty's words, I root my work on every actor's *somatic logos* upon *physical-vocal-verbal initiations* as they emerge from *points of contact* with the space and the others in a sequence of BMC-informed contact explorations. The awareness of what "zero of pressure" may mean in this sequence is shaped upon the practice of *cellular touch* or contact at a *cellular level* in BMC/IBMT somatic processes. Cellular awareness underlies a series of movement forms that Bonnie Bainbridge Cohen, the founder of BMC, identifies as *Basic Neurocellular Patterns (BNP)* (2012, 4–5). It emerges by attending, voicing and moving through an ongoing interrelation between each cell as a breathing part and one's embodied presence as a breathing whole. When cellular attention is infused into contact, as suggested in the opening invitation, the tactile communication aims at allowing a sense of mutual listening to self and other. In resonance with Merleau-Ponty's embodied transition, it challenges the distinctive receptive qualities one can broadly associate with each sense, helping towards experiential and expressive integration.

In the modified somatic contact explorations between each *actor-mover* and *actor-witness* in my teaching, cellular attention forms the first step towards negotiations of in-between-ness in pressure, weight and distance, full-body breath and communication. It can be manifested as *somatic logos* in every point of contact that could become the initiation of *vocal movement* through the roundness of every actor's ribcage-torso, the length of their spines and extremities. Upon this vocal roundness, movement and somatic attention, the actors are invited to ground the exploration of play text as becoming part of their own somatic logos while they establish mutual listening. They are prompted to understand verbal impulses not as something dictated by the author's text or an abstract concept but as felt *tactile initiations* in-between themselves, the stories they share, their partners and the space. These initiations become inseparable from actors' invisible contact with themselves, their shared creative ideas, imaginations, feelings and questions that are communicated not only in the experience of the acting explorations but also in first-person verbal reflections.

What I would like to focus on at this point is not the explorations in themselves (the *know how* in Robin Nelson's *praxical* vocabulary) but some underlying characteristics of *somatic logos* as I have witnessed them through the actors in training (the *know what*) (Nelson, 2013, 40–45). I currently reflect upon three main qualities that seem to support physiovocal integration and in-between somatic listening in actor training as developed in my own practice. These qualities are each actor's *somatic attention, somatic intention* and *somatic research*. *Somatic attention* in theoretical discussions is usually analyzed as a shift of concentration to one's present embodied self through movement and the senses, through dynamic relation with others and the space (see Csordas, 1993; Shusterman, 2008). In the field of experiential education that influenced the shaping of somatic pedagogies, John Dewey introduced an artist's *direct perception* and reflexive sensitivity to the world: "As we manipulate, we touch and feel, as we look, we see; as we listen, we hear" ([1934] 1980, 49). In BMC, Cohen refers to attention through touch as a mode of mutual support, knowledge and openness: "Through focusing attention on a place where someone simply doesn't move, they can become aware of that place and begin to move it themselves [...] I will go into that area of my own body to see. In the process I become more open also" (2012, 55). Developing this awareness in my work with actors, the practice of somatic attention through contact becomes about learning to be in active relation and response without making it only about the self or the other. It is about knowing that there is space for slowing down and parallel detailed observation while practising the ability to return to the simple qualities of contact in order to sustain focus and dynamic relation.

Mutual listening navigates *somatic intention* as the element of somatic logos that, in my perception, complements the way contact may be practised in other actor-training approaches such as contemporary Grotowskian traditions. As an actor-trainer, I help the emergence of this somatic consciousness in-between actor-mover and actor-witness by suggesting a subtle shift of responsibility to the latter who is prompted to attune to the actor-mover's investigation. Thus, the actor-witness is invited to hold the shared intention by trying not to direct the actor-mover's exploration. The exploration of this *listening through touch* requires clear points of contact without rushing the transition to a new impulse as well as "zero of pressure" before the interrelation moves to various expressions and dynamics. For a more familiar understanding of perceptive possibilities, I started likening somatic intention through contact to a verbal communication as if the actors perform a silent duologue that could softly and at any point transition to words. In that way, I suggest actor-witnesses to consider every point of contact as a word or phrase that emerges in response to the actor-mover's primary "monologue". In order for the actor-mover to *listen to* the tactile impulses that aim at supporting their own explorations, the points of contact need to be infused with clear intention and attention that can be transmitted. An "almost touch" and rushed changes without full engagement would equate to non-shaped or non-heard "words" that do not give actors space for in-between communication and parallel individual research.

After the completion of every improvisation, actors are given time for critical reflection that is primarily actualized through verbal sharings and questions. In comparison to other mainly intellectual modes of analyzing a dramatic text, a situation or a role, I identify this approach as *somatic research* in acting.[5] Shaping the ultimate component of *somatic logos*, somatic research in actor training integrates somatic attention and intention into a valuable source of cognitive knowledge. Prompted to use first-person language in grounding their words to their somatic experiences in present tense, actors are encouraged to an integral and ethical approach to listening to themselves and the others supporting their own multivocal somata and diverse self-learning in the group.

The significance of self-learning represents an important contribution of somatic movement pedagogies as have been applied or modified in actor training (such as Delsarte system of expression, Dalcroze eurhythmics, Laban movement analysis, Alexander Technique, Feldenkrais and more recently BMC).[6] Self-learning has also become an integral part of how I have been shaping my practice in relation to my own experience and active listening to the actors I am working with. As Cohen notices, this work "has to do with dialogue and openness, the imagination, to know how to trust that it is there already. You don't *teach* the reaction, you just allow" (2012, 151, original emphasis). Cohen's words become a sort of inner voice that orientates my ongoing self-learning and critical reflections while teaching actors as a somatically-informed trainer-witness. Inspired by the somatic vocabulary as used in the processes of BMC/IBMT and Authentic Movement, I complement the notions of actor-mover and actor-witness with the understanding of the *trainer-witness*. I do so in order to point out the dynamic yet not intrusive or hierarchical intentions of my own somatic logos in the classroom. As a researcher, I have also learned to root the shaping of this self-reflection in moments of resistance, challenge or change such as the one that triggers the following part of this discussion.

The somatic logos of the trainer-witness

I work with a group of first-year BA actors in a late afternoon class. I introduce an exploration on the interrelation of contact, breath, movement, weight and sound, by asking the help of a volunteer. I try to share a short version of the fluid structure of the process recognizing that "seeing" first (a prominent sense in traditional logocentric perception) makes some learners more secure. At the same time, I highlight that I do not intend to show an expected response as each shared exploration is unique. My partner and I sit down and turn around so we gradually meet, back to back. This first meeting sets up the ground of our mutual witnessing. I start searching for the whole surface of our backs as if I want to find every single point of this meeting from my sacrum up to the top of my head and from my spine out to the rounding edges of my sides and shoulders. As I do so led by my curiosity and the intentions of the practice, I verbalize the tracking of my experience, explaining every step and transition of my somatic attention. I wish to communicate the structure of the exploration while attuning to my emergent experience. Then I direct attention to our in-between breathing. I focus on listening to my own present lung breathing in relation to my partner and the undulation of our lungs. To further facilitate our meeting, I start integrating a very soft vibration through humming. I check if this transition is also present for my partner and I invite the emergence of movement through the blending of contact and sounding. I make clear that we do not have to keep the sounding throughout but only during the moments when this feels helpful. Still in relation to the ground and the movement of our lungs but allowing the ongoing shifting of our initial positions, we direct our attention to our weight and we start playing in-between very soft receiving-releasing each other's weight allowing the emergence of improvised shapes. I conclude this phase of the exploration by inviting the gradual return to our initial back-to-back position and the slow physical separation of our bodies. We find a transition to standing and we walk in the space making observations upon any possible shift in our presences. I check with the rest of the group if the intentions of the exploration are clear and I invite them to try out the practice ensuring that I am going to talk them through. Only a couple of minutes into their work, an actor exclaims "I don't understand. I just don't understand".

It is the second class of the first Term with the first-year actors in training at East 15 Acting School in London. The subject of our work is *Experiential Anatomy for Actors* explored through my modification of Cohen's *experiential anatomy* and *human movement development* processes into the needs of the modern actor. We develop the practice by integrating movement, contact and voice towards the embodiment of play texts and text-based characters. In the first Term, we focus on grounding somatic awareness, communication and expression by studying our *somata* as unities of expressive structures such as bones, muscles and organs that support different qualities in each actor's somatic logos. This learning process by itself can be quite challenging for actors in training usually coming directly from their secondary education and most likely with some expectations for what their actor training "should" be. I approach this potential challenge acknowledging the tension between somatic learning and logocentric problematics as outlined earlier and ingrained within the normative European education. Nevertheless, I do not use this awareness as an easy recourse but as a filter for questioning the ongoing development of my teaching in resonance with the learners' needs.

The discussed class aims at the understanding of breath as the ground of the actors' diverse physiovocal and embodied communication.[7] We focus on the experiential anatomy of breath into each actor's expression and the very first step towards the somatization of scripted text. Embracing the actors' gradual arriving into a new mode of perception, we start by visualizing the journey and movement of breath with the support of a three-dimensional human anatomy atlas software.[8] If "seeing" first can trigger helpful insights for the practice, I aim at revisiting the traditional use of anatomy in physiovocal actor training. Inspired by the way we studied experiential anatomy during my IBMT training, I use an interactive and dynamic tool which connects the learners' familiarity with technology with a fun way of seeing the roundness, volume, inner structures and movements of the anatomical body. As we do so, I name explicitly that the software depicts an objectified version of *the human body* and highlight the necessity of a parallel experiential mapping of the points discussed in our diverse bodies. I urge the actors in training to keep this individual awareness as we focus on the inner-outer "counterdance" between lungs and diaphragm in the physiology of breathing. This is followed by partner work during which each actor-witness offers cellular contact to an actor-mover studying together the size, volume, shape and movement of lungs in dynamic relation to the countermovement of our diaphragms. Thus, the anatomy software as a seemingly logocentric training tool becomes a way into diverse somatic attention and research.

By reflecting and writing in response to the actor's expressed frustration, I problematize whether I gave the group complex material quite early into their learning processes.[9] I take into consideration the tiredness of the whole day, given that the three previous classes were very well received, and the fact that every individual requires different time and attention. Nevertheless, shifting focus on my own role and somatic logos, the reaction of the learner stayed with me as I tested out the introduction of further material on breathing in the specific academic year. My objective was to check whether giving learners more possibilities in practical explorations would offer them additional space for personal engagement and curiosity. This choice may imply an opposition to the discussed processual learning but at the same time it could bring the teaching of somatic practice in drama schools more in sync to the general curriculum without losing its pedagogical philosophy.

Within this philosophy, after the actor's interruption, we paused the exploration and I apologized to the group in order to offer some extra time to the communication of the process. I did not mean to shut down the actor's confusion but at the same time I had to hold the group's multivocality. Instead of saying something along the lines of "don't worry, try to follow the invitations and your partner and maybe something will come up," I used once more my own somatic mapping to highlight contact and the effortless breathing as initiations of the process. In other words, I aimed at listening to the learner's uncertainty through my own witnessing and somatic logos. As part of that, I pointed out that somatic awareness is not something easy and, like every kind of skill, it requires practice and time. This aspect of training does not necessarily meet the logocentric fast rhythms and result-longing that dominate both the training time in drama schools and the contemporary rhythms of theatre productions. At the same time, it suggests ethical aspects of mutual responsibilities in-between trainers and trainees in the learning process. For instance, I move beyond the logocentric paradigm of the trainer as a singular authority of knowledge in the room and I approach learning as a process that requires each trainee's equal engagement. Therefore, somatic listening does not suggest only an understanding of in-between-ness among actors but also a simultaneous educational approach.

Part of my own ethical responsibility is to acknowledge that the discussed somatic reversibility is not easily accessible by every individual and requires time as it does not belong to conservatoire-trained actors' habitual perceptions, at times even contradicts them. Despite the fact that embodied and physiovocal integration is offered through various forms in actor training, somatic practice further values the identification of emergent knowledge, critical reflection and shaping of words that could allow experiences to become fuller. Moreover, somatic learning necessitates *in-between-ness* and the searching of *how* to be in relation, a premise that may sound as given in acting but with which learners may not be familiar or comfortable in the first place. This unfamiliarity could emerge somatically when contact is approached as an educational and expressive acting methodology. For this purpose, the grounding practice of cellular support becomes a significant preparation in my classes and an embodied metaphor for actors to learn to fully listen to each other's uniqueness: "As we experience the uniqueness of cells [...] we learn about individuality within the context of community" (Cohen, 2012, 5). This shared and diverse awareness should be first and foremost informed by the educator's own self-knowledge and continuous investigation.

In my present understanding, I notice that I may never be able to respond with certainty to some of my questions. At the same time, the ongoing process of self-reflection renders my practice flexible and responsive. My teaching material is never static and even though it has become more systematized, it maintains its pedagogical identity. In that way, I know with certainty that I can always be present for each actor, holding multiplicity and uniqueness, moments of confusion or uncertainty, avoiding the enforcement of change into the individuality of their somatic logos.

Somatic logos as listening methodology

I start singing from my contacted adrenal glands and I feel as if the wholeness of my voice's inner-outer space is supported by two small but clear and resourceful points of contact. I know that I can move and voice without my partner but I cherish that I find fuller presence and expression through his witnessing.

This reflective moment does not belong to my classroom witnessing, as above, but to the third year of my IBMT somatic training with Linda Hartley (December 2014). It emerged from the integrating phase[10] while working with a partner on the experiential anatomy of glands, as I followed my urgency to voice and sing through attention to the points of contact. Thus, it somehow became the anchor for my current somatic vocal awareness and gave me a sense of clarity; it prompted the expanding of the explorations on actors' diverse and multi-expressive somatic logos in my practice. I include it at this point, while I reach the end of this chapter, in order to indicate the transition to a broader understanding of somatic logos as a *listening methodology* in educational contexts, within and even beyond actor-training environments. This spectrum of possible applications lies in the fact that it offers a subtle experiential perspective that could complement the actual process of interrelational *listening as understanding*. Consequently, somatic witnessing in my praxis is not confined in a practical context but becomes a complementary support to theorizing, thinking and perceiving qualities of somatic logos. As Hartley notices, witnessing is "an embracing attitude which both guides and contains" (2004, 66). Exploring this process, I discuss the mover-witness or voicer-listener communication not on the premises of hierarchy, interdependency and unification but based on individual differences and inclusivity that support somatic resonance or ontological communication.

166 *Christina Kapadocha*

Going back to Merleau-Ponty's ideas, the philosopher notices:

> My left hand is always on the verge of touching my right hand touching the things, but I never reach coincidence; [...] Likewise, I do not hear myself as I hear the others, the sonorous existence of my voice is for me as it were poorly exhibited.
>
> (1968, 148)

Further developing this thinking through my somatic understanding, I would add that the voicer can recognize the experiential differences in the flow of the transitions and the presence of the other while simultaneously allowing self-listening. Hence, one can listen to self as clearly as to the other and vice versa. Linking this to the conceptual discourse in the field of voice studies, this chapter proposes how modified somatic witnessing as part of somatic logos in actor training can support the praxical understanding that voice is "a plurality – and the aural 'in-between' is the junction point for multiple encodings of experience to be negotiated and understood" (Thomaidis and Macpherson, 2015b, 4). Allowing the expansion in between the traditional confines that separate modes of experience and perception, I suggest that the amplification of a sense through the reflexive use of another, such as the witnessing of contact for voicing-listening, can incite a more in-depth critical understanding of one's vocal logos.

Notes

1. Available from https://en.oxforddictionaries.com/definition/apparatus [Accessed 1 April 2017].
2. The relationship between Stanislavski and science has been a subject of rigorous investigation in acting theory. See, among others, Roach (1985), Pitches (2006) and Whyman (2008).
3. My description of Merleau-Ponty's corporeal understanding of *logos as flesh* is based upon Gail Stenstad's choice of words in her article "Merleau-Ponty's Logos: The Sens-ing of Flesh" (1993, 52–61).
4. For this specific discussion, I draw mainly from my work as Movement Tutor at East 15 Acting School in London, particularly between the academic years 2014–2015 and 2016–2017.
5. Even though I introduce the notion of somatic research in actor training, it is a frequently used term in dance pedagogy (Green, 2007, 1119–1132).
6. I refer to somatic practices based on Martha Eddy's "mapping" of the "Founders of Somatic Movement Trainings and their Influences" (see Figure 1 Eddy, 2016, 2). François Delsarte (1811–1871) and Dalcroze (1865–1950) are in the periphery of Eddy's "somatic circles" as broader influences and in the center of this map she situates somatic progenitors such as Rudolf Laban (1879–1958), Heinrich Jacoby (1889–1964) and Elsa Gindler (1885–1961). She connects them with first-generation practitioners, including F.M. Alexander (1869–1955), Moshe Feldenkrais (1904–1984) and Irmgard Bartenieff (1900–1981). Cohen follows in the second generation through the impact of Laban and Bartenieff. For a critical reading on how some of these practices have been used in actor training, see Evans (2009, 2015), Hodge (2010), Murray and Keefe (2016).

7 The exploration of various approaches to breathing patterns for the practice of actors' inner-outer dynamics has a long tradition. For a concise overview of the use of the breath in actor-training approaches, see, among others, Nair (2007) and Boston and Cook (2009).
8 The software used at that point was *Human Anatomy Atlas-Visible Body©* by Argosy Publishing, Inc., 2007–2014.
9 In my current teaching of first-year students at East 15 (academic year 2019–2020), we study a further developed version of this material in the fifth out of nine classes in Term 1 of their studies. The reflective changes have had a very productive impact on the overall understanding of breathing as ground of physiovocal expression and communication in acting.
10 Integration in the IBMT training follows a meticulous theoretical and practical exploration of the studied subject. It is a phase during which learners, working individually or with a partner, release concentration and allow what Cohen identifies as "peaceful comprehension" in embodiment (2012, 157).

References

Argosy. (2007–2014) *Human Anatomy Atlas-Visible Body©* [software]. Newton, MA: Argosy Publishing, Inc.
Bainbridge-Cohen, B. (2012) *Sensing, Feeling, and Action: The Experiential Anatomy of Body-Mind Centering.* Northampton: Contact Editions.
Boston, J. and Cook, R. (2009) *Breath in Action: The Art of Breath in Vocal and Holistic Practice.* London: Jessica Kingsley.
Cavarero, A. (2005) *For More than One Voice: Toward a Philosophy of Vocal Expression.* Translated from Italian by Paul A. Kottman. Stanford, CA: Stanford University Press.
Csordas, T. (1993) Somatic modes of attention. *Cultural Anthropology*, 8(2) 135–156.
Derrida, J. ([1967] 1997) *Of Grammatology.* Translated from French by G. C. Spivak. Baltimore, MD: John Hopkins University Press.
Dewey, J. ([1934] 1980) *Art as Experience.* New York: Penguin Putnam.
Eddy, M. (2016) *Mindful Movement: The Evolution of the Somatic Arts and Conscious Action.* Wilmington: Intellect Ltd.
Evans, M. (2009) *Movement Training for the Modern Actor.* London: Routledge.
——— (2015) *The Actor Training Reader.* Abingdon, Oxon: Routledge.
Green, J. (2007) Student bodies: dance pedagogy and the soma. In: Liora Bresler (ed.) *International Handbook of Research in Arts Education.* Dordrecht: Springer, 1119–1132.
Gutekunst, C. and Gillett J. (2014) *Voice into Acting: Integrating Voice and the Stanislavski Approach.* London: Bloomsbury.
Hanna, T. (1970) *Bodies in Revolt: A Primer in Somatic Thinking.* New York: Holt, Rinehart and Winston.
Hartley, L. (2004) *Somatic Psychology: Body, Mind and Meaning.* London: Whurr Publishers Ltd.
Hodge, A. (2010) *Actor Training.* 2nd edition. London: Routledge.
Kapadocha, C. (2016) *Being an Actor/Becoming a Trainer: The Embodied Logos of Intersubjective Experience in a Somatic Acting Process.* PhD. Royal Central School of Speech and Drama, University of London.
Merleau-Ponty, M. (1968) *The Visible and the Invisible.* Translated from French by Alphonso Lingis and edited by Claude Lefort. Evanston, IL: Northwestern University Press.

Murray, S. and Keefe, J. (2016) *Physical Theatres: A Critical Introduction.* 2nd edition. London: Routledge.
Nair, S. (2007) *Restoration of Breath: Consciousness and Performance.* Amsterdam: Rodopi.
Nelson, R. (2013) *Practice as Research in the Arts: Principles, Protocols, Pedagogies, Resistances.* Hampshire: Palgrave Macmillan.
Pitches, J. (2006) *Science and the Stanislavsky Tradition of Acting.* London: Routledge.
Roach, J. R. (1985) *The Player's Passion: Studies in the Science of Acting.* Newark: University of Delaware.
Sellers-Young, B. (2010) Breath, perception, and action: the body and critical thinking. In: Per Brask and Daniel Meyer-Dinkgräfe (eds.) *Performing Consciousness.* Newcastle upon Tyne: Cambridge Scholars, 63–73.
Shusterman, R. (2008) *Body Consciousness: A Philosophy of Mindfulness and Somaesthetics.* Cambridge: Cambridge University Press.
Stanislavski, K. (2010) *An Actor's Work on a Role.* New York: Routledge.
Stenstad, G. (1993) Merleau-Ponty's logos: the sens-ing of the flesh. *Philosophy Today*, 37(1) 52–61.
Thomaidis, K. and Macpherson, B. (eds.) (2015a) *Voice Studies: Critical Approaches to Process, Performance and Experience.* Abingdon, Oxon: Routledge.
——— (2015b) Introduction: voice(s) as a method and an in-between. In: Konstantinos Thomaidis and Ben Macpherson (eds.) *Voice Studies: Critical Approaches to Process, Performance and Experience.* Abingdon, Oxon: Routledge.
Whyman, R. (2008) *The Stanislavsky System of Acting: Legacy and Influence in Modern Performance.* Cambridge: Cambridge University Press.

Part IV
Beyond the somatic in performance research

13 Mapping the burden of vocality

French seventeenth-century vocal lamentations, Japanese meditation and somatic intra-action

Elisabeth Laasonen Belgrano

Prologue

This chapter has been composed as a performative and in-the-moment narrative, based on a practice-led artistic investigation of a French seventeenth-century manuscript of vocal lamentations titled Leçons de Ténèbres by Michel Lambert (Lambert, c. 1662–1663; Massip, 1999, 215–244), somatic experiences from Alexander Technique lessons (Alexander, 1985, 1997) and feminist new materialist and physics agential realist theories (Barad, 2007, 2010, 2012, 2014; Arlander, 2014). Accordingly, this chapter is an intricate performance and a complex sample of thinking through praxis. The chapter also indicates how a diffractive methodology (Barad, 2007, 2014) can be used for articulating artistic and somatic praxis in an academic context. Rather than describing what has already occurred in the near or far past or reflecting comparatively on the practical aspects with already existing theories (as in practice-based research), words have been carefully selected and performatively shaped in order to meet the reader in the current moment. This allows for the writer and reader to engage, entangle and reason with both heads and hearts. The chapter is a bold attempt to dissolve all thresholds between any agents, including writer and readers. The theoretical terminology is exposed in more detail in endnotes and the text has consciously been framed and figured as an essayistic poetics rather than a regulated description of a practical process eagerly trying to fit into a theoretical standardized format. The notion of somatic as reconfigured in this chapter involves a materialization of thoughts, vocality, movements, physical practice and theory – creating a sensation of a psycho-physical whole: thoughts emerge as a matter of fact, as a burden or a weight, causing an inseparable reaction of body and mind. In other words, a thought becomes a physical matter impossible to separate from a vocal movement. Thought and vocal movement appear psycho-physically united as one.

Argomento

Let me tell you, dear reader, something very important. This chapter is not meant to explain anything. It will describe a series of events, yes it will. But most of all, this chapter is a performance based on somatic experiences. It is important to tell you this at the very beginning, since most probably you will find yourself both confused and wondering. You might think that explanations would have helped to clear out questions or theoretical concepts. Well, it is in fact the state of wonder I am trying to create in myself while writing and in you while reading. Through the words you are reading right now, we are entangled and actively part of a common dynamic landscape: our ways of breathing while writing and reading; the ways we move in and out of our habits and thoughts.[1] I am trying to make words come alive, breathe, move and grow. Like living bodies. Through words, I try to create meaning as somatic experiences. Allowing words to touch and perform, simply by appearing as words. The writing act can be compared to an act of performing vocal sound. When vocal sound appears, the result emerges as a somatic whole. It appears as a materialized burden produced by a voice practitioner.[2] What I try to accomplish with this chapter is to build a bridge between the somatic experiences of voicing and writing. Trusting that you as a reader can engage with these words as you do with a sounding voice. Allow yourself to be touched (and inspired). To let go of old habits (and critical ways of judging). To stop. And to let new directions move through your somatic self. Allowing you neck to be free, your head to move forward and up, to let your back be long and wide, to let ...

A seventeenth-century French vocal lamentation: a point of departure

I open the music manuscript (Figure 13.1) and scribbled signs appear on the page in front of me. Codes to be translated, reconfigured, decoded, analyzed, interpreted, described, explained and performed. Hierarchies are immediately constructed from this simple act of looking into the manuscript. We can decide that this is completely the way it should be, the way many of us are taught to live and learn about most things in life. In terms of two. In terms of oppositional dichotomies. In terms of separation. Categorically, there are many of us – particularly in Western societies – who at this moment are reasoning critically based on dualistic preconception. We have been accustomed within certain cultures to accept both separation and categorization. Body *and* mind. Me *and* you. Him *and* her. Us *and* them. Separated from one another. But, as an experiment, let us take a new look at the manuscript. Let us cut-every-act-apart-and-glue-it-together-in-the-same-breath. Cutting together-apart.[3] Let us start from the beginning.

I open the music manuscript and scribbled signs appear on the page in front of me. I touch the ink with my fingers. As if to make sure the black color has dried into the paper. I see codes that someone has drawn by hand, by body, by mind, by memory. A living movement finding structures on a paper. There is not a single line equal to another. The edge of a tool touching a surface. Fingers touching a paper. It is something in this very moment that

Mapping the burden of vocality 173

Figure 13.1 Score. Seventeenth-century manuscript Leçons de Ténèbres by Michel Lambert.

brings us all together. We are entangled through the score and through these words that we are all performing together while reading. We are all part of the same map and of the same event. As for our method, we are intra-actively diffracting, since we all are agents and actors in the same play.[4] Our eyes are not the same, but all eyes are part of the same apparatus.[5] The same can be said about our bodies and minds. We see, we sense, we reason and we unreason here and now. We are diffractively engaged through a seventeenth-century music score, shaped by a hand that was occupied with many different actions in a very different time than the time we live today. We are part of a historical time, where the past is inseparable from our present and our future.

What has been understood by the hand that placed the ink and the codes in the score does not only have to do with creating a musical score that should explain the ultimate reason for how to sing or play. The hand has lived a life as part of a living-sounding-speaking-moving-writing body. A body/mind has taught a hand to translate memories of living;[6] to silently sing the somatic awareness of a living being into codes and traces for others to take over; for voices to encounter across spacetimes and presumed boundaries. Somatically and diffractively, we all learn to decode the process of living, precisely because we are living and breathing. A hand becomes part of a voice reading/hearing/sensing a text. Because a voice, no matter if silent or sounding, cannot be separated from the living body/mind. Voicing then becomes the intra-acting tool of body/mind for translating the experience of sound. A tool for articulating and structuring the movement of thinking/breathing/acting.

Voicing: an act of transitioning from one place to another as part of the same apparatus

The sound that emerged from her throat was her issue, her task and her cause for action. The materialized yet silent waves passing through her body/mind as thoughts had to be transformed and translated into codes that could be read and understood. That could be listened to. That could be observed as knowledge structured and disseminated to the field for whomever would find the topic of interest. These codes of music on the seventeenth-century surface were not meant to be understood in the same way for everyone. They were meant to be understood and reconfigured individually, somatically, imaginably, speculatively over and over again.[7]

Her feet moved across the large wooden theatre floor. She had been told that her walk should not interfere with the upper part of her body. Only her feet should move. The rest of her body should float above. She searched to focus her eyes somewhere at the back of the stage. Somewhere in between the branches of the large tree painted on the wall at the back of the theatre space. *Suriashi*. This was the specific name of the very slow walk across the Noh stage. The whole foot caressing the floor until the toes at a certain point would leave the ground leading the rest of the foot into a very small step forward. An experiential fragment written by dancer and choreographer Skånberg-Dahlstedt emerged:

> I walk with my teacher, Nishikawa Senrei. Students call her Senrei sensei. The lesson had thus begun, manifested in and with suriashi. Suriashi coordinates our bodies and holds us together. The silence in the dance studio is emphasized through our serene walk. Under my skin however, it is all but quiet. There is an arch in my upper body, a vigorous muscular activation between, and at the back of, my shoulders, but this is not something easily noticed by the naked eye. A physical impetus disseminates my spine whilst I tilt my pelvis backwards and push my chest forwards and upwards. A considerable amount of energy is generated by the intense muscular activity. The posture, the kamae in Japanese, is all about action. Senrei sensi and I walk at the same pace, we turn at the same time. Our white tabis brush the floor, creating a smooth rhythm. Our bodies tremble inaudibly and imperceptibly on the inside from the physical challenge of keeping our rigorous posture.
>
> (Skånberg-Dahlstedt, 2017, 29)

Brushing the floor. The memory of the almost imperceptible touch while slowly sliding forward was now somehow translated into the reading of the music manuscript. The rigorous control of moving between musical notes had to be almost inaudible. The slides indicated in the vocal score had not been of such a great importance until the very moment she understood the movement of her body sliding through the brushing steps of *suriashi*. The *portamento* (the common seventeenth-century ornament allowing for a vocal sliding from one note to another) suddenly informed her how to pass from one place to the other.

> *Portaménto,* cariage, portage, bearing, bringing. Also sufferance. Also the cariage, behaviour or demeanour of a man. Also any fashion or habite of the body. Also any fashion or manner of garment or any this else.
>
> (Florio, 1611)

Her eyes were fixed on the painted tree on the wall, as her feet moved her body across the stage. She moved, with the speed and manner of a snail, into the branches of the tree in front of her. She remembered what she had been told earlier in a lecture about the Noh play. That the tree could be found at the back of all Noh theatres. It was painted as a reflection of a tree that had been planted outside the theatre building. This reflection now called for a reflective extension performed by her own body/mind. Curiously she, herself, became the invisible tree in the garden. She turned to her every-day-mantra, "to let the head go forward and up, to let the neck be free, to let the back be long and wide, to let...". These words came naturally to her body/mind after studying Alexander Technique for almost thirty years. They were part of her somatic system, very much in the same way as her legs and arms were physical extensions of her body. Without moving her upper body, she slowly allowed her arms to stretch into the clear air. Her arms had transformed into moving branches. Branches that made her forget about fixing herself and her breath throughout her action.

As a tree with branches stretching out into the sky, she moved between the notes in the manuscript. She could feel the air supporting her on all sides. Her voice had received the space required for making the path from one place to another. Transitioning between musical notes and experienced realities. Voice carried the air and the life of the tree she had consciously become. A tree firmly rooted in the ground but with branches sensitive to the force of the wind that moved and touched every surface exposed to any external encounter. Her movements were enacting the force of the wind. Slowly, not as a storm. She had become the wind itself. The somatic experience of moving between notes in the musical manuscript had become synonymous with the movement of the wind transitioning between the branches of the tree in the Noh theatre. The somatic experience of becoming a tree became the actual singing of the score (Figure 13.2).

176 *Elisabeth Laasonen Belgrano*

Figure 13.2 Breathing. © Elisabeth Belgrano.

Alexander Technique and the art of touching

The mantra taught to her throughout her many Alexander Technique lessons had become part of her everyday life. Every word in the mantra had become a touching act in itself. This mantra had been incorporated into all possible movements she carried out, in any situation. Into every meeting with any subject/object. The mantra had been a conscious act at the beginning, but over time it had unconsciously become a habit or rather a re-turning to a familiar space where she was allowing herself *to let go*. The space she had become accustomed to enter was not really a physical space. She used to call it her own specific somatic *spacetime* which she tried to explain as a moment of total sensuous awareness – both inward and outward. This awareness occurred to the recitation of the same words: *to let... to let... to allow... to let...* The simultaneous chanting of directions in the end had been reduced to thought provocations. Touches. Somehow these words triggered a realization in her somatic system to occur. Articulations for doing. The event in itself was continuous. Sometimes, she would ask herself how this somatic practice had turned into such groundbreaking stimulation. The continuous practice had allowed a psycho-physical growing initiated by a single touch in the form of a word, a hand or a sound.

> When two hands touch, how close are they? What is the measure of closeness? Which disciplinary knowledge formations, political parties, religious and cultural traditions, infectious disease authorities,

immigration officials, and policy makers do not have stake in, if not a measured answer to, this question? When touch is at issue, nearly everyone's hair stands on end. I can barely touch on even a few aspects of touch here, at most offering the barest suggestion of what it might mean to approach, to dare to come in contact with, this infinite finitude. Many voices speak here in the interstices, a cacophony of always already reiteratively intra-acting stories. These are entangled tales. Each is diffractively threaded through and enfolded in the other. Is that not in the nature of touching? Is touching not by its very nature always already an involution, invitation, invisitation, wanted or unwanted, of the stranger within?

(Barad, 2015, 1)

Touch was the key. The touch in her Alexander lesson, when her teacher had placed her hands at the front and back of her head, on the lower back, on her chest. Their spoken dialogue during the lessons had traveled into many different directions, often seemingly irrelevant to what was going on inside her body or in relation to her skin. It was the touch of the hands of her teacher (often unconsciously sensed in relation to the spoken words) she would always remember. A gentle touch. A touch reminding her that her body was so much more than simply just a body. And, when touched, she suddenly recalled a whole new field growing out of her being – simply due to a single touch. She sensed it as a field of aliveness. The measure of closeness was the actual vibration of warmth and care that gave life to new directions. The somatic experience materialized in every cell of her skin. It caused her to react emotionally and actively. Aroused by memories, sometimes touch made her weak and tearful. Sometimes, sensations caused her to see a light moving above her head or right in front of her eyes. As if someone kept telling "don't stop listening. If you care long enough, you will see. Make sure that you don't forget to breathe". While voices echoed inside her, the ongoing dialogue with her teacher kept moving on. It was as if voices gave hidden directions from behind the stage while she herself was busy acting out her role as an attentive student.

She turned her eyes back to the musical score. What her eyes did in that very moment was not so different from what the hands of her teacher did in the Alexander lesson when they moved on her body. Her eyes adapted the same force. They touched the page in an immediate glance. They carefully moved across lines, notes, words and indications of various vocal ornaments. Her eyes did not try to solve anything specific on the musical page. The page did not explain anything to her, but she knew she was part of a silent performance. Where was she meant to go? What and who would she encounter inside her musical adventure? What was hiding in the shadows behind the articulations – both musically and literary? She found specific points of interest she could not just leave. In her diffracted reading of the score, every detail intra-acted with her somatic self: the score with her eyes;

the indicated ornaments with her neck; the memories of the lyrical context (words, story, content – both vocal and narrative). Her somatic sensation of walking through the melody intra-acted with the sensation of her own experience of an expanding vocal somatic instrument. This whole experience was complex indeed and had to be investigated in all its complexity. Her desire for voicing and re-voicing over and over again made her stay and move further into the musical symbols. Each sound complemented the next one. She had to stop, touch and sense specific fragments. She had to explore the context that was not given. There was always something more and something else to learn and to live through. The score gave her impulses. The score opened up a window for her curiosity to continue moving.

Her sincere sensitivity to the act of touching was a necessary measurement for her practice as a singer and a researching artist. She used to look at herself and others. Being touched by minimal details in any situation triggered her to build structures and draw lines, throwing out invisible garlands to attract new attention. She would move around observing. Her garlands structured themselves into words and narrations. Into ornaments. Words entangling into sentences and eventually into short stories. She had become a critical monster. One who always kept looking under the table for the unexpected to be found. As Alexander points out, she had become one of them who had found out

> that the process gives them the opportunity for testing continuously the validity of their sensory observations and impressions of what is taking place, because all the time that they are consciously projecting the directions for the new and improved use they are obliged to go on *being aware* whether or not they are reverting to the old instinctive misdirection of their use which, associated with the sensory untrustworthiness, had led them originally to be deceived in what they were doing with themselves.
>
> (1985, 108, original emphasis)

Translated into her own words, she knew that every single one of her acts was never separated from her own processes of judging. Her process involved a continuous moving, removing, configuring, reconfiguring and translating. Every act included a row of continuous encounters or events that created a paradigmatic impact on all following acts. It was, as Erin Manning suggests, "an attunement to the differential of the minor gestures" (in Zegher et al, 2017, 367). Naturally, this kind of attunement followed her everywhere in her work as well as in her everyday life. Applied to her vocal studies, the sensitivity into the score made her realize that the manuscript in itself was only a fraction of what the whole musical experience could become. And what she saw when reading the score was a million and more stories enfolded into her own. Stories that she had to figure out in relation to her readings. In relation to the *spacetime* she inhabited. In relation to the

Mapping the burden of vocality 179

Figure 13.3 To let. © Elisabeth Belgrano.

roads she decided to walk. In relation to her companions. In relation to the community she belonged to. But also in relation to feelings, to silence, to longing and to vocal sounds that grew and dynamically evolved from inside her. She knew that her voice, so real and determined to her in all its aspects, was like an eternal yet limited story in a limitless *spacetime* (Figure 13.3).

Meditating as meaning-making

She followed the handwritten vocal melody on the music sheet. Connecting and translating. Never comparing. Only moving, relating, learning and growing based on a combination of previous experiences and a strong energy of desire. Melodic patterns became clear the more she intra-actively engaged in her practice. She started to understand the logic of disguising "irrationality" (Massip, 1999, 228).[8] Music was structured in such a way that nothing made sense at first, but slowly the score and the sound taught her about the process of meaning-making. The art of impatient learning for the sake of doing and becoming whole. Becoming alive in its stillness. She feared that her voice would make a boring impression, but what did that boringness and dullness mean? She had a feeling it had to do with a Western fear of missing out on the blissful and sparkling event a happening could be and become. Or what did a happening-encounter mean? She turned to the happening master Allan Kaprow for an answer. Jeff Kelley writes in the acknowledgments of Kaprow's book *Essays on the blurring of art and life:*

> If Dewey's influence upon Kaprow can be reduced to a single phrase, it would be that 'doing is knowing'. What Kaprow hopes to know is the meaning of everyday life. To know that meaning, he must enact it every day. This is where pragmatism becomes a practice. […]

A methodological verification of existence takes sustenance from Zen. Like Dewey's pragmatism, Zen mistrusts dogma and encourages education, seeks enlightenment but avoids formalistic logic, accepts the body as well as mind, and embraces discipline but relinquishes ego-centered control. In establishing discipline as a contemplative practice that opens the practitioner to knowledge, Zen loosely parallels the scientific method, in which controls are established in an experimental process that opens the researcher to phenomena. For Kaprow pragmatism is the mechanics of Zen, and Zen the spirit of pragmatism.

(2003, xxiv)

Kaprow found in the music of John Cage "the merger of Zen and science, of passive contemplation and active experimentation" (Ibid.). In her own study, seventeenth-century music allowed her practising exactly what Kelley describes. She experienced her own vocal existence while meditating herself through the musical score, while being engaged in a lively dialogue about the meaning of every sound, slide and movement. Her praxical exploration was a meditation on and study of being human.

She had made an appointment with a doctoral student at the University of Kyoto. He was studying Japanese philosophy as well as practising *zazen* – Zen Buddhist sitting meditation – in a temple in Kyoto. She would for the first time experience this form of meditation. A little anguished, she felt she was embarking on something very important but also something extremely new to her. She felt as if she was in no man's land. An in-between feeling. She set off in the morning allowing herself plenty of time to arrive. The temple was situated behind a large wall with a wooden gate. There was no possibility of getting a glimpse of the place from outside. While waiting outside the gate, questions kept coming to her: who was the person she would meet? Where would he take her? What would she experience? What kind of place was she about to enter? The wall kept all secretly away from her until the moment the gate opened and she was invited to step inside. She followed his steps along a path in the midst of a carefully raked garden. She found a sense of peace. They walked onto a wooden terrace that seemed to surround the main temple building. He indicated that she should take off her shoes. By mistake, she started to put on a pair of slippers but soon enough she realized that she had committed her first error. That memory stayed with her for a long time after she had left the temple. The memory of committing an error.

They turned to the main temple hall and went inside. She felt the soft wood under her feet and was suddenly recalling the memory of moving in *suriashi* across the theatre floor at the Noh Theatre in Tokyo. The two experiences of moving occurred simultaneously. Intra-actively entangled into one another. This sensation of being in an endless spacetime encounter blurred when she forced herself to focus on the fact that she was in a temple in Kyoto walking behind a person who was going to guide her into her first experience of *zazen*. There was a large Buddha seated in the middle of the

Mapping the burden of vocality 181

Figure 13.4 Meditation. © Elisabeth Belgrano.

room. Two places were prepared. One right in front of the statue, the other placed a little to the side and in a ninety degrees angle from the first place. The seats were arranged so that they could see each other.

The meditation session lasted all together thirty minutes divided in two separate parts. During the first part, they sat together counting their breath. In the second part, she sat on her own, meditating, while he was walking around the temple hall. The whole experience brought her into a silent engagement with stillness and motion. She later recalled the words of Thomas Hanna: "A soma is any individual embodiment of a process, which endures and adapts through time, and it remains a soma as long as it lives. The moment it dies it ceases to be a soma and becomes a body" (in Eddy, 2016, 5). Sitting in *zazen* became an active shaping of spacetime itself. Time had no great importance in her meditation. She knew that somehow her guide had full control over their time together and that she, through her breathing, kept a certain rhythm that indicated her spatial situatedness in time. Her somatic being *inside* time might have been her greatest sensation in the temple. Spatiality was acting through her whole being. Her silent voice sounded endlessly, bringing both a state of relief and a profound sensation of active wholeness. Meaning emerged as a sounding voice without voice (Figure 13.4).

Epilogue: mapping the somatic burden of vocality

After her meditation experience in the temple, she had found a translation of the word *sóma* in Florio's seventeenth-century Italian-French dictionary. Here, *sóma* was described as "any kind of load, burthen, fraught or charge that any beast doth beare. Used also for man's bodie or mortall vaile" (Florio, 1611). For some reason, the load and the burden related to the silent activity she had experienced while meditating in the temple. Soma belonged to the spatial encounter of breathing and hearing her silent voice vibrating through and around her. Soma was heavy and desired at the same time. It had aroused a sensation of living and hoping in her, even if it all happened in silence. No part of the experience had been separated or left aside. What had been materialized as part of the ontological experience relied on a psycho-physical unity. Burden became meaning-as-mattering or materializing-in-itself. The experience of soma had sedimented in her a sense of weight but in a mature and complementary way. The somatic burden was the sensation of a phenomenon produced by "the ontological inseparability/entanglement of intra-acting 'agencies'" (Barad in Arlander, 2014, 28). The somatic sensing of voice without voice and the lamenting meditation from the seventeenth-century score contributed as agencies producing load (*soma*) as intra-acting phenomena. Through the specific intra-action of these agencies, "the boundaries and the properties of the 'components' of phenomena become determinate and the particular material articulations in the world become meaningful" (Ibid.). The somatic burden made sense through its specific vocal materialization.

In her study of the vocal score, she realized that she had found yet another way of reading music. She had discovered that vocality was a somatic materialization of all intra-acting components emerging along the voicing research process. Her understanding of the load or burden of vocality was produced by readings and imaginative encounters, as part of her vocal acts, meditation and theories. The somatic burden she embodied through her voicing emerged as a fascinating sedimentation of vocal psycho-physical understandings. Somatic vocality could only become reality when all agencies intra-acted as one entangled unit. The agencies could never produce her understanding of somatic vocality as separated inter-acting "objects-in-themselves" (Ibid.). Instead, her understanding depended on the way she experienced everything around her and inside her as intra-actions rather than inter-acting components. She knew this was a significant key in her practice of voicing. Practice/theory could never be separated in order to produce her understandings. Nor could Eastern/Western meditative practices be separated in her meaning-making processes. Barad writes that

> [a]gency is 'doing' or 'being' in its intra-activity. It is the enactment of iterative changes to particular practices – iterative reconfigurings of topological manifold of spacetime-matter relations – through the dynamics of intra-action. Agency is about changing possibilities of change entailed in reconfiguring material-discursive apparatuses of bodily production, including the boundary articulations and exclusions that are marked by those practices in the enactment of a causal structure.
>
> (2007, 178)

Mapping the burden of vocality 183

The theory on intra-acting agencies helped her understand that her intra-active enactments, as a somatically-informed practitioner and a vocal performer engaged in critical research, produced her somatic vocality. Allowing agencies to somatically intra-act paved way for her voice to expand and for unexpected encounters to grow into a continuous meaning-making praxis.

Acknowledgments

The author acknowledges the support from Royal Academy of Music, The Royal Society of Arts and Sciences in Gothenburg, Sven and Dagmar Saléns Stiftelse, Helge Ax:son Johnsons Stiftelse, Gertrude and Ivar Philipsons Stiftelse and Japanstiftelsen.

Notes

1 The term entanglement can primarily be related to physics. Physics and feminist scholar Karen Barad uses the term in her agential realism theory while referring to "the ontological inseparability" of phenomena (2007, 308); "the notion of entanglement needs to be understood in terms of the relational ontology of agential realism" (Barad, 2007, 388–389). She is talking about entangled practices as dynamic intra-actions where agents are *part of* a process of understanding certain phenomena, rather than being removed – positioned as distant spectators – from the object of study. To be entangled means to be dynamically involved and *part of* a meaning-making process. In this chapter, the words I/we/us/our indicate an ontological inseparability, meaning that we are not any longer seen as separated individuals through our practice of writing/reading, but rather dynamically entangled in the process of making sense of the words we encounter. We are *part of* each other's practices of thinking, imagining or moving in our different ways of understanding and making sense of what we read, despite any physical or spatial distance. We are all part of an intra-active entanglement. For further discussion on the term intra-action vs. inter-action, see endnote 6.
2 I will return to the analogue between soma and the burden of vocality in the Epilogue of this chapter.
3 The term cutting together-apart is presented by Barad as follows: "[...] is about joins and disjoins – cutting together/apart – not separate consecutive activities, but a single event that is not one. *Intra-actions*, not interaction" (2010, 244, original emphasis). For the definitions of intra-action and inter-action, see endnote 4.
4 Barad explains intra-action and inter-action as follows:

> The notion of intra-action (in contrast to the usual 'interaction', which presumes the prior existence of independent agencies or relata) represents a profound conceptual shift. It is through specific agential intra-actions that the boundaries and properties of the components of phenomena become determinate and that particular concepts [...] become meaningful.
>
> (2007, 139)

Also see Arlander (2014). Another term that needs some clarification is diffracting or diffractive methodology: according to Barad, a diffractive methodology "is a critical practice of engagement, not a distance-learning practice of reflecting from afar. The agential realist approach [...] eschews representationalism and advances performative understanding [...] of knowledge-making practices" (2007, 90). Also, once more, see Arlander (2014).

5 "[A]*pparatuses are not mere observing instruments but boundary-drawing practices - specific material (re)configurings of the world - which come to matter*" (Barad, 2007, 140, original emphasis). Her terminology has been developed from Michel Foucault's use of the same term (2007, 199–201).
6 Throughout the chapter, you will find the use of slashes between words. They have consciously been used following Barad's theory "to denote a dis/continuity – a cutting together-apart" (2015, 12, n.6).
7 On the term *reconfiguring*:

> Scenes never rest but are reconfigured within and are dispersed across and threaded through one another [...] The reader should feel free to jump from any scene to another (is there any other way to proceed?) and still have a sense of connectivity through the traces of variously entangled thread [...].
> (Barad, 2010, 244–245)

8 The music has been described as being both "irrational" and at the same time very much to the point through distinct clarifications and highly specific details (Massip, 1999, 215–244).

References

Alexander, F. M. (1997) *Constructive Conscious Control of the Individual.* London: STAT Books.
——— (1985) *The Use of the Self.* London: Victor Gollancz.
Arlander, A. (2014) From interaction to intra-action in performing landscape. *Artnodes*, 14 26–34.
Barad, K. (2007) *Meeting the Universe Halfway. Quantum Physics and the Entanglement of Matter and Meaning.* Durham: Duke University Press.
——— (2010) Quantum entanglements and hauntological relations of inheritance: dis/continuities, spacetime enfoldings and justice-to-come. *Derrida Today*, 3(2) 240–268.
——— (2014) Diffracting diffraction: cutting together apart. *Parallax*, 20(3) 168–187.
——— (2015) When two hands touch, how close are they? On touching – the inhuman that therefore I am (v1.1) [pre-print] Published. In: Susanne Witzgall and Kerstin Stakemeier (eds.) (2018) *Power of Material/ Politics of Materiality.* Zurich: Diaphanes, 153–164. Available from: https://www.diaphanes.net/titel/on-touching-the-inhuman-that-therefore-i-am-v1-1-3075 [Accessed 17 October 2019].
Eddy, M. (2016) *Mindful Movement. The Evolution of the Somatic Arts and Conscious Action.* Wilmington, NC: Intellect Ltd.
Florio, J. (1611) *Italian/English dictionary: Queen Anna's new world of words.* Available from: http://www.pbm.com/~lindahl/florio/ [Accessed 17 October 2019].
Kaprow, A. (2003) *Essays on the Blurring of Art and Life.* Edited by Jeff Kelley. Berkley, CA: University of California Press.
Lambert, M. (1662–1663) *Leçon du Ténèbres.* Cycle I, Bibliotheque Nationale de France, département de la Musique, Rés. 585.
Massip, C. (1999) *L'art de Bien Chanter: Michel Lambert (1610–1696).* Paris: Société Française de Musicologie.
Skånberg Dahlstedt, A. (2017) Suriashi: a meditation on the local through artistic research. In: Louisa Greenfield, Myna Trustram and Eduardo Abrantes (eds.) *Artistic Research – Being There, Explorations into the Local.* Arhus: Nordic Summer University Press, 29–42.
Zegher, C., Gansterer, N. and Manning, E. (2017) Trialogue: thinking-making in relation. In: Nikolaus Gansterer, Ema Cocker and Mariella Greil (eds.) *Choregraphic Figures: Deviations from the Line.* Berlin: Walther de Gruyter, 367–373.

14 Intensive interaction

A lesson on *queered* voicing from children with learning disAbilities

Yvon Bonenfant

Prelude 1: on this chapter

In my 2010 article "Queer listening to queer vocal timbres" (Bonenfant, 2010), I postulated the beginnings of a theory of *how* and *why* queer people find each other through the timbre, or touch and texture, of vocal emanations. Essentially, I argued that queered bodies develop a kind of virtuosity of listening that enables them to reach out and feel out for, other, othered bodies, by attending to the voices produced by those bodies and their literal and symbolic touch qualities, as embedded in their timbral transmissions. I argued that the touch of vocal difference exerted a pull on other people who had uniquely queered bodies. Drawing from Thomas Csordas' (2006) theory of *somatic modes of attention*, crossed with readings of Sara Ahmed's (2006) notions of *queered spatial relations*, I argued that there exists a kind of *queer listening* that can listen out for and feel out for and revel in other queered bodies through the din of (hetero-) normative sound that dominates most of our quotidian space.

That article, however, limited its scope to the realm of the LGBTQI+-identified. Shortly after its publication, I developed interactive vocal art projects with primary school children (2012–ongoing, Bonenfant, 2018a, b). These raised many questions about how children's voices might be considered queered in culture – for children are routinely shut up, silenced, quietened, pacified and generally disciplined into shaping their vocalizations in "social" ways; their vocal emanations and the bodies they represent are rarely accorded the same respect as those of adults. This chapter goes a bit further and concentrates on a specific group of children who belong to the diagnostic and demographic category of profound and multiple learning disabilities (PMLD).

Drawing from a Research and Development (R&D) case study that took place at Rosewood Free School (Southampton, England, 2014–2015), I explore the intersection of three kinds of embodied practice: *intensive interaction*, *non-punctate* voicing and *extra-normal* voicing, within an unusual kind of somatic relationship.[1] This somatic relationship is one where a lead artist (myself), who has a non-disAbled body, is working with and relating to learning artists (children), whose bodies are understood by wider society to be disabled. The eventual goal was to enable the children artists to feel as much agency to explore their vocalities' creative potential as possible.

Through this writing, I hope to open up a dialogue about the questions and transformative potentials, raised by the exchange of vocal-somatic stimuli between bodies constructed as normative and others constructed as more extra-normal. Through so doing, I intend to stimulate thought about the future of the queered voice in an ever-queering culture.

Prelude 2: on somatic(s) in this chapter

Within the diverse constellation of somatic practices that animate the pages of this book, my own grounding in somatics comes from the perspective of both having been a client in and having been trained in variations on neo-Reichian approaches to body psychotherapy techniques, derived from practices of the schools of Gerda Boyesen (2018) (biodynamic psychology), Alexander Lowen (2013) (bioenergetic analysis) and Charles Kelly's radix body re-education (The Radix Institute, 2019). What all three of these approaches share is an understanding of the demonstrative expression of emotion as positive rather than pathological. In fact, to differing extents, these techniques see expressions such as sobbing, yelling, shouting, wailing, cursing and laughing out loud with uncontrolled, raucous joy as social activities rather than anti-social ones.

All of these techniques attempt to cultivate – in different ways – the capacity of the client or patient to access the felt experience of intensely expressive emotional states with increased ease. The goal is to take "command" of such states through immersing oneself in them and getting to know them and thereby consciously experience and engage with their flow. Thus, the discussed techniques assert that mastering intense emotions involves consciously experiencing their abreactive qualities from within one's own body and that expressive, emotional energy is a power to be harnessed, not sublimated or repressed.[2] The specific techniques also conceive of vocal expression as part of a whole-body somatic ecosystem, where eye contact, eye expression, gesture, movement and vocalizing are construed as inter-dependent. Therefore, they predispose one to feeling that non-verbal vocal material is of value.

There is less emphasis placed on self-calming, contemplation or meditative reflexivity in these three body psychotherapy techniques than in many other somatic practices. Whether or not this set of values regarding abreaction accords with the reader's, from a vocal perspective, it is clear that being a client or patient in these practices has a tendency to encourage one to generate non-verbal vocal material that might be termed "emotionally raw" and hyper-expressive. Because of this, the vocalizations produced in some of the sessions one might experience in these kinds of practices are most certainly queering, in that through exploring these expressive impulses overtly, one is counter-acting some of the mores and values of bourgeois Western culture – one is indulging in intense emotional expression in an environment where it is valued as creative, rather than silenced or criticized.

More importantly for the relationship with the children referred to in this chapter was my training in biodynamic massage, which one learns as part of training in biodynamic psychotherapy. It is one of the tools used in such therapy, but it is also practised as a relaxation massage technique, independently of psychotherapeutic contexts. Biodynamic massage is a technique developed by clinical psychologist and physiotherapist Gerda Boyesen (2002) from the physiotherapeutic interventions of Norwegian physiotherapist Adel Bülow-Hansen. During a biodynamic massage session, in most cases, extremely light touch is used, often on skin level and often over clothing, unlike Swedish massage or other oil-based more vigorous approaches. Most pertinent to this chapter, though, is the kind of attention to other bodies that is developed by the professional biodynamic massage practitioner.

This attention is enacted when a stethoscope is placed on the client's area of the large intestine and the sounds of the intestine are listened to as cues to whether they are "digesting" stress or other emotions (Bassal and Coster Heller, 2015, 159–160). Beyond questions on whether such assumptions about the sounds of one's digestive system have any scientific basis, the approach trains the practitioner to listen to the involuntarily produced sounds of the human body and to integrate these with the tactile feedback received through the hands-on work. Thus, when one learns this kind of massage, they practise – indeed, rehearse – listening to the non-verbal voice of the (digestive) body of other people, while trying to decode some of the system's secret song-like poetry. They simultaneously enter an extremely delicate touch relationship – a dance of skin-level contact that requires intense concentration. Attending to voice of the body and to the delicacy of the minute signals of the skin becomes a kind of virtuosic practice.

The sonic and corporeal relationship with the children with PMLD, as discussed in the following parts, was not "therapy". It was about vocal improvisation without, beyond or despite the absence of words, about mutual engagement of our sound worlds and bodies in a kind of kinetic, dancing relationship of play with vocalic difference. While I was attempting to act as a facilitator of the child's vocal sound, I was not trying to heal their trauma, better them in some way or improve their mind-body self-awareness. All I was trying to do was to hear their voices and be challenged by them; stimulate voice, and voice back.

An invitation to *profound* and *multiple* learning

In 2014, I was invited into Rosewood Free School to work on voice with the children. Rosewood is a state-funded school for children with PMLD. An arts specialist who worked in this school had heard of and seen parts of Your Vivacious Voice! (Bonenfant, 2013), a project of mine that developed interactive vocal performance for children aged 6–11. During that work, I had focused on eliciting non-normative voicing from the children and had set up frameworks within which they co-made intermedia vocal art from these "strange" voicings. The arts specialist said that she had an instinct that I should explore some kind of similar vocal art work for and with the children at Rosewood. She was particularly interested in how the explored interaction seemed to overtly celebrate the participants' vocal creativity and uniqueness, while it avoided "typical" singing practices. At that point though, I knew nothing about the nature of PMLD.

PMLD is an unusually complex and individual condition; we might even call it, in humanities terms, a condition of profound biophysical intersectionality, within which interwoven conditions (genetic, developmental, neurological, physical or psychological) co-exist to differing degrees and influence one another. It would be very rare for two children with PMLD to be identically disAbled. For these reasons, within the medical-educational environment, there has been a long debate around exactly how to define PMLD, beyond simply identifying the children as having extreme disAbility-related needs. Responding to this lack of clear definition, in 2010 Bellamy et al (2010) surveyed a wide range of stakeholders (such as care workers, parents, teachers, medical professionals) in PMLD-related environments in the UK, as well as existing literature, to attempt to distill some sense of accord about what exactly PMLD persons have in common from a symptomatic perspective. The overall understanding is that people with PMLD have the chance to engage and to achieve their optimum potential in a highly structured environment with constant support and an individualized relationship with a carer (Bellamy et al, 2010, 263). They also summarized the following general symptoms: delayed intellectual and social functioning, possible limited ability to engage verbally but response to cues (e.g. familiar voice, touch, gestures), need for support by their carers when communicating with others, frequent association with a medical condition such as neurological issues, physical or sensory impairments.

Situating the above in the school environment, it practically means that learners are often in wheelchairs or lying down. The degree to which their *profound* and *multiple* conditions influence these children is unique and individual. So, in addition to the more universal and typical ways in which all humans are unique, these people have extra layers of uniqueness woven within them. These extra layers of uniqueness, I assert, *queer* these children in the eyes of wider culture. Vocally speaking, they rarely use words to express themselves; though some do, but many routinely use vocal and other biophysical sound, like tapping and squeezing.

Setting up our *learning* process

The first time we went to the school, collaborating digital artist Kingsley Ash and I visited a music class. In the class, children in wheelchairs sat with a person beside them, seeing to their needs. As the children entered the classroom, a little gentle pat was given on the shoulder. We learned that at Rosewood, multi-sensory signals (words, touches, visual signals) are used to help the students know what might happen next and thereby to help them have a measure of predictability about the shapes of their days and experiences. In addition, the learners were addressed as much as possible in the first person, rather than talked "about". For instance, teachers did not say to us: "he likes the colour blue," but rather, "Rodney likes the colour blue, don't you, Rodney?" Continual efforts were made to de-medicalize the ways the children were treated, to actively include them in communication about them and to treat them like their views, preferences and expressions mattered.

Direct address and communication seem self-evidently important to the children's well-being. Nevertheless, this is not the case in the majority of care-provided environments. The children at Rosewood, subjected to and indeed needing *care* for most of their day, would be highly vulnerable to the objectifying medicalization of their bodies, with the consequent de-personalization and de-humanization of their somatic experiences of selfdom by persons wielding medical, educational and other forms of care "power". The school made concerted efforts to *not* do this. The children were *valued* as people with *desires, preferences* and *unique personalities.* Their differences were acknowledged and celebrated. We were moved by the attention paid to the whole-body modes of communication that seemed to be appropriate with most of the children. The voice was accompanied by touch, by intense eye contact, by a careful direction of attention to the senses of the student across registers of sensation.

We watched a music class during which children shook maracas, drummed and made little vocal sounds. Many of them smiled, giggled, growled, shook themselves, moved excitedly, danced to some rhythms, looked around, wriggled with their eyes and limbs to the sound. The children went out again, after a closing ritual to their session and careful orientation to the next event of the day. Our observation offered us new knowledge and lots of elements to reflect upon before beginning our process.

Kingsley Ash, a sound and intermedia artist, sound engineer and coder; Ricardo da Fonseca, a lighting designer, and I returned to the school together. Entering our work room, our intention was to transform it and make it feel somehow *magical.* To do so, we developed a light-color-sound interaction. We set up two microphones and we arranged for them to sound back through a digital interface and speakers. We also connected the microphones to a projector that would respond to the received sounds through color patterns and to lights shed on the walls. In this first phase of our work, we visited the school for three, two-day long improvisation sessions between myself and a child. A new child visited us almost every thirty minutes.

During each session, I held the microphones close to our mouths and we simply made sounds. Kingsley used live coding to echo these sounds back to us after a delay. The length and quality of the delay and reverb constantly varied; additional effects were sometimes added to the voices. He also used live coding to control the projected colors and the brightness of the lights on the walls. Everything responded to the vocal input. We started by looking at what in the Your Vivacious Voice! project, with the advice of renowned psycholinguist Prof. Catherine Best of Western Sydney University, we identified as *the voice-enhancing mirror principle*: the children's motivation to explore what *else* their voices can do, as induced by the discussed echoing (Bonenfant, 2018a, b). Working with the specific group of children, it soon became about the qualities of their sounds per se as well as the qualities in our interaction.

With one child, we developed a "duet" with her breath patterns only. She barely vocalized, but after fifteen minutes or so of copying her breath patterns with different echoing delays, she started to breathe out little groups of pulsed breaths into the microphone. That felt very much like a dialogue with me. She seemed to wait to hear the echoes, both those made by me and by the sound and light array we had set up. Another child made snore-like, tiny, gentle and sweet snort-sounds, which I imitated by echoing them as best I could, and with which Kingsley invented gentle and sensual landscapes of echo-sound that helped form a backdrop to our duet. Again, she, at some point, started phonating in response to me, even if at a very low volume. We became lost in a bliss of snort-like duets: pleasureful, funny, whimsical but somehow also profoundly serious. A few children did not make discernible vocal sounds. Sometimes, they were tired or under the weather; other times, it was just not a thing they usually did. Still, I sang to them with my own extra-normal vocal lexicon.

Sounds in queered (non-punctuate) time

Almost all the children responded to my invitations to vocalize in some way and almost none of them used standard words.[3] The sounds they made were, to my mind, glorious. Utterly glorious. I reveled in them. They made the widest variety of delightful utterances: delightful, at least, to a "professional" extra-normal vocalist. But how could I describe the sounds the children made? There is little vocabulary in English to describe the range of timbres, textures and breath-column variations that they were able to produce. Long, streaming joy-wails. Shorter, stuttering, churning columns of repeating peck-bocks. Curling, languid moan-laughter. Shallow, breathy sand-grunts. Sudden shout-dances. Quiet murmur-trails. Giggle-leaps. Jokey twists of labials. Long pauses, short pauses, scratchy dental sounds, singing-like scoop-notes. And once they realized they were being echoed – by me, by the digital apparatus or by both – about 60 percent of them became deeply exploratory, making sound, listening back, sometimes making more sound over the loop of delayed sound that was coming back to them. Some of them needed me to continue making sound; sometimes, I or we seemed to be enjoying making sound in echo or unison; some made sound to and with each other;[4] and others did not seem interested in further input from my voice once they understood the digital echoing setup.

In another context, these very sounds might have been construed as "ugly" or "embarrassing". They were sounds that most listeners do not usually associate with the volitional production of vocal communication and refined artistic cultures of vocal production. They were sounds that, in the not too distant past, would have been heard as embarrassing, awkward or uncouth. But when one has been exposed to Cageian aesthetics, the theatrical and musical extended voice traditions and the historic avant-garde's reconstruction of "all sound" as musical, or at least, meaningful;[5] if one is familiar with the challenging aesthetics of live/performance art, where the focus is on the process of making happening in front of you, rather than having been done before you arrive;[6] if one is interested in traditions of post-post-modern dance where *all* gesture, not just *beautiful* gesture, matters and carries aesthetic weight;[7] these sounds felt genuinely virtuosic. The children had particular propensities and talents that were unusual. One propensity was a seeming lack of need for pulse, rhythm, meter or predictable prosody in their sound. On a similar note, they demonstrated an ability to generate extremely long silences between utterances; silences that seemingly force the "typical" listener to contemplate the power and meaning of the preceding utterances. I connect both qualities with the concept of non-punctuate time in vocal utterance.

The concept of non-punctate musical time is not new. However, neuroscientific musicologist Alex Khalil (personal communication, June 3, 2019), though he has not yet written about this term, verbally coined it in order to sum up the concept of not needing, being wedded to or feeling a strong impulse to engage with typical notions of repetitive pulse and rhythm. He is studying populations of people whose relationships to the passage of sonic time are atypical and he needed a term to describe *how* this was so. I, personally, have found the term incredibly useful because of its onomatopoeic quality. To non-musically educated people, one can say: well, punctate time is punk, punk, punk, punk (four repetitive beats), but non-punctate time does not need a punk! They do not think in punk! Time speeds up, slows down, is fragmented, or the beats of the punks are so far apart or close together that typical listeners cannot detect a pulse anymore. Or, the time between the punks is constantly varying.

I hope that it is evident that this is an extra-normal relationship with the passage of sonic time and thus, that children with PMLD, in my understanding, are *virtuosic queerers* of the passage of time in vocal utterance. Their utterances invite us to cast aside our assumptions about the pace and prosody of vocal sound. For even sentences have notions of sonic time embedded in theme, thanks to sentence contour and prosody. We expect sentences to begin and end in certain ways and we expect certain words to be spoken with specific melodic qualities, situated with the patterns of speech we call our accents; without prosody and sentence contour, we lose our verbal cues to the passage of time.

Queer (intensive) interaction

With many children, I worked, at first, to stimulate a sense that any vocal sound would be permitted and found meaningful or beautiful. Some children seemed to respond with interest and vocalization only when I was in extreme physical proximity to them. I often had to use a form of ineffable somatic intuition, to tell me whether the child could tell that I, another vocalizer, was there echoing their sounds and I suppose, by extension, that their sounds mattered to me. This meant that I might put my cheek very near to theirs; or maybe a hand over their head to feel the heat coming from them; hoping they would feel heat coming from me; some children grabbed and played with my face or fingers, the way young babies might do, seemingly to explore who I was and what on earth I was doing there. Some children would respond with physical cues, cocking an ear to my low register, some to my high register and some to very different timbres and diaphragmatic impulses; some to consonants, some to words and some to the sound of their names, played with, stretched or expanded. Responses ranged from flickers of eyelids, to changed breathing patterns, to reaching towards me, to vocalizing with or in response to me.

Throughout this interactive process, a profound somatic attunement to their states was required, including rapid-fire, subconscious, intuitive readings of the micro-signals from their bodies, to decide how to approach the invitation to voice. I was paying attention to extremely unusual vocal cues, to my own sensations and to atypically configured bodies. I was learning to feel and listen and exchange vocal sound in new ways from these cues and bodies and I was loving it. At that point, I was neither aware of the term *intensive interaction* nor that I was doing a form of it. All I knew was that I was absorbed, hyper-attentive and yet generatively creative with my vocal gestures, in the *queerest* way, because I wanted to approach them without the obligation to speak words that made "sense".

Though I have used the phrase intensive interaction earlier in this chapter, I have not formally defined it. Like PMLD, there seems in fact not to be a clear, single definition of intensive interaction: it represents many different ways of approaching the use of body language, facial expression, non-verbal cues, mirroring and other strategies to signal to people with complex disabilities that their utterances, gestures, desires and interests matter to a listener-witness, in the hopes that such signals and communication will stimulate the person's own interest in communication (summarized from Caldwell, 2011). The technique is used widely in special schools in the UK, as is evidenced by Mouriere's and McKim's (2018) recent collection of case studies of intensive interaction leads in nine different schools (where it is used to relate to children with PMLD, Autistic Spectrum disOrders and mixed complex learning disAbilities). There is an enlarging body of discourse that has evolved, especially in the last fifteen years, exploring the benefits of and best practice in, the technique.[8] Caldwell's summary of what intensive interaction is and how it works describes the underpinning principles in the following way:

> The paradigm underlying Intensive Interaction is that of the Infant-Mother interaction, in which the infant initiates a sound or movement or rhythm and the mother responds in an imitative way. Once the baby's initiative is sufficiently confirmed they are able to move on and try out something else. *It is crucial to emphasise that in using Intensive Interaction we are not in any way infantilising our conversation partners, since for all of us, this non-verbal dialogue is a primary communication pathway, laid down in babyhood but remaining with us all our lives.* We continue to look for underlying confirmation throughout adulthood.
>
> (2011, added emphasis)

Caldwell moves on to point out that:

> Because interactions are all personal, each practitioner tends to develop their own style. Personally, since I find that it is easy to block intuitive perception with information that is not relevant to our current interaction, I tend not to take elaborate histories or go through long preliminary observations.
>
> (2011)

Own style, intuition, intuitive perception: the lexicons of art-making and of relational, vocal-somatic practices converge with the educational. Body language, pre-verbal utterances and intuition dance together in order to send an intensely meant message to a partner, a message of welcome to unusual voicings taking place in non-punctate time. Intense attention is paid to non-verbal cues; imitation of these cues, of sounds and of eye contact signals to the object of one's interactive impulses that one wants to engage in and cares about, the nature of the communication at play. And somehow, the goal is also to acknowledge that the child with PMLD is a child, without infantilizing them.

One way of doing this, I would assert, is by moving beyond the educational paradigm of intensive interaction to treat the child's vocal creativity as if it has aesthetic value and not just emotional, developmental or educational value: as if it were functionally useless, yet inconceivably beautiful. Valuing its content for its sonic beauty shifts the emphasis from the adult partner being a "helper" or "carer" to being a facilitator in a dialogue among aesthetic equals. This is a decidedly queer sort of somatic relationship, for it places value on unusual vocal utterance that moves beyond the relational qualities of such utterances and treats them as cultural production.

The work thus plunges us into a deeply queered, special and extra-normal relationship with vocalic material and unusual bodies. Indeed, we might even call this space a queered somaesthetic, subverting Shusterman's (2008) modernist somatic project. This is a performative space within which bodies seek to "better" their relationships with themselves along alternative lines of value, where non-verbal and idiosyncratic utterances of difference become queered vocal beauty and where voicing with and from embodied PMLD becomes a sublime form of queered vocal art.

The future of *queer voicing*

Out of the first six days of visiting the Rosewood school, it emerged that a small proportion of the children seemed to have already been developing an increasing sense of being in "control" of their experience from one session to the next. Once they began vocalizing, they would recognize that their volitional sound was creating the sound-light echo experience and would take over from me. They would play with their voicings more and more and show increasing interest in improvising in relation to their own echoing sounds. This would make me feel very moved, because these children seemed to have so few opportunities to take control of a sensory world. They would stop needing me to stimulate and respond to them and begin making soundscapes from their own vocalizations – long, resonant tails of echoes, formed by the vocal impulses of their uniquely configured, voicing bodies. These sounds later decayed and reverberated in echoing trails, moving away from us and into the seeming sonic distance. Listening to themselves through the sonic and visual "mirror" provided by me, by the digital sound and light apparatus or both, they would do their own thing and generate astonishingly unusual sounds.

I loved being in active interaction with these sounds. I might often have been having a more stimulating experience than the children were, because the sounds they made could be challenging for me to imitate. I had to use my whole body to try to echo them and to channel their unique vocal gestures through my corporeal system. I tried to enter their vocal worlds, not merely invite them into mine; yet, I also *used* mine. And at the end of each day, I felt absolutely exhausted and absolutely blissful. These were some of the best "performances" of my life. In a way, I felt like I had found my best-ever audience. They sang back to me; they took over from me; they did it exceptionally well, making sounds that were unique. And I found them not only *profoundly intelligent improvisers* but also *profoundly intelligent educators.* The learning from these six days of work became the underpinnings of the installation *Resonant Tails*, a voice-art enticement console, now enhanced with tactile feedback, currently in use in four UK schools that serve PMLD populations.[9]

What future possibilities are thus opened up by thinking about what we have to learn from experiencing (with our whole, attuned, somatically-active selves) the voicing of and voicing with children with PMLD? For me, there is, of course, the pleasureful technical challenge of grappling with the unique qualities of their sounds, trying to imitate them and the resulting, gratifying expansion of my own technical vocabulary. However, much more importantly, there is also the bliss. A very *queer* bliss. A kind of non-punctate, deeply felt, transformative bliss. The elation I experience when indulging in this bliss tells me that there is a kind of pleasure I am missing out on in my daily life: that is the pleasure of *intensive interaction* with people whose bodies and life experiences are configured in ways that are intensely *unlike mine*. Indulging in the time spent with these different bodies, just for the sake of exploring what beautiful territories we invent and echo together and of engaging in mutual vibration with our vocalic stimuli and vocal-aesthetic indulgences, while fleeing the strictures of punctate time, might help us experience togetherness, contact and the blissful, daring security of being different, together.

What of a completely reconfigured practice of extra-normal vocal art, where intensive interaction is used between the *non*-disAbled? Where the non-professional voices back to and with the professional, in a kind of complementary synchrony of the celebration of vocal idiosyncrasy? Where cheeks are one centimeter apart but the sounding voices are those of strangers? What would such a practice look like? Feel like? How would it function? The future of *queer voicing* might actually be not so much in bonding the queer with one another but bonding the queer and the "less" queer in a dance of somatic togetherness, where even the strangest vibrations, and no obligatory "punk, punk, punk," help us positively, generatively, intensely interact.

Notes

1 For the facilitation of the reading process, I offer at this point a navigating definition for the terms *intensive interaction, non-punctuate* and *extra-normal* voice:

Intensive interaction is a term used to describe a range of techniques developed for engaging with people who have special communication needs. These people appear to benefit from a kind of heightened, dramatized and intimate approach to the use of body language, verbal communication, prosody, eye contact and sometimes touch, to attract and generate interest in communication. While variations on the technique are used in many contexts, I specifically refer to the heightened quality of intensive interaction that is often used with people with PMLD. I will return to intensive interaction to discuss how it is understood further in the sixth part of this chapter.

Non-punctate is an adjective coined by my colleague in music studies, Alexander Khalil, to describe musical time without obligatory regular pulse or beat. *Non-punctate voicing* is thus "beatless" voicing (there is no currently available bibliography on Khalil's ideas and I draw here from personal communication). I extend the term to describe voicings within which regular and typical prosodic contour is not typically found. I return to this notion in the fifth part of this chapter.

Extra-normal *voice* is a phrase first used in a scholarly context by Edgerton (2004) to describe the range of atypical vocal sounds used by "extended technique" practitioners in contemporary art music. I have adopted this phrase from his writing because it intersects very well with contemporary notions of queerness and of the malleability and culturally relative nature, of the queered position in contemporary culture. Talking about voice interchangeably as both queered and extra-normal reinforces the fact that, when a vocal sound is construed as "not normal," this is always in relation to a set of deeply encultured expectations around what "normal" voicing is. One culture's scream is another's prayer; one culture's song is another's conversation; one culture's chanting is another's lilt.

2 On abreaction:

> In mental health, abreaction has come to mean an intense emotional release or discharge in an involuntary, vivid, sensory reliving or re-experiencing, of an event that was originally neurobiologically overwhelming (i.e., 'traumatic') and thus could not be remembered (or forgotten) in normal ways.
>
> (Peebles, 2010, 9)

For further information and the rest of Peebles' input on abreaction as a psychological term, see pages 9–11 in Weiner and Graihead (2010).

3 Due to ethical clearance, audio-visual recordings from the specific sessions could not be included here.
4 In some limited cases, we got to work with two pairs of children. The school staff call them "buddies" and "best friends". This is because some children already "like" each other vocally and "chatter" (improvise) with each other if they are together.
5 See Cage (1961, 1981), Cage and Kostelanetz (2000).
6 See Shusterman (2000).
7 See Daly (2002), Croft (2017).
8 See Heimann et al (2006), Nind and Hewett (2012), Weedle (2014), Hewitt (2018).
9 For a visual sense of how this installation looks like and for a short video on how children with PMLD and their carers interact with *Resonant Tails*, click on the following link: https://network.youthmusic.org.uk/introducing-resonant-tails.

References

Ahmed, S. (2006) *Queer Phenomenology: Orientations, Objects, Others*. Durham: Duke University Press.

Bassal, N. and Coster Heller, M. (2015) The Norwegian tradition of body psychotherapy: a golden age in Oslo. In: Gustl Marlock and Halko Weiss (with Courtenay Young and Michael Soth) (eds.) *The Handbook of Body Psychotherapy and Somatic Psychology* [Play Book]. Berkeley, CA: North Atlantic Books.

Bellamy, G., Croot, L., Bush, A., Berry, H. and Smith, A. (2010) A study to define profound and multiple learning disabilities (PMLD). *Journal of Intellectual Disabilities*, 14(3) 221–235.

Bonenfant, Y. (2010) Queer listening to queer vocal timbres. *Performance Research*, 15(3) 74–80.

——— (2013) Your Vivacious Voice! Available from: http://www.yourvivaciousvoice.com/ [Accessed 29 April 2019]

——— (2018a) Children's queered voicings: questions of voiced power. *Performance Research*, 23(1) 52–60.

——— (2018b) PAR produces plethora, extended voices are plethoric, and why plethora matters. In: Annette Arlander, Bruce Barton, Melanie Dreyer-Lude and Ben Spatz (eds.) *Performance as Research: Knowledge, Methods, Impact*. New York: Routledge.

Boyesen, G. (2018) *Entre psyché et soma: introduction à la psychologie biodynamique.* Paris: Payot.

Cage, J. (1961) *Silence: Lectures and Writings.* Middletown, CT: Wesleyan University Press.

—— (1981) *For the Birds, John Cage in Conversation With Daniel Charles.* Boston, MA: Boyars.

Cage, J. and Kostelanetz, R. (2000) *John Cage, Writer: Selected Texts.* Lanham, MD: Cooper Square Press.

Caldwell, P. (2011) Intensive interaction: using body language to communicate. Available from: http://www.intellectualdisability.info/how-to-guides/articles/intensive-interaction-using-body-language-to-communicate [Accessed 29 April 2019].

Croft, C. (2017) *Queer Dance: Meanings and Makings.* Oxford: Oxford University Press.

Csordas, T. (2006) *Embodiment and Experience: The Existential Ground of Culture and Self.* Cambridge: Cambridge University Press.

Daly, A. (2002) *Critical Gestures: Writings on Dance and Culture.* Middletown, CT: Wesleyan University Press.

Heimann, M., Laberg, K. and Nordoen, B. (2006) Imitative interaction increases social interest and elicited imitation in non-verbal children with autism. *Infant and Child Development*, 159(3) 297–309.

Hewitt, D. (2018) *The Intensive Interaction Handbook.* 2nd edition. London: Sage.

Khalil, A. (2019) On non-punctate musical time [personal communication]. Conversation with Yvon Bonenfant, June 3.

Lowen, A. (2013) *Pleasure.* Hinesburg, VT: The Alexander Lowen Foundation.

Mouriere, A. and McKim, J. (2018) *Integrating Intensive Interaction: Developing Communication Practice in Services for Children and Adults with Severe Learning Difficulties, Profound and Multiple Learning Difficulties and Autism.* Abingdon: Routledge.

Nind, M. and Hewett, D. (2012) *Access to Communication: Developing the Basics of Communication with People with Severe Learning Difficulties Through Intensive Interaction.* London: Routledge.

Peebles, M. J. (2010) Abreaction. In: Irving B. Weiner and W. Edward Craighead (eds.) *The Corsini Encyclopedia of Psychology.* 4th Edition, Volume 1. Hoboken, NJ: Wiley, 9–11.

Shusterman, R. (2000) *Performing Live: Aesthetic Alternatives for the Ends of Art.* Ithaca and London: Cornell University Press.

—— (2008) *Body Consciousness: A Philosophy of Mindfulness and Somaesthetics.* Cambridge: Cambridge University Press.

15 Vocal resonance and the politics of intercorporeality

Anita Chari

As a somatic practitioner, vocalist and political theorist, my work has traversed distinct landscapes that often feel as if they are worlds apart. I have immersed myself in the subtleties of physical sensation, the largely non-linguistic arena of movement practice and the world of the voice, with its emphasis on resonance, sound and the vibration of the flesh, learning to refine my sensate capacities and the forms of attention specific to the visceral realms of embodied practices. These practices often prioritize sensate experience over a theoretical analysis and an interest in the granular terrain of bodily gestures over the subtle refinement of linguistic distinctions.

As a counterpoint to these more viscerally attuned sites of practice, I have simultaneously worked as a political theorist. My research in the arena of political theory has also been concerned with somatics. Above all, I am interested in the ways in which forms of sensate dissociation permeate contemporary neoliberal society and become entangled with the ever-deepening forms of commodification and economic inequality that infiltrate all spheres of contemporary social life. My work as a political theorist interrogates the relationship between sensate experience and political experience, as well as, ultimately, the relationship between sensate domination and political domination in neoliberal society. In my work as a political theorist, I have searched for a language to describe the ways in which the dissociation from bodily sensation is an impediment to the practice of social and political freedom.

In 2011, I met the dancer and somatic pioneer Emilie Conrad, the creator of a vocal and movement practice called Continuum Movement. Conrad innovated the techniques of Continuum over the course of more than forty years of work in the areas of somatic therapy, poetry, dance and vocal practice. As I began first to practise Continuum and then to train as a facilitator of Continuum Movement as a form of therapeutic practice with Conrad, I was provoked and inspired by the ways in which this practice joined a sociopolitical vision of what I will call "embodied democracy," along with a set of deeply immersive, vibrational, sensate practices of movement and voice. Implicit in Conrad's work was an understanding of the relationship between the sensate dissociation predominant in contemporary society and the political domination of contemporary neoliberalism.[1]

In this essay, I discuss the significance of Continuum Movement as a critical vocal-movement practice for conceptualizing embodied democratic practices. In the course of this exploration, I discuss the ways in which Continuum Movement may speak both to current discussions in voice studies and to debates in political theory regarding the relationship between somatically-informed concepts of vocal resonance and critiques of contemporary neoliberal domination.

Continuum Movement and the somatic voice

First, I will describe in detail some of the key aspects of the Continuum practice, drawn from my own extensive practice, from my work with Conrad herself in workshops, as well as from Conrad's book on the story of Continuum's emergence, *Life on Land* (2007).

Multidisciplinary in nature, Continuum works directly with vocal resonance and with the materiality of vocal sounds to engage with embodied sensation and to orient practitioners to intercorporeal space. In Continuum, vocal resonance is used to potentiate and deepen sensation in the body. Practitioners studying Continuum learn a series of breaths and resonant sounds that engage with various patterns of awareness and systems within the body. Conrad's work with breath and sound involved a process of continual innovation. In the course of her work, she created a palette of well over fifty types of sounds and breaths to be used in the practice, ranging from variations on vowel sounds such as "O" and "E" sounds designed specifically for resonating certain tissues, such as the "bone breath" and the "cerebrospinal breath," and sounds influenced by vocalizations from various sound traditions, such as the "blur breath," which was a variation on the timbres of Tuvan throat singing adapted for somatic practice.

Rather than engaging with the voice primarily as the bearer of language, Continuum works directly with the vibrational character of the voice. Practitioners work with the shapes, sensations and textures initiated by different kinds of vocal registers, breath techniques, sound rhythms and timbres of sound. As one is sounding in a Continuum practice, they usually place their hands on different parts of the body to deepen the perception of physical vibration. The resonant vibrations of the voice, channeled through various tonalities and breaths, begin to potentiate subtle movement within one's physical body. Indeed, an important part of the practice is learning to cultivate a synesthetic capacity for perceiving sound as movement. What is initially perceived as vocal resonance then becomes a simultaneous perception of somatic resonance.

Continuum practitioners learn to attune to extremely subtle sensations and movements in the body, tracking them and refining the awareness of the flow and development of these subtle movements. Moment to moment, dwelling in sensation, one alternates between sounding into the body and into the space, and then pausing in states of open attention, where one listens with receptivity to the sensations that emerge in the body as the echoes of sound. In this open-attention state, one simply allows movement and sensation to emerge, tracking the development of subtle movements as they mutate and evolve from one moment to the next.

Vocality as the plural "in-between"

I suggest that the vocal and somatic innovations of Continuum have significant implications for the field of voice studies. Konstantinos Thomaidis and Ben Macpherson conceptualize voice studies through the paradigm of a plural "in between," at the nexus of body and language. As Thomaidis and Macpherson write in their introduction to the volume, *Voice Studies: Critical Approaches to Process, Performance, Experience*, "the 'in-between' of voice offers an interdisciplinary space for such plurality, wherein multiple renderings work together in a process of transition, passage, and transformation" (2015, 4). Continuum has much to offer for developing this approach to voice as a form of mediation in specifically somatic terms (Thomaidis and Macpherson, 2015, 3).

I suggest that the practical and theoretical insights that emerge from Continuum's sound and movement practice can serve in the project of challenging what Thomaidis and Macpherson name, "the fetishized voice-as-object," a critique shared as well by theorists such as Adriana Cavarero and Carolyn Abbate (Abbate, 1996; Cavarero, 2005). The fetishized voice-as-object refers to the tendency to understand the voice as localized solely in acts of sonic and vocal presence, rather than to sense the diffuse ineffability of voice in space, in silence and in plurality (Thomaidis and Macpherson, 2015, 4). Continuum's focus on the theory and practice of resonance can help to deepen the articulation of voice within this pluralistic and non-ontologizing framework.

Moreover, Continuum's approach to sound and movement makes manifest the continuity between vocal and somatic resonance. Making use of a complex palate of vocal shapes, timbres and syllables, Conrad's teachings focused on directing these vocal sounds into practitioners' physical bodies to potentiate one's capacities for sensation and movement. Conrad's work with vocal resonance ultimately led her to a more robust understanding of intercorporeal space, of what she as well as others working within somatic disciplines have called the "somatic field," a concept I will discuss in depth below. In Continuum, vocality and vocal resonance might be understood as the "in-between" of individualized bodies and intercorporeal space and therefore as a way of unsettling the distinction between vocal resonance and somatic resonance by perceiving the continuity between the two.

This destabilization of the distinction between vocal and somatic resonance reveals the relevance of Continuum to the field of voice studies and places into relief the importance of focusing scholarly attention on perceiving and conceptualizing forms of intercorporeal experience. The practices of Continuum reveal the chiasmatic relationship between vocal resonance, centered on sound and vocal production in the individualized body and somatic resonance, which focuses on the circulation of vocal vibrations within an intercorporeal, non-individualized field of awareness. Instead of fetishizing the individual voice, a conceptualization of resonance that emerges from the perspective of Continuum would rather focus its attention upon intercorporeal vocalities and resonances.

This emphasis on intercorporeality, which emerges through perceiving the continuity between vocal and somatic resonance, speaks to the relevance of voice studies to theorizing the practice of democracy in contemporary context. Within the field of political theory and feminist theory, there have been many explorations of the political implications of voice that focus upon the appearance of individualized or even collective voices as political actors, as well as upon the significance of the voice to a more expansive form of political communication (Young, 1997; Lorde, 2012). While these approaches are crucial for understanding the formation of political subjectivities of marginalized groups, I suggest that a perceptual exploration of the political potential of more affective and somatic forms of vocality can help to deepen these discussions of the relationship between vocality, embodiment and democracy.

In the context of the fetishization of individuality in neoliberalism, I would suggest that in order to grasp the significance of voice studies for a critique of neoliberalism, more attention should be paid to the ways in which vocality and vocal resonance can motivate and aid in the creation of capacities for perception of intercorporeal forms of experience. Such perceptive capacities can illuminate alternative forms of collectivity in contemporary society. In the following section, I explore the concept of intercorporeality through the notion of the somatic field in order to discuss how collective experiences in the practice of Continuum can inform the theory and practice of embodied democracy.

Perceiving intercorporeality and vocal resonance in the somatic field

That we feel less and less, that sensation is a challenge rather than a given in the bodies in which we dwell, is a reality I believe it is urgent to consider. The denial of sensation is a form of domination. It is the subjectivity of the digital. It is the logic of incarceration. It is the anchor of a world in which we feel the limits of our skin as the limits of our sense, in which individuality isolates. There is a sensate register in which the isolating and commodifying form of selfhood and subjectivity operates, as well as where it might be resisted: this register, I term, intercorporeality.

First, how am I using the term "intercorporeality"? In my practice, intercorporeality is a perceptive space between bodies, which is not delimited by an individualized form of consciousness or perception, though it coexists with the latter. Perhaps, using the terminology of Gilbert Simondon, we could begin to describe this intercorporeal space by referring to the notion of individuation, as a movement that goes from the pre-individual to the individual (Simondon, 2007). In this way, the intercorporeal allows us to conceive of a space that is pre-individual or at least in some sense not yet individual, in the sense that it allows for perceptive experiences that exceed the delimitations of individualized physical bodies.

A key term for understanding the phenomenology of intercorporeality is the concept of the "somatic field". With the term "somatic field," I am referring to a matrix of non-linguistic, resonant, embodied communication that happens in the interstitial tissue between bodies moving in space.[2] Conrad encountered the somatic field in the course of her somatic studies in biodynamic movement and its relationship with vocality. She noticed that slow, fluid movement, coupled with the use of resonant vocal sounds directed into the body heightened individuals' capacities to experience sensation within their bodies. She observed repeatedly that attention to bodily sensation invoked the possibility of a form of resonant communication between bodies. Conrad noted that practitioners would often take on similar patterns and shapes in the course of a collective movement exploration, without any external prompting and even without individuals looking at each other's movement at all (Conrad, 2007, Chapter 22). They were mirroring one another, not in any kind of uniform way, but through an entrainment process where movements began to spontaneously mirror and echo one another in a form of resonant improvisation. Individuals often noticed that in the process of engaging in movement in a collective context, as opposed to when they practised alone, their movement impulses were vastly amplified. Bodies were communicating non-linguistically, through the medium of a somatic field, initiated by the subtle attention of individuals to their own bodily sensations, as well as by the vibratory effect of the polyrhythmic prosody of their voices.

As individuality becomes weaponized in new and inconceivable ways towards the ends of neoliberal commodification, part of the issue one confronts, particularly in digitalized neoliberalism, is a complex yet palpable reduction of the sensory capacity to perceive intercorporeality and the somatic field. Perhaps this is in part due to where we direct our attention. As Dominic Pettman notes in his book *Infinite Distraction* (2015), the contemporary social media landscape fosters a hypermodulation of affect that forecloses the possibility of affective attunement or synchronization, because we are all outraged, impacted, affected by something slightly different than everyone else every single moment. But it is also due to the ways in which a solipsistically individualistic and entrepreneurial subjectivity increasingly permeates all aspects of life, particularly in postindustrial digitalized societies.

The theoretical significance of intercorporeal experience lies in the potential it contains for imagining and experiencing new forms of collective subjectivity. In my approach to thinking through the intercorporeal, the issue of perception is fundamental. Theoretical discussions of the significance of intercorporeal experience abound in the areas of political theory, philosophy and affect theory, for example, in the work of Erin Manning (2006) and Brian Massumi (2002). Yet throughout this body of literature, I suggest that not enough attention is paid to the question of the conditions of possibility for intercorporeal experience to emerge, what kinds of techniques and practices foster this register of experience, and how these kinds of perceptive techniques can then be brought to bear on political and theoretical work. Techniques of intercorporeality, in my experience, often come from marginal, experimental, artistic and non-theoretical spaces. The praxical focus of a voice studies approach can illuminate practices that foster intercorporeal perception. Below, I highlight the relationship between somatic practices and vocal resonance in Continuum Movement and the way in which vocal resonance is generative of intercorporeal perception.

Sensation

What is the significance of vocal resonance to intercorporeal experience? Within the context of Continuum, Conrad understood the key to the relationship between vocality and intercorporeality to lie in the way in which vocal resonance potentiates embodied sensation. One of the most important aspects of the Continuum vocal-movement practice, as well as other related somatically-informed therapeutic practices such as Biodynamic Craniosacral Therapy, Somatic Experiencing and Body-Mind Centering, is the refinement of a set of capacities on the part of practitioners for perceiving subtle sensation in one's own physical body and ultimately for perceiving sensation as a process within the physical body.[3] This involves refining the capacity to perceive sensation in one's own physical body from moment to moment, as well as to perceive these sensations in their unfolding. Now more, now less, shifting, moving, modulating rhythms and locations in the body, sensation can be perceived as a process rather than as a static or segmented impression.

In the course of Continuum practice, one comes to understand the conditions of possibility for perceiving more subtle and complex sensations in one's system, by learning about the history of perceptual development in each unique body. Perhaps one person perceives more when they can see; another person may feel much more when they close their eyes. For a person who is very cognitive in their orientation, there may be more of an attunement to perceiving the physical and sensate movements of thought than of visceral perception. Perhaps one person's sensations are more ethereal, for another more fleshy and carnal. Sensation is never just sensation. And so when we describe sensation in theoretical or even in neurobiological terms, there is the danger of neglecting the fact that the history of sensate perception in every individual is somewhat different, something that demands subtle inquiry. We cannot speak of sensation in the abstract.

Perceiving subtle sensation is a fundamental aspect of invoking experiences of intercorporeality. It opens up possibilities for the entrainment of one's physical and emotional body to the body of another. Individualized sensation is a bridge and transition point to perceiving in the register of intercorporeality. Emilie Conrad's innovation in the Continuum practice was to see the fundamental link between vocal resonance and physical movement and sensation. She detailed her explorations of the nexus between vocality and embodiment in her extraordinary book, *Life on Land*. She writes: "One of the miracles of the human voice is that it can modulate and nuance sound [...] sound is one of the most efficient and immediate ways of changing density and thereby liberating movement" (2007, Chapter 15). Vocal resonance, therefore, potentiates somatic resonance, movement and sensation, and ultimately opens perception to the intercorporeal realm.

Relational attunement

Continuum Movement involves a set of practices of relational attunement that are perceptive and sensate in nature and which foster an invocation of intercorporeal space. While its relational dimensions are implicit rather than explicit, Continuum shares with the other somatic therapeutic practices I mentioned earlier an engagement with relational attunement. In Continuum, this attunement occurs through the medium of vocal resonance.

In Conrad's practice, the modulation of the voice and its vibrational qualities itself was a form of contact, both with one's own body and with other bodies in a shared space. For example, if I were working with the sound of "O" in a dive, a sound that is often used in a Continuum sequence, I would work with finding the right volume, the proper timbre and the necessary amplitude of vibration to feel that I am making contact with my own body. I would play with the shape of my mouth to find a sound that could penetrate into my tissues. And then the vocal resonance of the "O" sound would also exceed my own body, entering intercorporeal space and merging with the symphony of vibrations in the room. The merging of sounds within intercorporeal space becomes a form of negotiation of contact, sometimes conscious and often improvised and alchemical. Sometimes, my sounding is a direct engagement with the vocalizations of others within the somatic field.

To summarize, while at the beginning of a Continuum exploration, one begins to make vocal sounds that are directed primarily into one's own physical body, all the while observing sensation as a process of unfolding within one's body, potentiated by vocal resonance, this individualized focus then shifts, intermittently and fluidly, to a perception of intercorporeal somatic resonance. The perception of individualized sensation gives way at some point in the exploration, either intentionally or unintentionally, to "the field" which one may perceive within the space in the room. Vocal resonance within one's own body morphs into a form of somatic resonance within the field, between and among bodies in the room, and also within the interstitial space in between. Vocal resonance therefore becomes a means of access to and relationship with sensation as movement in one's physical body, as well as a bridge to a perceptual orientation towards intercorporeal space. Practising this, one learns to refine perception of resonance not only in one's bounded, individualized physical body but also in a shared somatic field.

In the following section, I link this understanding of vocal and somatic resonance to the field of contemporary political theory and a critique of neoliberalism.

From vocal and somatic resonance to political resonance

Shifting the discussion to the register of political theory, I now want to explore some critical issues surrounding concepts and practices of resonance from two political theorists who have explored the implications of resonance in the contemporary political context, William Connolly (2005) and Romand Coles (2011). The perspective of political theory is significant to my discussion because it helps one to understand the potential dangers of resonance in the political sphere, for example, by illuminating the ways in which resonance plays into the current global resurgence of right-wing populism in the US, Europe, South America and beyond. Yet simultaneously, discussions of resonance in political theory show its potential to foster receptivity and to disclose alternative forms of social and political possibility that are crucial to the practice of embodied democracy.

The perils of resonance in the political sphere

From a relational, intersubjective and political perspective, rather than from a purely sonic one, resonance could be understood as an experiential state in which the movements of self and other enter a zone of indistinction without altogether erasing the perceptual boundary between self and other. Resonance entails a vibratory continuity in which the actions of one person become part of a continuity with the actions of another, such that the individual is no longer the sole originator of their actions. In such a resonant state, I am mover and I am moved, partaking in what the political philosopher Hannah Arendt (1998) described as the non-sovereign character of action. For example, in Continuum, through the process of merging my voice with others in intercorporeal space, my sounds become part of a collective process of improvisation. New sonic possibilities arise and dissipate through contact with the vocalizing of others. My body is moved by my own sounding as well as by the sounds of others. The movements of my body and the sounds that I vocalize are expressive but they are also a form of working through my history, completing patterns that have lived in and shaped my physical body and nervous system. In both of these senses, as a form of individual and collective expression, as well as through the completion of somatic patterning in my body and nervous system, intercorporeal resonance induces a possibility-disclosing state.

The theoretical collective, the Invisible Committee, articulates furthermore the capacity of resonance to shape progressive political action through non-linear, non-sovereign, rhythmic movement:

> Revolutionary movements do not spread by contamination but by resonance. Something that is constituted here resonates with the shock wave emitted by something constituted over there. A body that resonates does so according to its own mode. An insurrection is not like a plague or a forest fire – a linear process which spreads from place to place after an initial spark. It rather takes the shape of a music, whose focal points, though dispersed in time and space, succeed in imposing the rhythm of their own vibrations, always taking on more density.
>
> (2009, 12–13)

If indeed resonance involves a state in which modes of non-sovereign, collective action emerge, it becomes crucial to inquire into the political ends to which this kind of resonant action might be deployed. For while the Invisible Committee emphasizes the centrality of resonance to progressive political movements, the reality is that contemporary right-wing movements have also made use of political resonance in the service of authoritarian and exclusionary projects.

With this dimension of the contemporary politics of resonance in mind, the political theorists Connolly and Coles have pointed to the ways in which resonant, affectively driven forms of political action have been involved in the right-wing populist resurgences that have emerged in recent years in the US and globally. Focusing on the US context, Connolly articulates the ways in which resonance has played out in a right-wing political formation he calls, critically, the "evangelical-capitalist" resonance machine (2005, 869). For Connolly, resonance allows one to understand dimensions of political ascription that are precognitive and which are not simply based on the interests of various political actors, but instead entail the interpenetration and imbrication of various viewpoints and commitments through affective and vibrational means. As Connolly writes:

> [I]n politics diverse elements *infiltrate* into the others, metabolizing into a moving complex – Causation as resonance between elements that become fused together to a considerable degree. Here causality, as relations of dependence between separate factors, morphs into energized complexities of mutual imbrication and interinvolvement, in which heretofore unconnected or loosely associated elements *fold, bend, blend, emulsify and dissolve into each other*, forging a qualitative assemblage resistant to classical models of explanation.
>
> (2005, 870, original emphasis)

This sonic and vibrational model of resonance helps us to see the mutual imbrication of diverse elements of an assemblage, and the way in which they come to amplify and dissolve into one another.

Connolly emphasizes that it is not so much shared doctrines that link the various strands of the capitalist-Christian assemblage; more importantly, it is "affinities of sensibility" that connect them and that resonate together into a larger movement (2005, 871). Resonance helps to explain the ways in which affect, more than intellect, drives the affinities that Connolly observes in the linkage between neoliberal capitalism and evangelical Christianity. He writes:

> The affect-imbued ideas that compose them are installed in the soft-tissues of affect, emotion, habit, and posture as well as the upper reaches of the intellect. These sensibilities trigger the responses of those imbued with them even before they begin to think about this or that event. This is particularly so when complementary dispositions loop back and forth in a large political machine, with each constituency helping to crystallize, amplify, and legitimize the dispositions of the whole.
>
> (Connolly, 2005, 873)

There are obvious dangers inherent in this mode of affectively driven type of political sensibility, as is clear from the racist, exclusionary and violent forms of political collectivity that have marked the public sphere of the US since 2016.

Working in dialogue with Connolly's work, the political theorist Romand Coles emphasizes therefore that one needs to be attentive to the ways in which relationships of intercorporeal resonance, though occurring in a register that is prior to linguistic cognition, are by no means outside the operations of power. As he writes:

> Intercorporeal resonance is itself not innocent of inequalities and the toxic politics of (in)difference but rather *is itself a target of and imbued with modes of power.* This has likely always been true, but in present times the relationship between our capacities for inter-corporeal resonance and contemporary practices of power is particularly salient and intense due to the ways in which such power is enmeshed with and borne by technologies and asymmetries of resonance itself.
>
> (Coles, 2011, 274, original emphasis)

Like Connolly, Coles observes that it is the political Right that has invested its time and organizing efforts into taking advantage of resonant media. Coles poses the question of whether it is possible to envision a progressive, democratic politics of resonance. How might radical democratic political movements make use of resonant practices? How might they forge a politics of counter resonance, reconceiving resonant practices in a radical democratic mode as "a vital element of the ethos and power of an engaged, hospital and ecological democracy"? (Coles, 2011, 276).

Addressing these questions, Coles makes a crucial distinction between two forms of resonance. He distinguishes between forms of resonance that are entangled with exclusionary politics, and forms of resonance that can be deployed towards democratic ends. He calls the former "deceptive resonance," and the latter "receptive resonance". Deceptive resonance refers to practices that shut down and diminish relationships that would disclose new political possibilities and reveal the plurality and complexity of the world (Coles, 2011, 281). Receptive resonance by contrast "opens and intensifies 'acknowledgement' of others – which is as much a condition for agonistic negotiation as it is a condition for more harmonious processes" (Coles, 2011, 282).

Coles' distinction between receptive resonance and deceptive resonance is important, I believe, because it allows one to see the political potential of resonance while being aware of its dangers in the context of contemporary nativist right-wing politics. The exclusionary forms of resonance that Connolly discusses in his theory of the capitalist-evangelical resonance machine are perhaps not best described as forms of somatic resonance at all. Perhaps they are better understood as forms of practice and communication that forestall somatic resonance of the kind that one sees in practices such as Continuum, though these exclusionary practices do rely on emotional forms of resonance.

The "dampening" of resonance that Coles describes in reference to the capitalist-evangelical resonance machine, I would argue, is an expression of emotional resonance but not an expression of somatic resonance. At stake in this distinction is the possibility of grasping and recuperating resonance as a form of critical practice, one that is not reducible to the exclusionary and nativist practices of current right-wing populist movements. Thus, a critical theory of resonance must see that there is no parallelism between the critical resonant practices that Coles wishes to incorporate into a radical democratic habitus and the right-wing forms of "deceptive resonance" that are the target of Connolly's critique. Holding these terms separate is crucial to recuperating an understanding of somatic resonance that could motivate emancipatory politics in the present.

Concluding reflections on shock and resonance

I would take Coles' claims about deceptive resonance even further to argue that in fact what we confront in the conjuncture of contemporary right-wing populist political movements is a form and effect of political shock rather than a form of resonance. Coles refers to this state of affairs as one of "dampened resonance," which he claims is "cyclically entangled with an extremely dimmed sense for relational possibilities, be they cooperative or agonistic or both" (2011, 284). Within the neuroscientific framework that Coles references, the human mirror neuron system is seen as the locus of resonant intersubjectivity. Mirroring allows for experiences of entrainment and heightened receptivity to emerge that provide the basis for embodied democratic practices. In a state of dampened resonance, individuals, and indeed society grasped more generally, lack the relational capacities for mirroring that would create the conditions for somatic resonance to take place. If we begin to think these neuroscientific frameworks at a societal level, through the lens of what I would call a "societal nervous system,"[4] we can begin to understand that the right-wing political formation that Connolly and Coles criticize is better understood as the *discharge* of shock or freeze in the societal nervous system, rather than a state of somatic resonance.[5] In other words, a state of dampened resonance may involve movement, but that movement is more an expression of discharge than of resonant intersubjectivity.

Conrad explored the phenomenon of somatic shock extensively in her work. She found that vocal sounds could function as a powerful form of mirroring back to one's body and nervous system the lack of movement that characterizes a state of shock. Moreover, the mirroring that occurred through the medium of the somatic field in the context of a collective movement exploration included not only the mirroring of movement but also the mirroring of stasis, of shock and of freeze. Many practitioners experience extended periods of deep stillness, sometimes for several hours. These phases of apparent non-movement are an important part of the process. The reflection of stasis from one body to another within the medium of the somatic field creates traction for something phenomenologically and perceptually new to occur when the cycle of suspension is complete. I believe that these processes in which apparent non-movement becomes reflected back to one's body are significant for understanding such moments of political stasis, shock and disorientation of the kind that we arguably confront in the present. Vocal sound, sensate awareness and somatic relational attunement provide an underexplored perceptual path and method for inquiring into states of dampened resonance.

To conclude, I believe that the vocal and somatic practices of Continuum provide a method of inquiry into and practice of what Coles theorizes as a practice of "receptive resonance". As Coles argues, a practice of receptive resonance is a possibility-disclosing practice that intensifies the sensate acknowledgment of others. Moreover, I want to highlight that part of what characterizes a practice of receptive resonance is that such practices open subjects up to a perception of intercorporeal space, decentering the bounded, atomized forms of subjectivity predominant in neoliberal society. Receptive resonance practices create space for the perception of the possibility of new forms of collective subjectivity. Though these forms of practice may not themselves be tied to the formation of social movements or collective forms of political struggle, they create the perceptual and subjective conditions that might articulate new forms of political movement and of political subjectivity. The subtle awareness of the development of movement within one's own body and within the somatic field hones the capacity for perceiving potency and the pluripotent nature of time and space. It trains the capacity to perceive at a collective level what the critical theorist Ernst Bloch calls, the "not-yet," the emergent forms of collectivity that are latent within the present (Bloch et al, 1995).

Notes

1 Recent scholarship has defined the term neoliberalism by reference to three salient features. The first is that neoliberalism originated as a set of ideas put forth by a group of economic theorists in the 1930s and 1940s, including economists such as Alexander Rüstow, Walter Eucken and Friedrich von Hayek. Second, neoliberalism also refers (perhaps retroactively) to a set of policies adopted from the late 1970s by politicians and elites such as Margaret Thatcher and Ronald Reagan, who selectively put aspects of neoliberal theory into practice. The foundation of these neoliberal policies was the deregulation and liberalization of economic life. Third, and relatedly, neoliberalism, or, more accurately, "neoliberalization," also refers to a political-economic process whereby the boundary between economics and politics is transformed in ways that allow for greater intervention of the state in market processes while simultaneously obscuring that role. Neoliberalization entails the retreat of the State from social welfare functions even as the State takes a more interventionist role in market processes.
2 On the concept of the field from an affect-theory perspective, see Chapters 3 and 6 of Brian Massumi, *Parables for the Virtual: Movement, Affect, Sensation* (2002, 68–88, 144–161). For a more biological take on the notion of the field, see Rupert Sheldrake, *The Presence of the Past: Morphic Resonance and the Memory of Nature* (2012).
3 Related somatic practices would include Somatic Experiencing (SE), a practice developed by Peter Levine; Biodynamic Craniosacral Therapy, a practice which emerged from cranial osteopathy and is carried on by numerous practitioners, including Michael Shea, John and Anna Chitty, Franklin Sills and Hugh Milne; and Body-Mind Centering, developed by Bonnie Bainbridge Cohen. Conrad was in dialogue with these various related somatic practices, especially later in her career as Continuum took a more therapeutic turn.
4 Chapter 3 of my manuscript in progress entitled *Intercorporeality: Field Consciousness and Sensate Democracy.*
5 I am translating terms such as "discharge" and "freeze" into a political framework from Peter Levine's work on trauma and the nervous system. See Levine and Frederick (1997).

References

Abbate, C. (1996) *Unsung Voices: Opera and Musical Narrative in the Nineteenth Century.* Princeton, NJ: Princeton University Press.
Arendt, H. (1998) *The Human Condition.* 1st edition. Chicago, IL: University of Chicago Press.
Bloch, E. (1995) *The Principle of Hope, Volume 1.* Translated from German by Neville Plaice, Stephen Plaice and Paul Knight. Cambridge: MIT Press.
Cavarero, A. (2005) *For More Than One Voice: Toward a Philosophy of Vocal Expression.* Stanford, CA: Stanford University Press.
Coles, R. (2011) The neuropolitical habitus of resonant receptive democracy. *Ethics and Global Politics* (Special issue: A politics of receptivity), 4 273–293.
Connolly, W. E. (2005) The evangelical-capitalist resonance machine. *Political Theory,* 33(6) 869–886.
Conrad, E. (2007) *Life on Land: The Story of Continuum, the World-Renowned Self-Discovery and Movement Method* [Kindle]. Berkeley, CA: North Atlantic Books.

Invisible Committee. (2009) *The Coming Insurrection.* Cambridge: MIT Press.
Levine, P. A. with Frederick, A. (1997) *Waking the Tiger: Healing Trauma.* 1st edition. Berkeley, CA: North Atlantic Books.
Lorde, A. (2012) *Sister Outsider: Essays and Speeches.* Reprint edition. Toronto: Crossing Press.
Manning, E. (2006) *Politics of Touch: Sense, Movement, Sovereignty.* Minnesota: University of Minnesota Press.
Massumi, B. (2002) *Parables for the Virtual: Movement, Affect, Sensation.* 1st edition. Durham, NC: Duke University Press Books.
Pettman, D. (2015) *Infinite Distraction.* 1st edition. Cambridge: Polity.
Sheldrake, R. (2012) *The Presence of the Past: Morphic Resonance and the Memory of Nature.* 4th edition. South Paris, ME: Park Street Press.
Simondon, G. (2007) *L'individuation Psychique et Collective: A la Lumière des Notions de Forme, Information, Potentiel et Métastabilité.* Paris: Editions Aubier.
Thomaidis, K. and Macpherson, B. (2015) Introduction: voice(s) as a method and an in-between. In: Konstantinos Thomaidis and Ben Macpherson (eds.) *Voice Studies: Critical Approaches to Process, Performance and Experience.* Abingdon, Oxon: Routledge.
Young, I. M. (1997) *Intersecting Voices: Dilemmas of Gender, Political Philiosophy and Policy.* Princeton, NJ: Princeton University Press.

16 The somaesthetic in-between
Six statements on vocality, listening and embodiment

Ben Macpherson

Introduction

In the introduction to his 2012 work *Thinking through the Body*, the pragmatist philosopher Richard Shusterman suggests that: "Art enchants us through its richly sensuous dimensions, perceived through the bodily senses and enjoyed through embodied feelings" (2012, 1). Over the past decade, this truism has been explored in numerous publications, acknowledged in what is commonly referred to as "the embodied turn" in scholarship. In some cases, this is linked to the "cognitive turn," seen in explorations of the relationship between performance and neurobiology (McConachie and Hart, 2006; McConachie, 2008), considered on the basis of practice-led research (Marshall, 2008) or praxical inquiry (Reeve, 2013) or embodied performance and applied pedagogy (Scott, 2017). Within this context, Shusterman's further assertion that "philosophical aesthetics largely neglects the body's role in aesthetic appreciation" (2012, 1) may seem somewhat alarming. Yet over half a decade after this claim was made, it remains largely accurate; while cognitive studies, performance studies and the fields of pedagogy and applied practice have all considered the centrality of embodied experience, this has not always been the case in the field of philosophical discourse.

Following the acknowledgement of this omission, Shusterman critiques the aesthetic theories and practices of key western philosophers who, he argues, marginalized the body in their conceptions of aesthetic beauty, privileging structural approaches to artistic discourse or appreciation over sensorial experience. Unsurprisingly, the aesthetic thought of eighteenth-century enlightenment philosopher Immanuel Kant is singled out early on. After all, in *The Critique of Judgment*, Kant suggests that taste and experience are largely cognitive, involving "not what gratifies in sensation but merely by what pleases by its form," separate from the "empirical delight" of bodily senses (1987, 65–67). While it would be remiss to suggest that the body is entirely absent in scholarship on the experience of art and performance, this philosophical preoccupation with form and taste is problematic, especially when it comes to those "richly sensuous dimensions" of what vocal coach and somatic scholar Anne Tarvainen has broadly termed "vocal art forms" (such as singing, dramatic spoken text and extended vocal practice) (Shusterman, 2012, 1; 2018, 125). Through a series of six statements in this chapter, then, I am interested in exploring how western philosophies of somatic knowledge can *enhance* our understanding of vocal experience, and simultaneously, how vocal practice – of speech, song and those forms in-between – might, in turn, help address the relative paucity of philosophical discourse relating to the body. As the final part of this chapter will demonstrate, this investigation also says something – not just about the way we speak or sing – but also about the way we listen.

First, a broad historical statement marks my point of departure, offering a context for the rest of the discussion.

Statement 1

The problematic status of the soma in western philosophical aesthetics has its origin in antiquity.

Plato's problem

In *Phaedo*, Plato proclaimed the body as "the prison-house of the soul" (n.d.), and on this basis, sociologist Henri Lefebvre has exclaimed: "Western philosophy has *betrayed* the body; it has actively [...] *abandoned* the body; and it has *denied* the body" (1991, 407). In *Performing Live: Aesthetic Alternatives for the Ends of Art* (2000), Shusterman explored this denial and the metaphysical dissatisfaction with the body as an "organon" of communication still present in contemporary thinking, perhaps derived nowadays from neo-Platonic deference to Cartesian maxims of the mind-body dualism.[1] As we know, Plato wished to ban theatrical performance from the *Republic* (1995) because its appeal to spectators did nothing to enhance the reasoning and rational *logos* of the soul.

However, while Plato evidenced a mistrust of the body, marginalizing it in all respects – even *abandoning* it if Lefebvre does not overstate the case in the aforementioned quotation – the very act of this ideological silencing of dramatic performance and poetry (including vocal performance in its various forms) implicitly demonstrated its acknowledged impact on the audience. It may not have enhanced the formal properties of *logos,* but as *Republic* makes clear, Plato was fully aware that performance appealed to the *thumos* (senses) through its "richly sensuous dimensions," and the *ethos* – which performance theorist Graham Ley directly relates to the material; the body (1999, 21). His desire to ban this from the *Republic* was a political act, but viewed somatically, it is also paradoxical, as this chapter will consider. In any case, such an acknowledgement from Plato forms the second key statement in this chapter.

> **Statement 2**
>
> Performance – including vocal performance – must be understood in somatic terms.

Indeed, performers of all forms, and in this case vocal agents of various genres or traditions, have two things in common: "they are all alive, and they all have bodies" (Lutterbie, 2012, 21). As Tarvainen notes, "the artist's body is strongly present" in vocal performance, often becoming the "object of experience" for audiences or listeners through its sensuous and somatic properties (2018, 120). In fact, Tarvainen's recent chapter "Reflections on Vocal Somaesthetics" (2018) explicitly uses the concept of *proprioceiving* to engage with the performance of vocal acts such as speaking and singing through the body. As I have argued elsewhere, voice does indeed act as "the paradoxical keeper of both linguistic utterance, and the bodily presence of the speaker/singer" (Macpherson, 2012, 43). Previously, I have tried to encapsulate these ideas by using the term "corporeal vocality" in a challenge to the often-paradoxical Lacanian perspectives of Mladen Dolar in *A Voice and Nothing More* (2006).[2] In fact, the performer's body may be so "strongly present" (Tarvainen, 2018, 120) that it can even be understood as implicit in the very notation of vocal music, from marking to indicate breath in neumatic notation to technological visualizations of voice in real time (see Macpherson, 2015).[3] Here, however, I wish to extend this through an explicit focus on the audience member or listener as an embodied receiver of vocal performance. To better understand this, I want to outline a critical framework that I am here calling "Somaesthetic Performance Analysis". It is broadly based on the pragmatist philosophy of Shusterman, and provides a means to challenge Kant's focus on form to better understanding the inevitability of "corporeal vocality," or what might be more accurately "somaesthetic vocality" in this context, extending this inquiry to consider the role of the body in the experience of vocal practice (2012, 43).

Somaesthetic performance analysis

In his 2008 volume *Body Consciousness: A philosophy of mindfulness and somaesthetics* (2008), Shusterman defines somaesthetics (or "body consciousness") as the "critical study and meliorative cultivation of how we experience and use the living body (or soma) as a site of sensory appreciation (aesthesis) and creative self-fashioning" (2008, 1). This definition comprises two elements. First, sensory appreciation through experience. Second, self-fashioning through use.[4] Shusterman's objective is therefore to use body consciousness as a way of understanding oneself and the world more completely, a goal he sees as the entire *raison d'etre* of philosophy at large

(2008, 3). He divides his project into three branches: *analytic, pragmatic* and *performative somaesthetics*. The latter relates to bodily training, while in focusing on the pragmatist aspect, Shusterman essentially frames it as an applied use of the analytic branch, which seeks to understand the body and its place in the world.[5] He writes:

> Our bodies [...] help create a sense of common space. When I see your body, I focus on a place and object that is also the focus of your experience, even though your experience of your body is from a different perspective. In the same way, bodies provide a common place for the meeting of minds, whose intentions, beliefs, desires, and feelings are expressed [...] bodily.
>
> (2008, 145)

This "common space" results from, and relies on, bodily sensations, and this is most clearly expressed by William James in *Essays on Radical Empiricism* (1976). "The world experienced," writes James, "comes at all times with our body as its centre, centre of vision, centre of action, centre of interest" (1976, 86). As Lefebvre has elsewhere suggested, "[t]he body serves both as point of departure and as destination" (1991, 194) and in this sense, the body is what Shusterman calls a "unifying space" between external and internal experience, acting as an "integrator of such sense perceptions" (2008, 143). When viewed from the combined position of analytic and pragmatic somaesthetics, this "unifying space" allows for the world to be experienced on the basis of "Somaesthetic Performance Analysis" as a critical model or framework.

Considering this model, which both draws on and extends beyond Shusterman's philosophical concerns, the rest of this chapter will consider how Somaesthetic Performance Analysis might offer a framework for articulating what might be called "somaesthetic vocality," further centralizing the role of the body in philosophical discourse and in the production and experience of voicing and vocality. We begin with the third statement of this chapter.

Statement 3

Somaesthetic vocality must be placed within given cultural contexts or conditions.

Cultural conditioning

Experiences are determined by both nature and nurture, internal and external factors which are then "unified" to configure our reactions. Shusterman suggests that "one's body [...] incorporates its surroundings" (2008, 214), echoing the words of Ludwig Wittgenstein when he wrote that bodily action and somatic consciousness may only be understood in relation to context and cultural mediation; "the whole hurly-burly of human actions, the background against which we see any action" (1967, 577). Wittgenstein's discussion of artistic experience (along with that of John Dewey) explicitly entails a reciprocal process of "doing and undergoing" in which the subject's embodied experience mixes with the external environment to constitute aesthetic sensations (Dewey, 1980, 43–45).

On this basis, somaesthetic vocality is produced and experienced within the context of cultural conditioning. Indeed, neurobiologist Antonio Damasio notes that internally, we operate through "stereotyped patterns" of behavior (2000, 55) and despite the problematic vagueness of this term, he elsewhere qualifies it somewhat by suggesting that "social psychology has produced massive evidence for nonconscious influences in the human mind and behaviour" (2000, 297). As listeners, then, our responses to voice are determined by what we *allow* ourselves to feel, governed both by genetics and by social conditioning. In her now-ubiquitous study *The Human Voice*, Anne Karpf wryly notes that "I speak with my voice, but my culture speaks through me" (2006, 182). We might think in this case of Judith Butler's concept of performativity ([1990] 2006) and the constructions of social types, even inviting Jungian ideas of "archetypes" to join the party ([1947] 2001).

A predominant exemplar of this relationship between voice and culture is the "stereotyped or encultured patterns" that proffer explicit or implied connections between body, voice, listener and *race* in American culture. Karpf and others have discussed the complicated notion of race as biologically innate in vocal production, but the effect of cultural conditioning on the listener's experience becomes particularly telling in this case. Considering the way in which "race is heard" through speech or song, Jennifer Lynn Stoever asserts that voice "enables listeners to construct and discern racial identities" on a sonic color line that she expressly defines as a "socially constructed boundary that codes sonic phenomena such as vocal timbre, accents, and musical tones" as inherently indicative of race, ancestry or area (2016, 11). Stoever uses examples of nineteenth-century trade adverts which drew explicit distinctions between the timbral qualities of "civilized" white slave owners with the "coarse," "loud" qualities of black slave voice (2016, 29–30). Culturally, voice was viewed as indicative of race and therefore class and status, within an implied biological component borne of prevailing neo-Darwinist ideals of natural selection and white superiority. The white listeners' body filtered the voice through by incorporating their social and political surroundings, as Shusterman indicates.

Reflecting on such culturally-politicized notions, Jacob Smith has similarly examined how white American minstrel performers of the early twentieth century viewed certain inflections or qualities as "markers of authentic black voice," assuming a heavy faux-dialect with a performance infused with "occasional whoops and laughs, and a syncopated delivery" in a performance of "blackvoice" (2008, 141).[6] In other words, what the white voices did evoked "stereotypes" of the African-American race for white listeners. Stoever hears this as "auditory imaginings of blackness" experienced by the "embodied ear" of the listener; the means by which what one hears is "shaped by [...] experience, historical context, and physicality" (2008, 1, 15). Cultural conditioning – whether positive or pejorative – therefore has an overt ability to impact a listener's understanding of voice. It is notable that in the aforementioned examples, the persistent references to vocal texture, dynamics and inherent musicality of style all relate to the biological production of sound; notwithstanding the cultural markers of race here, the voice is still experienced through corporeal properties that become central to the listening experience.

Elsewhere, the cultural symbol of the singing mother soothing her baby to sleep has become an "archetypical ideal" of socially-constructed motherhood, "a perfect combination of body and voice" which – through bodily vibration and intimate touch borne of vocal tone and timbre – reinforces the mother-child bond in the early stages of infancy (Fleeger, 2014, 1). The mother's voice is, according to Michel Chion, stronger than even the umbilical cord, and is a "sound bath" that catalyzes an infant's development (Anzieu, 1989, 6; Chion, 1999, 61). As a result of this, when Jennifer Fleeger chose instead to play her baby recordings of Michael Jackson or Geraldine Farrar as music to soothe and serenade, it caused such anxiety that it inspired Fleeger to write a monograph on the "mismatch" between cultural expectations and the recorded female voice.[7] Aside from issues of race, the body is again at the center of concerns regarding vocality, related in this instance to child development and gender.

In just these two representative instances, responses to voice – and the implied centrality of the body in its experience and production – are conditioned by prevailing social and political ideals. With regard to voice, one further prevailing condition that is perpetuated in western society is the "segregation" of training methodologies that approach the training of speaking and singing "as if they were separate entities," in what Paul Barker has termed a "tyranny of understanding" (2015, xx, xxiv) – one which separates the rational from the emotive and the experiential from the efficacious. Such dislocated thinking about voice in western pedagogy is indicative of a broader dislocation between sensorial experience and rational thought. In fact, Scott Miller is even more dogmatic than Barker in his observation about this subject, claiming that contemporary western society has "civilised 'full-bodied emotion' out of people" through such approaches, suggesting that this is one reason that heightened forms of vocal performance such as opera and musical theatre may be overwhelming in the way they offer direct and emotional expressivity (2007, 1; Sontag, 1964).[8] Personal taste and choice in entertainment notwithstanding, however, Plato's mistrust of performance in *Republic* was precisely because of its capacity for eliciting embodied responses in its audience. With attendant acknowledgement of western societal and cultural norms, how might the inevitable feeling and experience of voice be understood through the "unifying space" of the body – especially when emotional response is still viewed with suspicion or mistrust? The answer to this question can be found by further consideration of the relationship between voice, body and neurological experience – or cognitive engagement, if one wishes to appease Plato, Kant and Descartes. As we will see, this relationship is more complicated that Plato first thought.

Neurological experience

Taken as a trilogy of sorts, three key texts from neuroscientist Antonio Damasio – *Descartes' Error* (1994), *The Feeling of What Happens: Body, Emotion and the Making of Consciousness* (1999) and *Self Comes to Mind: Constructing the Conscious Brain* (2012) – represent a collective scientific challenge to the mind/body dualities seen in Platonic, Cartesian and Kantian thoughts. For Damasio, "consciousness begins as the feeling of what happens when we see or hear or touch […] that accompanies the making of any kind of image […] within our living organisms" (2000, 26). Consciousness – the opportunity for sensory experience and self-knowledge – begins here as an expressly corporeal event, induced by factors external to our biological machinery, from which electro-chemical and neurological *images* may be produced within our minds, resulting in chemical changes occurring within our bodies. Damasio, in effect, suggests that "I am, therefore I think". In other words, Damasio claims primacy for somatic "sensory appreciation" before (over, above or beyond) cognitive or epistemological understanding.

Together, these processes of sensation and understanding form what Shusterman has defined as (body) consciousness, the reciprocal awareness of self in relation to the external world and sensory appreciation experienced through bodily sensation (or, "somaesthetics"). The conscious experience of vocal acts, then, does not begin with an epistemological image in the mind or a rational appreciation of form but with the "empirical delights" of the listener's engagement with the voice as a physical and embodied form, a sound experienced by bodies in space through reverberation, echo and atmospheric wave forms. As Lynne Kendrick might put it, such sonorous properties of vocal acts "become the co-ordinates by which we understand [external] space" (2017, 63).[9] If consciousness "begins as the feeling of what happens when we […] hear" (2000, 26), then our conscious – or cognitive – understanding of voice is expressly determined by our embodied response to external physical properties *in the first place*, with the "unifying space" of the listeners' body functioning as an active, somaesthetic "integrator of […] sense perceptions" (Shusterman, 2008, 143). After all, as William James wrote, no matter what sensorial maelstrom of information we may have to negotiate, it is all one through "the obvious nucleus of every man's experience, his own body [as a] true, continuous percept" (1890, 33). Such an observation constitutes the fourth statement in this discussion.

> **Statement 4**
>
> Somaesthetic vocality is experienced by means of the ontological primacy of somatic sensation over cognitive understanding.

This statement – and the evident philosophical links that might be identified between cognitive experience and bodily sensation – is particularly provocative when considering the two aforementioned philosophical discourses. First, in the case of Plato, the fourth statement suggests that the "prison-house" of the body does not simply illicit sensory delights but is expressly instrumental in the formation of the conscious and rational cognitive experience he championed. Far from a Platonic paradox, this may simply be Platonic paranoia. Second, while Kant claimed that the experience of art derives chiefly from its rational or cognitive form rather than visceral sensations, a neurobiological perspective suggests that such a purely epistemological perspective is flawed. Simply put, if Damasio's construction of consciousness is correct, then ontological sensation leads to (or is at least concomitant with) neurological "images" of experience. Having established this neurobiological perspective and a challenge to philosophical discourses, however, how might this enhance our understanding of the relationship between vocal acts and somatic experience?

We have already seen that the voice is corporeal, produced by a body. As numerous scholars have noted – including in the pages of this collection – vocal acts and vocal art forms are expressly somatic; borne of the bodies which bring them forth.[10] Performance theorist Erika Fischer-Lichte has noted that when detached from language "the voice emerges as the opposite of *logos*" (2008, 127). As sound without semantic attribution, such voices therefore become "dangerous and seductive" precisely because they emerge from (and are implicitly connected to) the body that produces them; they become the very object of Platonic mistrust (Fischer-Lichte, 2008, 127). Yet, given that the focus of this chapter is on the listener rather than the vocalist, how are listeners' bodies involved in the somaesthetic vocality?

It is clear from Plato's paradox that, at its base, his anxiety was borne of an understanding that audience members at performances are effected somatically by what they see and hear. By definition, such somaesthetic appreciation must extend to listening practices as well as the visual reception of performance. In fact, the experience of what might be termed "embodied listening" (as well as embodied, somaesthetic vocality) is present in reception studies and sound studies alike. Fischer-Lichte already hints at the phenomena of somatic listening when she writes that voices "physically take hold of the listeners" (2008, 127), a word picture expanded by sound studies scholar Salome Voegelin in her description of vocal exchange as noise: "My voice meets his voice not through language but through both our fleshness:

screaming, screeching, yelling and croaking, shouting the corporeality out of our bodies" (2011, 73).

Expressing the corporeality of vocal exchange through "fleshness" indicates the intensity of somatic *experience* in the act of listening, producing a consciousness through hearing a sound felt by bodies in space. Steven Connor's further assertion that voice is "not simply an emission of the body," but is its own corporeality in production seems apt here (2004, 158). In fact, such a position allows for the fifth and penultimate statement of this chapter.

Statement 5

If vocality is corporeal at the point of production, negotiated by means of the primacy of the body, then listening must also, *a posteriori*, be a corporeal act.

However, while I have suggested that somaesthetic vocality has an affective equivalence in the act of listening, this raises the final question considered in this chapter: what happens between these two states – in sonorous space?

While Thomaidis, Voegelin, Fischer-Lichte and others all express confidence in the somatic qualities of voice and the conditions of its auditory reception, this duality of somaesthetic vocality and listening is not universal. For example, reflecting on speech acts, Mladen Dolar's Lacanian position suggests an ambivalence about what happens when a voice gives voice, arguing that voice all at once belongs to – and is separate from – the body, a position echoed by Ella Finer when she suggests that sounded "voice carries a body and no body simultaneously" (2015, 184). In other words, once a voice leaves a body, does it engage in an act of denial, as Lefebvre early suggests is the presumptive prejudice in western philosophical thought? In other words, are echoes, reverberations and auditory waves in space ontologically ineffable when it comes to ideas of the "vocal body" (Thomaidis and Macpherson, 2015, 6)? Transient they may be, but these intensely felt sensations accord with Voegelin's notion of the "fleshness" of vocality: the colliding of sonic bodies in the production and reception of voice (2010, 73). Yet, is this affective philosophy supported beyond the ideals of somaesthetic analysis?

Between leaving a body and taking hold of listeners (Fischer-Lichte, 2008, 127), voice in space might be understood to exist as a sonic in-between. Along with Konstantinos Thomaidis, I have suggested that the idea of vocal "in-betweenness" is a useful way to consider voice as an experience shared by both speaker/singer and listener. Defining the aural "in-between" as "the junction point for the multiple encodings of experience to be negotiated and understood" (2015, 4), the combination of cultural conditioning and neurobiological experience and sensation can be better articulated, allowing for a space in which operative voice can evoke supersensory emotion (Poizat, 1992; Tomlinson, 1999) or rasp can produce an "auditory imagining of blackness" (Stoever, 2016). Yet, there has to be more to this than theoretical rhetoric or discourse. In fact, two specific facets of vocality and voicing suggest that the sonorous space between voice and its reception is likewise expressly somatic.

A sonorous, somatic in-between

First, as Lynne Kendrick (2017) notes, the sonorous space between the producer and receiver of sound is filled with physical reverberations, echoes and atmospheric wave forms that materially change the space. In other words, upon being received by the listener, the sound produced by a voice *physically* envelops them, as Fischer-Lichte suggests earlier. Through such sonorous properties, vocal acts "become the co-ordinates by which we understand [external] space" (Kendrick, 2017, 63), negotiating these through the "unifying spaces" of the listeners' bodies (Shusterman, 2008, 143). Sound, then, affects us corporeally, mediated by cultural expectations that condition how we feel about *what* we hear, somaesthetically.

Second, neuroscientific research suggests that such somatic affect by sonic material (the somaesthetic vocality of the one giving voice) has specific consequences in the body and mind of the listener. Debates surrounding the existence of mirror neurons in the brain suggest that a direct relationship can be formed in the aural space between vocalist and listener. Damasio discusses the function of mirror neurons through reference to the "as-if body loop" (2010, 101–107):

> [A]s we witness an action in another, our body-sensing brain adopts the body state we would assume were we ourselves moving, and it does so [...] by a pre-activation of motor structures – ready for action [...] in some cases by motor simulation.
>
> (2010, 104)

This idea of a neurobiological loop between performer and audience member/listener also corresponds to other versions of a similar embodied phenomenon, elsewhere termed "inner mimicry" or "vicarious enactment" (Martin, 2002).[11]

While this has been applied to various performance disciplines – most notably in the field of dance studies – it is particularly interesting to note that motor simulation – whether mapped synaptically, or directly experienced through motor-evoked potentials – simulates embodied movements. In the case of somatic vocality, such "inner mimicry" or "motor simulation" is what allows us to feel be moved by a soprano, relax at the sound of a crooner, cringe at a cackle or feel anxious at an infant's cry. The particular type of somaesthetic consciousness involved in engaging with voice, then, relies on a reciprocal process between somaesthetic vocality, somaesthetic listening *and* a sense of the embodied "in-between" that allows a person's voice to touch another human being. Expressly and specifically, this reaction – borne of culturally conditioned listening, physical changes to the space that carries the voice and our own neurobiology – is somatic: experienced within our bodies as they respond to the "richly sensuous dimensions" of a voice. Prior to a summary and final commentary, this is the sixth statement of this chapter.

> **Statement 6**
>
> The moment in between "somaesthetic vocality" and "somaesthetic listening" is also expressly and explicitly somatic, and the point at which corporeality of voice is culturally mediated.

In summary

With a specific focus on the listener or audience member, this chapter has explored the ways in which western philosophies of somatic knowledge can enhance our understanding of vocal experience and "vocal art forms". Six key statements drew out and articulated the interrelationships between philosophical thought, embodied experience, corporeality, vocality, cultural conditioning and somatic listening. Taken together, these statements are as follows:

- The problematic status of the soma in western philosophical aesthetics has its origin in antiquity.

However,

- Performance – including vocal performance – must be understood in somatic terms.
- Somaesthetic vocality must be placed within given cultural contexts or conditions.
- Somaesthetic vocality is experienced by means of the ontological primacy of somatic sensation over cognitive understanding.
- If vocality is corporeal at the point of production, negotiated by means of the primacy of the body, then listening must also, *a posteriori*, be a corporeal act.
- The moment in between "somaesthetic vocality" and "somaesthetic listening" is also expressly and explicitly somatic, and the point at which corporeality of voice is culturally mediated.

By means of these statements, a tripartite process of embodied experience can be established, flowing from the vocalizer, through the in-between of space, to the corporeal listener. This experiential paradigm is facilitated through Somaesthetic Performance Analysis, derived from pragmatist philosophical discourses and supported by means of neurobiological and sociological concepts. In this case, a somatic understanding of vocal acts borne of such an analytical framework also suggests that this approach to vocal practice – of speech, song and those forms in-between – might not only enhance our understanding of somatics and voice, but, in turn, the very act of somaesthetic vocality or somaesthetic listening may also implicitly challenge – and help to address – the relative paucity of philosophical discourse relating to the body in western aesthetic thought.

Notes

1 Such marginalizing of the corporeal has often been attributed to the transcendent and metaphysical vocal aesthetics of opera. Seminal discussions of this subject by scholars, including Michel Poizat (1992) and Carolyn Abbate (1991, 2001), along with Gary Tomlinson's excellent survey of voice and nomenal and phenomenal in *Metaphysical Song* (1999).
2 Drawing on Lacanian's psychoanalytic perspectives, Dolar's consideration of the "object voice" (or a vocal *objet petit a*) suggests that voice is the unattainable object of desire, which serves to tie language to the body but which is, nevertheless, "part neither of language or of the body" (2006, 73). In other words, from Dolar's psychoanalytical position, the voice is liminal – no part of the body or of language, but reliant on both.
3 Even Dolar continues to suggest, in a seeming contradiction to his assertion cited in endnote 2, that "there is no voice without a body" (2006, 60).
4 In Shusterman's definition of somaesthetics here, he suggests that his philosophy focusses on the "soma," a term conventionally held to represent the body as distinct from mind, psyche or emotion. While the application of somaesthetics in Shusterman's work is, in reality, more inclusive than this, his specific emphasis here enables the development of a model that ensures the primacy of the body in lived experience. In this sense, the portmanteau "somaesthetics" comprises *soma* (the material body) and *aesthetics*: sensory and emotional experience and appreciation. Throughout this chapter, then, I employ this term in relation to my understanding of it as a holistic and embodied concept. Specifically, in this reading, the terms "soma" and "corporeal" relate to the body as an autonomous entity; the idea of embodied experiences, allied to the concept of "somaesthetics," imbues such bodily experiences with cognitive, sensory or emotional characteristics.
5 This application includes discussions of the Alexander technique and the Feldenkrais method, and here we might draw connections between the philosophy of pragmatic *somaesthetics* and recent discourses on voice and voice training through practices from the so-called field of somatics (Lutterbie, 2012; Kjeldsen, 2015; Wragg, 2017).
6 Specifically, Smith's text focuses expressly on the way in which listening habits and practices have been culturally mediated or conditioned concomitant with the developments of sound recording from the late nineteenth century to the present day.

7 If Stoever and Smith have identified culturally constructed ideals of voice and body in relation to race (and, elsewhere, gender), Fleeger's experience of dislocation between bodily experience and recorded voice also hints at a further facet of the relationship between voice and body that cannot be considered in this chapter due to space – the impact of technology on somatic experience.
8 We might even think of the pejorative use of Susan Sontag's (1964) definition of "camp" in this respect, and its association with traditional musical theatre vocal aesthetics as over-the-top and too direct in their expression of emotions and feelings.
9 Steven Connor's assertion that voice is "not simply an emission of the body" but is its own corporeality in production seems apt here (2004).
10 In fact, Konstantinos Thomaidis (2013, 2014) has expressly employed the terms "physiovocality" and "The Vocal Body" in his work on performance practice.
11 For further discussion of this idea of a somatic and embodied relationship between performer and audience (member), see also Maaike Bleeker (2002), Amy Cook (2007) and Corrinne Jola (2010). For an explicitly vocal perspective relating to popular performance styles such as musical theatre, see Millie Taylor (2012).

References

Abbate, C. (1991) *Unsung Voices: Opera and Musical Narratives in the Nineteenth Century*. Princeton, NJ: Princeton University Press.
Abbate, C. (2001) *In Search of Opera*. Princeton, NJ: Princeton University Press.
Anzieu, D. (1989) *The Skin-Ego*. New Haven and London: Yale University Press.
Barker, P. (2015) Foreword (With one voice: Disambiguating sung and spoken voices through a composer's experience) in *Voice Studies: Critical Approaches to Process, Performance and Experience*. Abingdon, Oxon: Routledge.
Bleeker, M. (2002) Disorders that consciousness can produce: bodies seeing bodies on stage. *Critical Studies (Bodycheck: Relocating the Body in Performing Art)*, 17 131–160.
Butler, J. ([1990] 2006) *Gender Trouble* (Routledge Classics). London and New York: Routledge.
Chion, M. (1999) *The Voice in Cinema*. New York: Columbia University Press.
Connor, S. (2004) The strains of the voice. In: Brigitte Felderer (ed.) *Phonorama: Eine Kulturgeschischte der Stimme als Medium*. Berlin: Matthew and Seitz, 158–172.
Cook, A. (2007) Interplay: the method and potential of a cognitive scientific approach to theatre. *Theatre Journal*, 59 279–294.
Damasio, A. (1994) *Descartes' Error: Emotion, Reason and the Human Brain*. London and Basingstoke: Picador.
——— (2000) *The Feeling of What Happens: Body, Emotion and the Making of Consciousness*. London: Vintage.
Damasio, A. (2011) *Self Comes to Mind: Constructing the Conscious Brain*. London: Vintage.
Dewey, J. (1980) *Art as Experience*. New York: Perigee.
Dolar, M. (2006) *A Voice and Nothing More*. Cambridge: MIT Press.
Finer, E. (2015) Strange objects/strange properties: female audibility and the acoustic stage prop. In: Konstantinos Thomaidis and Ben Macpherson (eds.) *Voice Studies: Critical Approaches to Process, Performance and Experience*. Abingdon, Oxon: Routledge, 177–187.

Fischer-Lichte, E. (2008) *The Transformative Power of Performance: A New Aesthetics*. Oxford and New York: Routledge.
Fleeger, J. (2014) *Mismatched Women: The Siren's Song Through the Machine*. New York and Oxford: Oxford University Press.
James, W. (1890) *The Principles of Psychology*. Cambridge, MA: Harvard University Press.
——— (1975) *Essays in Radical Empiricism*. Cambridge, MA: Harvard University Press.
Jola, C. (2010) Research and choreography: merging dance and cognitive neuroscience. In: Bettina Blasing, Martin Puttke and Thomas Schack (eds.) *The Neurocognition of Dance: Mind, Movement and Motor Skills*. Hove: Psychology Press, 203–234.
Jung, C. ([1947] 2001) *On the Nature of the Psyche* (Routledge Classics). London and New York: Routledge.
Kant, I. (1897) *Critique of Judgment*. Translated from German by Werner S. Pluhar. Indianapolis, IN: Hackett.
Karpf, A. (2006) *The Human Voice: How the Extraordinary Instrument Reveals Essential Clues About Who We Are*. London and New York: Bloomsbury.
Kendrick, L. (2017) *Theatre Aurality*. Basingstoke: Palgrave Macmillan.
Kjeldsen, T. (2015) Learning to let go: control and freedom in the *passaggio*. In: Konstantinos Thomaidis and Ben Macpherson (eds.) *Voice Studies: Critical Approaches to Process, Performance and Experience*. Abingdon, Oxon: Routledge, 38–48.
Lefebvre, H. (1991) *The Production of Space*. Translated from French by D. Nicholson-Smith. Oxford: Blackwell.
Ley, G. (1999) *From Mimesis to Interculturalism*. Exeter: Exeter University Press.
Lutterbie, J. (2012) *Towards a General Theory of Acting: Cognitive Science and Performance*. Basingstoke: Palgrave Macmillan.
Macpherson, B. (2012) A voice and so much more (or when bodies say things that words cannot). *Studies in Musical Theatre*, 6(1) 43–57.
Macpherson, B. (2015) Body musicality: the visual, virtual, visceral voice. In: Konstantinos Thomaidis and Ben Macpherson (eds.) *Voice Studies: Critical Approaches to Process, Performance and Experience*. Abingdon, Oxon: Routledge, 149–161.
Marshall, L. (2008) *The Body Speaks: Performance and Expression*. 2nd edition. London: Methuen.
Martin, J. (2002) Characteristics of the modern dance. In: Michael Huxley and Noel Witts (eds.) *The Twentieth-Century Performance Reader*. 2nd edition. London and New York: Routledge, 295–302.
McConachie, B. (2008) *Engaging Audiences: A Cognitive Approach to the Spectating at the Theatre*. Basingstoke and New York: Palgrave Macmillan.
McConachie, B. and Hart, E. (eds.) (2006) *Performance and Cognition: Theatre Studies and the Cognitive Turn*. Abingdon, Oxon: Routledge.
Miller, S. (2007) *Strike Up the Band: A New History of Musical Theatre*. New Hampshire: Heinemann.
Plato (n.d.) *Phaedo*. Available from: http://classics.mit.edu/Plato/phaedo.html [Accessed 18 January 2019].
——— (1995) Republic, Excerpts from Book III (386-398b), and Book X (595-608b). In: Alex Neill and Aaron Ridley (eds.) *The Philosophy of Art: Readings Ancient and Modern*. USA: McGraw-Hill Inc., 466–487.

Poizat, M. (1992) *The Angel's Cry: Beyond the Pleasure Principle in Opera*. Ithaca and London: Cornell University Press.
Reeve, S. (ed.) (2013) *Body and Performance (Ways of Being a Body)*. Bridport: Triarchy Press.
Scott, J. A. (2017) *Embodied Performance as Applied Art, Research and Pedagogy*. Basingstoke: Palgrave Macmillan.
Shusterman, R. (2000) *Performing Live: Aesthetic Alternatives to the Ends of Art*. Ithaca and London: Cornell University Press.
——— (2008) *Body Consciousness: A Philosophy of Mindfulness and Somaesthetics*. Cambridge and New York: Cambridge University Press.
——— (2012) *Thinking Through the Body: Essays in Somaesthetics*. Cambridge and New York: Cambridge University Press.
——— (2018) *Aesthetic Experience and Somaesthetics*. Lieden and Boston, MA: BRILL.
Smith, J. (2008) *Vocal Tracks: Performance and Sound Media*. Berkeley, CA: University of California Press.
Sontag, S. (1964) Notes on "Camp". Available from: http://faculty.georgetown.edu/irvinem/theory/Sontag-NotesOnCamp-1964.html [Accessed 20 December 2018].
Stoever, J. (2016) *The Sonic Color Line: Race and the Cultural Politics of Listening*. New York: New York University Press.
Tarvainen, A. (2018) Singing, listening, proprioceiving: some reflections on vocal somaesthetics. In: Richard Shusterman (ed.) *Aesthetic Experience and Somaesthetics*. Lieden and Boston, MA: BRILL, 120–142.
Taylor, M. (2012) *Musical Theatre, Realism and Entertainment*. Farnham: Ashgate.
Thomaidis, K. (2013) The vocal body. In: Sandra Reeve (ed.) *Body and Performance*. Devon: Triarchy Press, 85–98.
——— (2014) Singing from stones: physiovocality and Gardzienice's Theater of musicality. In: Dominic Symonds and Millie Taylor (eds.) *Gestures of Music Theater: The Performativity of Song and Dance*. New York and Oxford: Oxford University Press, 242–258.
Thomaidis, K. and Macpherson, B. (2015) Introduction: voice(s) as a method and an in-between in *Voice Studies: Critical Approach to Process, Performance and Experience*. Abingdon, Oxon: Routledge.
Tomlinson, G. (1999) *Metaphysical Song: Essays in Opera*. Princeton, NJ: Princeton University Press.
Voegelin, S. (2010) *Listening to Noise and Silence: Towards a Philosophy of Sound Art*. New York and London: Bloomsbury.
Wittgenstein, L. (1967) *Zettel*. Oxford: Blackwell.
Wragg, G. (2017) *Towards Vocal Freedom: Alexander Technique and the Use of the Singing Voice*. Graz: Mouritz.

Part V
Beyond this book

17 Beyond our somatic voices

Christina Kapadocha

When I set up the proposal of this project, I explicitly expressed that it would be

> developed upon intentions of diversity, openness, relationality and inclusion that try to challenge traditional binaries, not only between bodies and vocalities but also between traditional somatic practices and modern embodied processes that interrogate somaticities, theoretical and practical research in academia and *beyond*.
>
> (Kapadocha, 2017b, added emphasis)

As I allowed the project to evolve around these intentions, I have been simultaneously researching what this *beyond* could be and become during and after introducing somatic voice studies as a new area of vocal and somatic praxis. Due to the experiential, voice-sensitive, polyvocal and praxical identity of this research, the most pertinent way to test out the *beyond* in the creative process of this publication was to organize a series of group research activities. They took place at East 15 Acting School in London, where I am currently a member of the teaching and research team and culminated with a two-day praxical symposium (July 19–20, 2019) from which I draw for shaping this closing chapter.[1]

Organizing a gathering that could bring together in one place the contributors of this volume had been an imperative for me since the beginning of the project. The fact that I was able to host it at East 15 as a conservatoire environment aimed at additionally contributing to this collection's praxical, multivocal and multidisciplinary nature. As an experiment within the creation of this collection, it gave me a strong opportunity to also explore the *beyond* potentialities of the project within current praxical investigations on polyvocal and intermedia writing. This writing includes embodied voices or, as I introduced in Chapter 12, diverse *somatic logos*. Returning to Thomaidis' and Macpherson's notion of in-betweenness as a theoretical framework for multimodality and multivocality in critical voice studies: "Acknowledging the in-betweenness of voice is a provocation to methodological multiplicity" (2015b, 7). As outlined in the Introduction of this book, this methodological multiplicity is evident throughout the body of the collection through the combination of various formats and narratives. Could I though take this praxically (practically and theoretically) a bit further?

For the shaping of the gathering activities and how they could inform the completion of this book, I aimed at embracing existing advancements in praxical research while also suggesting new directions. For instance, I have been inspired by how Thomaidis and Macpherson held the polyphonic conclusion to the *Voice Studies* volume, around multiple responses to the question "What is voice studies?" (2015a, 203–216). Given that I could use the symposium activities as a practice-research framework, I was interested in checking whether there would be space for further shared polyphony to emerge. I started by considering the praxical nature of the gathering based on three *beyond* possibilities. First, as the contributors to this collection, we could meet in one place and somatically share our works *beyond* our own research. Second, we could open up the "book as experience" prior to its publication to the public, *beyond* our group. Finally, we could create a *third*[2] space in-between us, the authors in this collection and the symposium participants offering them space for their own contributions *beyond our somatic voices*. This intended structure along with all the relevant details outlined below was, of course, communicated first to the authors of this book.

In the call for participation to the symposium, I explained to the possible participants that the activities would follow the structure of this volume and therefore unfold in four main parts, including an Introduction and an Epilogue. I added the four main overarching questions, one for each part, as they appear in the Introduction of this book (see p. 8). Practitioner-researchers, artists and PhD candidates in Arts and Humanities were invited to offer their own brief contributions on any of the project's navigating question that would be pertinent to their own present interests and inquiries. It was noted that their contributions could be prepared in advance and/or be emergent responses to the offered seminars by the volume contributors in line with the contingent nature of practice research. Transferring this praxical polyphony to the conclusion of this book, I wish to focus on how the "voices" of the six *contributing participants*[3] interacted with the gathering activities and my own witnessing of this further development of the project. I do so by interweaving my narrative in a standard format and the "voices" of the participants in italics acknowledging them in this way as an inextricable part of a "polyvocal authorship".

I would like to clarify that my own "voice" as the author of this chapter is not meant to convey a shared perception or other individuals' views. It is unavoidably filtered through my own experience of the project, understanding and research interests. In the same way, I "filter" the contributions as it is also practically challenging to include here everything that was voiced.[4] Nevertheless, I aim at containing this filter by including, to the extent it is possible, the "voices" of the participants themselves instead of making them entirely part of my own narrative. In the order of their contributions, these "voices" belong to Judah Attille (2019), Fabiano Culora (2019), Natusha Croes (2019), Daron Oram (2019b), Carmen Wong (2019) and Faye Rigopoulou (2019).[5] This is also combined with polyphonic audiovisual material developed in-between contributors and participants in the end of the gathering and a multivocal score inspired by the same practice as a visual ending of this chapter.

With the chosen interconnected modes of writing voices, I wish to share how somatic vocalities and somatic modes of witnessing voices offer multiple *in-between* potentialities of diverse *somatic logos*. This advanced theoretical understanding of logos as integrated, interrelational, individual and also innately polyvocal suggests new ways of understanding and disseminating embodied experiences. In that sense, it can go *beyond this book* and somatic voice studies by informing embodied research as an overall methodology. *Somatic logos* also resides in the very nature of praxical research that necessitates practice in order to actualize and deepen the undergoing investigations. To this end, I organized and held the gathering activities. As Judah Attille, who opened the participants' contributions, noted in the end of the first day of the symposium:

It is so brilliant to have this space together with the writers to explore some issues that are going to be fresh by the time you go to print and beyond […] It's almost like we are talking about the beyond of the book now.

Somatic voices: day 1

Heightening my sense of somatic listening as integrated and interrelational experience, I noticed that from the first responses of contributing participants (after my Introduction and the seminars offered by Andrea Olsen-Chapter 2 and Patricia Bardi-Chapter 4), dynamics between somatics and beyond possibilities came up. It was soon obvious that the communication of the inquiries of this project triggered curiosity and discussions on urgent ethical and sociopolitical issues that innately reside within multiple and co-existing somaticities.

This vividly resonated with the inquiry that was brought in by the filmmaker and PhD candidate at University of Arts, London, Judah Attille. Attille connected her past experiences in somatic practices (such as Tanya Fitzpatrick's Align Somatics) and voice therapy that she underwent due to voice strain as a secondary-school teacher, by sharing that this process:

Has really opened me up to the possibility of the body-voice-breath and the potential for narrative […] I also realized that the tensions around the body which add to the throat are ongoing changing process depending on the environment we are in. As a body of color those changes in environment become more perceptible as I travel through different spaces. So, in terms of my filming, I'm very aware of my power to capture other people's images and whether or not they consent to that happening. Doing this research, I'm very aware of this ethical position and the idea of consent.

Overall, why this moment is important to me Christina, is because it is an opportunity to think about the methodology and the theories that inform my practice. For example, Homi Bhabha [see Bhabha, 2012] *back in the 80s–90s, he spoke about the space of colonialism; of not just the colonizer and colonized in two separate places but colonizer-colonized in the same space. So, we occupy the same language but we hold different positions within that space. Moving on from that, I'm interested in Derrida's theory of hospitality* [see Derrida and Dufourmantelle, 2000]; *the role of the host, the role of the guest, the terms of engagement between host and guest to ensure there isn't hostility. The gestures of hosting and the gestures of being a good guest.*

I was particularly drawn to Derrida's ideas on hospitality Attille added to the project for multiple reasons. Beyond the way I employ the philosopher's definition of logocentrism in relation to problematics I challenge in my research, I felt that *hospitality* as notion and experience also resonated a lot with the intentions of my role in this project as well as its overall vision outlined in the opening of this discussion. Fabiano Culora, somatic movement educator and therapist, attuning to the offered space for emergent investigations shared:

That's something I really appreciated, to be responsive to the moment. I really don't know what this question is but it's a question coming out from being with you both [referring to Andrea Olsen and Patricia Bardi].

As soon as I hear your voice Andrea and see you moving my body starts responding. For the last few years my work and my research interest is being around the body relational practices and what happens in the space between us; maybe I'm not just this body sound but maybe that's appropriated. So I'm interested in how the cells of my body are generating in your presence as a memory of work.

[...] If there was a question there is something about "How do you experience that in your work as an artist working with people, being in the world?" That resonance that is timeless. What really struck me was that, Patricia, I haven't been in your presence for many years and it was only a two-day workshop but as soon as I hear you and see you moving something also draws me back to that moment [...] somehow shared between us. It wasn't just my memory [...] My impression is what happens is beyond us that's been co-created or trans-created.

In the group reflection that followed, I noticed that the experience of a hosted co-creation somehow remained as an underlying current while I was drawn to themes of in-between witnessing, boundaries and community. Receiving the expressed ideas, it became significant for me to acknowledge that using the word community or setting up one (like the one shaped for the ground

Beyond our somatic voices 233

of this project) does not mean that we automatically overcome issues of exclusion, unless the emerged community is enveloped by a genuinely porous membrane that allows permeability by *different* members. Derrida's notion of *différance* (see, among others, Derrida, 1982) that acknowledges the ongoing overlapping between presence and absence could support this awareness. In other words and in some sort of resonance with the philosopher's criticism upon any kind of community (see Derrida, 1995), I was as much mindful of the people who were present in the studio (and this project) as of the people who were not, of the project's potentialities as well as limitations. So, the thoughts that came up for me were: we can create new communities and discuss issues but do we actually make a change? What really needs to happen for that *beyond*?

Whatever this *beyond* may become in relation to various environments and processes, this project suggests that it lands within our *somata* and is directly associated with our ability to listen or the lack thereof. Hence, adding to existing discussions in voice and sound studies (see, among others, Idhe, 2007; Voegelin, 2010; Thomaidis and Macpherson, 2015a; Eidsheim and Meizel, 2019), listening is approached as an inherently somatic and relational activity that can become a chosen practice or methodology towards ethical awareness and sociopolitical change. As it becomes evident in the length of this book and the cited work, somatic listening as methodology is a growing process in the fields of artistic research and education. Thus, after the Second Part of the gathering activities and the contributions of Ellen Foyn Bruun (Chapter 5), Leticia Santafé (Chapter 6), Amy Mihyang Ginther (Chapter 8) and Stephen Paparo (Chapter 7),[6] it was exciting to receive the responses of the multimedia artist Natusha Croes and the Senior Lecturer in Voice at Royal Central School of Speech and Drama (RCSSD, London) Daron Oram.

Originally from Oranjestad (Aruba, Caribbean Sea) with ongoing experience in audiovisual arts and recent studies in the MA Performance Making at Goldsmiths (University of London), Croes brought in the following:

I am into the morphology or the potential of transformation that the body has, especially tapping into practices that have sort of tuned me into experiencing the body as more than just flesh and joints and the physical barriers of skin. I'm really interested in the vastness of the body. So I started the year with a first stimuli which was through Butoh [...] I started reading a lot about Sondra Fraleigh and Shin Somatics [Chapter 3][7] *and that got me into this chain reaction of exploration. So, I'm not a dancer, not a singer. I'm not an artist and performer. It is constantly shape-shifting.*

I am very interested in perhaps from this grounded state [referring to the impact of the workshop with Stephen Paparo] *to tap into an exploration. I was thinking, oh, I want to investigate "What is the potential of the voice as a guiding vehicle to hold space for us to give permission; to give the agency to our bodies?" Just beginning from here, right now, without needing to think* about the "what if" or "how" or "where" or "who". So, from this grounded state [...] I just want to invite you or facilitate or offer, if that's wanted, a state of letting go or releasing to the sensation of the floor; of the gravity. Just kind of surrender to the sensation of touch, of contact with the surface beneath you, with the texture beneath you; allow conversation to unfold with the curiosity to the sensation of touch; to the sensation of allowing your skin, allowing your body to be a receptor, to take in information of the surface beneath you. Listening carefully as well to this chain reaction to the sound.

This organically transitioned to the emergent sharing of Oram:

I teach voice, I spend my time thinking and talking and doing voice. And I've spent the last week writing about my thinking and talking and doing voice. So today for me became about listening and receiving. My research has been around power value systems and pedagogy and it's been a heuristic research process so immersion of myself into those questions and at the heart of that process has been learning to listen deeply, to listen through the skin. So, I set myself a Practice-as-Research question at the beginning of today: "Could I attend today from a deep listening place?"

And in a way it's useful to go "What is not a deep-listening place?". So, not a deep-listening place for me, as I sit here as a queer man from a royal training institution, who grew up with a family with limited cultural and economic capital, is to hear things and immediately go: "I know that" or "that's wrong" or "I don't like that" or "that feels bad" or "why am I here?" or "what's this doing?" And those immediate responses as I listen inscribe a circle around me which becomes my value system [...] Whereas deep listening is acknowledging that that thought is happening but staying with listening to what's going on here [circling his hand on top of his belly area] *[...] And then an interesting thing happens that I'm in relationship to whatever is happening in the room but I'm also in relationship to my own value system and I can just about make it out a little bit about what that is.*

[...] So, in my research one of the things I did was set up a focus group with my students to talk about their experiences of the training. I didn't run the focus group I had a facilitator so that they were a little bit outside of my power dynamic and they spoke very freely and a young black working-class student of mine talked very emotively about how damaged he was by the training, how much he'd been hurt by the training. I couldn't respond because I wasn't there so I couldn't defend my values. So, I was moved deeply by him and I was taken to another place [moving to another spot in the space] *where I was with the recording and I was able to begin to see myself and I started in that moment to see my own whiteness, to see what that was and that's become a process over the last few years and what I call decolonizing my lesson.*[8]

And the reason I came to that today was because I was reminded when I was listening to Amy [Ginther]. *That I felt a discomfort and I didn't go to the thinking-analyzing, rejecting/accepting place. I just stayed with the discomfort and was taken to another place in relationship to Amy, in relation to myself* [he moves to another spot] *[...] and that practice has fed into my teaching [...] So today what the Practice-as-Research question has given me is a way of understanding the process I've been doing for the last three years which I haven't quite got hold of until just now. So, thank you everyone because everyone's contributed to that experience.*

In my understanding, it was not random that in the end of the day and while exploring modes of somatic listening, we returned to ideas of "colonialism".[9] It is a current theme in various discussions and publications,[10] was brought in by Attille and, as Oram noted, is discerned through alternative vocabulary in this volume, primarily in the work of Amy Mihyang Ginther. Would this already be an indication of the *beyond*? Could somatic methodologies of listening bring change when applied beyond educational or therapeutic contexts? Not only to be seen or examined in relation but being applied in the *doing* of research methodologies? What if, for instance, somatic listening was collectively practised in contexts of significant decision making? Would this practice help with the understanding of listening as not only a one-sided but an interrelational or in-between responsibility? Would that make any difference or would it seem inappropriate?

Somatic voices: day 2

On the second day of the symposium activities, there was time for two sharings by contributing participants after seminars offered by Tara McAllister-Viel (Chapter 9), Christina Gutekunst (Chapter 10), myself (Chapter 12) and Anita Chari (Chapter 15). There were some shifts in the group as a few people could not attend both days but this, as noticed by both contributors and participants, did not affect the continuous development of the inquiries. This time, the sharings were specifically prompted to focus on aspects beyond performance environments and two additional perspectives were brought in.

Carmen Wong, a performance maker and PhD candidate at the University of Warwick, UK, shared:

So, my research is how we perform belonging through food, in particular in migrant diaspora; how we make substitutes, how we translate-interpret recipes, body language with the making of foods that feed us and how I guess arrive home. So my research question was "Can we eat our way home?" [...]

You want to go somewhere different? Pick a travel partner and bring your phones. You need your self-phones to take selfies and photos. So the idea is that we walk around this studio space as if we've arrived through a new land and we have our travel buddy and we're now exploring [...] Everybody, take a moment to find something that is familiar to you in the space and take a photo of it [...] so now take a photo or a selfie of something that is just really alien to you, you've never seen before and you think it's just strange [...]

Now, I wanted us to go through that [...] of course I dramatized it a little bit and talk through actually one particular time when I did a self-made residency with a collaborator and friend in India. And I asked for different kinds of publications from my artist friends, and they came from all over the different kinds of disciplines. And this particular one came from a friend, Bill [indistinct surname] he is a photographer in DC [...] And his question and publication was "When you're in this other place, when you know that you're other and also actually when you're at home [...] can you allow an image to come to you instead of to take?" And then another dear friend, Sharon Steward, who is a musician and songwriter, she was the one that led me to Deep Listening, which I want to do a very short exercise with this today. And then afterwards, see if that helps us allow an image.

It's quite simple. Be in a comfortable position, ideally sort of alert but grounded [...] And we begin by listening to our breathing. Of course closing eyes helps with that focus of listening. You may wish for some tactile assistance to locate your heart beat so that you can touch it and then begin to listen [...] Expand your listening, front, back, up and down [...] How can we welcome all sounds as we enter this listening sphere? Expand this sphere even further. Outside the studio, further than you think your eye could reach [...] And then see if you can allow an image with this Deep Listening technique [...] Can you take a picture? Do you even want to take a picture?

The second perspective was offered by Faye Rigopoulou, a Musical Theatre director and PhD candidate at the University of Exeter, UK:

[...] I am researching the embodied vocalic presence of the female ageing performers in Musical Theatre and the space where this identity is formed; not only in terms of the roles that they are provided but also with the experience that is being experienced; where is Fabiano? [in reference to an expression that was offered the day before by Culora] And that makes me an inside researcher cause I was a Musical Theatre performer, I moved to Musical Theatre directing, I engage myself with voice studies and I am ageing [...]

It is a fact that the twenty-first century Musical Theatre is praising youth. And everything is about the perfection of the bodies and the beautifulness of the bodies and the voices and very difficult physiovocal performances. Musical Theatre is political, it explores different things but hasn't touched the intergenerational problem with the performances. And we do have some roles for female ageing performers, and emphasis on some, but they are within the *stereotypical image of the old women [...] And this is a problem because female performers, especially female ageing performers, they bring that gravitas and the voices are settled and they have a lot of things to offer, so they shouldn't be obsolete in their prime.*

So biologically speaking [...] by the age of 65, and I'm saying in facts, the entire laryngeal skeleton, where our vocal folds reside, ossifies; our vital capacity, which is the amount of the air that we use when we breathe (and we talk a lot about breathing here) [...] to speak and to sing eventually, it reduces; and with this so does our ability to hold longer notes; and for us female sex hormones wreak havoc on our vocal bodies, especially after mesopause. But is this a fact? Does voice age? I mean, why do we have to see it as ageing and not as changing? And why don't we embrace this change as we did with different aspects we worked on these two days? And reflecting on my research then it became obvious why Christina gave me this space; because I feel now, after experiencing these two days, that somatic practices can actually be very useful in ageing studies.

In my understanding, *attending* to somatic experiences (especially the ones that are not familiar to ourselves due to the imperative significance of human difference) and organically allowing fluid porosity in-between diverse communities, practices and ideas can surely trigger *third* or *beyond* possibilities. Considering the invaluable symposium sharings that emerged from *beyond our somatic voices* as main contributors of this volume, the final group reflection at the gathering and this project as a whole, it becomes apparent that there are multiple beyond potentialities in somatic voice studies and that this is the ground of a much wider international body of work. Returning to the notion of hospitality as inspired by Attille's input, my role was to host this enactment through various invitations, including this publication as an invitation to each one of you, the readers of this book. The impact of this work, which I resemble to a living organism, is now open to *how* it will be received and will grow.

In line with *intending* to open up this space of attentive possibilities and mutual listening, for the completion of the symposium activities, I also offered a very last invitation. Going back to my practice and the way I have been inspired by processes used in Authentic Movement, I invited a long circle (see Hartley, 2004, 67–70) during which each mover-voicer could allow emergent responses to the phrase "my somatic voice is ...". Despite the word-based invitation, the responses could be open to each person's present availability, from the pre-verbal to the verbal, from participation to silent witnessing.[11] To bring this epilogue and book into a closure, I would like to offer a witnessing of a compilation of these responses in a video, the audio recording from the video and a score (see Figure 17.1). In the editing of the audiovisual material, I focused on moments that could be somehow transmitted to the viewer-listener, given the ongoing challenge of contingent practice-research documentation through "discreet" modes. Figure 17.1 reflects how I visualized the responses in the practice as an alternative polyvocal score.

238 *Christina Kapadocha*

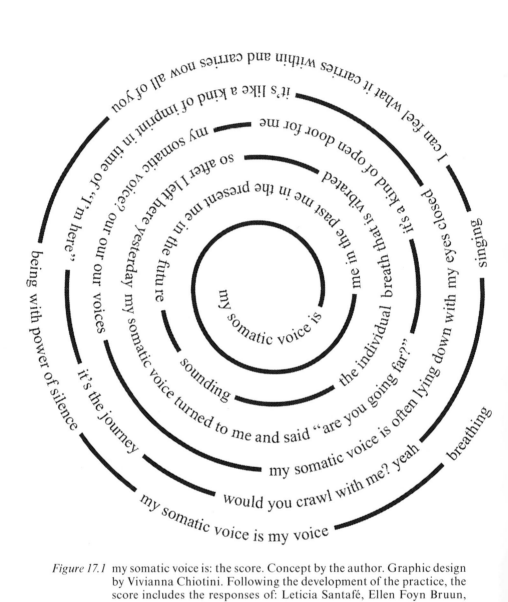

Figure 17.1 my somatic voice is: the score. Concept by the author. Graphic design by Vivianna Chiotini. Following the development of the practice, the score includes the responses of: Leticia Santafé, Ellen Foyn Bruun, Jeremy Finch, Judah Attille, Jinyoung Kim, Christina Kapadocha, Fabiano Culora, Lisa Lapidge, Vicky Wright, Andrea Olsen, Anita Chari, Faye Rigopoulou, Amy Mihyang Ginther and Aphrodite Evangelatou. © Christina Kapadocha.

Beyond our somatic voices 239

For your witnessing, I choose not to complement the material with an annotated guidance as I genuinely believe the multiple expressions "voice" for themselves.[12] The only element I would like to point out is that I have not intervened in the order of the events, something that in my understanding indicates shifts in the shared or in-between group listening throughout the time of the circle. We ended the circle with some shared breathing, something I have also borrowed from my training with Linda Hartley. Both video and audio recordings are available on the volume's webpage through the RVS website, under the titles_my somatic voice is_(video) (7:14) and_my somatic voice is_(audio) (7:03), respectively. You may wish to access both, you may find interesting to listen to the recording before watching the video, you may as well have a look at Figure 17.1. So, without any further written exegesis or *logos-as-reason* (Thomaidis, 2014, 82) but integrating all that is included in this book and allowing the communication of diverse *somatic logos* "my somatic voice is …".[13]

Notes

1 The other two events were the five-hour workshop with Patricia Bardi (November 17, 2018) which informed the shaping of the interview with the practitioner for Chapter 5 of this volume and the guest seminar by Ben Macpherson (May 4, 2019) inspired by his discussion for Chapter 16.
2 The *third* here is inspired by Jessica Benjamin's recognition theory (2018), especially based on the way she discusses the necessity of "understanding and negotiating differences" (2018, 95) towards co-creation and "the holding of multiplicity" (Ibid., 100).
3 This is a term I started using in order to challenge the dividing lines between contributors and participants. I combined this intention with offering a multivocal space of sharing and receiving while accepting our differentiation. Through this approach, I also aimed at revisiting defensive language in disseminating research (i.e. defend an argument) and hierarchical structures usually associated with such contexts in academia (i.e. the dividing line between speakers and listeners).
4 The contributions as included in this chapter have been transcribed from the video documentation of the activities. As suggested in other parts of this collection (see Table of Contents and Introduction), you can access these videos through the following CHASE webpage: https://www.chasevle.org.uk/archive-of-training/archive-of-training-2019/somatic-voices/. Due to a mistake on the webpage, please note that: Response #1 by Judah Attille is video no 5 and Response #2 by Fabiano Culora is video no 4.
5 Relevant citations are included in the list of references.
6 This change in the order was requested by the contributors on the day for reasons that do not relate to the cohesive development of the gathering activities, hence of this collection.
7 It became very interesting to me that even contributors to the project who could not attend like Sondra Fraleigh were still very much present through the strong influence of their work.
8 Oram had also recently published an article under the title "Decolonizing Listening: Towards an Equitable Approach to Speech Training for the Actor" (2019a). This is in line with numerous discussions on decolonizing the curriculum in various UK-based institutions originally generated in impactful educational

environments such as Soas University of London (see, among others, Decolonising Soas Blog, 2018) and University College London (see UCL, 2014). This initiative activated a series of "Why is my curriculum white?" discussions between students and academic staff (such as the Decolonizing the Curriculum Network hosted by Exeter University in collaboration with Brunel University and Plymouth University, 2017 onwards), many institutional events (such as the Decolonizing the curriculum: what's all the fuss about? at Birbeck, University of London, February 1, 2019 and Decolonizing the Curriculum conference at Kent University, March 20, 2019), artistic research discussions (such as the executive panel on Decolonizing Theatre, Dance & Performance at Theatre and Performance Research Association – TaPRA – 2019 conference) and publications (see, among others, Peters, 2015; Waghid, 2017). I should add through my experience that this critical awareness and attention is an innate aspect of the identity and ongoing activities of East 15 Acting School (i.e. subject of discussions in staff meetings based on the students' views) and University of Essex (see Why is my curriculum white? Essex University, 2016). More active shifts are currently underway particularly in response to the Black Lives Matter movement.
9 I choose at this point to use the word within inverted commas due to the gravitas of its historical complexity and its metaphorical use in the context of this discussion.
10 Decolonization of voice has been present in various publications on literature (Smith, 2018), cultural (Andersen, 2018), museum (Onciul, 2015), religious (Nono, 2016) and theatre studies (Magnat, 2016; Mitra, 2016). At the same time, the decolonization of listening has been an ongoing parallel discussion in music, sound and voice studies (see, among others, Viveros Avendaño, 2017; Przybylski, 2018; Magnat, 2019; Salois, 2019).
11 I should highlight that silent witnessing, as any form of witnessing inspired by somatic practices, does not indicate disengaged, distant or inactive presence but an entirely involved-relational activity through one's own integrated attention and intention (on the role of the silent witness in Authentic Movement, see Adler, 2002, 65–76). For more information on somatic witnessing and the way I use it in my work, see Kapadocha (2016, 66–70; 2017a, 217–218; 2018, 206–208).
12 I do though include subtitles in case this could facilitate your witnessing.
13 In order of appearance in the video, the material includes the responses of Leticia Santafé, Ellen Foyn Bruun, Jeremy Finch, Judah Attille, Jinyoung Kim, Christina Kapadocha, Fabiano Culora, Lisa Lapidge, Vicky Wright, Andrea Olsen, Anita Chari, Faye Rigopoulou, Amy Mihyang Ginther and Aphrodite Evangelatou.

References

Adler, J. (2002) *Offering from the Conscious Body: The Discipline of Authentic Movement*. Rochester: Inner Traditions.
Andersen, C. (2018) *Decolonizing the mind* [online]. European Colonial Heritage Modalities in Entangled Cities. Available from http://projectechoes.eu/keywords [Accessed 20 September 2019].
Attille, J. (2019) Shadow voices [participating contribution]. *Somatic Voices in Performance Research and Beyond: A Two-Day Praxical Symposium*, East 15 Acting School, London, 19–20 July.
Benjamin, J. (2018) *Beyond Doer and Done to, Recognition Theory, Intersubjectivity and the Third*. [Google Play Book]. London: Routledge.
Bhabha, H. K. (2012) *The Location of Culture*. Abington, Oxon: Routledge Classics.

Croes, N. (2019) Untitled participating contribution. *Somatic Voices in Performance Research and Beyond: A Two-Day Praxical Symposium*, East 15 Acting School, London, July 19–20.

Culora, F. (2019) Untitled participating contribution. *Somatic Voices in Performance Research and Beyond: A Two-Day Praxical Symposium*, East 15 Acting School, London, July 19–20.

Decolonising Soas Blog (2018) London: Soas. Available from https://blogs.soas.ac.uk/decolonisingsoas/ [Accessed 20 September 2019].

Derrida, J. (1982) *Margins of Philosophy*. Translated from French by Alan Bass. Chicago, IL: University of Chicago Press.

——— (1995) *The Gift of Death: Religion and Postmodernism*. Translated from French by David Wills. Chicago, IL: University of Chicago Press.

Derrida, J. and Dufourmantelle, A. (2000) *Of Hospitality: Anne Dufourmantelle Invites Jacques Derrida to Respond*. Translated from French by Rachel Bowlby. Stanford, CA: Stanford University Press.

Eidsheim, N. S. and Meizel, K. (eds.) (2019) *The Oxford Handbook of Voice Studies*. Oxford: Oxford University Press.

Hartley, L. (2004) *Somatic Psychology: Body, Mind and Meaning*. London: Whurr.

Idhe, D. (2007) *Listening and Voice: Phenomenologies of Sound*. 2nd edition. Albany: State University of New York Press.

Kapadocha, C. (2016) *Being an Actor/Becoming a Trainer: The Embodied Logos of Intersubjective Experience in a Somatic Acting Process*. PhD. Royal Central School of Speech and Drama, University of London.

——— (2017a) The development of Somatic Acting Process in UK-based actor training. *Journal of Dance and Somatic Practices*, 9(2) 213–221.

——— (2017b) *Routledge Voice Studies: Proposal for Edited Volume* [unpublished book proposal].

——— (2018) Towards witnessed thirdness in actor training and performance. *Theatre, Dance and Performance Training*, 9(2) 203–216.

Magnat, V. (2016) Decolonizing Performance Research. *Études Anglaises – revue du monde anglophone*, 69(2) 135–148.

——— (2019) *The Performative Power of Vocality (Routledge Voice Studies)*. Abingdon, Oxon: Routledge.

Mitra, R. (2016) Decolonising immersion: translation, spectatorship, rasa theory and contemporary British dance. *Performance Research: A Journal of the Performing Arts*, 21(5) 89–100.

Nono, G. (2016) *Decolonizing Voice: A Talk-Performance by Grace Nono*. [talk-performance]. School of Social Work Building, LSA International Institute, University of Michigan, April 12.

Onciul, B. (2015) *Museums, Heritage and Indigenous Voice: Decolonising Engagement*. New York: Routledge.

Oram, D. (2019a) Decolonizing listening: towards an equitable approach to speech training for the actor. *The Voice and Speech Review*, 13(3) 279–297.

——— (2019b) Untitled participating contribution. *Somatic Voices in Performance Research and Beyond: A Two-Day Praxical Symposium*, East 15 Acting School, London, July 19–20.

Peters, M. A. (2015) Why is my curriculum white? *Educational Philosophy and Theory*, 47(7) 641–646.

Przybylski, L. (2018) Bilingual hip hop from community to classroom and back: a study in decolonial applied ethnomusicology. *Ethnomusicology*, 62(3) 375–402.

Rigopoulou, F. (2019) Untitled participating contribution. *Somatic Voices in Performance Research and Beyond: A Two-Day Praxical Symposium*, East 15 Acting School, London, July 19–20.

Salois, K. R. (2019) Listening towards decolonisation. *Sound Studies: An Interdisciplinary Journal*, 4(2) 217–220.

Smith, V. E. (ed.) (2018) *Voices of Ghana: Literary Contributions to the Ghana Broadcasting System, 1955–1957*. 2nd edition. Oxford: James Currey.

Thomaidis, K. (2014) The revocalization of logos? Thinking, doing and disseminating voice. *Studies in Musical Theatre*, 8(1) 77–87.

Thomaidis, K. and Macpherson, B. (eds.) (2015a) *Voice Studies: Critical Approaches to Process, Performance and Experience*. Abingdon, Oxon: Routledge.

────── (2015b) Introduction: Voice(s) as a method and an in-between in *Voice Studies: Critical Approaches to Process, Performance and Experience*. Abingdon, Oxon: Routledge.

UCL (2014) *Why is my curriculum white?* [online video]. Available from https://www.youtube.com/watch?v=Dscx4h2l-Pk [Accessed 21 September 2019].

Viveros Avendaño, I. C. (2017) *Sounding Out Tarima Temporalities: Decolonial Feminista Dance Disruption* [blog entry]. 18 September. Sounding Out!: Sound Studies Blog. Available from https://soundstudiesblog.com/tag/iris-c-viveros-avendano/ [Accessed 21 September 2019].

Voegelin, S. (2010) *Listening to Noise and Silence: Towards a Philosophy of Sound Art*. New York: Continuum.

Waghid, Y. (2017) Does a white curriculum matter? *Educational Philosophy and Theory*, 49(3) 203–206.

Why is my curriculum white? Essex University (2016) *Why is my curriculum white? Facebook page* [facebook] Available from https://www.facebook.com/Why-is-my-curriculum-white-Essex-University-1563387630648678/ [Accessed 21 September 2019].

Wong, C. (2019) Scoring, voicing migration (adapted practice with a deep listening score by Ximena Alarcón) [participating contribution]. *Somatic Voices in Performance Research and Beyond: A Two-Day Praxical Symposium*, East 15 Acting School, London, July 19–20.

Index

Note: *Italic* page numbers refer to figures and page numbers followed by "n" denote endnotes.

actor training 120–121, 158; impulses and psycho-physical actions 131; logocentrism 155–159; pedagogies 132; postcolonial 99; practices 108; somatic research, notion of 166n5; touch in training, use of 117; and voice practices 7; vocal integration 131–132
adoptees: translingual 99, 103, 109n5; transnational 99; transracial 98, 99, 100, 102
affect theory 203, 210n2; somatic affect 221
Ahmed, S. 101, 102; queered spatial relations, notions of 185
Alexander, F. M. 16; conscious-controlled behavior 124; directing awareness 121; hands-on approach 115; orders 122, 123; re-education, concept of 116, 124, 126
Alexander Technique (AT) 7, 115, 130, 223n5; art of touching 176–177; Frederick, Michael 78; to let 175; Williams, Elaine 78
Alker, G. 101
American Method 121
Amkpa, A. 101
anatomy: experiential anatomy and human movement development processes 28, 52, 163, 165; as foundation for phenomenological experience 119–121; functional anatomy of voice 58
Anderson, R. 65
Anglo-American voice training 116, 123
Arendt, H. 205
Aristotle 157

Asian: Experimental Theatre program 116; modes of training 116, 119, 121; modes of practice 116; physical disciplines (Yoga and T'ai Chi) 16, 17, 39, 41, 130; martial arts 16
Asma, S.: *Evolution of Imagination* 22–23
aural in-between 166; definition of 220–221
Authentic Movement 16, 17, 237, 240n11; inner witness 35n10; principles 157; Whitehouse, M. 7
autoethnography 64, 70–71
autonomic nervous system (ANS) 33–34, 58, 77
autobiophony xx
awareness 126; attentive 123; cellular 159–160; of creative self-empowerment 59; cultivating ki as 124; embodied 28–35; expanded awareness 16; kinds of 142; kinesthetic 19, 20; racialized 102; sense of 121; somatic 18, 18–20, 66, 67, 76, 78, 86; students' awareness 122, 123; touch as, use of 121, 123; "zero of pressure" 159; *see also* self-awareness
Awareness Through Movement® (ATM) 90, 95; in-person ATM/FI lessons 95

Bainbridge-Cohen, B. 77, 78, 210n3; experiential anatomy and human movement development processes 163; founder of BMC 159–160
Bakhtin, M. M. 39, 45; phenomenology 42
Barad, K. 182; intra-action and inter-action 183n4
Barker, P. 41; tyranny of understanding 217

Index

Barry, C. 52
Barton, R. 21
Basic Neurocellular Patterns (BNP) 77, 160
Bateson, M. C. 20
Batson, G. 16
Benedetti, R. 21
Benjamin, J.: recognition theory 239n2
Berry, C. 115, 122, 130
Bioenergetics 17; analysis 186; Lowen, A. 186
Bloch, E. 209
blogs, research-oriented 10n14
Body and Earth (Olsen) 7
body xxi, xxiii; bodymind 3, 5; body-mind-voice integration 76–86, 124; body/voice 115–127; map 6, 98–109; I-body xxii, xxvin1; moving body 3, 51–60; object-body xxv, 119, 122
Body-Mind Centering® (BMC®) 7, 16, 78, 157, 203, 210n3
Bourdieu, P. 3; *nomos* 99, 100
Boyesen, G. 186, 187
Brave Kids project 152n2
breath: *Active Breath* 56; in actor-training approaches 163, 167n7; *anima spiritus,* breath and soul 18; bone breath 199; blur breath 199; cellular respiration 31, 160; cerebrospinal breath 199; full-body breath 160; patterns 29, 190; reverse breathers 31; shallow breathers 31
breathing xxiv, 18, 29–31, 65–68, 77, 125, 126, 136–138, 158, 160, 162–164, 172, *176,* 181, 182, 192, 237; breathing in impulse 136; breathing in other person 136; breathing rhythmicity center 29; "reverse breathing" xxii; "see-saw breathing" xxii; shared breathing 239
Brown, N. G. 10n5
Brown, T. 52
Bülow-Hansen, A. 187
burden: vocality 171–184; somatic burden 181–183
Butler, J.: concept of performativity 216
Butoh 7, 39, 45–46, 48, 233
Bryon, E. 9n1

Cage, J. 180
Caldwell, P. 192–193
Carey, D.: *Vocal Arts Workbook and DVD* 117
Cavarero, A. 37, 73; criticism on devocalization of logos 158
cellular: awareness 159–160; contact 156, 163; respiration 31; support 164–165; text 156–157; touch 159
central nervous system (CNS) 66, 79
chakra, throat 41
CHASE webpage 10n15, 239n4
Chekhov, M. 132, 139n2
Chion, M. 217
Cixous, H. 59
Clark Carey, R.: *Vocal Arts Workbook and DVD* 117
cognitive turn 212
Coles, R. 205, 206, 207; dampened resonance 208; deceptive and receptive resonance 208, 209; mirroring 208–209
colonial embodiment 101–102
colonialism 99, 101, 102, 108, 235
communication 3, 29, 32, 34, 43, 63, 72, 73, 86, 101, 116, 119, 158, 160, 164, 165, 167n9, 189, 192, 193, 201, 202, 208, 213, 231, 239; and direct address 189; diverse physiovocal embodied 163; exploring 136–137; somatic communication 42, 163; verbal communication 66, 161, 195n1; vocal communication 79–81, 84, 131, 191
Connolly, W. 205, 206, 207
Conrad, E. 198, 210n3; Continuum Movement 198; *Life on Land* 199, 204; phenomenon of somatic shock 209; somatic field 200, 202; vocal resonance 200
consciousness 16, 20, 21, 23, 29, 38–40, 42, 102–103, 131, 143, 148, 159, 214–215, 218, 220, 222, 224
Consciousness in Action (Hurley) 21
contact 42, 84, 91, 92, 118, 155–157, 159, 161–166, 177, 187, 195, 204, 205, 234; at cellular level 159; Contact Unwinding 39, 42, 43; eye contact 81, 83, 186, 189, 193, 195n1; improvisation 52, 153n9; somatic contact 157, 159, 160
Continuum Movement 7, 198–199
Coordination Technique (CT) 140, 152n2
corporeality 45; of vocal exchange 220
corporeal vocality 214
Costello, E.: Narrow daylight 68, 71
Craniosacral Therapy 41; Biodynamic Craniosacral Therapy 203, 210n3
Csikszentmihalyi, M. 21
Csordas, T. 185; and cellular attention 160

culture, cultural 24, 29, 40, 48, 118, 172, 196, 216; cross-cultural 41, 76; cultural conditioning 28, 215–216; dimensions of somatics 147, 150; hegemonic culture 108; Indian music culture 57; metaphors 23; queering 186; semiotic forms of 152, 157; or social environment 23; vocal production 191; Western culture 57, 106, 187

Damasio, A. 15, 20, 131; consciousness, definition 20; *Descartes' Error* 218; *The Feeling of What Happens: Body, Emotion and the Making of Consciousness* 218; function of mirror neurons, "as-if body loop" 221; self and consciousness 131, 218; *Self Comes to Mind: Constructing the Conscious Brain* 218; somatic markers 21, 22
dance: background of PB 51–52; dance-voice artist 51–52; teaching process 45
decolonization of voice 240n10
decolonizing the curriculum 239n8
Derrida, J. 157–158; différance, notion of 233; hospitality theory 232; logocentrism, definition of 157, 232; notion of deconstruction 157–158
Descartes 218; body *vs.* mind paradigm 15–16
destructuring-restructuring 65–68
Dewey, J.: artistic experience 216; direct perception 160; experiential education and reflexive sensitivity 160; influence upon Kaprow 179–180
Dharma talk 121, 127n2
difference, significance of 5, 239n2
Di Matteo, P. 45, 100, 101, 105, 142; idea of *tracing sound back* 45
diversity, diverse 2–5, 8, 15, 41, 43, 51, 52, 56, 57, 117–119, 127, 130, 137, 140, 144, 151, 157–159, 161, 163, 165, 186, 206, 229, 231, 237, 239; multicultural and diverse training environments 118
documentation: audio-visual material 9; video documentation 10n15, 51, 239n4
Dolar, M. 220; object voice 223; *A Voice and Nothing More* 214
dreambody, dreamvoice 140; Ilona Kraczyk 140–144; Kernels of the voice (Ben Spatz) 149–152

dualism (mind and body dualism, mind-body dualism) 159, 213
Du Bois, W. E. B. 106; double consciousness 102

East 15 Acting School 1, 9, 10n12, 35n1, 51, 54, 130, 163, 166n4, 229, 240n8
Eddy, M. 5, 102; soma, definition 100
education: contemporary somatic education 7; experiential education 160; "re-education" 116, 124, 126, 186; somatic educational program 53–54
embodied: cognition 15–16; democracy 198, 201, 205; "the embodied turn" 212; listening 219; logos 159; performance 212; voice 103, 105, 116, 142
embodiment: cognitive 23; colonial 101–102; peaceful comprehension in 167n10
emotions 29, 30, 34, 43, 58, 63, 82, 85, 86, 93, 104, 121, 130, 187, 208, 218, 221, 223n4, 224n8; "emotionally raw" 186; "faked" emotions 132–133; fluid flesh in movement 79–80; 'full-bodied emotion' 217; in verbal communication 66
empathy 37, 46–47, 125, 126
enworlding sound 48; engaging in world/living the world 38; *Enworlding (verweltlichung)* 40; *see also* Husserl, E.
Espinosa, M. 117
ethos, ethical 3, 37, 43, 46, 158, 161, 164, 207, 213, 231, 233
exploration 4, 7, 9, 15, 17–22, 24, 25, 33, 41, 52, 57, 65, 77, 89, 93–95, 139n3, 141, 151n10, 166n7, 167n10, 199, 201, 202, 204, 209, 212; attitude of 20–22; *cellular text* 156; of organs 53–54; Reeve on conscious exploration xxii; self-exploration 90, 94, 148
extra-daily training 124–125
extra-normal voicing, voice 185, 186, 190, 191, 193, 195–196n1

Faber, R. 16
Fanon, F. 106; *Black Skin, White Masks* 102; racialized awareness, third-person consciousness 102
Farnell, B. 3
Feldenkrais, M. 7, 16, 17, 38, 89, 90, 92, 94, 95, 157, 161, 166n6; *Awareness Through Movement* 90; *Body and Mature Behavior* 90

246　Index

Feldenkrais Method® (FM) 7, 223n5; awareness of oneself in action 93; Awareness Through Movement® 90, 95; freedom of expression 93; Functional Integration® 90; National Association of Teachers of Singing and Voice 95; pedagogical principles and strategies 92–94; practice sessions, voice lessons and choral rehearsals 91–92; self-discovery, new options 94; Speech Trainers Association 95; teachers of voice 94; voice studios and choral rehearsals 94, 95
Finer, E. 220
Fischer-Lichte, E. 219, 220, 221; in relation to somatic listening 219
Fitzmaurice, C. 71–72; founder of FV (*see* Fitzmaurice Voicework® (FV))
Fitzmaurice Voicework® (FV) 8; destructuring-restructuring 65–68; Teacher Certification Program 69; tremorwork® 66; in vocal "forest of Arden" 63–64; vocal freedom and focus of expression 63–64
Fleeger, J. 217
Foucault, M. 3
Frederick, M. 78
Functional Integration® (FI) 90; *see also* Feldenkrais Method® (FM)

Gallagher, S. 15
Gallese, V. 23
Gardner, H. 17, 22
Gazzaniga, M. 15
Gillett, J: *Voice into Acting* 26n5
Goldsmiths (University of London) 233
Goodman, M. 52
Gronbeck-Tedesco, J. 21
Grotowski, J. 140; movement as/of perception 145; quality of expressive receptivity 144; *see also* post-Grotowskian practice/s
grounding 29, 66, 147, 156, 161, 163, 165, 186

Hakomi Method 16
Hanna, T. 4, 181; definition of soma 157; soma, as self-regulating and self-sensing unity 69
Hart, R. 109n1; *see also* Roy Hart Method
Hartley, L. 7, 165, 239; IBMT training 157, 167n10; Integrative Bodywork and Movement Therapy (IBMT) 7, 157, 167n10
Hawkins, E. 52
Heidegger, M. 38; *Being and Time* 39–40; worlding 39
Heller, J. 18
Homi Bhabha 232
Hook, D.: colonial embodiment 101–102
Hurley, S.: *Consciousness in Action* 21
Husserl, E. 38; engaging in world/living the world 38; "the environing world" 39; *Enworlding (verweltlichung)* 40; enworlding sound 48; intentionality 47; "lifeworlds" 39; *Sixth Cartesian Meditation* 40

imagery, images 9, 41, 45, 56, 65–73, 77, 79, 90, 108, 146, 148, 150, 151, 156, 231–232, 236, 237; breath, exploration and 17–18; cognitive embodiment 23; electro-chemical and neurological 218, 219; and engagement 135; *ideokinesis* 24; image-based units 65; multimodality 23; power of 22–25
imagination 18, 22, 23, 40, 47, 68, 74, 130, 135, 149, 156, 160, 162; active imagination 65, 66
improvisation 20, 43, 46, 52, 55, 58, 98, 104, 105, 106, *106*, 107, 140, 141, 143, 144, 146, 153n9, 155, 156, 161, 187, 189, 202, 205
in-betweenness 4, 157; in-between (Thomaidis and Macpherson) 4, 157, 166, 200–201, 220–222, 229; multimodality and multivocality 229; potentialities of diverse somatic logos 231
individuation, notion of 202
Ingold, T. 39–40; *Being Alive* 40
Integrative Bodywork and Movement Therapy (IBMT) training 7, 157, 167n10
intensive interaction: description 195n1; invitation to profound and multiple learning 187–188; learning process 188–190; queer (intensive) interaction 192–194
intercorporeality 201–203
intercultural 58
interdisciplinary 3, 53, 141–142, 200
intuitive inquiry 64–65

James, W. 218; *Essays on Radical Empiricism* 215
Järviö, P. xxiv

Joan of Arc 33
Johnson, D. H. 5; *Diverse Bodies, Diverse Practices: Towards an Inclusive Somatics* 5; inclusive somatics 5
Johnson, M. 24; *Philosophy in the Flesh* 23
Jonathan Hart Makwaia (JHM) 98, 99, 104–108
Journal for Artistic Research (JAR) 10n14
Journal of Dance and Somatic Practices 10n5, 10n13
Jung, C.: active imagination, notion of 65; archetype of rebirth 67; ideas of "archetypes" 216
Jungian concept of the unconscious, dream analysis 142
Jungian-inspired phenomenology 64

kalarippayattu 116
Kant, I. 218; "corporeal vocality" 214; *The Critique of Judgment* 212; epistemological perspective 219
Kaprow, A.: *Essays on the blurring of art and life* 179–180
Karpf, A.: *The Human Voice* 216; notion of race 216
Kazuo, O. sensei 39, 48–49
Keeling, E. 52
Kelley, J. 179
Kelly, C.: radix body re-education 186
Kemp, R. 16
Kendrick, L. 218, 221
Khalil, A. 191
ki cultivation 116, 119, 121–126
Kim, E. J.: coherence of self-identity 103; multiple consciousness 106; racialization 102–103
King, Martin Luther 33
Klein, S. 52
knowledge 1, 5, 15, 20, 47, 72, 76, 92, 109n5, 125, 161, 164, 174, 189; of body 25, 37, 53, 118; formations 76, 176; potential of somatic 25, 60, 213, 222; racialization through 101; self- 56, 60, 165, 218; somatic knowledge, potential of 25; on transformative potentialities 64; voice knowledge 1
Korea, Korean 105, 106, 107, 109n5, 109n9, 109n10; adoptees 102–103, 109n2; Korean National University of Arts (KNUA) 121; Korean Seon (zen) 127n2
Kornaś, T. 145
Krall, D.: Narrow daylight 68, 71

Kristeva, J. 59
Kurtz, R.: Hakomi Method 16

Lakoff, G. 23–24; *Philosophy in the Flesh* 23
LAMDA (London Academy of Music and Dramatic Art) 120
lamentation vocal 171, 172–174
lamenting meditation 182
Land to Water Yoga 39, 41; Chakra Unwinding 41; lock jaw 41
LeDoux, J. 15
Lefebvre, H. 213, 215
Levine, P. 210n3, 210n5
Ley, G. 213
Lincoln, A. 33
Linklater, K. 8, 18, 115, 119, 130; Linklater methodology 77; Linklater Voice Training 8
listening methodology 157, 159, 217, 223n6, 234, 236, 239; decolonization of 239n8, 240n10; embodied listening 219; listening as understanding 165; mutual listening 160, 161, 237; self-listening 166; somatic listening 63, 160, 164, 165–166, 219, 220, 222, 223, 231, 233, 235
lock jaw 41
logocentrism xxv, 157, 158–159, 162, 163, 164, 232
logos 213, 219; criticism on devocalization of 158; exegesis/logos-as-reason 37, 238, 239; logos as flesh 158n3; logos-as-language xxv; potentialities of diverse somatic 231; reasoning and rational 213; somatic (*see* somatic logos); understanding of 158
Loukes, Rebecca 10n7
LoVetri, J. 4; Somatic Voicework™ 4
Lowen, A. 186; *see also* Bioenergetics
Lugones, M. 101, 102; "Towards a Decolonial Feminism" 101
Lutterbie, J. 16, 24

Maathai, W. 33
McAmis, C. 95n1
McCallion, M. 78, 115, 117
McGilchrist, I.: brain function 131; *The Master and his Emissary – The Divided Brain and the Making of the Modern World* 131
McKim, J. 192

Macpherson, B. 4, 7, 10n4, 10n13, 38, 200, 230; "the fetishized voice-as-object" 200; the in-between 4, 157, 166, 200–201, 220–222, 229; *Journal of Interdisciplinary Voice Studies* 10n2, 10n4; *Voice Studies: Critical Approaches to Process, Performance, Experience* 200, 230
magic *if*, organic voice: creative connector 135; exploring 135–136; sensory experience 135
Maisel, E. 116, 127, 127n1
Mandela, N. 33
Mani, C. xxiv
Manning, E. 203
Massumi, B. 203
meditation *181*; *zazen* 180–181; *see also* Zen meditation
meditative breathing 119
medullary rhythmicity center 35n3
Meehan, E. 10n5
Meehan, N.: PB modern dance technique with 52
Merleau-Ponty, M. 166; embodied transition 160; logos as flesh 158, 166n3; *The Visible and the Invisible* 158
Miller, S. 217
mind-body paradigm shift, neuroscience and somatics 15–17
Mindell, A. 142, 143; notion of dreambody 142; primary and secondary processes 143; processwork 140, 147–148
Minton, S.C. 16
Mouriere, A. 192
movement, moving: movement-voice interrelation 15; moving-voicing-acting-thinking 8; voice and movement styles 18
multicultural, multiculturalism 77, 116, 117; multicultural and diverse training environments 118
multidisciplinary polyphony, voice studies 4
multiple, multiplicity 3, 4, 165, 229, 230, 231, 239, 239n2; learning 187–188; methodological multiplicity of writing 8; scripts xxv; somaticities and expressions 158; vocal experiences 4
multivocality 157, 164, 229

Nagatomo, S.: conception of nature of body knowledge 25
Nagrin, D. 52

Nelson, L. 52
Nelson, R. 69, 103; defines praxis 109n6; *know how, know what* 160; *praxical* vocabulary 160
neoliberalism 210n1
Neuro-Linguistic Programming 16
neurolinguistics 109n5
neuroscience, neurology, neurological xxiv, 18, 90, 188; embodied cognition 15–16; experience 218–221; mind-body/voice-body 15; neurophysiology 77; vocal integration 131–132
nomos (Pierre Bourdieu) 99, 100
non-punctuate time 190–191, 195n1

objective: in acting 137–138
Ocampo-Guzman, A. 117
Olsen, B. 3
Oram, D. 239n8
organic voice: actor's intellectual and creative mind 131–132; definition 132–133

p'ansori 116
Paxton, S. 52
pedagogy, pedagogical: actor-training 99, 132; dance 17, 166n5; engaged 100, 103; somatic xxiii, 8, 39, 160, 161; voice 95, 98, 99–100, 108, 115, 147, 148
Performance as Research (PAR) 64, 71, 73
performance: induced anxiety 76; performative narrative 171–172; praxis 2 (*see also* praxis); pre-performance anxiety 82; somaesthetic performance analysis 214, 223; training 18
Perry, B. 80
Pettman, D.: *Infinite Distraction* 202
phenomenology 38–42, 64, 65, 157
physiologically-based voice exercises 120
physiovocal actor training 9n1
Piaget, J.: idea of reflexive action 141
Plato 157, 218; Platonic paranoia 219; prison-house of body 219; problem 213–214; *Republic* 213, 217
polyphony 1, 2, 4, 8, 45, 157, 230
polyvocal: authorship 230; collection 9; and intermedia identity 9; writing, authors' 8
Porges, S.W. 80; polyvagal theory 80; social engagement system 34
post-Grotowskian practice/s 144–147; theatre 152n1; *see also* Grotowski, J.

post-Stanislavskian traditions 7; work of Christina Gutekunst 8; *see also* Stanislavski, K.
Practice as Research (PaR) 98, 99, 140, 142, 157
practice-led research 212
practitioner-researchers 140, 230
praxical inquiry 212; investigations 229; methodologies 2
praxis 103; 157, 165; definition 10n3; 109n6; vocal 2; vocal and somatic 229
process, process-oriented, processual 8, 153n11; acting 130, 131, 132, 133; attitude of exploration 20–22; butoh processes 39; devising process 65, 68, 69, 72, 144; learning processes 64, 66, 89, 94, 95, 115, 158, 159, 163, 164, 188–190; metamorphic process 48; process-oriented approach 153n11; research process 9, 64, 65, 66, 68, 70, 81, 182; somatic processes 3, 15–26, 39, 41, 55, 157, 159; voicework 141, 142, 143, 147, 148, 149, 153n11; work (processwork) 142–144
processwork 140, 142, 143–144, 147, 148, 149
profound and multiple learning disabilities (PMLD) 185
proprioceiving 214
psychotherapy 7, 17

queer, queered: listening 185; somaesthetic 193; voicing 191

racialization 101
Reeve, S. xxii
resonance: dampened resonance 208; deceptive and receptive resonance 208, 209; intercorporeal resonance 207; political resonance 7, 205, 206; shock and resonance 208–209; vocal and somatic resonance 200–201
respiratory rhythmicity center 35n3
Responsive Voice: somatic partnering process 43
Ricoeur, P.: *Freedom and Nature: The Voluntary and the Involuntary* 47; phenomenology of choice 48
Rockwell, B. H. 101
Rodenburg, P. 115, 119
Romanyshyn, R. 65
Routledge Voice Studies (RVS) website 9, 10n2, 10n4, 10n13

Royal Central School of Speech and Drama (RCSSD) 233
Roy Hart Method 8; actors and singers 108; Centre Artistique International Roy Hart 98; inspired pedagogies 104; principles of 98; voice work 98, 104, 107, 109n11

Sahn, S. 121
Scott, S. 77
self-awareness 56, 95, 149, 159, 187
self-exposure 68, 69
self-learning, significance of 161–162
sensation 203–204
Shakespeare, W.: *As You Like It* 63, 71
Shin Somatics (Fraleigh) 7
Shusterman, R. xxiv, 2, 3, 16, 193–194; *Body Consciousness: A philosophy of mindfulness and somaesthetics* 214; (body) consciousness, definition 218; definition of somaesthetics 223n4; *Dynamic Embodiment for Social Theory* 3; philosophical concerns 215; somaesthetics 7; *Thinking through the Body* 212
Simondon, G. 202
singing 33, 34, 37, 175
Skånberg-Dahlstedt, A. 174
Smith, J. 216
social engagement system: vagal brake 34
societal nervous system 209
soma, somata 2, 4, 146, 157, 163, 233; body (soma) 131, 133; definition 4, 100, 157, 181–182; experienced bodymind 5; female vocal soma 59; in Florio's seventeenth-century Italian-French dictionary 181; in Greek 2; Hanna's notion as self-regulating and self-sensing unity 69; integrated 15, 16; racialized 102; re-introduced, Hanna 4; in Shusterman's somaesthetics 223n4; the structural self, or actual physical system, and the imaginal/social self/images of world 17; the structural self, or actual physical system, and the imaginal/social self/images of world 17
somaesthetic in-between 7; cognitive experience and bodily sensation 219; cultural conditioning 215–218; listening 222; neurological experience 218–221; Plato's problem 213–214; somaesthetic performance analysis 214–215; sonorous, somatic

in-between 221–222; vocality 215, 220, 222
somaesthetics 218; analytic, pragmatic and performative somaesthetics 215
SOMart 7
somatic: attention 160–161; intention 161; logos 160; research 161; state of being/having a living body 3; turn 2–3; in twenty-first century 3
Somatic Acting Process® 7, 157
Somatic Experiencing (SE) 203, 210n3; attending to 237
somatic field 200, 202
somaticity 2, 10n6; racialized 102, 106; transracialized 105, 107, 108
somatic lineages 5
somatic logos 158–159, 229; for acting pedagogies 159; against objectification and unification 158; against universal characteristics and "truths" 157; from one logos to 157–159; from somatic attention, initiating 155–157; as listening methodology in educational contexts 165–166; in physiovocal actor training 159–162; of trainer-witness 162–165
somatic partnering process 43
somatic research 8, 161, 166n5
somatic vocality/ies 2, 3, 182, 231
somatic voice/s 238, 239; beyond our somatic voices 9, 229–239; mapping somatic voices 4–5; my somatic voice is 9, 239
somatic voice studies 5; map 7; moving-voicing-thinking 2, 8; as a new area of voice and somatic research 4; research process 1–2, 9; significance of polyphonic voicing 2; source of theoretical advancements 4; vocal praxis, expansion of 2; voice training 2
somatics 2, 5, 37, 146; and medical sciences 8; model of inclusive somatics 5; Shin Somatics 7; written dissemination 5
Song of the Goat Theatre 140, 141, 145, 148, 152n2; inner life, notion of 152n3
sonorous 166, 218, 221–222
Sontag, S. 224n8
sounding: body/mind 173–174; enworlding sound itself 48; grounding before 29; metamorphic intention 46–47; response 107; sounding other 48–49; transforming 46–48; values of morphic intentionality 47

stage fright 77–81
standpoint epistemologies 103
Staniewski, W.: Gardzienice Theatre 145
Stanislavski, K. 132, 158; acting elements 133; *An Actor's Work* 158; criticism 132; episteme 158; practice foundation of my work with voice 139n2; quintessential components 135; and science, relationship between 166n2; techniques of 130
Stoever, J. L. 216, 217
Sweigard, L. 24; *ideokinisis* 24

T'ai Chi 16, 130
taiqiquan 116
Taoist and Buddhist philosophy 16–17
Tarvainen, A. 212–213, 214; vocal art forms 212–213
Taylor, A.: It's good to see you 69
Thelen, E. 16, 21
Thomaidis, K. 1, 4, 10n4, 10n13, 37, 38, 200, 220, 230; Cavarerian project 73–74; "the fetishized voice-as-object" 200; idea of vocal in-betweenness 4, 157, 166, 200, 220, 229; *Voice Studies: Critical Approaches to Process, Performance, Experience* 200, 230
thumos (senses) 213
time collecting 209; non-punctuate time 190–191, 195n1
Tomlinson, G. 153n10
touch, touching: Alexander lessons 176–178; in BMC 160; breathing and being breathed 122–124; Cohen's views 160; as directing awareness 116, 121; inside/outside 120–121; listening through touch 161; multicultural and multilingual contexts in 116; revisiting touch 126–127; touched, touching in Merleau-Ponty 159, 166; "the touch of sound" (Linklater) 79; as "universal" human experience 119–120; voice as touch 31
trainer-witness 162–164
training: multicultural and diverse training environments 118; physical-vocal 15; physiovocal, physio-vocal 9n1, 159–162; process of 15
transformative, transformational. transforming 8, 17, 46–47, 53, 149; ego transformation 143; embodiment approaches 5; Fitzmaurice Voicework® 63–64; potentialities 37, 68, 186
transracialized somaticities 98–108

US actor-training programs 117
utterance, level of 45

vagus nerve/s 34, 58, 80–81, 83–86
vibration, vibrational 32, 40, 46, 49, 53, 55, 77–79, 84, 86, 92, 116, 141, 177, 195, 198, 199, 201, 204, 206, 217
Vital Movement Integration Bodywork (VMIB) 56
VMI practice and training 54–59
vocal: agents 214; art forms 212–213, 222; body 220; discovery 105–107; gestural language 18; homecoming 68, 69, 74; in-betweenness 35n8, 220; individuation 73; integration 130, 131; mannerisms 132; organic response 130; polyphony 2; praxis 1, 2, 4, 8; resonance 198–210; somaticities 5; transformation 63; urgency and awareness 8
Vocal Dance 52, 54–56, 58
Voegelin, S. 220; notion of fleshness of vocality 220; vocal exchange as noise 219–220
voice: authentic voice, recovering 33; and truth telling 41–42
"voice box" 31
Voice into Acting (Gutekunst and Gillett) 26n5
Voices of the Disappeared 15

voice studies 230; contemporary 2, 4, 63; critical and multidisciplinary 4
voice therapy 231

Warren, I. 120
Whatley, S. 10n5
Whitehouse, M.: Authentic Movement 7; *see also* Authentic Movement
Williams, E. 78
Wilson, M. 16; embodied cognition 16
witness, witnessing 43, 51, 58, 78, 82, 83, 84, 85, 108, 157, 165, 166, 231, 239; actor-witness 155–156, 160, 161; inner 33, 35n10; listener-witness 192; silent 237, 240n11; trainer-witness 157, 159, 162–164
Wittgenstein, L. 216
Wolfsohn, A. 106, 109n1
Wood, K. 10n5
worlding: "a gathering dance" 38; in phenomenology 39–40
worlding voice 38, 39, 42–45

Yang-ming, W. 125
yoga 3, 7, 16, 17, 39, 66, 130; *Land to Water* 41
Yoo, J.: training mind through body 124

Zarrilli, P. 120
Zen meditation 116, 121, 127n2, 180

Taylor & Francis eBooks

www.taylorfrancis.com

A single destination for eBooks from Taylor & Francis with increased functionality and an improved user experience to meet the needs of our customers.

90,000+ eBooks of award-winning academic content in Humanities, Social Science, Science, Technology, Engineering, and Medical written by a global network of editors and authors.

TAYLOR & FRANCIS EBOOKS OFFERS:

- A streamlined experience for our library customers
- A single point of discovery for all of our eBook content
- Improved search and discovery of content at both book and chapter level

REQUEST A FREE TRIAL
support@taylorfrancis.com

Printed in the United States
By Bookmasters